A GUIDE TO
Microsoft® Windows NT®
Server 4.0
in the Enterprise

Jeffrey Williams
David Johnson

Contributing Authors:
Christopher Budd
J. Michael Stewart
Steven Linthicum
Jonathan Taylor
Pete Schwatka

COURSE
TECHNOLOGY

ONE MAIN STREET, CAMBRIDGE, MA 02142

an International Thomson Publishing company I(T)P®

Cambridge • Albany • Bonn • Boston • Cincinnati • London • Madrid • Melbourne • Mexico City
New York • Paris • San Francisco • Singapore • Tokyo • Toronto • Washington

A Guide to Microsoft® Windows NT® Server 4.0 in the Enterprise is published by Course Technology.

Managing Editor:	Kristen Duerr
Senior Product Manager:	Jennifer Normandin
Production Editor:	Melissa Panagos
Development Editor:	Ann Shaffer
Technical Editor:	Nicholas A. DiTirro
Composition House:	GEX, Inc.
Text Designer:	GEX, Inc.
Cover Designer:	Wendy J. Reifeiss
Marketing Manager:	Tracy Foley

© 1999 by Course Technology—I(T)P®

For more information contact:

Course Technology
One Main Street
Cambridge, MA 02142

ITP Europe
Berkshire House 168-173
High Holborn
London WCIV 7AA
England

Nelson ITP Australia
102 Dodds Street
South Melbourne, 3205
Victoria, Australia

ITP Nelson Canada
1120 Birchmount Road
Scarborough, Ontario
Canada M1K 5G4

International Thomson Editores
Seneca, 53
Colonia Polanco
11560 Mexico D.F. Mexico

ITP GmbH
Königswinterer Strasse 418
53227 Bonn
Germany

ITP Asia
60 Albert Street, #15-01
Albert Complex
Singapore 189969

ITP Japan
Hirakawacho Kyowa Building, 3F
2-2-1 Hirakawacho
Chiyoda-ku, Tokyo 102
Japan

Trademarks

Course Technology and the Open Book logo are registered trademarks and CourseKits is a trademark of Course Technology. Custom Edition is a registered trademark of International Thomson Publishing.

I(T)P® The ITP logo is a registered trademark of International Thomson Publishing.

Some of the product names and company names used in this book have been used for identification purposes only and may be trademarks or registered trademarks of their respective manufacturers and sellers.

Disclaimer

Course Technology reserves the right to revise this publication and make changes from time to time in its content without notice.

ISBN 0-7600-5876-8

Printed in the United States of America

1 2 3 4 5 6 7 8 9 BH 02 01 00 99 98

BRIEF TABLE OF CONTENTS

TABLE OF CONTENTS

CHAPTER THREE
Configuring Windows Protocols and Protocol Bindings   **51**

CHAPTER SIX
Configuring and Protecting Hard Disks   **155**

PREFACE

To know a little bit about technology is dangerous. This book aims to close the gap between basic familiarity with Windows NT Server and true understanding of Windows NT Server. At the same time, this book will prepare you for Microsoft's Certification Exam 70-068, "Implementing and Supporting Microsoft Windows NT Server 4.0 in the Enterprise." The Enterprise exam is the most difficult and comprehensive of the four core exams required for the Microsoft Certified System Engineer (MCSE) certification. Passing it is a major milestone on the road to becoming an MCSE.

As Windows NT Server has matured over time and through its various revisions (do you remember Lan Manager?), powerful functionality has been added, giving an administrator new opportunities as well as introducing new complexities. By completing this book, you will gain a better perspective on what is possible using Windows NT, how to make that happen, and what to do if it doesn't go perfectly.

Overcoming challenges at the enterprise level is one of the most rewarding experiences in the careers of most administrators. This is likely due to the satisfaction associated with demonstrating such a high level of competence and understanding such complicated systems.

Because textbook explanations alone will not prepare a technician for working at the enterprise level, this book contains a number of features aimed at maximizing the learning experience. Each chapter includes hands-on projects that walk you through the various tasks step-by-step, giving you hands-on experience. In addition, each chapter contains case studies that place you in the role of problem solver, requiring you to think through the concepts of the chapter in order to provide a successful solution. Also, each chapter contains review questions aimed at preparing you to complete the certification exam successfully.

Chapters 1 and 2 introduce you to the concepts and planning associated with networking Windows NT at the enterprise level, including security, interoperability, and domain structure. Chapter 3 builds on this by covering networking protocols and protocol bindings as they apply to Windows NT Server.

Beginning with chapters 4 and 5, you will focus on the application layer with Windows NT core and optional services, including very comprehensive coverage of Remote Access. In chapter 6 you will learn how to configure and protect your online storage.

Chapters 7 through 9 take you through the management side of Windows NT at the enterprise level. You will learn how to manage clients and servers as well as utilize user and group accounts, profiles, and system policies.

Chapters 10 and 11 cover some of the interoperability aspects of the enterprise, such as connections to NetWare and Appletalk networks. Also, installation and configuration of multiprotocol routing are discussed at length to further extend your knowledge of your connectivity options.

The remaining four chapters take what you have learned to a higher level by applying it to troubleshooting and optimization. Optimization and baselining help you determine how your network is performing, and the troubleshooting chapters teach you how to choose appropriate resolutions for problems related to each of the topics covered in the book. Special attention is paid to resolving the most difficult of problems, such as those involving Routing and Remote Access Services, and troubleshooting and debugging STOP errors (also known as the "Blue Screen of Death").

FEATURES

To help you fully understand Windows NT concepts, there are many features in this book designed to improve its pedagogical value.

- **Chapter Objectives** Each chapter in this book begins with a detailed list of the concepts to be mastered within that chapter. This list provides you with a quick reference to the contents of that chapter as well as a useful study aid.

- **Illustrations and Tables** Numerous illustrations of server screens and components help you to visualize common setup steps, theories, and concepts. In addition, many tables provide details and comparisons of both practical and theoretical information.

- **Hands-On Projects** Although it is important to understand the theory behind server and networking technology, nothing can improve upon real-world experience. To this end, along with theoretical explanations, each chapter provides numerous hands-on projects aimed at providing you with real-world implementation experience.

- **Chapter Summaries** Each chapter's text is followed by a summary of the concepts it has introduced. These summaries provide a helpful way to recap and revisit the ideas covered in each chapter.

- **Review Questions.** End-of-chapter assessment begins with a set of review questions that reinforce the ideas introduced in each chapter. These questions not only ensure that you have mastered the concepts, but also are written to help prepare you for the Microsoft certification examination.

- **Case Project** Located at the end of each chapter are several case projects that ask you to solve real-world, enterprise problems.

TEXT AND GRAPHIC CONVENTIONS

Wherever appropriate, additional information and exercises were added to this book to help you better understand what is being discussed in the chapter. Icons throughout the text alert you to additional materials. These icons are described below.

The Note icon is used to present additional helpful material related to the subject being described.

Each hands-on activity in this book is preceded by the Hands-on icon and a description of the exercise that follows.

Tips provide extra information about how to attack a problem, how to set up Windows NT Server for a particular need, or what to do to in certain real-world situations.

The cautions are included to help you anticipate potential mistakes or problems so you can prevent them from happening.

Case project icons mark case projects at the end of each chapter.

INSTRUCTOR'S MATERIALS

The following supplemental materials are available when this book is used in a classroom setting. All of the supplements available with this book are provided to the instructor on a single CD-ROM.

Electronic Instructor's Manual. The Instructor's Manual that accompanies this textbook includes:

■ Additional instructional material to assist in class preparation, including suggestions for lecture topics, suggested lab activities, tips on setting up a lab for the hands-on assignments, and alternative lab setup ideas in situations where lab resources are limited.

■ Solutions to all end-of-chapter materials, including the Project and Case assignments.

Course Test Manager 1.1. Accompanying this book is a powerful assessment tool known as the Course Test Manager. Designed by Course Technology, this cutting-edge Windows-based testing software helps instructors design and administer tests and pre-tests. In addition to being able to generate tests that can be printed and administered, this full-featured program also has an online testing component that allows students to take tests at the computer and have their exams automatically graded.

PowerPoint presentations. This book comes with Microsoft PowerPoint slides for each chapter. These are included as a teaching aid for classroom presentation, to make available to students on the network for chapter review, or to be printed for classroom distribution. Instructors, please feel at liberty to add your own slides for additional topics you introduce to the class.

Simulations. Featured on the Instructor's Resource Kit CD-ROM are several simulations, written in Visual Basic, which animate key concepts including starting a server service; sharing a folder as a network resource; setting up a network (shared) printer; setting up TCP/IP network protocol properties; creating and modifying user accounts for network management; setting up network account policies (password and account lockout management policies); setting up account auditing; setting up rights policies; and installing the Network Monitor Agent. Also, the Windows NT Server Installation Simulator, which simulates an actual installation, is provided. These simulations work in conjunction with many of the hands-on exercises in the book, and can be run in a 16-bit or 32-bit environment. The host workstation operating system and setup are unaffected by running the simulation software.

TRANSCENDER CERTIFICATION TEST PREP SOFTWARE

Bound into the back of this book is a disk containing Transcender Corporation's Implementing and Supporting Microsoft Windows NT Server 4.0 certification exam preparation software with one full exam that simulates the Microsoft exam (Exam 70-067).

ACKNOWLEDGMENTS

Jeffrey Williams: I owe a great deal to a great many. The greatest thanks go to my wife, Amanda, for her tolerance and exceptional forbearance in a project that grew from naught to infinity overnight. Mea culpas and acts of contrition are forthcoming.

A special thanks to Kristen Duerr for the opportunity to challenge myself in a new way, Ann Shaffer for helping me along that way (and making sure I could always keep up), and Jennifer Normandin for holding up the light that led me the last few miles. Extra thanks to our technical editor, Nick DiTirro of Lakeland Community College; to reviewers Joe Gannon of New Hampshire Technical College and Connie Batten of the University of Minnesota, who always made sure that my i's were dotted and my t's were crossed; and to Christopher, who in addition to his contributions to the book, made sure I never lost sight of what was most important.

David Johnson: First, I would like to thank Ann Shaffer, Jennifer Normandin, and the staff at Course Technology for making this rather arduous project a success. It has been a difficult time, to say the least, and you pulled it off successfully. I would also like to thank the staff at LANWrights for making sure I had the time to work on this book and continue the path we've chosen. Finally, my vast appreciation goes out to J. Michael Stewart, without whose help this book would not be possible.

DEDICATION

This book is dedicated to Raymond, who taught me how to see; to my parents, who taught me how to be; and especially to Amanda, who taught me how to feel.

— Jeff Williams

I'd like to dedicate this book to Ahnon, my best friend and confidant. You remind me of what life can be.

— David Johnson

PREPARING FOR MICROSOFT CERTIFICATION

Microsoft offers a program called the Microsoft Certified Professional (MCP) program. Becoming a Microsoft Certified Professional can open many doors for you. Whether you want to be a network engineer, product specialist, or software developer, obtaining the appropriate Microsoft Certified Professional credentials can provide a formal record of your skills to potential employers. Certification can be equally effective in helping you secure a raise or promotion.

The Microsoft Certified Professional program is made up of many courses in several different tracks. Combinations of individual courses can lead to certification in a specific track. Most tracks require a combination of required and elective courses. One of the most common tracks for beginners is the Microsoft Certified Product Specialist (MCPS). By obtaining this status, your credentials tell a potential employer that you are an expert in a specialized computing area such as Personal Computer Operating Systems on a specific product, like Microsoft Windows 95.

How Can Transcender's Test Prep Software Help?

To become a Microsoft Certified Professional, you must pass rigorous certification exams that provide a valid and reliable measure of technical proficiency and expertise. The disk contained in this book, Transcender Corporation's Limited Version certification exam preparation software, can be used in conjunction with the book to help you assess your progress in the event you choose to pursue Microsoft Professional Certification. The Transcender disk presents a series of questions that were expertly prepared to test your readiness for the official Microsoft Certification examination on Implementing and Supporting Windows NT Server 4.0 (Exam 70-067). These questions were taken from a larger series of practice tests produced by the Transcender Corporation—practice tests that simulate the interface and format of the actual certification exams. Transcender's complete product also offers explanations for all questions. The rationale for each correct answer is carefully explained, and specific page references are given for Microsoft Product Documentation and Microsoft Press reference books. These page references enable you to study from additional sources.

Practice test questions from Transcender Corporation are acknowledged as the best available. In fact, with their full product, Transcender offers a money-back guarantee if you do not pass the exam. If you have trouble passing the practice examination included on the enclosed disk, you should consider purchasing the full product with additional practice tests and personalized feedback. Details and pricing information are available at the back of this book. A sample of the full Transcender product is on the enclosed disk, including remedial explanations.

The Transcender product is a great tool to help you prepare to become certified. If you experience technical problems with this product, please e-mail Transcender at *course@transcender.com* or call (615) 726-8779.

Want to Know More about Microsoft Certification?

There are many additional benefits to achieving Microsoft Certified status. These benefits apply to you as well as to your potential employer. As a Microsoft Certified Professional (MCP), you will be recognized as an expert on Microsoft products, have access to ongoing technical information from Microsoft, and receive special invitations to Microsoft conferences and events. You can obtain a comprehensive, interactive tool that provides full details about the Microsoft Certified Professional program online at *www.microsoft.com/train_cert/cert/certif.htm*. For more information on texts at Course Technology that will help prepare you for certification exams, visit our site at *www.course.com*.

When you become a Certified Product Specialist, Microsoft sends you a Welcome Kit that contains:

- An 8½ × 11" Microsoft Certified Product Specialist wall certificate. Also, within a few weeks after you have passed any exam, Microsoft sends you a Microsoft Certified Professional Transcript that shows which exams you have passed.

- A Microsoft Certified Professional Program membership card.

- A Microsoft Certified Professional lapel pin.

- A license to use the Microsoft Certified Professional logo. You are licensed to use the logo in your advertisements, promotions, proposals, and other materials, including business cards, letterheads, advertising circulars, brochures, yellow page advertisements, mailings, banners, resumes, and invitations.

- A Microsoft Certified Professional logo sheet. Before using the camera-ready logo, you must agree to the terms of the licensing agreement.

- A Microsoft TechNet CD-ROM.

- A 50% discount toward a one-year membership in the Microsoft TechNet Technical Information Network, which provides valuable information via monthly CD-ROMs.

- Dedicated forums on CompuServe (GO MECFORUM) and The Microsoft Network, which enable Microsoft Certified Professionals to communicate directly with Microsoft and one another.

- A one-year subscription to Microsoft Certified Professional Magazine, a career and professional development magazine created especially for Microsoft Certified Professionals.

- A Certification Update subscription. Certification Update is a bimonthly newsletter from the Microsoft Certified Professional program that keeps you informed of changes and advances in the program and exams.

- Invitations to Microsoft conferences, technical training sessions, and special events.

- Eligibility to join the Network Professional Association, a worldwide association of computer professionals. Microsoft Certified Product Specialists are invited to join as associate members.

A Certified Systems Engineer receives all the benefits mentioned above as well as the following additional benefits:

- Microsoft Certified Systems Engineer logos and other materials to help you identify yourself as a Microsoft Certified Systems Engineer to colleagues or clients.

- Ten free incidents with the Microsoft Support Network and a 25% discount on purchases of additional 10-packs of Priority Development and Desktop Support incidents.

- A one-year subscription to the Microsoft TechNet Technical Information Network.

- A one-year subscription to the Microsoft Beta Evaluation program. This benefit provides you with up to 12 free monthly beta software CDs for many of Microsoft's newest software products. This enables you to become familiar with new versions of Microsoft products before they are generally available. This benefit also includes access to a private CompuServe forum where you can exchange information with other program members and find information from Microsoft on current beta issues and product information.

Certify Me!

So you are ready to become a Microsoft Certified Professional. The examinations are administered through Sylvan Prometric (formerly Drake Prometric) and are offered at more than 700 authorized testing centers around the world. Microsoft evaluates certification status based on current exam records. Your current exam record is the set of exams you have passed. To maintain Microsoft Certified Professional status, you must remain current on all the requirements for your certification.

Registering for an exam is easy. To register, contact Sylvan Prometric, 2601 West 88th Street, Bloomington, MN, 55431, at (800) 755-EXAM (3926). Dial (612) 896-7000 or (612) 820-5707 if you cannot place a call to an 800 number from your location. You must call to schedule the exam at least one day before the day you want to take the exam. Taking the exam automatically enrolls you in the Microsoft Certified Professional program; you do not need to submit an application to Microsoft Corporation.

When you call Sylvan Prometric, have the following information ready:

- Your name, organization (if any), mailing address, and phone number.

- A unique ID number (e.g., your Social Security number).

- The number of the exam you wish to take (70-67 for the Implementing and Supporting Microsoft Windows NT Server 4.0 exam).

- A payment method (e.g., credit card number). If you pay by check, payment is due before the examination can be scheduled. The fee to take each exam is currently $100.

READ THIS BEFORE YOU BEGIN

To the Student

This book comes with an NT Server installation simulator, available from your instructor, that enables you to practice the installation steps from any computer with Windows 3.1 or higher. Your instructor also can provide electronic simulations to help you practice important server setup activities. Each chapter of the book ends with review questions, Hands-on projects, and case assignments. Your instructor can provide you with answers to the review questions and additional information about the Hands-on projects. When you complete the case assignments you can submit them electronically or in written form.

To the Instructor

Please refer to the Instructor's Resource Kit that accompanies this text for more details.

Setting up the classroom or lab file server To complete the projects and assignments in this book, the students will need access to a Windows NT server. To maximize the learning experience, it is recommended that you have two or more file servers which can be dedicated for classroom use. (You'll need to be able to modify the servers' configuration frequently.) These servers need not be expensive models, but should be on Microsoft's Hardware Compatibility List. The advantage in having several servers for student projects is that the students have more flexibility in their practice. (The ideal would be one server per student.) Every server should be equipped with Microsoft Windows NT Server 4.0 with Service Pack 3 and have enough licenses for all students who need to access them. The Instructor's Resource Kit contains many suggestions about how to set up a lab, including how to equip and manage a lab in which there are limited resources. It also contains alternative projects and assignments for students.

Internet Assignments A few projects require Internet access for information searches and for downloading files. Although these projects are not mandatory, they will help train the student in using this resource as a prospective server administrator.

System Requirements All hardware, especially the server hardware, should be included on Microsoft's Hardware Compatibility List. The recommended software and hardware configurations are as follows:

Workstation Clients:

- Windows 95 or Windows NT Workstation 4.0 (if an NT Workstation computer is used, it must be a member of the NT Server's domain)
- 486 or higher processor with 16 MB of RAM (Pentium or higher preferred with 32+ MB of RAM)
- VGA monitor
- Mouse or other pointing device
- Network interface card cabled to the classroom file server
- Hard disk with at least 100 MB free
- At least one high density 3.5-inch floppy disk drive
- Internet access and a browser (recommended but not required – used for selected assignments)

Windows NT Server:

- Windows NT Server 4.0 with Service Pack 3 and Network Monitor installed, configured as a Primary Domain Controller
- 32-bit bus computer with an 80486 25 MHz or faster processor
- VGA or better resolution monitor
- Mouse or pointing device
- High density 3.5-inch floppy disk drive
- CD-ROM drive
- 32 MB or more memory
- One or more hard disks with at least 500 MB of disk storage (three additional unused hard drives will be necessary to complete exercises using Disk Administrator)
- Network interface card for network communications (two network interface cards – preferably attached to different networks - are needed for some projects)
- Tape system (recommended but not required)
- Two identical modems (if these modems are external, additional serial ports may be required)
- Printer (to practice setting up a network printer)

Other recommended equipment:

- A second Windows NT Server with a modem (required for some exercises)
- Two or more phone lines
- One or more Macintosh computers accessible on the network
- A Novell NetWare server running Version 3.x (or 4.x in bindery emulation mode) and an account with Supervisor rights

System Requirements for Transcender Corporation's Test Prep Software:

- 8 MB RAM (16 MB recommended)
- VGA/256 Color display or better
- 3.5-inch disk drive
- Microsoft Windows 3.1, Windows for Workgroups 3.11, Windows NT 3.51, Windows NT 4.0, or Windows 95

Upgrade to the full version of EnterpriseCert 4.0 Limited

What you get with the full version:

- Three full-length exams
- Detailed answer explanations for every question
  - *each explanation gives specific citations to common study references for easier study*

- Documentation that includes a study outline
- Money Back if You Don't Pass Guarantee
  - *see our website for guarantee details*

NetCert 2.5 is one of an entire line of Microsoft exam simulations designed to help you attain Microsoft certification. Transcender offers simulations of exams for every certification – MCSE (Microsoft Certified Systems Engineer), MCSD (Solution Developer), MCPS (Product Specialist) and MCT (Trainer). See our website at **http://www.transcender.com** for detailed product information and to download product demos.

To order your upgrade, mail us:
The coupon below, filled out with your information (no reproductions or photocopies please)

A check or money order, made out to Transcender Corporation, for $129, plus $6 shipping ($25 outside U.S.)

Terms and Conditions:
Maximum one upgrade per person. Prepayment by check, money order, or credit card, payable to Transcender Corporation. For your own protection, do not send currency through the mail. Allow 4–6 weeks for delivery.

Send to: Upgrade Program
 Transcender Corporation
 242 Louise Avenue
 Nashville, TN 37203

Please send me the EnterpriseCert 4.0 Upgrade. Enclosed is my check or credit card number, payable to Transcender Corporation for $129 plus $6 ($25 outside U.S.). TN residents add $10.64 for sales tax.

Name _____   School_____

Address_____   Credit Card: VISA   MC   AMEX   DISC

City_____State _____   CC# _____

Zip _____Country _____   Expiration _____

Phone _____   Name on Card _____

E-Mail _____   Signature_____
 _____ CRS3398

Transcender Corporation
SINGLE-USER LICENSE AGREEMENT

This is a legal agreement between you, the end user, and Transcender Corporation. BY BREAKING THE SEAL ON THE ENVELOPE AT THE BACK OF THIS BOOK, YOU ARE AGREEING TO BE BOUND BY THE TERMS OF THIS AGREEMENT. IF YOU DO NOT AGREE TO THE TERMS OF THIS AGREEMENT, YOU MAY RETURN THE PRODUCT TO THE PLACE OF PURCHASE AND, UPON RECEIPT OF THE UNOPENED PACKAGE, THE PURCHASE PRICE WILL BE REFUNDED AS LONG AS NONE OF THE COMPONENTS ARE MISSING, ALTERED OR DAMAGED.

Transcender Corporation Software License

1. **Grant of Single-User License.** Transcender Corporation grants to you a **single-user**, non-exclusive, non-transferable license to use this copy of the enclosed Transcender Corporation product, *EnterpriseCert 4.0 Limited* (the "Software"), on a single computer. You may not install this copy of the Software on a network server or allow multiple users. If you wish to put the Software on a network server or allow any other user or multiple users, you must purchase a network or multiple-user license for the Software.

2. **Copyright.** This product, including the program and the manual, is copyrighted. You may install the Software on your hard disk and/or make an archival copy by installing the Software on another floppy disk, but the program and manual may not, in whole or in part, be copied, photocopied, reproduced, translated or reduced to any medium, electronic or otherwise, or machine readable form without prior consent, in writing, from Transcender Corporation.

3. **No Transfer.** You may not sell, rent, lease, sublicense, disclose or otherwise transfer the Software or the documentation, in whole or in part, to any third party.

4. **Term.** The term of this Agreement and the license granted to you pursuant to this Agreement shall commence upon opening of this package and shall terminate after three years or upon your discontinuing the use of the software, whichever comes first.

5. **Title.** Title in and to the software and documentation remain exclusively in Transcender, subject to the express, limited and non-exclusive license granted to you pursuant to this Agreement.

6. **Governing Law.** This Agreement shall be construed, interpreted and governed by the laws of the State of Tennessee.

BY YOUR OPENING OF THIS SEALED PACKAGE, YOU ACKNOWLEDGE THAT YOU HAVE READ AND UNDERSTAND THE FOREGOING AND THAT YOU AGREE TO BE BOUND THEREBY.

CHAPTER ONE

INTRODUCTION TO THE ENTERPRISE NETWORK

In this chapter, you will learn the benefits of using Windows NT Server 4.0 in an enterprise network. An **enterprise network** is one in which users, servers, and resources are divided into at least two administrative groups, called **domains**. (You will learn more about domains in Chapter 2.) A network of this type encompasses multiple servers in multiple domains and locations, with the Internet being the largest enterprise network currently in existence. While managing an enterprise network is similar to managing a single-domain network, some problems are unique to the enterprise environment. In this chapter you will learn how to use Windows NT to solve some of these problems. First, to better understand the nature of Windows NT, you will learn about some historical events that helped shape enterprise networking in general, and Windows NT in particular.

AFTER READING THIS CHAPTER AND COMPLETING THE EXERCISES YOU WILL BE ABLE TO:

- Discuss the history of network computing
- Explain why Windows NT is portable, scalable, and approachable
- Explain the interoperability of Windows NT, and describe the networks and environments with which it can communicate
- Explain why Windows NT is considered secure

A Brief History of Windows NT

Two events related to market demands over the last 15 years have shaped the way we share information today. The first of these events, the client/server revolution, affected the way individual computers are connected to create networks. The second event, the GUI revolution, changed how users interact with the information stored on these networks. Together, the client/server and GUI revolutions set the stage for a new age of network computing, in which end users can access information quickly and easily, without having to be concerned about where that information is stored.

The Client/Server Revolution

In the early 1980s, most large companies relied on mainframe computers. In a **mainframe** environment, one or more primary hosts effectively centralize all processing and data gathering. (A **host** computer is a central computer resource on which data and applications are stored for access by users.) The only necessary interface is a **dumb terminal**—a screen and keyboard that connect, via a standard asynchronous connection or telephone line, to the mainframe. Keystrokes are sent to the mainframe for processing, and the mainframe returns the text to the dumb terminal. All database processing takes place on the mainframe.

With the widespread adoption of the Personal Computer (PC) in the late 1970s and early 1980s, the stage was set for a revolution in data processing. Instead of using expensive, proprietary mainframes, companies began connecting individual PCs to create networks in which the processing load was shared, rather than concentrated in a single computer. PCs on the network that acted as the central repositories of documents and applications were called **servers**. Other PCs on the network that functioned as terminals providing access to information on the servers became known as **clients**.

This transition from dumb terminal/mainframe environments to desktop PCs and servers is sometimes called the **client/server revolution**. In the modern client/server environment, one computer acts as a **client** or a requestor of services. A server provides these services by responding to client requests, using a predefined method of communication, or **protocol**. Many messages are sent between clients and servers, requiring a high level of cooperation between computers.

PCs require an **operating system**—that is, software that makes it possible to run programs, store data, and communicate with networks. In the business world, **DOS** (Disk Operating System) was widely used for desktop PCs. Many of the early networks were connected via **Novell NetWare**, a popular DOS-based network operating system. NetWare was relatively easy to set up and use, and performed the required tasks effectively and inexpensively.

Because the client/server design is already part of its operating system, a computer running Windows NT can act as both a client and a server. A network of computers that act as both client and server for one another is known as a **workgroup**. The individual computers within the workgroup are known as **workstations**. Each workstation can access resources on any other workstation by using its workstation service to connect to the server service on the other machine. Thus, to share information with users on another workstation, you can simply share the folder that contains the information by using the server service on your workstation.

Two versions of Windows NT exist: Windows NT Server, and Windows NT Workstation. Windows NT Server provides a variety of basic (or core) features, as well as numerous optional services. Windows NT Workstation provides only Windows NT Server's core features, and can accommodate only 10 clients simultaneously.

THE GUI REVOLUTION

As powerful and useful as the PC turned out to be, the appearance of its DOS screen (known as an **interface**) was not easy for the average user to master. To solve this problem, the graphical user interface (GUI) was developed. GUI relies on pictures, or graphics, rather than lines of text. It first began to show real promise in the 1970s, when a group at the Xerox Palo Alto Research Center (PARC) developed the Alto, a GUI-based computer. The Alto, which was the size of a large desk, provided a "What You See Is What you Get" (WYSIWYG) display on its monitor that used graphics rather than command lines. While touring PARC in 1979, Steven Jobs (president of Apple Computers) recognized the future of personal computing in the Alto. Much of the interface of the Apple Macintosh computer, which employed a GUI interface, relied heavily on the work done at PARC.

Apple adopted the mouse as a point-and-click device for navigating the GUI. The ease of use associated with the GUI made Apple's Macintosh line of computers a favorite for schools. Children found it much easier to navigate in a computer environment that required them to click on pictures, rather than entering complicated commands via the keyboard.

To maximize productivity and remain competitive, businesses running PCs needed a DOS-based GUI interface. Realizing the potential for such a product, Microsoft introduced one of the first DOS-based GUIs for the PC called Windows. Gone were the days of cryptic DOS commands like "dir" and "cd." Best of all, users could still use their old DOS programs, which generally ran well in the Windows environment. Business users did not have to invest in new hardware or new GUI applications to replace DOS-based ones. Because switching to Windows represented a cost-effective upgrade for most businesses, the GUI revolution helped change the PC marketplace. Figure 1-1 illustrates the difference between the DOS interface and the Windows interface.

INCREASED ACCESS TO INFORMATION

Over the next few years, Windows-based, client/server networks became increasingly popular in the business world. As the individual networks grew larger, the task of managing user accounts and security became more costly and time-consuming. Information systems (IS) managers began to install additional servers to keep up with the demand for information, which in turn meant that more user accounts had to be created and managed on those servers. Because each server had its own security system, however, users had to enter a valid user name and password for each server they attempted to access. End users struggled to remember multiple logon IDs and passwords, and administrators tried to meet the challenge of managing such fragmented networks. The problem was especially acute in the enterprise environment, where geographical distance made managing multiple servers even more difficult.

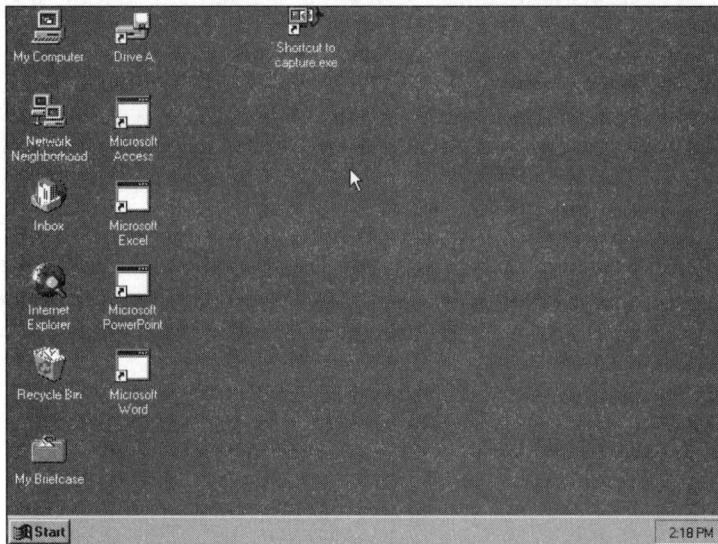

```
C:\>dir d:/w
Volume in drive D is NTS
Volume Serial Number is ECE5-A9E1

Directory of D:\

[CA]            [data]          [Inetpub]       [MSSQL]         pagefile.sys
[Program Files] [TEMP]          [WINNT]
           8 File(s)        46,137,344 bytes
                            914,237,440 bytes free

C:\>dir
Volume in drive C is DOS
Volume Serial Number is 1335-11E6

Directory of C:\

09/30/93  06:20a                  54,619 COMMAND.COM
12/12/97  10:57a                       0 CONFIG.SYS
12/12/97  10:57a                       0 AUTOEXEC.BAT
12/12/97  11:02a        <DIR>            I386
12/12/97  12:24p        <DIR>            InetPub
01/26/98  06:37a                       0 OCIWrapper.log
12/12/97  12:47p        <DIR>            hypersnap
12/12/97  12:47p        <DIR>            art
12/21/97  03:12p        <DIR>            hold
12/21/97  03:33p        <DIR>            college
12/21/97  03:37p        <DIR>            COLLWIN
12/26/97  12:05p                   1,225 mpssetup.log
01/24/98  10:37a        <DIR>            download
          13 File(s)        55,844 bytes
                        283,222,016 bytes free

C:\>
```

Figure 1-1   DOS interface and Windows interface

What was needed was a way to centralize network administration—something similar to the old mainframe environment, in which all user accounts were centralized, permitting easy management from one location. Network users demanded an enterprise network operating system that would allow users to log in once and gain immediate access to all servers and shared resources. In the ideal information system, end users would not have to be concerned with where the information was stored—only with getting the information quickly, easily, and seamlessly.

Probably the single largest leap toward this ideal information system occurred with the release of a new desktop (that is, non-server) operating system, Windows 95. Designed with networking in mind, Windows 95 provides powerful information-gathering tools to end users, such as simple terminal emulation software, dial-up networking, and the ability to accommodate multiple simultaneous network clients. Windows NT Server 4.0 is modeled on the popular GUI employed by Windows 95.

Because Windows NT is capable of being both a Microsoft client and a NetWare client, end users need not be concerned with whether a file is on a NetWare server or a Microsoft server. Drive D may be **mapped** (assigned) to a volume on a NetWare Server, while drive E is mapped to a **share** (a local designator for a remote resource) on a Windows NT server. Because the user no longer needs to create a link and separately log onto a variety of different network servers, the connection is said to be "transparent." Even though the underlying communication methods are vastly different, the end user sees none of these differences, and can easily access information on servers in the same office—or around the world.

Market pressures continue to change the way we use computers. The ideal information system was only partially realized with the release of Windows NT Server 4.0. New technologies, such as Active Directory, Active Desktop, and Internet/Intranet Integration, will be released in Windows NT Server 5.0 and should further simplify the task of gathering information from dissimilar sources. Windows 95 and Windows NT might also be blended into a single operating system. Preliminary versions of Windows 98 and Windows NT Server 5.0 already appear to be strikingly similar. It would not be surprising to hear that, after the introduction of Windows 98, only Windows NT will be upgraded.

WINDOWS NT IN AN ENTERPRISE ENVIRONMENT

Now that you understand the history of Windows NT, you can appreciate the features that make it so useful and powerful in an enterprise environment.

PORTABILITY

One of the most useful features of Windows NT is its portability. A **portable** operating system is not designed for a specific hardware platform, but rather adapts itself to operate on many different processor platforms in many different configurations.

Historically, servers were built to run a specific, proprietary operating system—usually an operating system that was written by the same company that built the hardware. These operating systems are not portable; therefore they can be run only on the hardware platform for which they were designed. Because it is completely portable, however, Windows NT works on both existing and newly introduced hardware.

> ⚠️ **Caution** Even though Windows NT is extremely portable, a word of warning: before attempting to install it, make sure both your computer and its network interface card are included on Microsoft's hardware compatibility list. You will have an opportunity to complete this task in the Hands-On Projects at the end of this chapter.

The secret to the portability of Windows NT lies in its **hardware abstraction layer (HAL)**, which hides many platform differences from the operating system. Where great differences in processors occur, Windows NT provides a different HAL. Figure 1-2 illustrates the HAL.

Windows NT Server

HAL.DLL

Intel 386

DEC ALPHA

PowerPC

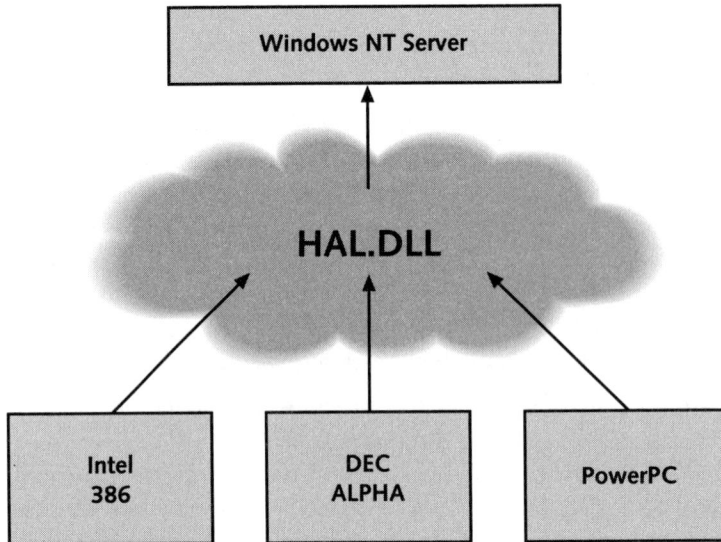

Figure 1-2   The HAL hides platform differences from the operating system

SCALABILITY

Windows NT is also scalable. A **scalable** operating system takes full advantage of multiple processors by balancing the processing load and ensuring optimal performance; it can therefore accommodate small or large networks. By using more processors, Windows NT can handle a large network. By using fewer processors, a scalable operating system can accommodate a small network. The need for a scalable operating system became apparent as inexpensive Intel-based network servers became more popular and data-intensive applications stretched the limited capacity of single Intel processors. While Intel processors were inexpensive to make and easy to mass-produce, they lacked the powerhouse performance required by many large data-processing companies.

Windows NT solves this problem by allowing several Intel-based processors to work together and share the processing workload. Using a process called **symmetric multiprocessing (SMP)**, it schedules operating system tasks to be processed on processors that are free when the process is initiated, thus distributing the load to idle processors. Out of the box, Windows NT Server 4.0 supports as many as 4 processors. With modifications and special drivers provided by the equipment manufacturers, it can conceivably support as many as 32 processors in the same system.

WINDOWS NT INTEROPERABILITY

In large enterprise environments, dissimilar information systems are bound to exist. These differing systems require special communication methods. Communication between such networks is facilitated by another important feature of Windows NT—its interoperability. As illustrated in Figure 1-3, the term **interoperability** refers to the ability of an operating system to communicate, share data, and cooperate with dissimilar network servers and workstations.

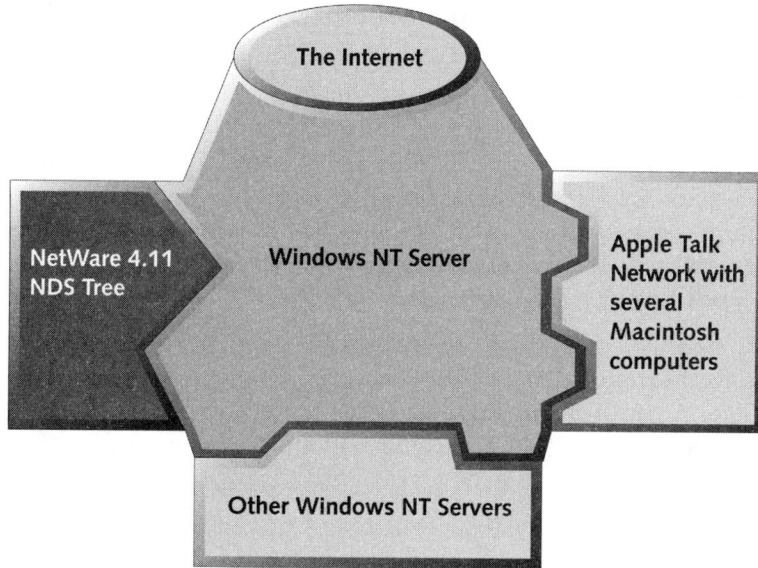

Figure 1-3   Interoperability of Windows NT

Windows NT Server 4.0 is interoperable with all major network and workstation operating systems, including systems running NetWare 3 and 4 systems, Macintosh computers, and mainframes. Because Windows NT includes industry-standard protocols such as TCP/IP and DLC, and as well as proprietary protocols such as IPX/SPX and AppleTalk, you can use it to link even dissimilar network servers. (You will learn more about protocols in Chapter 3.) The following sections summarize the interoperability capabilities of Windows NT.

Interoperability with NetWare

NetWare 3 stores security and connection information in a flat database, called the bindery, and communicates through Novell's proprietary IPX/SPX protocol. Although NetWare 4 also supports bindery emulation, it implements a structured objects database called NetWare Directory Services (NDS) as well. Because nearly 80% of the local area networks installed in the United States include a NetWare server, the interoperability of Windows NT is very important, especially in an enterprise network.

Two Windows NT services provide connectivity to NetWare 3 and 4: Client Services for NetWare (CSNW) and Gateway Services for NetWare (GSNW). **CSNW** is a core service provided with Windows NT Workstation that allows it to connect seamlessly to NetWare volumes and access information, provided that a valid user account has been created on the NetWare server. **GSNW**, which is available only with Windows NT Server, allows Windows NT Server to link to a NetWare volume through a single NetWare user account and then reshare that volume with all Microsoft clients on the NT network.

Interoperability with AppleTalk (Macintosh) Networks

Macintosh clients dictate a unique series of connectivity requirements, which pose a challenge for many administrators. NT Services for Macintosh allows a server to act as an AppleShare File Server, thus enabling Macintosh clients to save and share data on a Windows NT shared folder. Windows NT can also act as an AppleTalk print server, by translating PostScript print requests from Macintosh clients into bitmap images that can be sent to any non-PostScript printer. This feature is automatically installed for each shared printer on the Windows NT Server upon the installation of Services for Macintosh. Furthermore, administrators can configure a shared print queue on the server that allows non-Macintosh clients to print to AppleTalk printers.

Finally, Services for Macintosh enables Windows NT to be configured as an AppleTalk multi-homed router. A **multi-homed router** is simply a Windows NT computer with two or more network interface cards (NICs), a configuration that permits the computer to act as a node on two or more networks. Routing is designed to physically separate two networks, and can be quite useful in reducing traffic on busy AppleTalk networks.

Interoperability with OS/2 Networks

Because OS/2 servers use the same communication methods and protocols as Microsoft networks, no special additions or client software is required when connecting to OS/2 servers. Client for Microsoft Networks is all that is required. You can even use the Windows NT password change utility to alter passwords on OS/2 domains. Security account databases remain separate, however, requiring a valid log-on ID and password to be presented when connecting to an OS/2 shared resource.

Interoperability with Other Systems

Windows NT offers several ways to access other systems such as Mainframes, IBM AS/400s, and Unix-based servers for which there is no dedicated Windows NT subsystem. These methods include Remote Access Service (RAS, which is discussed in Chapter 5), terminal emulation, and also through add-on products such as Microsoft SNA Server (SNA Server ships as a part of Back Office).

With each of these software-based connections, the NT Server connects as a gateway. This type of connection does not give the same interoperability and security as those connections that have a dedicated subsystem.

Interoperability with the Internet

Microsoft included a simple Web browser (Internet Explorer) as part of the Windows 95 operating system; it also provided client software to establish dial-up networking connections directly to the Internet through an Internet service provider (ISP). Windows NT Server 4.0 provides the familiar Windows 95 interface, plus some of the same tools for using the Internet.

Windows NT 4.0 also includes Remote Access Service (RAS) which facilitates the connection of remote networks either by modem, ISDN, X.25, or another linking method. RAS can be used to link your internal network to the Internet. It is often used in conjunction with Microsoft Proxy Server to establish a secured, single point of connection to the Internet.

SECURITY

Yet another important feature of Windows NT relates to its security. Any network is vulnerable to security breaches. In most companies, certain kinds of information should not be made available to all personnel. The Human Resources department, for example, may store employee performance reviews in a secured area, so that they are viewable only by designated managers and administrators.

Windows NT provides the ability to effectively provide security without compromising the ability to share data when needed. When configured properly, the attributes and characteristics of the network security system can be transferred across multiple domains and networks. Combining interoperability with security, Windows NT even allows administrators to restrict access to resources to authorized users on dissimilar networks at both the resource and file level.

Another security feature of Microsoft Windows NT is its ability to manage security for an entire enterprise from a single location. Even when a wide area network (WAN) separates domains, specially defined relationships between domains, known as trust relationships, provide the framework for centralized administration. This strategy can potentially reduce the cost of network administration. (You will learn more about trust relationships in Chapter 2.)

Table 1-1 lists some Windows NT Security features.

Table 1-1   Security Features of Windows NT

Feature	Description
Restrictive primary file system	Provides restrictive access to specified users, while allowing them to share data with other specified users
Fault tolerance	Ensures that, in the event of a power failure or other abnormal system shutdown, data that were in transit during the failure are not lost
Event logging	Maintains a record of user actions, ensuring user accountability
No "undelete" utility	Ensures that a file is completely erased when it is deleted

APPROACHABILITY

The last key feature of Windows NT is its approachability. The term **approachability** refers to the ease of using a new network operating system for the first time. A truly approachable network operating system is so easy to use that it doesn't require continuous training, and allows a novice administrator to complete most tasks.

Microsoft Windows NT Server 4.0 is considered very approachable. While other network operating systems require the administrator to use cryptic command lines, Windows NT is based on the familiar Windows 95 interface. It can be comfortably used by almost anyone who is already familiar with Windows 95. For the most part, Windows NT is completely self-tuning. The operating system automatically makes changes in usage, network traffic, and disk space availability that would normally require intervention by network administrators.

CHAPTER SUMMARY

- An enterprise network is one in which servers are divided into at least two administrative groups, called domains. A typical enterprise network encompasses multiple servers in multiple domains and locations. Two principal events helped make enterprise networks what they are today.

- The first of these events, the client/server revolution, occurred when businesses switched from expensive, proprietary mainframe computers to networks of inexpensive personal computers (PCs). These PCs relied on operating system software (usually DOS) to run programs and store data. In the modern client/server environment, one computer acts as a client or a requestor of services. A server provides these services by responding to client requests, using a prearranged method of communication, or protocol. A computer running Windows NT can act as both a client and a server. A network of computers that acts as both clients and servers is known as a workgroup. The individual computers within the workgroup are known as workstations.

- The second event, the GUI revolution, occurred when operating systems switched from a text-based interface to a pictured-based, graphical user interface (GUI). The GUI was first widely used in Apple computers, along with the point-and-click device known as a mouse. To avoid the expense associated with the new Apple technology, businesses running PCs demanded their own GUI interface: Windows. Because changing to Windows represented a cost-effective upgrade for most businesses, the GUI revolution dramatically changed the PC marketplace.

- As Windows-based, client/server networks proliferated, businesses turned to Windows 95, and then to Windows NT, as a means to centralize network administration and help network users find needed information. Windows NT is now widely used as a network operating system, thanks to several key features.

- First, Windows NT is portable, which means that it adapts itself to many different platforms in many different configurations. Its portability is made possible by its hardware abstraction layer (HAL), which hides many platform differences from the operating system. Windows NT is also scalable, so that it takes full advantage of multiple processors by balancing the processing load and can therefore accommodate small or large networks. Using a process called symmetric multiprocessing (SMP), Windows NT schedules operating system tasks to be processed on processors that are most available when the process is initiated, thus distributing the load to idle processors. Windows NT is also interoperable, which means that it can communicate, share data, and cooperate with all major network and workstation operating systems, including AppleTalk, OS/2, mainframes, and NetWare 3 and 4. Yet another feature of Windows NT, its security, allows administrators to maintain security for an entire enterprise network from a single location without compromising the ability to share data. Finally, Windows NT is approachable, which means that it is relatively easy for new network administrators to master and use.

KEY TERMS

- **approachable** — Term used to describe the ease of using a new network operating system for the first time.

- **client** — In early networks, a computer that functioned as a terminal providing access to information on servers. In modern networks, a computer that acts as a requestor of services.

- **client/server revolution** — The transition from dumb terminal/mainframe environments to desktop PCs and servers.

- **Client Services for Netware (CSNW)** — A service provided with Windows NT Workstation that allows it to connect seamlessly to NetWare volumes and access information, provided that a valid user account has been created on the NetWare server.

- **domain** — An administrative group of servers and resources.

- **DOS (Disk Operating System)** — An operating system widely used on early PCs that requires the user to type lines of commands. DOS is available through emulation in Windows NT.

- **dumb terminal** — A screen and keyboard that connect, via standard asynchronous or telephone line, to a mainframe computer.

- **enterprise network** — A network that encompasses at least two domains.

- **Gateway Services for NetWare (GSNW)** — A Windows NT Server feature that allows Windows NT Server to link to a NetWare volume through a single NetWare user account and then reshare that volume with all Microsoft clients on the Windows NT network.

- **GUI** — Graphical user interface. A screen display that requires the user to use a mouse to point at and click on pictures (graphics) rather typing lines of commands.

- **GUI revolution** — The transition from text-based interfaces, such as DOS, to graphics-oriented interfaces, such as Windows.

- **HAL** — Hardware abstraction layer. A layer of the Windows NT operating system that hides many differences in hardware platforms from the operating system.

- **host** — A host computer is a central computer resource on which data and applications are stored for access by clients.

- **interoperable** — Term used to describe an operating system that can communicate, share information, and cooperate with other network servers and devices.

- **mainframe** — An environment in which one or more primary servers (usually called mainframe computers) effectively centralize all processing and data gathering. Users communicate with the mainframe computer via dumb terminals.

- **map** — To assign a local designator to a remote resource. For example, you could map a storage resource to a drive letter.

- **multi-homed router** — A Windows NT computer with two or more network adapter cards, enabling the computer to act as a node on two or more networks.

- **Novell NetWare** — A DOS-based network operating system.

- **operating system** — Software that allows a computer to run programs, store data, and communicate with networks.
- **overhead** — Resource utilization on a network.
- **portable** — Term used to describe an operating system that adapts itself to many different processor revisions and hardware platforms.
- **protocol** — A prearranged method of communication between computers.
- **scalable** — Term used to describe an operating system that takes full advantage of multiple processors by balancing the processing load and ensuring optimal performance. A scalable operating system can accommodate both large and small networks.
- **server** — In early networks, a PC that acted as the central repository of documents and applications. In modern networks, a computer that provides services by responding to client requests.
- **share** — A local designator for a remote resource.
- **symmetric multiprocessing (SMP)** — An operating system process that takes full advantage of multiple processors in the same machine by balancing the operating load across all of them.
- **workgroup** — A network of computers that act as both clients and servers.
- **workstation** — A computer within a workgroup.

REVIEW QUESTIONS

1. What is a portable operating system?
   a. an operating system that will work on a portable computer
   b. an operating system that can be networked and provide portable data transfer
   c. an operating system that can adapt to a variety of processor types and platforms
   d. an operating system that uses more than one of the same type of processor

2. What is a scalable operating system?
   a. An operating system that is easy for first-time users to master
   b. An operating system that can operate on individual computers of any physical size
   c. An operating system that can take full advantage of multiple processors by balancing the processing load and ensuring optimal performance
   d. An operating system that can manage individual programming functions so that they can be effectively monitored

3. The term symmetric multiprocessing refers to:
   a. a server with two or more processors.
   b. the relationship between a dumb terminal and a mainframe computer.
   c. an as-yet-unavailable feature that will probably be included in Windows 98.
   d. the situation in which an operating system schedules tasks to be processed on idle processors

4. A computer running Windows NT:

   a. can act only as a server.

   b. can act only as a client.

   c. acts as a dumb terminal unless specially configured to act as a server.

   d. can act as both a client and server.

5. "GUI" is short for _____.

6. One concern with using Apple Macintosh computers in an enterprise business environment was:

   a. their incompatibility with the PCs already in use.

   b. their picture-based interface was difficult for first-time users to master.

   c. their text-based interface was difficult for first-time users to master.

   d. they could not be connected to create a network.

7. The term interoperability refers to:

   a. the ability of a computer to act in multiple capacities.

   b. the ability of an operating system to use multiple programming languages.

   c. a computer system that can access the Internet.

   d. the ability of a computer to communicate, share information, and cooperate with other existing or legacy network servers and devices.

8. The _____ hides many platform differences from the operating system.

9. Windows NT is interoperable with all major network and workstation operating systems, including _____, _____, and _____. It is also interoperable with the _____.

10. Security on a Windows NT enterprise network:

   a. must be managed from multiple locations throughout the networks.

   b. compromises the ability to share data.

   c. does not allow administrators to limit resources to authorized users on dissimilar networks.

   d. can be managed from a single location.

11. The term approachable refers to:

   a. the cost associated with instituting a network within acceptable tolerances.

   b. a measure of the ease of using a new network operating system for the first time.

   c. a network operating system that can communicate with other computers running a variety of different operating systems.

   d. a measure of the ease of linking workgroups into an enterprise network.

12. The term client/server revolution refers to:
    a. the transition to WYSIWYG interfaces.
    b. the transition from approachable to portable operating systems.
    c. the transition from mainframe environments to desktop PCs and servers.
    d. the transition from desktop PCs and servers to mainframe environments.
13. Which of the following factors was most instrumental in launching the client/server revolution?
    a. the availability of low-cost PC workstations
    b. the shortage of mainframe computers
    c. the development of network operating systems
    d. the decision by Apple to maintain a proprietary operating system
14. In Windows NT, all changes in network traffic, usage, and disk availability:
    a. always require intervention by network administrators.
    b. generally do not require intervention by network administrators.
    c. are made automatically by the operating system.
    d. both b and c.

HANDS-ON PROJECTS

For one or all of these projects you will need a Windows NT Installation CD (either Server or Workstation), a Windows NT Server and Windows 95 computer, one of which has access to the Internet.

PROJECT 1-1

The purpose of this project is to provide you with a practical understanding of how Microsoft implements portability into Windows NT. It is designed to demonstrate how the Windows NT installation CD segregates the installation files and folders, depending upon the platform used as the NT server. To complete this hands-on project, you will need the Windows NT Server or Workstation 4.0 installation CD and a computer that can access the installation CD.

Throughout this book, the term "left mouse button" signifies the primary mouse button and "right mouse button" signifies the secondary mouse button. When you are instructed to "right-click" the mouse, click the secondary mouse button.

1. Place the CD in your CD drive and close the drive. If the installation window opens automatically, close it.
2. Click **Start**, point to **Programs**, then click **Windows NT Explorer**.
3. In the left pane of Windows NT Explorer, double-click the **CD drive**.
4. Note the number of folders located on the root directory of the installation CD.
5. Double-click the **I386 folder** to display its contents in the right pane of Windows Explorer. Note the number of subfolders.
6. Right-click the **System32 folder icon** to open the Shortcut menu, then click **Properties**. How many files are contained in this folder?
7. In the left pane of Windows Explorer, double-click the **Alpha folder** in the root directory of the installation CD. How many folders do you see? How many files are contained in this folder?
8. Compare the folders and files in the Alpha and I386 folders to see if you can identify which folders are the same and which ones are different. This can be a lengthy project. If you are working with fellow students, share this responsibility.

PROJECT 1-2

This project involves ascertaining whether your computer is on Microsoft's hardware compatibility list. The most up-to-date source for this information is Microsoft's Web site. You will need Internet access to complete this project.

1. Determine the make, model, and processor type of your computer. Also identify the make and model of the network interface card (NIC) installed in your computer.
2. Use your Web browser to access Microsoft's Web site at *www.microsoft.com*.
3. Click the **Search button** located on Microsoft's home page.
4. In the text box, type **HCL and NT**.
5. From the search results, select **Windows NT Hardware Compatibility List (HCL).**
6. Use this page's form to determine if your computer and NIC card are on the Microsoft hardware compatibility list. If they are not, does it mean that Windows NT will not run on your computer? If both the computer and NIC card are on the list, does it mean that Windows NT will necessarily operate properly on your computer?

PROJECT 1-3

This project provides you with a guided tour that highlights some differences between the screens you will see when operating in a Windows NT and a Windows 95 environment. It assumes that the Windows 95 computer is set up to provide user access to a Windows NT domain. Comparison screen shots are provided in case you do not have access to Windows NT and

Windows 95 at the same time. If you have access to only one of the operating systems, perform the steps for Windows NT or Windows 95, and read the steps for the operating system you lack.

1. Turn on a Windows 95 workstation and a Windows NT computer.

2. On the Windows 95 workstation, you see the Enter Network Password dialog box. Enter the user name and password, and then select the domain you wish to log into.

3. On the Windows NT computer, you see the Begin Logon dialog box. Press **Ctrl+Alt+Delete** to log on. The Logon Information dialog box opens. Enter the user name and password, and then select the domain you wish to log into.

4. Answer the following questions:

   ▪ Why does Windows NT require you to press Ctrl+Alt+Delete to log on?

   ▪ Why can't you insert a domain name into the Logon Information dialog box on a Windows NT computer like you can in the Enter Network Password dialog box of a Windows 95 computer?

5. On both the Windows 95 and Windows NT computers, click the **Start button**, then point to **Programs**. Figure 1-4 illustrates the Windows 95 Programs menu. Figure 1-5 illustrates the Windows NT Programs menu.

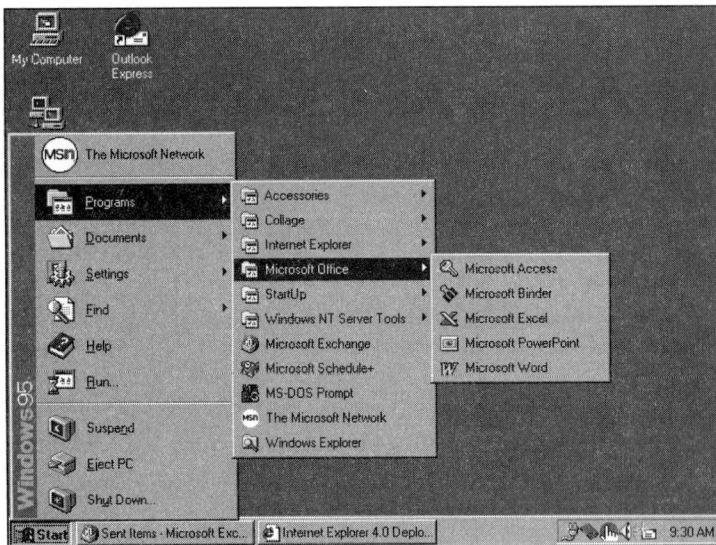

Figure 1-4   Windows 95 Programs menu

6. Note the "Administrative Tools (Common)" option on the Windows NT Programs menu. It is not available on the Windows 95 programs menu. Why not?

7. On the Windows NT menu, click Administrative Tools (Common) and note the 13 Administrative Tools utilities. To test your current familiarity with Windows NT, describe in general terms the function of each utility. (Limit your descriptions to a single sentence for each utility.)

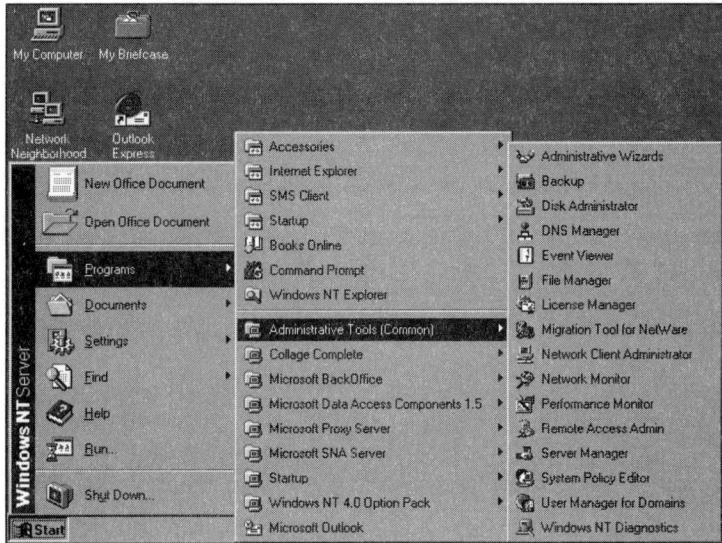

Figure 1-5   Windows NT Programs menu

8. On both the Windows NT and Windows 95 computers, click the **Start button**, point to **Settings**, then click **Control Panel** to open the Control Panel. Figure 1-6 shows a Windows 95 Control Panel, while Figure 1-7 shows a Windows NT Control Panel. Note that your Control Panel may differ from the figure.

Figure 1-6   Windows 95 control panel

Figure 1-7   Windows NT control panel

9. Which icons are common to both Control Panels? Which icons are included in the Windows NT Control Panel but not the Windows 95 Control Panel? Which icons are included on the Windows 95 Control Panel, but not the Windows NT Control Panel? Note the absence of the Add/Remove hardware icon from the Windows NT Control Panel. How do you add or remove hardware when operating in an NT environment?

10. On both the Windows 95 and Windows NT computers, double-click the **System icon** on the Control Panel. Figure 1-8 shows the System Properties dialog box for Windows 95. Figure 1-9 shows the System Properties dialog box for Windows NT. Note that your System Properties dialog boxes will differ from the figures.

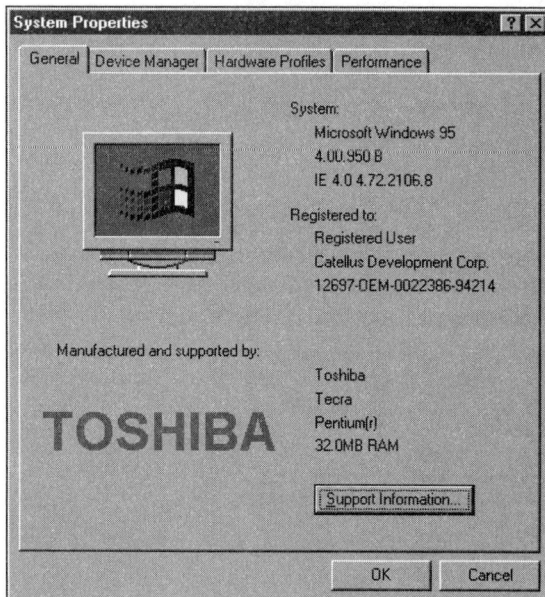

Figure 1-8   Windows 95 System Properties dialog box

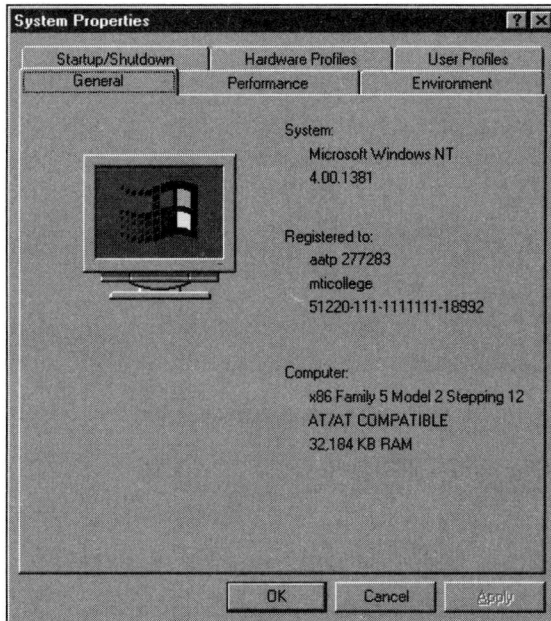

Figure 1-9   Windows NT System Properties dialog box

11. Which tabs are common to both dialog boxes? Which tabs are included in the Windows NT System Properties dialog box but not the Windows 95 System Properties dialog box? Which tabs are included in the Windows 95 System Properties dialog box but not the Windows NT System Properties dialog box? Note the absence of the Device Manager tab in the Windows NT system dialog box. How do you determine what hardware is installed and configured in Windows NT?

PROJECT 1-4

The purpose of this project is to compare Windows NT security features under a Windows NT file system with those available in a FAT file system.

1. Figure 1-10 shows the options for using a Windows 95 computer to share files across a network with other users. Note the single tab of options, with limited security settings.

2. What security choices do you have regarding a shared folder on a Windows 95 computer? What type of security is this?

3. Figures 1-11, 1-12, and 1-13 show the options available for a folder on a Windows NT server. Note the number of security configurations available.

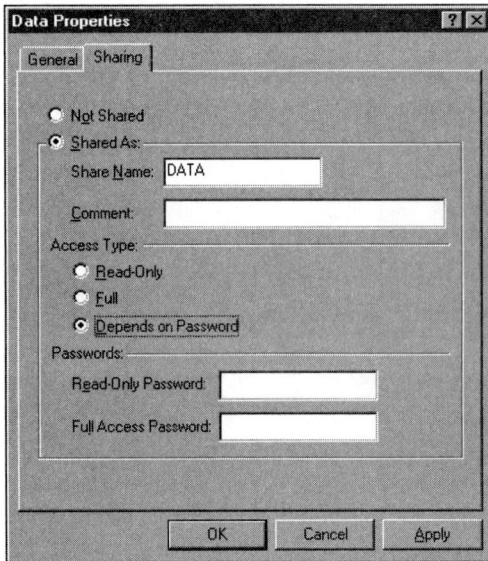

Figure 1-10   Windows 95 Data Properties dialog box

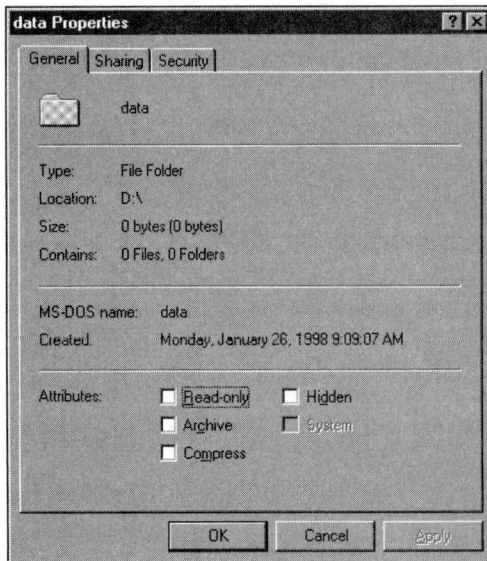

Figure 1-11   General tab of the data Properties dialog box

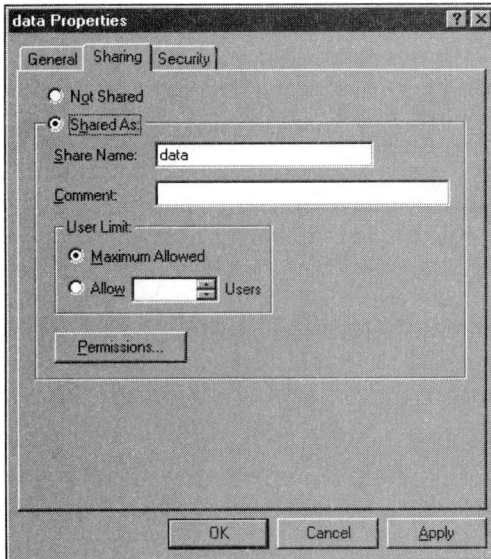

Figure 1-12   Sharing tab of the data Properties dialog box

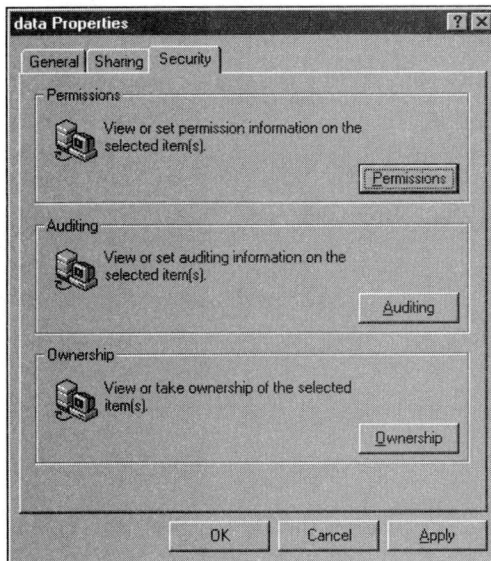

Figure 1-13   Security tab of the data Properties dialog box

4. What security choices do you have regarding a shared folder in Windows NT?

CASE PROJECTS

1. You have been hired as a consultant for Repro, a company that sells reproductions of antique lighting fixtures. Your job is to analyze the existing network system and create a plan that will allow the company to expand easily from a single office with customers drawn from the local metropolitan area to a nationwide mail-order firm. Repro may eventually acquire at least two competing companies, each with its own existing network. Repro's current network is a mainframe environment with 20 dumb terminals located at employee stations. The interface is text-based, which necessitates that new employees undergo a long training period. Write four to five paragraphs explaining the advantages of a Windows NT network. Which of the features described in this chapter are especially important for this expanding company? Why? Include explanations of these features in your report.

2. You are the Information Systems manager for a small, but growing marketing firm with a Windows NT network. Your company relies heavily on consumer preference research performed by researchers around the country. To speed the acquisition of research data, you would like to connect directly to your researchers' networks. The president of your company has asked you to prepare a short report (five to six paragraphs) explaining how Windows NT would make this connection possible. Explain the concept of interoperability, and then describe the networks and operating systems to which your company could connect via Windows NT.

3. You have been hired to analyze the security of a computerized cash register and inventory network for a chain of music stores. After evaluating the network, you have become convinced that it is extremely vulnerable. The company risks losing valuable sales data in the event of a power failure. It's also possible for employees to conceal the theft of cash or merchandise because the current network operating system does not adequately track user actions. Using the information in Table 1-1, write a short report (three to four paragraphs) explaining how Windows NT could be used to solve the company's network security problems.

PLANNING A WINDOWS NT ENTERPRISE NETWORK

One primary goal of a network is to hold information and make it available to users at the click of the mouse. As companies grow larger and become more complexly organized, however, this goal is often compromised. In a newly expanded company, employees often cannot find or access the information and resources they need. In most cases, this is because the network was poorly planned. As you will learn in this chapter, a carefully planned network is one that meets the needs of a small organization but can also grow to accommodate a much larger, more complicated organization. The keys to network organization are domains, and the relationship between domains, known as trust relationships.

AFTER READING THIS CHAPTER AND COMPLETING THE EXERCISES YOU WILL BE ABLE TO:

- Plan a network
- Explain the concepts of a one-way domain and a two-way domain
- Create a trust relationship and explain its purpose
- Explain and diagram the five domain models
- Explain the uses and limitations of Directory Services

PLANNING A NETWORK

The first step in planning a network (or reengineering a defective network) is to analyze the needs of the people who will use the network. A properly conducted needs analysis will go beyond the present business needs and focus on future needs, such as the anticipated addition of branch offices. The ideal goal for a network plan is one that is flexible enough to permit such growth. Unfortunately, in the real business world, network planning does not get the attention it deserves. A number of reasons for this disinterest in planning are issues such as financial limitations and the lack of experience and knowledge on the part of the systems engineers. Critical decisions about a network are often "knee-jerk reactions" to current inadequacies, rather than carefully orchestrated, long-term strategies.

When planning an enterprise network, you need to consider the following:

- The present number of network users

- The predicted number of network users over the next five years

- Ways the network could be divided into domains, such as by department or geographical location

- Preferences for centralized or decentralized management

THE WINDOWS NT DOMAIN

In a Windows NT network, a **domain** is a collection of users, resources, and servers. A domain must include at least one Windows NT server, and it may contain workstations and peripheral devices, such as printers. It must have one (and only one) primary domain controller. The **primary domain controller** maintains the domain's central security database, which lists users who are members of the domain, as well as those users' rights and privileges regarding resources on the domain. This database is commonly referred to as the **Security Accounts Manager (SAM) database**. The SAM database is a Windows NT Registry hive that stores all user account, group account, and security policy information for a Widows NT computer or a Windows NT domain. You'll learn more about the SAM database later in this chapter.

Depending upon its size, the domain may have one or more servers designated as backup domain controllers. **Backup domain controllers** are designed to handle much of the load associated with the **security authentication** (logon process) of domain users. They maintain a copy of the primary domain controller's security database in a "read-only" form. If a backup domain controller is available when a user logs into the domain, it will handle the user authentication process. This strategy reduces the load on the primary domain controller, allowing it to devote more of its network resources to maintaining the domain's security database and other necessary processes.

You create a domain while installing Windows NT on a server. Near the end of the installation process, you are asked to specify the server's function. The act of designating the server as a primary domain controller and then specifying a domain name creates the domain. (You will learn more about the installation process in the next section.)

> **Note** Keep in mind that the equipment and management costs associated with multiple domains make them inappropriate for small businesses with 25 or fewer workstations at a single location.

From a network management perspective, using domains as the building blocks of a network allows you to divide the network resources into groups that make sense logically, and that are therefore easier to manage as the network grows. For example, it may make sense to divide a network into two domains, one for users and one for network resources.

Another approach is to divide a business network into domains based upon geography. For example, suppose two parts of a wide area network (WAN), one in Detroit and one in Minneapolis, are connected via a modem or other slow connection. If both locations are part of the same domain, Minneapolis users may have difficulty accessing the domain controller in Detroit. As a result, the log-in process may be slow or nonresponsive. One solution to this problem may involve placing a backup domain controller at both locations. This approach could potentially create additional traffic across the modem link, as the domain controllers would have to communicate continuously with one another to maintain a consistent security database. A more efficient approach to this problem may be to establish a separate domain for each physical location. In this way you could maintain security databases independently for each domain, avoid the overhead of security database replication across a slow modem connection, and still allow users from one domain to access resources located on the other domain.

Multiple domains can also be used on a single local area network (LAN) as a security management tool. This approach does not separate the part of the network physically, but simply manages the security of each domain independently, through separate domain controllers. For example, you might establish a number of domains for a large corporate network based upon departmental structure. In this situation, the names selected should make sense logically—for example, "Sales" for the Sales Department domain, "Marketing" for the Marketing Department domain, and so on. This strategy greatly simplifies the process of managing the network resources, as well as users' rights and privileges. For example, a network administrator could see instantly that users in the Human Resources domain probably don't need to have access to a product inventory database located on a server in the Sales domain.

The creation of multiple domains is sometimes necessitated by limitations associated with Windows NT. From a practical standpoint, having more than 10,000 users in a single domain, for example, will result in unacceptable log-in times, even with the use of a large number of backup domain controllers. Later in this chapter you will learn how to organize multiple domains according to established domain models and recognize the limitations associated with each domain model.

In an enterprise environment, the use of a carefully planned domain system provides the following benefits:

- Reduction of the overall IS staff required in each remote office
- Central account administration
- Local administration of the resources in remote offices
- Quicker resolution of network problems
- Uniformed implementation of Windows NT throughout the network

In the next section you will learn about the roles a server can play in a domain environment.

WINDOWS NT SERVER ROLES

When installing Windows NT on an enterprise server, you must specify the server's role in the domain. You can choose one of three roles: primary domain controller, backup domain controller, and member server. Once you make this selection, you cannot reverse it, except by reinstalling Windows NT.

PRIMARY DOMAIN CONTROLLER

As you've already learned, the primary domain controller (PDC) plays the most important role in the domain. In fact, no domain exists without a PDC. A domain can include only one PDC, which maintains the SAM database. Because the PDC is responsible for this task, it is also responsible for authenticating users as they log on to the domain. Finally, the PDC synchronizes the copies of the database on the backup domain controllers (BDCs).

BACKUP DOMAIN CONTROLLER

As its name implies, the backup domain controller acts as a backup to the PDC. The SAM database is copied to the BDC and updated automatically with new information; it is charged with aiding in user authentication and taking over if the PDC fails or becomes unavailable. Unlike with the PDC, there can be any number of BDCs, although Microsoft recommends less than 200 per domain. According to the Microsoft guidelines, a BDC should be installed for every 2000 users in a domain. Because the BDC maintains only a read-only copy of the account database, no changes can be made through this controller. By maintaining a current copy of the account database, the BDC can authenticate users when it receives a request. This ability is especially helpful when the PDC is located at another site or in another building; the BDC can authenticate the user without waiting for the PDC to respond.

In the event that the PDC becomes unavailable or fails, the BDC will continue to authenticate users as usual. Although the domain will function without a PDC, it is often necessary to have one—for example, when you need to add a user or modify a group's access permissions. In such a case, the BDC can be promoted to become the PDC. It will then perform the PDC's functions and the domain can continue. When the original PDC is ready to return to the domain, it can be added as a BDC, then promoted to the new PDC. This promotion is done through the Computer menu in the Server Manager, which is part of Administrative Tools (Common).

> **Note**
> When you define a PDC (and thereby create a domain), the new domain is automatically assigned a security identifier (SID), which is a permanent and integral part of the operating system. (The same is true of user accounts, as you will learn in Chapter 8.) BDCs are assigned the same domain SID when they are created. Because a SID is permanent, it cannot be changed. As a result, a domain controller cannot be moved to an existing domain without reinstalling the operating system.

MEMBER OR STAND-ALONE SERVER

While stand-alone servers and member servers can perform the same tasks, a definite distinction separates the two. **Stand-alone servers** are Windows NT Server computers that participate in a workgroup network, rather than in a domain. Because these servers are not part of a domain, they are not part of an enterprise environment.

Member servers are part of a domain, but are treated as workstations and do not participate as domain controllers. As a result, they cannot authenticate user logons or take over in the event of a PDC failure. This limitation arises for two reasons. First, the member server does not have a copy of the account database. Second, and perhaps most important, member servers are assigned unique SIDs upon their creation. That is, the member server's SID is different from the domain's SID. While this structure means that the member server cannot participate as a domain controller, it can be moved between domains, like any other workstation.

Member servers are used to dedicate more resources, such as CPU and memory, to providing services, rather than authenticating users and managing groups' access rights. While these services can be run on the PDC, it is often a better strategy to dedicate servers to providing these services. Some examples of this type of configuration follow:

- Database server—Provides dedicated access to a database such as Microsoft's SQL Server.

- Remote access server (RAS)—Provides dedicated access for remote users.

- Internet information server—Provides Internet/intranet services for clients.

- Fault-tolerant file services—Run high-overhead, fault-tolerant systems such as RAID-5. (As you will learn in Chapter 6, fault-tolerant systems protect against data loss.)

> **Note**
> The most important thing to remember regarding server roles is that PDCs and BDCs remain locked into their domain. Although you can change the domain name, you cannot move the computers themselves to another existing domain. Member servers can switch domains, but they can never be domain controllers. To make either of these changes (PDC/BDC to an existing domain, or member server to domain controller), you must reinstall Windows NT.

MAKING THE RIGHT SELECTION

In evaluating the number and types of servers in your domain, you should consider the role the servers will play, their physical locations, and the resources they will provide.

In a large enterprise network, the PDC's responsibilities should be limited to account database authentication and management. The more users, groups, and BDCs in the domain, the more taxing the PDC's job. As the domain decreases in size, the PDC can perform more services, such as providing backups and file services.

The existence of a BDC in a domain guarantees the effectiveness of the network in the event of a PDC failure and speeds the authentication process. The number and location of BDCs depends on two things: the layout of the network and the number of users. As stated previously, at least one BDC should be added for every 2000 users. If your network consists of six sites connected by 56K lines, however, each site should have its own BDC to decrease the time it takes to log on. Forcing users to connect over a slow WAN link to the PDC for logon authentication will only lead to frustrated users. If the link is slower than 56K, a separate domain is preferable to a BDC. The number of BDCs must be balanced against the load on the PDC. For example, imagine a network where all 50 computers are Windows NT servers—1 PDC and 49 BDCs. While users will always be authenticated, the PDC will spend every moment synchronizing the account database to the BDCs. For such a small network, one PDC and one BDC are sufficient.

Member servers perform a very specific function in the enterprise domain environment—they provide dedicated resources to specific services. These types of servers are most often found in large networking environments and fall into two categories: file or print servers, and application servers. In a network that overtaxes its PDCs and BDCs, member servers can more efficiently service requests than can domain controllers, allowing the domain controllers to focus on user authentication, rights, and permissions.

In addition to planning the roles your servers will play within domains, you need to plan the connections between domains. The next section explains these connections, which are commonly known as **trust relationships**. After you become familiar with trust relationships, you will learn how to use them along with domains to build an enterprise network.

TRUST RELATIONSHIPS

Trust relationships (or simply **trusts**) provide a management tool for sharing resources across domain boundaries. A trust functions as an administrative link between two separate domains, enabling users in one domain to access resources in another domain without establishing a user account in the other domain.

The term "trust relationship," as used in the Windows NT environment, is similar to legal concepts associated with financial trusts. When a lawyer creates a trust, three players are typically involved: a trustor, a trustee, and a beneficiary. The *trustor* creates the trust (generally the client with the money). The *trustee* assumes responsibility for managing trust assets (often-times a bank or other corporate trustee). The *beneficiary* can spend the money, subject to the terms of the trust. The terms of the trust are administered by the trustee.

Trust relationships in an NT environment work in much the same manner. There is a trustor (known as the trusting domain), a trustee (known as the trusted domain), and beneficiaries (users in the trusted domain who can access resources in the trusting domain). The **trusting domain** includes resources (such as files, printers, or modems) that users from another domain need to access. The **trusted domain** manages access to the trusting domain's resources by users in the trusted domain.

The relationship between the trusted domain and the trusting domain is typically illustrated by an arrow pointing from the trusting domain to the trusted domain, as in Figure 2-1. In the figure, the arrow points from the trusting domain (i.e., the resource) to the trusted domain (i.e., the user who wants to access the resource). Thus the user is trusted by the resource—not the other way around, as you might be initially inclined to think. To avoid confusion about which way the arrow points, you must understand the relationship between trusting and trusted domains. Simply recognize that the trusting domain provides resources made available to users of the trusted domain.

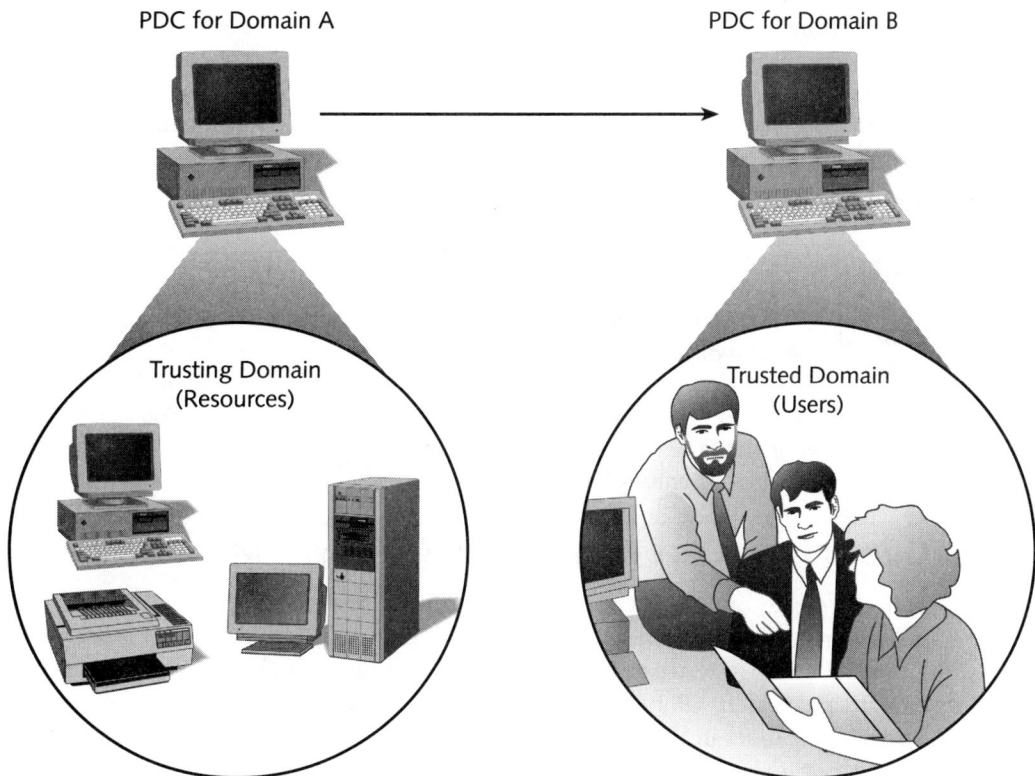

PDC for Domain A

PDC for Domain B

Trusting Domain
(Resources)

Trusted Domain
(Users)

Figure 2-1   Relationship between the trusting domain and the trusted domain

One key characteristic of trust relationships is that they are nontransitive. To understand what this property means, consider Figure 2-2.

In the figure, Domain A trusts Domain B. As a result, users in Domain B can access resources located in Domain A. Domain A is the trusting domain in this relationship and Domain B is the trusted domain. Domain B, in turn, trusts Domain C. As a result, users in Domain C can access resources in Domain B. Here Domain B is the trusting domain and Domain C is the trusted domain. Because trust relationships are not transitory, users in Domain C cannot access resources in Domain A.

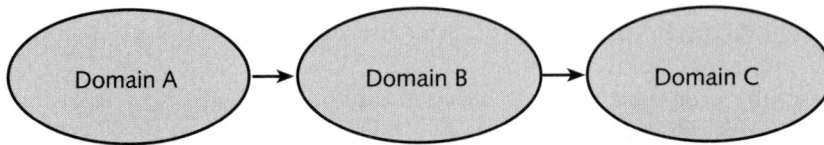

Figure 2-2 Nontransitive nature of trusts between multiple domains

The trust relationship illustrated in Figure 2-1 is known as a one-way trust. In a **one-way trust relationship**, users in one domain can access resources in the other domain; because trust relationships are not transitory, the reverse is not true. That is, while users in Domain B can access resources in Domain A, users in Domain A cannot access resources in Domain B. To enable equal sharing of resources, you must create a **two-way trust relationship**, which is really just two one-way trust relationships. In a two-way trust relationship, Domain A trusts Domain B, and vice versa. The two-way trust allows users in two or more domains to access resources in a multi-domain environment.

> **Note**
> If you are familiar with the Gateway Services for NetWare (GSNW) product that ships with Windows NT, you already have experience with trust relationships. GSNW establishes a user account on the NetWare server, putting the user in a special group called NTGateway. Rights and permissions for the user (who is generally an administrator on the NT domain) are based upon the associated rights and permissions given to members of the NTGateway group by a supervisor on the NetWare network. As a result of this process, the NetWare network becomes essentially a "trusting domain."

CREATING ONE- AND TWO-WAY TRUSTS

You can create one- and two-way trusts via the User Manager for Domains utility. In the following steps, you will use two separate domains known as Registration and Admissions. To create a one-way trust, you must first determine which domain will act as the trusting domain and which will be the trusted domain. Because users in the Admissions domain need access to resources in the Registration domain, Registration will be the trusting domain and Admissions will serve as the trusted domain. Next, to begin establishing the trust, you need access to a domain controller on the trusted domain, and then to a domain controller on the trusting domain.

To create a one-way trust:

1. Using the domain controller on the trusted domain, click **Start**, point to **Programs**, click **Administrative Tools (Common)**, then click **User Manager for Domains**. The User Manager window opens, as shown in Figure 2-3.

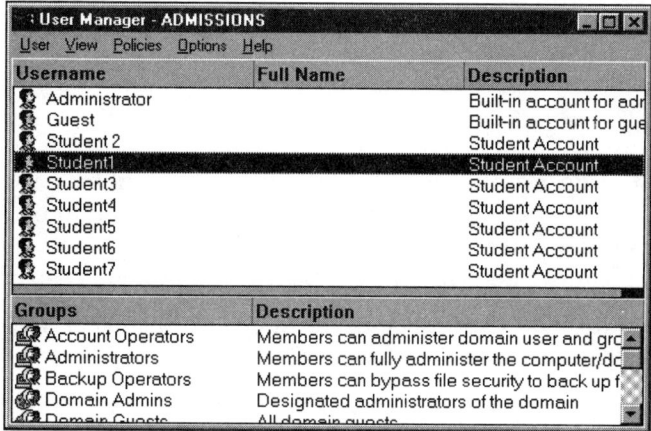

Figure 2-3   User Manager window

2. Click **Policies** on the menu bar, then click **Select Trust Relationships**. The Trust Relationships dialog box opens, as shown in Figure 2-4.

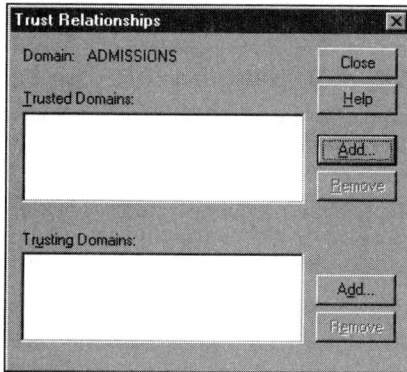

Figure 2-4   Trust Relationships dialog box

3. Click the **Add button** located to the right of the Trusting Domains list box. The Add Trusting Domain dialog box opens, as shown in Figure 2-5.

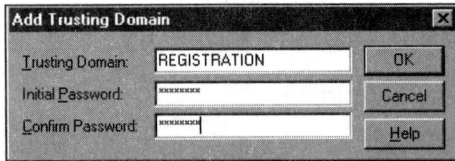

Figure 2-5   Add Trusting Domain dialog box

4. In the Trusting Domain text box, type **Registration**. In the Initial Password text box, type a password of your choosing; retype the same password in the Confirm Password dialog box. Do not share this password with anyone other than the administrator on the other domain (in this case, the Registration domain).

5. Click **OK** to close the Add Trusting Domain dialog box, then click **Close** to close the Trust Relationships dialog box.

6. Exit User Manager for Domains. You have now completed one-half of the steps required to establish a one-way trust relationship. The remaining steps closely mirror the previous steps, but must be completed on a domain controller located on the trusted domain.

7. Using the domain controller on the trusting domain, click **Start**, point to **Programs**, click **Administrative Tools (Common)**, then click **User Manager for Domains**. The User Manager for Domains dialog box opens.

8. Click **Policies** on the menu bar, then click **Select the Trust Relationships**. The Trust Relationships dialog box opens.

9. Click **Add** located to the right of the Trusted Domains text box. The Add Trusted Domain dialog box opens, as shown in Figure 2-6.

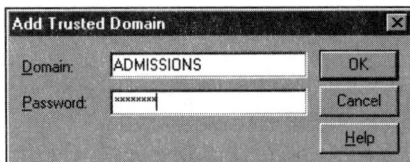

Figure 2-6   Add Trusted Domain dialog box

10. Type **Admissions** in the Domain text box, then type the password used in Step 4 in the Password text box.

11. Click **OK** to close the Add Trusting Domain dialog box, and then click **Close** to close the Trust Relationships dialog box.

12. Exit User Manager for Domains.

> The preceding steps were performed first on a domain controller located on the trusted domain and then on a domain controller located on the trusting domain. While you can establish a trust relationship by performing these steps on the trusting domain first, the establishment of the trust may be somewhat slower (normally no more than 15 minutes).

Remember, a two-way trust simply consists of two separate one-way trusts. To create such a trust, simply repeat the steps outlined above, but substitute Admissions as the Trusting Domain and Registration as the Trusted Domain. It's a good idea to use the same password for both trust relationships.

ADMINISTERING TRUST RELATIONSHIPS

The key to gaining the benefits associated with trust relationships in an enterprise network is planning. Effective planning demands that you analyze trust relationships on a cost-versus-benefit basis. If only a few users in one domain need to access resources in another domain, the more simplistic approach of establishing user accounts in both domains for these users probably makes more sense than establishing a domain-wide trust relationship. On the other hand, if a large number of domain users must access resources located on another domain, setting up user accounts on both domains can be too time-consuming. The same result could be achieved by creating a one-way trust relationship between the two domains.

When properly implemented, trust relationships can simplify network administration. For example, consider an enterprise environment where network users can browse the network and see available resources grouped into logical resource domains. Rather than mapping resources to multiple independent servers that do not identify themselves clearly, you can narrow a user's search for resources by grouping related resource servers into the same domain. In this case, descriptive domain names (such as "Printers" for a domain of printers) can prove very helpful.

Enterprise networks commonly comprise two types of domains: user domains and resource domains. The **user domain** is devoted to handling user accounts, while the **resource domain** manages network resources. In this configuration, user accounts and global group configurations are stored in a central location. User accounts are easily managed because they are maintained at a central location in the enterprise. At the same time, locating particular network resources is simplified because resources are located in logically named domains, in conjunction with similar network resources.

Now that you are familiar with the various relationships between domains, you are ready to learn about several models for associating domains within a network.

DOMAIN MODELS

A **domain model** describes the way domains are associated in a network. There are four basic domain models:

- Single domain model
- Single master domain model
- Multiple master domain model
- Complete trust model

Large enterprise environments sometimes use a combination of the four basic models. In the following sections you'll learn about the four basic domain models. Then you will learn about one of the hybrid domain models, commonly known as the Independent Domain model.

SINGLE DOMAIN MODEL

As you might expect, in the **single domain model**, an entire network is considered one domain. All user accounts, computer names and groups are created and administered within this single domain. Thus this domain does not differ from the actual physical network. The single domain model contains only one primary domain controller (PDC), with possibly one or more backup domain controllers (BDCs). PDCs and BDCs are used for account verification and resource access purposes. Their functionality is covered in depth in Chapters 3 and 5.

Because the single domain model includes only one domain, trust relations are not necessary. A single domain model is quite simplistic in thought and execution, and is often the best choice for some networks.

Use the single domain model when an organization:

- Is small or medium in size and operates from a single physical location.
- Requires central administration.
- Requires easy, low-cost administration.

The benefits associated with the single domain model may be outweighed by slow network performance as the network expands. The alternative models (explained in the following sections), however, require additional equipment and administrative time—both of which can prove costly. For this reason, businesses usually wait to implement a multiple domain strategy until the network speed becomes intolerably slow.

SINGLE MASTER DOMAIN MODEL

The **single master domain model** uses more than one domain. In this model, the **master domain** acts as a central administrative unit for user and group accounts in the other domains, which are known as **resource domains**. The single master domain model allows a company to divide its physical network into separate logical networks, thus providing an

2

organizational framework for managing users, groups, and resources in an enterprise environment. With the single master domain model, virtually all user accounts are located in one domain so that they can be administered centrally.

The master domain has a PDC and, usually, multiple BDCs. The PDC maintains the security database for user accounts and global groups. The BDCs provide user authentication services, maintaining a copy of the PDC's security account database. Because the master domain handles user account authentication, the PDC on a resource domain provides quite limited authentication services. The security database on a resource domain's PDC typically contains data related to which local groups have access to specific network resources.

The manner in which a master domain user account accesses a file located on the resource domain is best illustrated by way of example. Suppose a user named Mary belongs to a global group called Sales created on the master domain's PDC. A trust relationship exists between the resource domain (i.e., the trusting domain) and the master domain (i.e., the trusted domain). The resource domain has been configured so that a local group called Reports can access the company's accounts receivable database. The global group, Sales, is a member of the local Reports group on the resource domain. Thus Mary has access to the company's accounts receivable database.

While almost all of the user accounts are created and maintained in the master domain under this model, the computer accounts are generally created within a resource domain. Because resource domains remain separate from the master domain, it is possible to create a group of users that can administer only the resource domain, without exerting any control over the master domain. Consequently, less-skilled personnel can act as **resource domain administrators**, whose responsibilities are confined to relatively simple GUI-based tasks, such as creating shares and computer accounts. This setup, in turn, frees more highly trained personnel to focus on the more complicated task of administering the master domain, in the capacity of **domain administrators**. By dividing administrative duties in this way, the single master domain model balances the requirements for centralized account security with the need for individual departments to maintain their own network resources.

For a successful implementation of the single master domain model, each resource domain must establish a one-way trust relationship with the master domain. That is, you must create a trust relationship in which the resource domains act as trusting domains and the master domain acts as the trusted domain. Figure 2-7 illustrates the trust relationships in the single master domain model.

> **Note** Trust relationships are often considered a difficult subject on the Microsoft Windows NT in the Enterprise certification exam. Many students wonder why the master domain is the trusted domain. The reason is this: master domain users need access to resources located in the resource domains. Thus, the resource domains must trust the master domain administrators to exercise discretion in granting users access to those resources. Another way to think of it is that the master domain is trusted (by the resource domains) to use resources carefully and efficiently.

Figure 2-7   Single master domain model

Because the master domain is trusted by all resource domains, user accounts having domain administrative rights in the master domain will have those same rights in the resource domains. Consequently, master domain administrators have access to all resources on the enterprise network.

One benefit of this model is that it allows the grouping of resources into a logical configuration—for example, all marketing department printers might reside in the Marketing domain. It also enables network administrators to restrict access to special hardware devices that relatively few users need—for example, you could restrict the use of a color printer to users in the Sales Department domain. In addition to preventing indiscriminate, company-wide use of an expensive resource, this strategy holds only the Sales department accountable for all color printer costs. This pinpointing of responsibility can motivate department managers to manage their resources more effectively.

One drawback to the single master domain model is the potential for heavy traffic within one domain. All users must log onto the network via the single master domain. If a great number of users attempt to log on simultaneously, server response may be slow, just as in the single domain model. Another drawback relates to the higher administration costs associated with trust relationships and the establishment of multiple domains.

A third potential disadvantage is the limitation on the number of users, which results from the fact that Windows NT stores the directory database in **nonpaged pool memory** (RAM that is reserved and cannot be paged out to disk to free up space for other data). To understand why this problem arises, consider the fact that only 32 MB of system RAM can be allocated to the nonpaged pool. A directory database with 40,000 user accounts is roughly 26 MB in size, leaving only 6 MB of nonpaged pool memory for other system processes. Because additional user accounts would consume too much nonpaged pool memory for other processes to function correctly, domain models that store all user accounts in one domain (such as the single master domain model) are limited to no more than 40,000 users. If the domain also contains computer and user accounts, this number is reduced to 26,000 users. Keep in mind, however, that these numbers are only theoretical limits. Practically speaking, a domain with 40,000 users, or even 26,000 users, would be virtually impossible to manage.

> **Tip**
>
> When implementing the single master domain model in a network that already has domain administrators, you must divide the administrators into resource administrators and domain administrators. This goal can be accomplished by removing the resource administrators from the domain administrator group and adding them to a specially created global group. If you leave any resource administrators in the domain administrators group by mistake, they will have access to areas of the network that you may prefer to keep off-limits.

To summarize, the single master domain model offers the following benefits:

- Centralized account management
- Decentralized resource management
- Resources grouped in a logical manner
- Management of resources by the people responsible for them

The single master domain model has the following disadvantages:

- Slow network performance as the number of users increases
- A limit to the total possible number of user accounts
- Implementation of trust relationships that complicate network access issues

If the single master domain model does not meet your company's needs, you might want to consider the multiple master domain model.

MULTIPLE MASTER DOMAIN MODEL

The **multiple master domain model** resembles the single master domain model in that it divides resources into resource domains. As its name implies, however, the multiple master domain model uses two or more master domains. In this model, every master domain must have a two-way trust relationship with every other master domain. Each resource domain must then establish a one-way trust relationship with each master domain. The trust relationships within the multiple master domain model are illustrated in Figure 2-8.

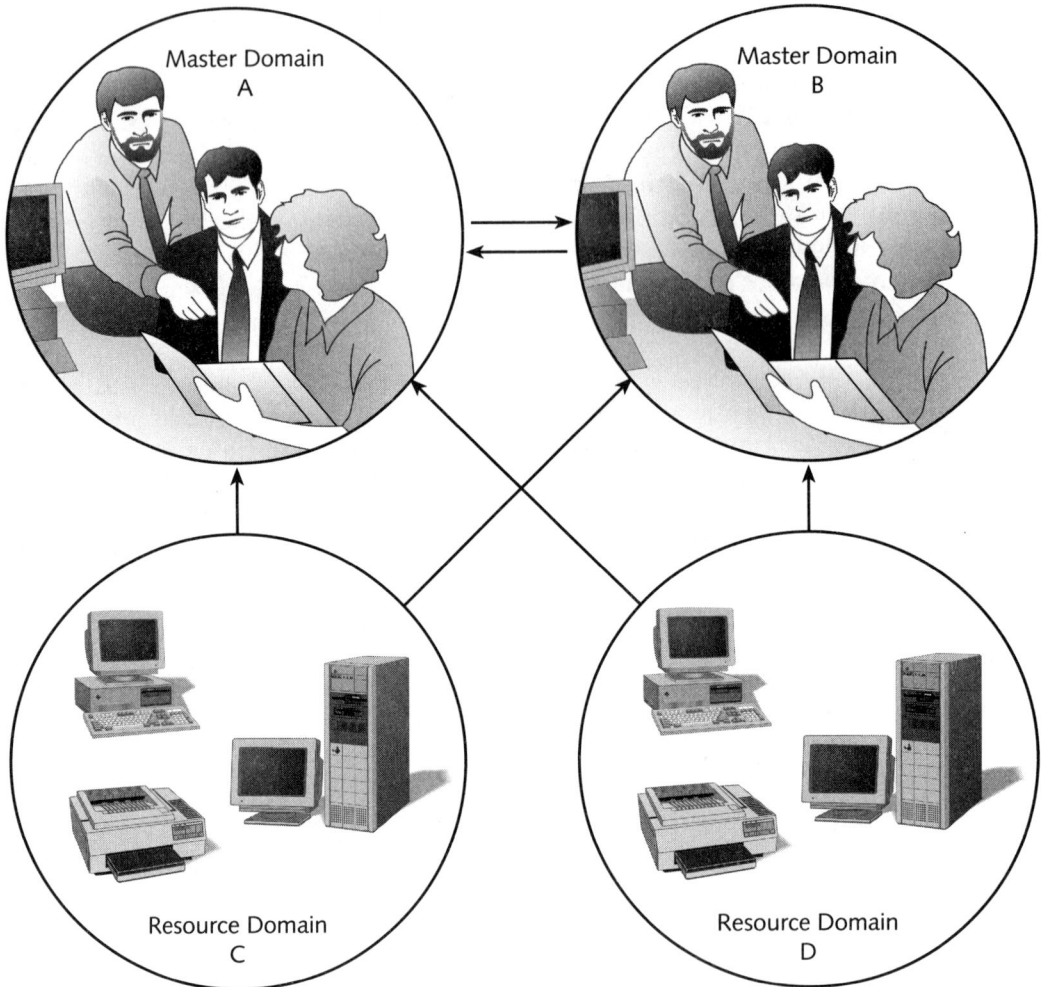

Figure 2-8   Multiple master domain model

The multiple master domain model is useful in large or expanding networks that span more than one physical location. It allows user accounts to be spread across different master domains, while still allowing a particular user to access resources in any resource domain, regardless of the master domain in which the user account was created. User accounts can be distributed between master domains based upon specific criteria, such as the user's department or geographic location. This model is completely scalable; as a company grows, new domains can be neatly tucked within the existing architecture. As with the single master domain model, resource domains are not configured to store or manage user accounts.

The multiple master domain model offers the following advantages:

- Mobile users can log on from anywhere in the network.
- Both centralized and decentralized administration schemes are possible.

- The domain structure can mirror the company's organization.

- Individual users can navigate easily through a potentially large number of domains.

One disadvantage of the multiple master domain model is the difficulty of establishing the trust relationships correctly. If the appropriate trust relationships are not implemented, the network will not function properly. Keep in mind that the network with the fewest number of trusts is the easiest and least expensive to maintain, because it involves a minimal amount of troubleshooting. Another disadvantage is the potential for errors within the network as more master domains are added.

To calculate the number of trust relationships required in this model, use the following formula, in which M is the number of master domains and R is the number of resource domains:

$$\text{Total number of trusted relationships} = M * (M - 1) + (R * M)$$

COMPLETE TRUST MODEL

In the **complete trust model**, every domain on the network has a two-way trust relationship with every other domain on the enterprise. An example of this configuration is shown in Figure 2-9.

Figure 2-9   Complete trust model

The principal benefit of this arrangement is that it enables decentralized management. The obvious drawback is that it can become unmanageable very quickly as the network grows, because a large number of trusts must be created. For example, a 5-domain network would require as many as 20 trust relationships, while a 10-domain network would require as many as 90 trust relationships. It is easy to see why the complete trust model could quickly become unwieldy as the number of domains increases, requiring costly administration time.

INDEPENDENT DOMAIN MODEL

In some situations, security is so important that a department cannot allow itself to be accessible in any way. Such a group would still need a physical connection to the network, but a logical tie, such as a trust relationship, to its domain would be forbidden. This situation requires the independent domain model, in which a single domain is attached physically to the network (that is, the domain is on the same wire as the rest of the network), but not logically (i.e., by a trust relationship). To maintain complete security, the domain's user and computer accounts would be created from within the independent domain. For example, you might designate Human Resources as an independent domain that resides on the same physical network as the other domains. To protect the extremely sensitive information (such as employee raises and bonuses) stored in the Human Resources domain, you would not create any trust relationships between this domain and the other domains on the network.

The problem with this arrangement is that it can encourage a false sense of security. In situations where security is extremely critical, it probably makes sense to create a entirely separate network.

CHOOSING A DOMAIN MODEL

When choosing the most appropriate domain model for a particular situation, you should consider a number of factors, including the existing and potential numbers of users, the existing and potential network site locations, and the number of existing and potential network resources. Table 2-1 summarizes these considerations.

Table 2-1

Feature	Single Domain	Single Master Domain	Multiple Master Domain	Complete Trust Domain	Independent Domain
<40,000 users	X	X			X
>40,000 users			X	X	
Centralized Resource Management Account Management MIS Department	X X X	 X X	 X 		X X X
Decentralized Resource Management Account Management MIS Department		 X 	 X X	 X X X	

DIRECTORY SERVICES

The Windows NT features used to manage domains are called **Directory Services**. Directory Services, which run at all times, allow various tasks to be delegated to computers on the network. One of the most important components of Directory Services is the Security Accounts Manager (SAM) database. Each account in a domain—whether it is for a user, group, computer, or other resource—is stored as an object in the SAM. Other components of Directory Services are explained in the following sections.

NET LOGON

The **Net Logon Service**, which is installed automatically along with Windows NT, is used to authenticate user accounts during the log-in process. It works via a process called **pass-through authentication**, in which a request for user account authentication is passed to the domain controller on which the account was created. For authentication to occur, the user account must be included within the SAM database. The SAM database loads into the memory of the PDC and BDCs and then verifies that the user logging into the network is valid. Each domain keeps an active list of its own SAM database. When users from a trusted domain log onto a computer located in a trusting resource domain, however, the user's account is located on neither the local machine's SAM database nor the resource domain's SAM.

The process of pass-through authentication is as follows:

1. The user presses Control+Alt+Delete on the keyboard, then enters the requisite information in the log-on dialog box, including the user account name, password, and domain name where the user account is located. (The user does not enter the domain where the log-on computer is configured as a resource.)

2. The Security Account Manager checks for the account in the local SAM database.

3. If the account is local, the local user accounts database processes it. If no local account is found, then the local Net Logon service passes this authentication process to a domain controller in its domain.

4. The domain controller determines whether the user's domain is a trusted domain; if it is, the domain controller passes the authentication to a domain controller located in the user's domain.

5. This domain controller handles the authentication process. Assuming the user has sufficient rights to log onto a computer in the other domain, the domain controller retrieves the user and group **Security Identifier** (**SID**) for the user account.

6. The SID information is passed back to the local domain controller, which in turn passes that information to the Net Logon Service for the local computer.

DIRECTORY SERVICES FOR NETWARE

Directory Services for NetWare copy the user and group account information from Novell's networking operating system, Netware, to the Windows NT server. The server then transmits the data back to the NetWare servers incrementally—that is, as changes are made. This strategy enables administrators to centrally manage user accounts in both the NetWare and Windows NT environment through one network operating system.

DIRECTORY DATABASE SIZE

When planning your domain model, keep in mind that all user, computer, and group accounts are recorded in the SAM database. If the SAM becomes too large, network performance will suffer. (A user account occupies 1.0 KB in the database. Each computer account occupies 0.5 KB of space within the SAM database, and a typical group account may occupy roughly 4 KB of space.) Although Microsoft has tested a SAM database with a total record size of 40 MB, the performance of a network with such a database would probably be unacceptable. It would take too long for users to log onto the network and for accounts to be replicated. The network traffic created by replication of this database from the PDC to BDCs would also be unacceptable. The secret to good network performance in a multiple domain environment is to keep the SAM database as small as possible, while using an adequate amount of RAM and a fast CPU. You should also limit the activities of the domain controller so that it focuses on only domain management.

CHAPTER SUMMARY

- A carefully planned network is one that meets the needs of a small organization but can also grow to accommodate a much larger, more complicated organization. When planning an enterprise network, you need to consider the following issues: current and future numbers of network users; ways in which the network could be divided into domains; and preferences for centralized or decentralized management.

- The keys to network organization are domains, and the relationship between domains, known as trust relationships. A domain is a collection of users, resources, and servers. A domain must include at least one Windows NT server; it may also include workstations and peripheral devices, such as printers. A domain must have one (and only one) primary domain controller. This controller maintains the domain's central security database, which lists users who are members of the domain, as well as their rights and privileges regarding resources on the domain. This database is commonly referred to as the Security Accounts Manager (SAM) database. Depending upon the size of the domain, it may have one or more servers designated as backup domain controllers. Backup domain controllers are designed to handle much of the load associated with the security authentication (the logon process) of domain users. These controllers maintain a copy of the primary domain controller's security database.

- You actually create a domain when installing Windows NT on a server. In large businesses, the use of domains as the building blocks of a network enables network

2

resources to be divided into groups that make sense logically (such as by department or geographical location) and that are therefore easier to manage as the network grows.

- The relationship between two domains is known as a trust relationship (or simply a trust). A trust relationship consists of a trusting domain and a trusted domain. The trusting domain has resources (such as files, printers, or modems) that users from another domain need to access. The trusted domain manages access to the trusting domain's resources by users in the trusted domain. The relationship between the trusted domain and the trusting domain is typically illustrated by an arrow pointing from the trusting domain to the trusted domain. One key characteristic of trust relationships is their nontransitive nature. In a one-way trust, users in one domain can access resources in the other domain; because trust relationships are not transitory, the reverse is not true. A two-way trust relationship is really just two one-way trust relationships.

- In Windows NT, you can create one- and two-way trusts with the User Manager for Domains utility. To establish a one-way trust, you must first determine which domain will act as the trusting domain and which will act as the trusted domain. Next, you need access to a domain controller on the trusted domain, and then to a domain controller on the trusting domain. To create a two-way trust, simply create two one-way trusts, using the same password for both trust relationships.

- A domain model describes the way in which domains are associated in a network. Five basic domain models exist, each of which has its own benefits and drawbacks. In the single domain model, an entire network is considered one domain. The single master domain model uses a master domain, which acts as a central administrative unit for user and group accounts in the resource domains. The multiple master domain model also divides resources into resource domains, but employs two or more master domains, each of which must have a two-way trust relationship with every other master domain. Each resource domain must then have a one-way trust relationship with each master domain. In the complete trust model, every domain on the network has a two-way trust with every other domain on the enterprise. In the independent domain model, a single domain is attached physically to the network (via the same wire as the rest of the network), but not logically (by a trust relationship). When choosing the most appropriate domain model for a particular situation, you must consider factors such as the existing and potential numbers of users, the existing and potential network site locations, and the number of existing and potential network resources.

- The Windows NT features used to manage domains are collectively known as Directory Services. One especially important component of Directory Services is the Security Accounts Manager (SAM) database. Each account in a domain is stored as an object in the SAM. When planning your domain model, keep in mind that all user, computer, and group accounts are recorded in the SAM database. If the SAM becomes too large, network performance will suffer. Another component of Directory Services, the Net Logon Service, authenticates user accounts via a pass-through authentication process. In pass-through authentication, a request for user account authentication is passed to the domain controller on which the account was created. Yet another component of Directory Services, Directory Services for NetWare, copies the user and group account information from Novell's networking operating system, NetWare, to the Windows NT server.

KEY TERMS

- **complete trust model** — A network structure in which every domain has a two-way trust relationship with every other domain.

- **Directory Services** — The Windows NT features used to manage domains.

- **Directory Services for Netware** — The Windows NT service that copies user and group account information from a Novell network to a Windows NT server.

- **domain** — In a Windows NT network environment, a collection of users and network resources in which security is managed by a primary domain controller.

- **domain administrators** — Personnel responsible for managing the master domain.

- **domain model** — A description of the way domains are associated in a network.

- **master domain** — In a network with more than one domain, the domain that acts as a central administrative unit for user and group accounts in other domains.

- **member server** — A server that is part of a domain but does not participate in the domain controller process.

- **multiple master domain model** — A network structure that divides resources into resource domains, and uses two or more master domains.

- **Net Logon Service** — The Windows service that is used to authenticate user accounts and provide pass-through authentication.

- **nonpaged pool memory** — RAM that is reserved and cannot be paged out to the hard disk to free up space for other data.

- **one-way trust relationship** — The simplest form of trust relationship, in which one domain (the trusting domain) grants users in another domain (the trusted domain) access to its resources.

- **pass-through authentication** — The process by which a request for user account authentication is passed to the domain controller on which the user account was created.

- **resource domain** — A domain containing resources that users in other domains need to access.

- **resource domain administrators** — Personnel responsible for relatively simple, GUI-based tasks, such as creating shares and computer accounts.

- **Security Accounts Manager (SAM) database** — The security account database located on a domain's primary domain controller, containing user and resource security data.

- **security authentication** — The process by which users log onto the network.

- **Security Identifier (SID)** — A unique number assigned to a user, group, or computer account in the SAM database.

- **single domain model** — A network structure in which the entire network is one domain, with a single primary domain controller for the entire network.

- **single master domain model** — A network structure in which the master domain acts as a central administrative unit for user and group accounts and controls access in other domains (resource domains).

- **stand-alone server** — Similar to a member server, a stand-alone server is not part of a domain, but provides server functions in a workgroup network.

- **trust relationship** — A relationship between two or more domains, in which one domain (the trusting domain) allows users in another domain (the trusted domain) to access its resources.
- **trusted domain** — In a trust relationship, the domain containing users who need access to resources in the trusting domain.
- **trusting domain** — In a trust relationship, the domain containing resources that can be accessed by the trusted domain.
- **two-way trust relationship** — Two one-way trust relationships, in which both domains act as both trusted and trusting domains.
- **user domain** — A domain devoted to managing user accounts.

2

REVIEW QUESTIONS

1. A principal goal of networking is _____ sharing.
2. What is the maximum number of PDCs that a single domain can have?
   - **a.** 64
   - **b.** 4
   - **c.** 2
   - **d.** 1
3. Which of the following is a major drawback to a single domain network in which parts of the network must communicate via a modem?
   - **a.** Resources will be available only to users on the local segment.
   - **b.** Users will be able to log onto only servers located on their local segment.
   - **c.** Low-speed connections often create logon delays and other problems associated with the need for PDCs and BDCs to communicate with one another.
   - **d.** No problems are encountered as a result of this configuration.
4. Which of the following are good reasons to change from a single domain model to one of the multiple domain models? (Choose all that apply.)
   - **a.** The network has grown to more than 5000 users.
   - **b.** The company has expanded from a single location to multiple locations.
   - **c.** The number of users and computers on the network has increased so that management is becoming overly complex.
   - **d.** The IS department is not good at managing trust relationships.
5. Where is the SAM database stored?
   - **a.** in nonpaged pool memory
   - **b.** on the local area memory pool
   - **c.** on the master browser's hard disk
   - **d.** in a secure file located on an NTFS partition of the user's NetLogon directory
6. What is the maximum number of users in a single NT domain?
   - **a.** 64,000
   - **b.** 40,000
   - **c.** 32,000
   - **d.** 4000

7. Which of the following is a symptom of having too many user accounts on a single domain?

   a. slow log-on processing

   b. conflicts in user names

   c. unauthorized sharing of network resources due to faulty log-on processing from an overloaded PDC

   d. the periodic dropping of network connectivity to a workstation

8. When configuring a multiple domain environment in which domains are based upon physical locations, it's a good idea to use domain names that correspond to the city in which the domain is located. True or False?

9. In the multiple master domain model, all domains share the same primary domain controller (PDC). True or False?

10. The multiple master domain model requires at least one two-way trust. True or False?

11. The multiple master domain model allows for centralized administration of users via a user domain that remains separate from the resource domains. True or False?

12. Two-way trusts can be created between a PDC and a BDC in different domains. True or False?

13. What is the common name of the domain providing resources for users on another domain via a trust relationship?

    a. the principal domain

    b. the secondary domain

    c. the trusting domain

    d. the trusted domain

14. In a two-way trust, what role does each domain play? (Choose all that apply.)

    a. a resource domain

    b. a principal domain

    c. a trusting domain

    d. a trusted domain

15. What is the principal limiting factor associated with the multiple master domain model?

    a. the monetary cost associated with its implementation

    b. the number of trusts it necessitates

    c. the network overhead created as a result of domain controller database replication

    d. the limitation on the number of users allowed

16. Once you have established a network as a single master domain model, you can no longer reconfigure it as a multiple master domain model. True or False?

17. A trust relationship is transitive. True or False?

18. Pass-through authentication concludes when a user account is finally validated by the local computer. True or False?

19. In a multiple master domain model, user authentication is accomplished by a domain controller located on the domain where the user's account is located. True or False?

20. Which of the following does not perform user authentication in a domain environment? (Choose all that apply.)

    a. primary domain controller

    b. member server

    c. stand-alone server

    d. backup domain controller

21. While a PDC cannot be moved to an existing domain, a BDC can be moved to an existing domain. True or False?

22. The tool used to promote a BDC to a PDC is called _____.

23. Which of the following statements does *not* accurately describe the role of a member server in the domain?

    a. A member server is part of the domain, but is treated like a workstation.

    b. A stand-alone server is a workgroup implementation of a member server.

    c. A member server has the same SID as the PDC and BDC for that domain.

    d. A member server provides dedicated access to resource-intensive services.

24. One responsibility of a BDC is to authenticate users when the PDC is unavailable. True or False?

HANDS-ON PROJECTS

For one or all of these projects you will need two Windows NT Server computers configured as PDCs in separate domains.

PROJECT 2-1

In this project you will create a trust relationship between two domains. Remember that when creating a trust relationship, you need access to a domain controller on both domains. If you are working on a single domain, you can practice the steps associated with creating the trust, even if you cannot actually complete the trust.

This project is best accomplished with a partner. Ideally both of you should log onto a PDC in different domains. In addition, both domains should be physically connected.

    1. In the spaces below, write the information you'll need to create the trust relationship:

        Trusting Domain: _____   Trusted Domain: _____

        PDC Name: _____   PDC Name: _____

        Password: _____

2. On the domain controller for the trusted domain, open the User Manager window and follow the steps outlined in the chapter to specify the trusting domain and the password.

3. On the domain controller for the trusting domain, open the User Manager window and follow the steps outlined in the chapter to specify the trusted domain and the password.

PROJECT 2-2

In this project you will use the trust relationship developed in Project 2-1. You will create a user account in the trusted domain, a folder in the trusted domain, and, acting as an administrator in the trusted domain, grant the new user access to the newly created folder.

1. Log onto the trusting domain as an administrator. On an NTFS partition located on the trusting domain's primary domain controller, create a folder called TestTrusts. Using Notepad, create a file named Welcome, typing a message of your choice in this text file. Set the permissions on this file so that access is limited to administrators with full control.

2. On the PDC on the trusted domain, log on as an administrator. In User Manager for Domains, create a user named TestUser. From NT Explorer, go to Network Neighborhood, then to the domain name for the trusting domain, then to the PDC. Locate the TestTrusts folder.

3. Right-click the **TestTrust folder**, then click **Properties** in the shortcut menu. Click the **Security tab**, then click **Permissions**. Give TestUser full access to the folder. Log off of the PDC on the trusted domain and immediately log back on as TestUser.

4. Attempt to access the TestTrust folder on the trusting domain's PDC. Were you successful? Why or why not?

5. Log on as an administrator on the trusting domain's PDC, and then try to access resources (folders and files) on the trusted domain's PDC. Were you successful? Why or why not?

PROJECT 2-3

In this project you will build upon the trust relationship developed in Project 2-1, creating a "reverse" trust relationship so that both domains trust one another. In this project, the trusting domain becomes the trusted domain, and the trusted domain becomes the trusting domain.

1. On the domain controller for the trusted domain, open the User Manager window and follow the steps outlined in the chapter to specify the trusting domain and the password.

2. On the domain controller for the trusting domain, open the User Manager window and follow the steps outlined in the chapter to specify the trusted domain and the password.

PROJECT 2-4

This project is designed to show that users in either domain can access resources in the other domain through a two-way trust relationship. In Project 2-2, you saw that users in one domain could access resources in the other domain. You also saw that administrators in the trusting domain could not access resources in the trusted domain.

1. Log on as an administrator on the trusting domain's PDC, and then try to access resources (folders and files) on the trusted domain's PDC. Were you successful? Why or why not?
2. Create another folder on the PDC where you created TestUser in Project 2-2. Give this resource a unique name.
3. Create a user account on the PDC where you created the folder in Project 2-2. Give this account a unique name. Through Windows NT Explorer, access the folder you just created and set its permissions so that the new user can access the folder.
4. Log off and then log on again as the newly created user. Can you access the newly created folder? Why or why not?

CASE PROJECTS

1. You have been hired by Apple Valley, a realty firm that has just merged with Smith Realty, another firm located in the same building. Fortunately both firms are utilizing Windows NT Server 4.0 as their network operating systems. The company president has explained that he would like to keep the businesses separate, but also wants employees of Smith Reality to have access to files and other resources in the Apple Valley network, and vice versa. Write a short report (three to five paragraphs) explaining how you would organize the network. Explain the domain model you would employ, as well as its advantages and disadvantages. Describe the required trust relationships. Illustrate the trust relationships in a diagram.
2. You have been retained by a large law firm. Because of previous consolidations, the law firm is actually an association of four smaller firms that have banded together for purposes of sharing resources (such as office space and equipment). Each law firm maintains its own network. As luck would have it, they are all operating in a Windows NT environment. It has been suggested that the new firm could save money by combining administrative functions on these separate networks. The firm wants to keep the networks separated (for legal reasons) but also desires a centralized administration structure. Write a short report (three to five paragraphs) explaining how you would organize the network. Explain the domain model you would employ, as well as its advantages and disadvantages. Describe the required trust relationships. Illustrate the trust relationships in a diagram.

3. The manager of Springfield Organic Grocery has called you about problems with the store's network, which is actually three separate networks. The former network administrator set up three servers, each in a separate domain. Files in the Accounts Payable domain can be accessed from the Management domain. In addition, files in the Accounts Receivable domain can be accessed from the Management domain. Unfortunately, neither the Accounts Receivable users nor the Accounts Payable users can access files located in the others' domain (which they need to do). Write a short report (three to five paragraphs) explaining how you would organize the network. Explain the domain model you would employ, as well as its advantages and disadvantages. Describe the required trust relationships. Illustrate the trust relationships in a diagram.

4. You have been hired to reengineer a poorly planned network with no more than 20 domains. A user account has been created for you on the IT domain. As you move throughout the building, however, you meet individuals who have the same power as you. These individuals are not part of the IT domain, but they are able to change your password. Write a short report (three to five paragraphs) explaining the existing domain model. Suggest alternative models, explaining the situation in which each would be appropriate.

5. A large international bank is planning to roll out Windows NT in all of its offices worldwide. Its offices, with the number of employees and workstations at each location, are listed in Table 2-2.

Table 2-2

Location	Users	Workstations
New York	15,000	10,000
London	1000	750
Paris	500	400
Los Angeles	750	500
Hong Kong	200	100
Moscow	100	50
Fargo, ND	1000	500

The bank's MIS department is located in New York. The network should be configured so that all user accounts are maintained at that location. The bank's data-processing center is located in Fargo, where all accounting database information is stored. Each site will have on-site network managers who maintain local resources on the network. Write a short report (three to five paragraphs) explaining how you would organize the network. Explain the domain model you would employ, as well as its advantages and disadvantages. Describe the required trust relationships. Illustrate the trust relationships in a diagram.

6. Your network consists of four sites connected via T-1. Each of the three remote sites consists of 300 to 340 workstations, while the central office has 3500 computers connected throughout a skyscraper downtown. You are currently providing remote access services and Internet access through NT servers. Write a short report (one to two paragraphs) describing the optimum server configuration for your network.

CHAPTER THREE

CONFIGURING WINDOWS PROTOCOLS AND PROTOCOL BINDINGS

Windows NT Server 4.0 is an extremely flexible network operating system that interacts seamlessly with other network operating systems and a diverse range of hardware and software. This flexibility primarily comes from its use of **network protocols**, which allow Windows NT to understand and, in turn, be understood by every node on the network. Protocols are a set of rules that govern the way data are interpreted by a network.

This chapter focuses on **transport protocols**, which define how data should be presented and organized across the network to ensure that the information is delivered intact, in sequence, and error-free. In this chapter you will learn how to install, configure and troubleshoot the five transport protocols supported by Windows NT Server 4.0: NetBEUI, NWLink (IPX/SPX), TCP/IP, DLC, and AppleTalk. (You will learn about an additional, specialized protocol, Remote Access Service, in Chapter 5.) Assigning protocols to network adapters and services is known as **binding**. Using a mixture of protocols on one LAN is not only possible, but also often necessary in today's heterogeneous networking environments.

As this chapter will demonstrate, you cannot competently establish and maintain a network without thoroughly understanding the nature of network protocols.

AFTER READING THIS CHAPTER AND COMPLETING THE EXERCISES YOU WILL BE ABLE TO:

- Explain how network protocols correspond to layers in the OSI model
- Describe the characteristics and uses of NetBEUI, NWLink, TCP/IP, DLC, and AppleTalk
- Identify the core protocols of TCP/IP and explain their functions
- Install and configure the five protocols
- Bind multiple protocols
- Identify and troubleshoot problems associated with network protocols

NETWORK PROTOCOLS AND THE OSI MODEL

You should already be familiar with the **Open Systems Interconnection (OSI) model**, which defines seven hierarchical layers of network tasks, from the Physical (hardware) layer to the Application (user-interface) layer. One reason that Windows NT Server can provide such a high degree of interoperability is because its services are based on the OSI model and are therefore modular. Microsoft's networking model can be divided into five layers, which correspond to the OSI model layers as follows:

- **Application/File System Drivers Layer**—Roughly equivalent to the Application and Presentation layer of the OSI model. This layer holds the two **application programming interfaces (APIs)**, Winsock and NetBIOS. Both Winsock and NetBIOS provide services, such as workstation or server service, that enable applications to access the network services that operate in the lower layers of the networking hierarchy.

- **Transport Driver Interface (TDI) Boundary Layer**—Roughly equivalent to the Session layer of the OSI model. This layer handles requests to and from the lower protocol layer; it also provides session services.

- **Protocols Layer**—Roughly equivalent to the Transport and Network layers of the OSI model. The protocols discussed in this chapter work in this layer. These protocols translate data so that other operating systems can understand them. In Windows NT, you have the choice of using one or all of the available protocols on a single adapter card, a capability known as **multiple protocol binding**.

- **Network Driver Interface Specification (NDIS) Boundary Layer**— Roughly equivalent to the Data Link layer of the OSI model. This layer provides the interfaces between the protocols and the Adapter Card Drivers layer.

- **Adapter Card Drivers Layer**—Roughly equivalent to the Physical layer of the OSI model. This layer handles the formatting of data to facilitate physical access to the **network interface card (NIC)** and the network wire.

Figure 3-1 illustrates the relationship between the Microsoft Networking model layers and the OSI layers.

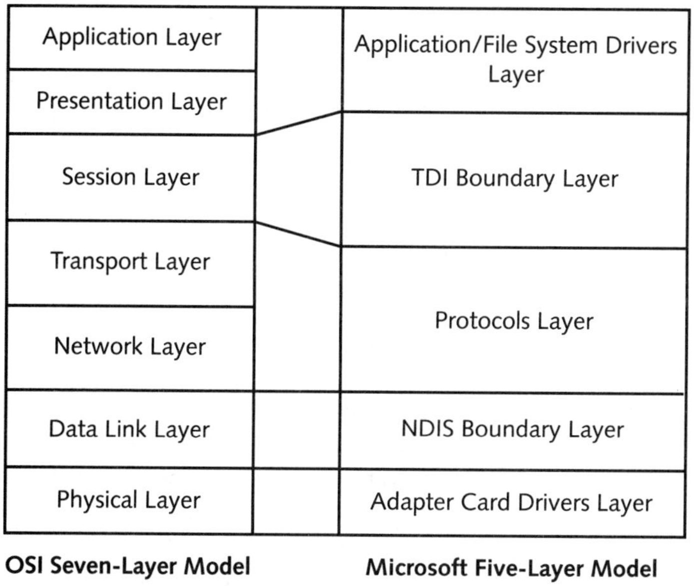

OSI Seven-Layer Model	Microsoft Five-Layer Model
Application Layer	Application/File System Drivers Layer
Presentation Layer	
Session Layer	TDI Boundary Layer
Transport Layer	Protocols Layer
Network Layer	
Data Link Layer	NDIS Boundary Layer
Physical Layer	Adapter Card Drivers Layer

OSI Seven-Layer Model   **Microsoft Five-Layer Model**

Figure 3-1   Comparison of OSI seven-layer and Microsoft Networking models

FIVE TRANSPORT PROTOCOLS

The five transport protocols supplied with Windows NT Server 4.0 have different histories, specialties, and strengths. They vary by speed, transmission efficiency, utilization of resources, ease of setup, and compatibility. In addition, protocols vary as to whether they can span multiple LAN segments. Protocols that have this ability are considered **routable**, because they carry network layer and addressing information that a **router** can interpret.

When choosing which protocols to use in your enterprise network, you must weigh each of these characteristics against the needs of your particular network. For example, you should not use nonroutable protocols in large, enterprise-wide networks, because they do not scale well and will therefore limit the size of the network. In addition to the size of the network, you must consider its interconnection requirements, data security needs, and the level of personnel available to administer the network. Most networks use more than one kind of protocol because they possess a mixed hardware and/or software infrastructure, so it is important not only to know how each protocol operates, but also how the protocols work together.

The following sections introduce the five transport protocols that ship with Windows NT Server 4.0.

NETBEUI

NetBIOS Enhanced User Interface (NetBEUI) is the Transport layer driver developed by Microsoft that was initially intended for networks using LAN Manager or Windows for Workgroups. NetBEUI is based on the original Network Basic Input Output System

(NETBIOS) protocol developed by IBM. When you install Windows NT, NetBEUI automatically binds to the network card and needs no further configuration to work (in fact, Windows NT doesn't offer any user-configurable parameters for NetBEUI). This fast and efficient protocol consumes few network resources, provides excellent error correction, and requires no tuning. It will support as many as 254 connections. Its weaknesses include poor security and an absence of a network layer, which makes this protocol, by itself, nonroutable. (It can be emulated or encapsulated by other protocols, then routed, if necessary.) NetBEUI is suitable for small, homogenous, Microsoft-reliant LANs where technical expertise is scarce. Today it is most commonly used to integrate legacy, peer-to-peer networks.

NWLINK

NWLink is Microsoft's implementation of Novell's native **Internetwork Packet Exchange/ Sequenced Packet Exchange (IPX/SPX)** protocol. It is required for interoperability with LANs running NetWare versions 3.2 and lower; it can also be used with LANs running higher versions of the NetWare operating system. It automatically binds to the network card when you install Windows NT. NWLink requires little or no configuration, depending on which of its capabilities you want to use. (You will have the opportunity to configure NWLink later in this chapter.) Because this protocol includes network addressing information, it is considered routable. Routability provides a significant advantage for NWLink over NetBEUI, allowing NWLink to span many LAN or WAN segments.

TRANSMISSION CONTROL PROTOCOL/INTERNET PROTOCOL (TCP/IP)

TCP/IP is not simply one protocol, but rather a suite of protocols, including TCP, IP, UDP, ICMP, and others. (These protocols are discussed in detail later in this chapter.) Most network administrators refer to the entire group as "TCP/IP." TCP/IP's roots lie with the United States Department of Defense, which developed the precursor to TCP/IP for its Advanced Research Projects Agency network **(ARPAnet)** in the late 1960s. Thanks to its low cost and its ability to communicate between a multitude of dissimilar platforms, TCP/IP has become extremely popular. A de facto standard on the Internet, it is fast becoming the protocol of choice on LANs connected to the Internet. Although it is a routable and flexible protocol, its flexibility requires significant configuration. When you install Windows NT Server, TCP/IP is selected as the default transport protocol.

DATA LINK CONTROL (DLC)

Unlike the protocols discussed earlier, **Data Link Control (DLC)** is useful in only a few specialized situations. This IBM mainframe transport protocol can provide host connectivity from the Windows NT server to an IBM mainframe or midrange computer such as the AS/400. It can also be used with remote print servers such as the HP JetDirect. DLC allows JetDirect printers to connect directly to the network cable instead of requiring a dedicated PC to drive the printer. Because both of these connectivity needs can now be addressed by

TCP/IP, however, the use of DLC is not recommended if TCP/IP is available. DLC is not a routable protocol and therefore cannot pass through a router. Thus a printer connected via DLC can be used only by clients on the same network segment.

APPLETALK

AppleTalk is the protocol that enables Windows NT to support Apple Macintosh clients. Through AppleTalk, Macintosh users can share files on a Windows NT server and print to Windows NT networked printers. AppleTalk is the protocol that Services for Macintosh uses to route information and configure zones. Although it is not installed and bound to the network card by default, it requires very little configuration when you do install it. Services for Macintosh is discussed in Chapter 7.

TCP/IP COMPONENTS

Now that you know something about the five transport protocols that ship with Windows NT, you can focus on the most important of these protocols, TCP/IP. Because TCP/IP is such a popular and widely used networking protocol, you need to be familiar with its components so as to properly configure and support it in a Windows NT environment. TCP/IP is a broad topic, spanning theoretical, historical, and practical issues. If you plan to take Microsoft's exam on TCP/IP, you should invest in a book solely devoted to this suite of protocols, such as *A Guide to TCP/IP on Microsoft Windows NT 4.0*, published by Course Technology.

The following section provides an overview of TCP/IP's most important concepts.

THE TCP/IP PROTOCOL SUITE

TCP/IP is often discussed in terms of a four-layer model known as the TCP/IP Protocol Stack. The layers of the TCP/IP Protocol Stack correspond roughly to the layers in the OSI model as follows:

- **Application Layer**—Roughly equivalent to the Application and Presentation layers of the OSI model. Applications gain access to the network through this layer, via protocols such as Winsock API, File Transfer Protocol (FTP), Trivial File Transfer Protocol (TFTP), Hypertext Transfer Protocol (HTTP), Simple Mail Transfer Protocol (SMTP), and Dynamic Host Configuration Protocol (DHCP).

- **Transport Layer**— Roughly corresponds to the Session and Transport layers of the OSI model. This layer holds the Transmission Control Protocol (TCP) and User Datagram Protocol (UDP). All service requests use one of these protocols.

- **Internet Layer**— Equivalent to the network layer of the OSI model. This layer holds the Internet Protocol (IP), Internet Control Message Protocol (ICMP), Internet Group Message Protocol (IGMP), and Address Resolution Protocol (ARP). These protocols relate to message routing and host address resolution.

- **Network Interface Layer** —Roughly equivalent to the Data Link and Physical layers of the OSI model. This layer handles the formatting of data and transmission to the network wire.

Figure 3-2 compares the OSI model with the TCP/IP model.

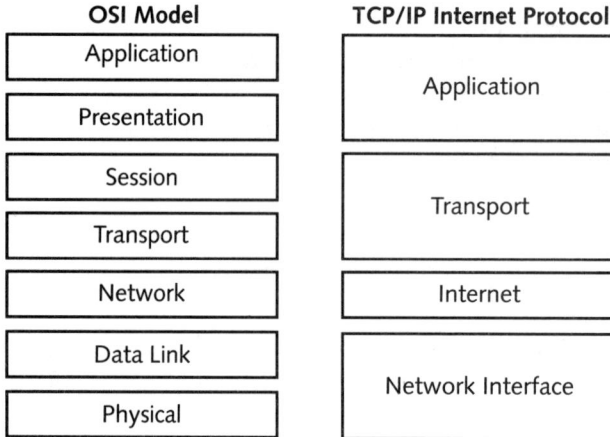

OSI Model	TCP/IP Internet Protocol
Application	Application
Presentation	
Session	Transport
Transport	
Network	Internet
Data Link	Network Interface
Physical	

Figure 3-2   Comparison of OSI seven-layer and TCP/IP model

TCP/IP CORE PROTOCOLS

To fully understand and support TCP/IP in the Windows NT environment, you need to examine the core protocols, or subprotocols, of the TCP/IP suite. The **TCP/IP core protocols** are designed to operate in the Transport or Internetwork layer, where they enable hosts on a network to communicate. They also provide services to the protocols in the Application layer, the highest level of the four-layer model. As you might guess, TCP and IP are the most significant core protocols in the TCP/IP suite.

Internet Protocol (IP)

Internet Protocol (IP) provides information about how and where data should be delivered. This information is contained in the **IP header**, which is a maximum of 20 octets long and contains a number of fields, including the packet destination address, source address, **Time To Live** (**TTL**; the maximum number of router hops a packet can traverse before it becomes unusable, or dies), IP version, packet length, transport protocol, and reliability specifications. This information, which routers interpret, makes the TCP/IP protocol routable. IP is an unreliable, connectionless, Internet-layer protocol, which means it does not guarantee delivery of data. Higher-level protocols of the TCP/IP suite, however, can use its information to ensure that data packets reach the proper addresses. IP's one concession to delivery reliability is a checksum that verifies the integrity of the routing information in the IP header. **Checksum** is an algorithmic method of determining whether data corruption occurred during transmission. If the checksum accompanying the message does not have the proper value when the packet is received, then the packet is presumed to be corrupt; it is therefore discarded, and a new packet is sent.

Transmission Control Protocol (TCP)

Transmission Control Protocol (TCP) is a **connection-oriented** Transport-layer protocol, which means that it provides reliable delivery of data between two points. The TCP header contains a maximum of 20 octets and includes information about source and destination ports, sequencing, error control, flow control, and packet **acknowledgment (ACK)**. It also provides a checksum feature to validate header and data accuracy. TCP is used by most Internet applications, such as Web browsers, FTP, and Telnet.

User Datagram Protocol (UDP)

User Datagram Protocol (UDP) is sometimes considered the inverse of the TCP protocol. UDP is a connectionless Transport-layer protocol that does not guarantee delivery of packets. The term **connectionless** means that UDP does not offer any assurance that packets will be received in the correct sequence. In fact, this protocol does not guarantee that the packets will be received at all. Furthermore, it provides no error checking or sequence numbering. UDP headers specify only source and destination ports, packet length, and checksum. Because UDP supports sending packets from a single sender to multiple receivers, it is used to transmit broadcast messages. It consumes much less overhead than the TCP protocol does, so its direct impact on network traffic is small. This protocol is suitable for use with sophisticated applications that provide their own connection-oriented functionality.

Internet Control Message Protocol (ICMP)

While IP ensures that packets reach the correct destination, **Internet Control Message Protocol (ICMP)** notifies the sender that something has gone wrong in the transmission process and that packets were not delivered. A Transport-layer protocol, ICMP does not provide error control. Instead, it simply reports which networks were unreachable and which packets were discarded because the allotted time for their delivery (that is, their TTL) expired. ICMP is used by several diagnostic utilities, such as PING and TRACERT. (You will learn more about these diagnostic utilities later in this chapter.)

Address Resolution Protocol (ARP)

TCP/IP uses a numerical addressing scheme to give each computer on the network a unique identity. While it might seem that computers communicate through their TCP/IP addresses, in reality they communicate through their physical hardware addresses, commonly known as **media access control (MAC) addresses**. These unique numbers are hard-coded (in effect, branded) onto the NICs by the computer manufacturer. No two computers have the same MAC. A MAC address is considered a physical address, whereas a TCP/IP address is considered a logical address.

Address Resolution Protocol (ARP) is an Internet-layer protocol that obtains the MAC (physical) address of a host and then creates a local database that maps this MAC address to the host's IP (logical) address. ARP works very closely with IP, because IP must have the address of a destination host before it can direct the message to it. A sending host accomplishes this goal by broadcasting an ARP request containing the destination host's IP address.

If a host on the local subnet receives an ARP request for its IP address, it responds with an ARP reply broadcast to the sender. The reply packet contains the physical address of the destination host.

Other TCP/IP-Related Protocols

A number of Application-layer protocols used by Windows NT Server are covered in detail in other chapters of this book. They include Dynamic Host Configuration Protocol (DHCP), Serial Line Interface Protocol (SLIP), Point-to-Point Protocol (PPP), and Point-to-Point Tunneling Protocol (PPTP).

The modular structure of Windows NT allows applications to take advantage of APIs to access TCP/IP protocols and their utilities. As a systems engineer, you do not need a detailed understanding of the contents of APIs. You merely need to understand their purpose, which is to allow an application to interact seamlessly with another program.

Routing Information Protocol (RIP), which is discussed later in this book, is used by TCP/IP as well. It provides routers with a communications protocol, enabling them to exchange **routing** information as network conditions change. RIP is used in situations where a Windows NT server is configured to function as a router. Routers not using RIP (with IP forwarding) must employ manually configured routing tables.

TCP/IP ADDRESSING

Hosts configured with TCP/IP, which may include computers or devices such as printers that are directly attached to the network, are assigned IP addresses. Each **IP address** is a unique 32-bit number, divided into four groups of **octets** (or 8-bit bytes) that are separated by periods. An example of a valid IP address is 144.92.43.178. Each IP address has two types of information: network and host. The first octet identifies the network class. Three types of network classes are commonly used: Class A, Class B, and Class C.

Table 3-1 summarizes the three commonly used classes of TCP/IP networks.

Table 3-1   Commonly Used Classes of TCP/IP Networks

Network Class	Beginning Octet	Number of Networks	Host Addresses per Network
A	1–126	126	16,777,214
B	128–191	>16,000	65,534
C	192–223	>2,000,000	254

The IP numbers of all nodes on a Class A network share the same first octet, consisting of a number between 1 and 126. Nodes on a Class B network share the same first two octets, and their IP addresses all begin with a number between 128 and 191. Class C network IP numbers share the same first three octets, with their first octet being a number between 192 and 223.

3

Because only 126 Class A networks are available on the Internet, most Class A networks are reserved for use by large corporations or governments. In addition, some IP addresses are reserved for network functions and cannot be assigned to machines or devices. Notice that 127 is not a valid first octet for any IP number. The range of addresses beginning with 127 is reserved for loopback information. The IP address 127.0.0.1 is called a "loopback address"; you can use this address, along with the PING diagnostic tool, to send a test message to your own machine. (PING is explained in more detail later in this chapter.)

A company can request a class of network addresses from the **InterNIC**, the current Internet naming authority, or its Internet service provider (ISP). Alternatively, if a **firewall** (a device designed to prevent external intrusion) protects the network, administrators can make up their own IP addressing scheme without regard for InterNIC standards. When the clients on those networks connect to the Internet through the firewall however, they must be assigned valid Internet IP addresses. This solution provides certain management benefits (for example, all machines on the third floor of an office building could be assigned an address beginning with 10.3.) and allows an organization to use more IP addresses than it could if InterNIC-sanctioned numbers were assigned to each machine.

A secondary number, known as a **subnet mask**, is also assigned as part of the TCP/IP configuration process. A subnet mask allows large networks to be subdivided into smaller subnetworks known as **subnets**. It notifies the network operating system about which addresses are on the same local network and which ones need to be contacted through a router. Subnetting is a complex, but highly useful tool of TCP/IP networking. Refer to a book devoted to the TCP/IP protocol suite to learn more about this topic.

IP address data are sent across the network in binary form, with each of the four octets consisting of eight bits. For example, the IP address 131.127.3.22 is the same as the binary number 10000011 01111111 00000011 00010110. Converting from the dotted decimal notation to a binary number is a simple process when you use the scientific calculator that comes with Windows NT and Windows 95.

To convert the first octet (131) of the previously given IP address to a binary number:

1. On a Windows 95 or Windows NT computer, click **Start**, point to **Programs**, point to **Accessories**, then click **Calculator**.

2. Click **View**, then click **Scientific**. Make sure that the **Dec option button** is selected.

3. Type **131**, then click the **Bin option button**. The binary equivalent of the number 131, 10000011, appears in the display window.

You can reverse this process to convert a decimal number to a binary number.

Every host on a network must have a unique number, as duplicate addresses will cause problems on a network. One benefit of Windows NT is that it can use ARP to detect such duplicate IP addresses. Because ARP does not cross routers, however, repeated addresses can be detected only on the local subnet. If a host is added to a network and its IP address is already in use by another host on the subnet, an error message will be sent to the new client and its TCP/IP stack will be disabled. The existing host will also receive an error message, but can continue to function normally. You can assign IP addresses manually, but you must take care to avoid assigning duplicate addresses. By using a DHCP server to automatically assign IP addresses, duplicate-addressing problems can be eliminated. (DHCP is described in detail in Chapter 4.)

INSTALLING AND CONFIGURING PROTOCOLS

The process of adding protocols to the Windows NT system is the same for each protocol. The only difference involves the amount of configuration needed. NetBEUI and DLC involve no configuration, while NWLink may require some. Only AppleTalk and TCP/IP definitely require configuration. The following steps guide you through the process of installing a protocol. Remember that NetBEUI, NWLink, and TCP/IP would already be present on your Windows NT server and bound to the NIC after installation, unless the administrator manually removed them.

The following steps describe the process for installing the NetBEUI protocol, which requires no configuration. The steps for installing other protocols would be identical, except that you might have to configure the protocol after installing it.

To install a protocol:

1. Log on to the server as an Administrator.

2. Right-click the **Network Neighborhood** icon, then click **Properties** on the shortcut menu. The Network Neighborhood Properties dialog box opens.

3. Click the **Protocols tab**.

4. Click **Add**. The Select Network Protocol dialog box opens, as shown in Figure 3-3.

5. Click **NetBEUI Protocol** in the Network Protocol list, then click **OK**. The Windows NT Setup dialog box appears, asking for the location of the Windows NT installation files.

6. Type the appropriate path to the installation files (typically the I386 directory on the installation CD-ROM), then click **Continue**.

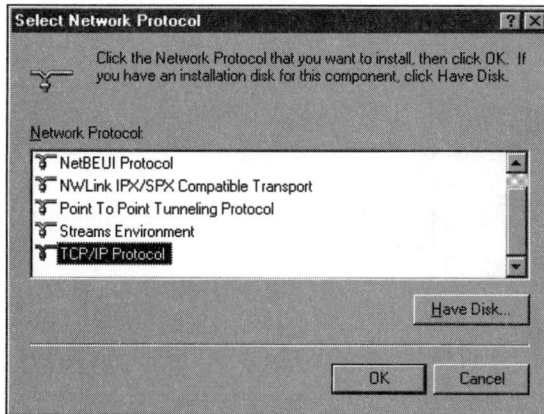

Figure 3-3   Select Network Protocol dialog box

7. Click **OK**. You will be prompted to restart your server to allow the changes to take effect.

8. Click **Yes** to restart your server.

When installing DLC or NetBEUI, you simply follow the previous set of steps to complete the installation. When installing NWLink, TCP/IP, and AppleTalk, you must configure the protocols after installing them. The following sections explain how to configure these protocols.

CONFIGURING NWLINK

In some cases, NWLink will work properly without any configuration. If your network uses multiple frame types or NICs, if you want to use Microsoft's IPX routing capabilities, or if your server will run File and Print Services for NetWare, then you will need to adjust the NWLink properties.

To configure NWLink:

1. Log on as an Administrator.

2. Right-click the **Network Neighborhood** icon, then select **Properties** from the menu.

3. Click the **Protocols tab**.

4. Click **NWLink IPX/SPX Compatible Transport protocol** in the Network Properties dialog box, then click **Properties**. The NWLink IPX/SPX Properties dialog box opens. The General tab should be displayed, as shown in Figure 3-4.

5. Refer to the explanations in the following section regarding NWLink's options, then make changes according to your network's needs.

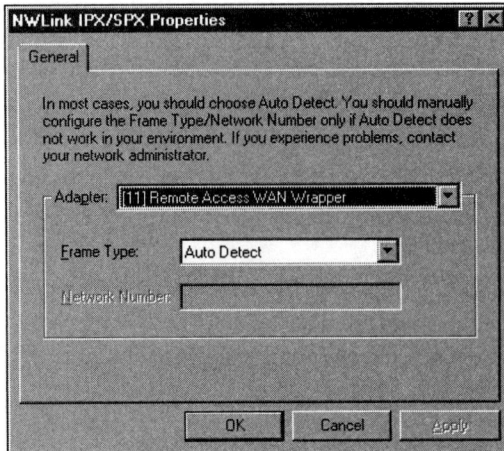

Figure 3-4   General tab of the NWLink IPX/SPX Properties dialog box

6. Click **OK**. You will be prompted to restart your server to enable the changes to take effect.

7. Click **Yes** to restart your server.

NWLINK'S CONFIGURABLE PARAMETERS

Perhaps one of the most important properties of NWLink is the internal network number. This unique, eight-digit hexadecimal number allows the server to communicate with servers running Novell's NetWare operating systems. The internal network number is equivalent to the IPX number on Netware server nodes, identifying that server in a multiple-network environment. To avoid potential addressing conflicts on the network, it is a good practice to change this value from its default value of zero to a unique, eight-digit hexadecimal number when you initially set up the Windows NT server.

Another important configurable NWLink parameter is the frame type. By default, Windows NT uses Auto Detect to determine which Ethernet frame type to support. Auto Detect will set the frame type equal to the first frame it receives and will not look for additional frame types. If you have only one NIC in your Windows NT server, and that server connects to only one NetWare server, Auto Detect will suffice. If your network environment is more complex, you will need to select Manual Frame Type Detection from the General Properties tab, then click Add to see the list of frame types available. Four frame types will appear: Ethernet 802.2, Ethernet 802.3, Ethernet II, and Ethernet SNAP. NetWare versions 2.x and 3.x use Ethernet 802.3, while NetWare versions 4.0 and higher use Ethernet 802.2. If you have more than one NIC on your server, you will need to select the adapter from the Adapter list box before choosing its frame type.

With Windows NT Server 4.0, you can use the server as a router or bridge to connect two different networks. This approach, however, will compromise your Windows NT server's performance. The server cannot match the routing capabilities of a dedicated router whose hardware and software are optimized for this function. If your server has more than one NIC, and you have configured the frame type and internal network number, you can enable IPX routing. (Chapter 11 explains how to enable IPX routing.)

CONFIGURING TCP/IP

TCP/IP requires significant configuration, unless you are using DHCP. DHCP is a service that automatically assigns unique IP numbers to network clients. (See Chapter 4 for information about configuring DHCP to work with Windows NT server.)

To configure TCP-IP:

1. Log on as an Administrator.

2. Right-click the **Network Neighborhood** icon, then select **Properties** from the menu.

3. Select **Microsoft TCP/IP** protocol, then click **Properties**. The Microsoft TCP/IP Properties dialog box appears, with five configuration tabs. The IP Address tab should be displayed, as shown in Figure 3-5.

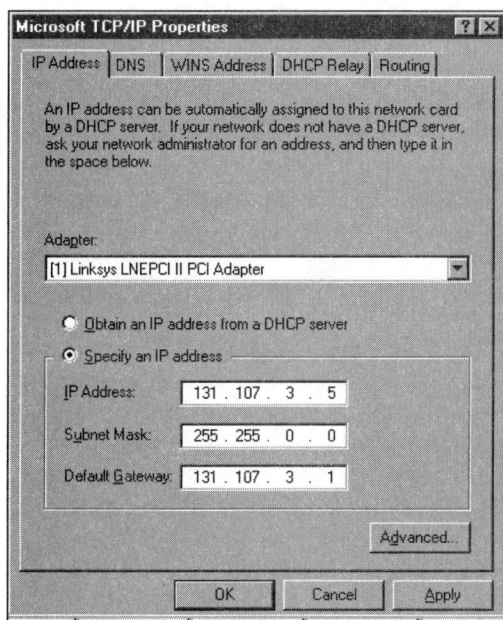

Figure 3-5   Microsoft TCP/IP Properties dialog box

4. Type the server's IP address, subnet mask, and **gateway** (if necessary) in the appropriate text boxes.

5. If you will be connecting with a Domain Naming Service (DNS), Windows Internet Naming Service (WINS), DHCP Relay, or RIP for TCP/IP, modify those tabs accordingly. Refer to the explanations in the following sections, or in Chapter 4, for more information about these services.

6. Click **OK**. You will be prompted to restart your server to enable the changes to take effect.

7. Click **Yes** to restart your server.

TCP/IP's Configurable Parameters

You configure TCP/IP using the five tabs of the Microsoft TCP/IP Properties dialog box. As you saw in the previous set of steps, the IP Address tab is used to identify the server's IP address and subnet mask number. If you plan to connect your Windows NT server to the Internet, you will need to configure its DNS properties using the DNS tab of the Microsoft TCP/IP dialog box.

In the Host Name text box, type the name of your server. In the Domain text box, type your Internet domain name. Domain names are a more user-friendly version of unique numerical addresses assigned to whole networks of computers. An example of a domain name is microsoft.com. Click the Add button under DNS Server Search Order to add IP addresses for your network's DNS server(s). The order in which these addresses appear is the order in which Windows NT will poll the DNS servers to find information about other domains and hosts. If you like, you can add domain suffixes under the Domain Suffix Search Order heading. A domain suffix is a domain name that will be appended to any host names that the server tries to look up. If you use one, make sure to type it correctly; otherwise the server will waste valuable time searching for a domain that doesn't exist.

If your network is using a WINS server, you will need to configure the WINS Address tab in the Microsoft TCP/IP Properties dialog box. A WINS server maintains a database that correlates each client's computer name, or NetBIOS name, with its IP address. If you have more than one WINS server, you can enter the IP addresses of the primary and secondary servers. You can also use DNS for WINS Resolution, although this option is not recommended on large networks because of its excessive maintenance requirements. WINS servers are discussed in more detail in Chapter 4.

You use the DHCP Relay agent tab to configure the DHCP Relay properties, which allow the Windows NT server to forward DHCP requests through a router. This service can support only clients on the server's local subnet. To use DHCP Relay, first make sure that the DHCP Relay Agent is installed in the Network Neighborhood Properties dialog box. Then, in the DHCP Relay tab, click the Add button and enter the IP address of your DHCP server.

In NWLink properties, you had the option of configuring the Windows NT server to route IPX data. In the same way, the Windows NT Server 4.0 server can act as a router for IP by implementing routing or IP Forwarding. The server must have multiple NICs, have the RIP for IP protocol installed, and have its TCP/IP properties correctly configured. You can then select Enable IP Forwarding from the Routing tab. Routing through Windows NT Server 4.0 is not recommended because it drains server resources.

CONFIGURING APPLETALK

Before you can configure AppleTalk, verify that Services for Macintosh are installed in the Network Neighborhood Properties dialog box.

To configure AppleTalk:

1. Log on as an Administrator.

2. Right-click the **Network Neighborhood** icon, then click **Properties** in the menu.

3. Click **AppleTalk** in the Network Neighborhood properties box, then click **Properties**. The Microsoft AppleTalk Protocol Properties dialog box opens, as shown in Figure 3-6.

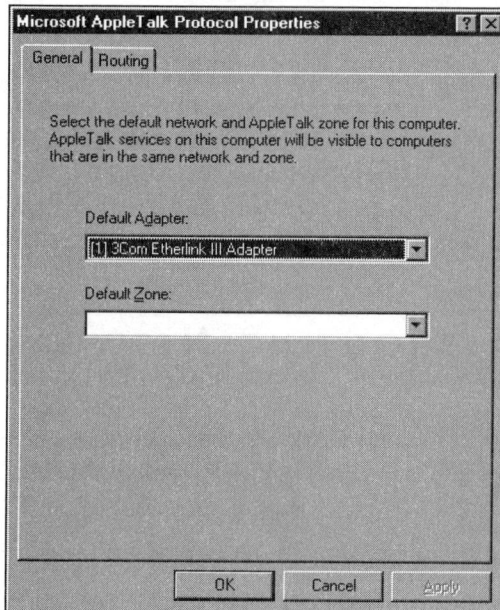

Figure 3-6   Microsoft AppleTalk Protocol Properties dialog box

4. On the General tab, select the network adapter to which AppleTalk will be bound, then choose the default AppleTalk zone (the zone in which the Windows NT server and printers will appear when Macintosh users select them through the Chooser function). As with IP and IPX, Windows NT 4.0 can function as a router for AppleTalk. Use the Routing tab to add and remove zones.

5. Click **OK**. You will be prompted to restart your server to enable the changes to take effect.

6. Click **Yes** to restart your server.

7. Before Macintosh clients can use files on the Windows NT server, you must create a volume that is visible to AppleTalk. To do this, run the **File Manager** program. Choose **Create Volume** from the Macfile menu and name the Macintosh volume. Leave the password and confirm password boxes empty, and leave the Volume Security and User Limit settings at their defaults.

8. Click **OK** to save your changes.

BINDING MULTIPLE PROTOCOLS

Binding is the process of assigning one network component to work with another. Protocols must be bound to the services and NICs on which they will run. To obtain the optimal network performance, you should adjust the **protocol binding** order so that the most heavily used protocol appears first on the list. To change the binding order, select a binding from the Bindings tab in the Network Properties dialog box, then click on the Move Up or Move Down buttons to adjust its priority.

Although you can bind multiple protocols on a server, you should install (or keep installed) only the protocols you need, because each protocol uses memory and further complicates the configuration. For example, because NetWare 4.11 servers can use TCP/IP, you should consider using only TCP/IP to communicate with a NetWare server, rather than NWLink. The same applies to Macintosh clients, which can use TCP/IP.

IDENTIFYING AND TROUBLESHOOTING NETWORK PROTOCOL PROBLEMS

In troubleshooting any kind of network problem, you must first analyze the nature of the problem. This rule applies to protocol problems as well. When a problem occurs, begin by asking these questions:

- Is the entire network affected? Only one subnet? Only one workstation?

- What changed prior to the problem's appearance? For example, did the workstation's properties change?

- Was a new application installed on the server? Did the server receive a hardware upgrade? Has the server or workstation been moved? Have network cables been moved?

- Can the user log on normally at another workstation?

- Can other servers or workstations "see" the affected server or workstation in Network Neighborhood?

- If a workstation is the problem, has it *ever* worked "normally"?

The majority of network problems, even if they appear to be protocol-based, probably result from changes to the system, either in software or hardware. For this reason, you should first examine the Physical-layer components, such as the network cable and NIC, for any changes. Then do the same for any software components. If these tactics fail to uncover the problem, examine the Transport-layer protocols, as explained in the following sections.

TROUBLESHOOTING NETBEUI

As noted earlier, the NetBEUI protocol does not contain addressing information and therefore is not routable. This characteristic makes it less prone to cause errors on the network, but more difficult to troubleshoot if errors do occur. NetBEUI transmits data in a broadcast manner, hitting every MAC address in its way. Therefore, it is nearly impossible to isolate NetBEUI traffic on the wire without a protocol analyzer. A protocol analyzer is a software- or hardware-based system that can capture and analyze network traffic. A hardware-based protocol analyzer is called a sniffer. Examples of software-based protocol analyzers include Microsoft's Network Monitor and Network Associates' Net X-Ray. Network monitor is a protocol analyzer that ships with Windows NT Server, as explained in Chapter 12.

TROUBLESHOOTING NWLINK

If you are using multiple network adapters in your Windows NT server or are connecting to NetWare servers that use multiple frame types, then the first step in troubleshooting NWLink is to check its configuration parameters. One server may have four or more adapters and support as many as four Ethernet frame types, so the possibility of error can be great. Another potential pitfall with NWLink is assigning two network devices the same internal network number. Every device running IPX/SPX should have a unique internal network number.

Once you have ruled out configuration errors, your best option is use a protocol analyzer, as described in the previous section. Although NWLink does contain addressing information, it does not come with its own diagnostic utilities, unlike TCP/IP. If you are using IPX/SPX to transport NetBIOS packets between network segments, you must use a protocol analyzer to track down protocol problems.

TROUBLESHOOTING TCP/IP

Among the Windows NT protocols, TCP/IP carries the highest potential of causing problems, because it requires the most configuration. For this reason, TCP/IP comes with a complete set of troubleshooting tools that allow you to track down most TCP/IP-related problems without a protocol analyzer. You should be familiar with the use of the following tools and their switches, because if you use TCP/IP you will need these diagnostics regularly. Each of these utilities can be typed at the command prompt from the server or client.

IPCONFIG

This utility displays local host TCP/IP configuration details. By viewing a machine's IPCONFIG data, you can determine all the TCP/IP settings from the Network Neighborhood properties (if configured manually) or the DHCP server. Figure 3-7 shows an example of IPCONFIG output.

```
Command Prompt                                                    _□×
<C> Copyright 1985-1996 Microsoft Corp.

C:\>ipconfig /all

Windows NT IP Configuration

        Host Name . . . . . . . . . : rpstax
        DNS Servers . . . . . . . . :
        Node Type . . . . . . . . . : Hybrid
        NetBIOS Scope ID. . . . . . :
        IP Routing Enabled. . . . . : No
        WINS Proxy Enabled. . . . . : No
        NetBIOS Resolution Uses DNS : No

Ethernet adapter LNEPCI21:

        Description . . . . . . . . : Novell 2000 Adapter.
        Physical Address. . . . . . : 00-20-78-11-DB-D9
        DHCP Enabled. . . . . . . . : No
        IP Address. . . . . . . . . : 131.107.3.5
        Subnet Mask . . . . . . . . : 255.255.0.0
        Default Gateway . . . . . . : 131.107.3.1
        Primary WINS Server . . . . : 131.107.3.5

C:\>
```

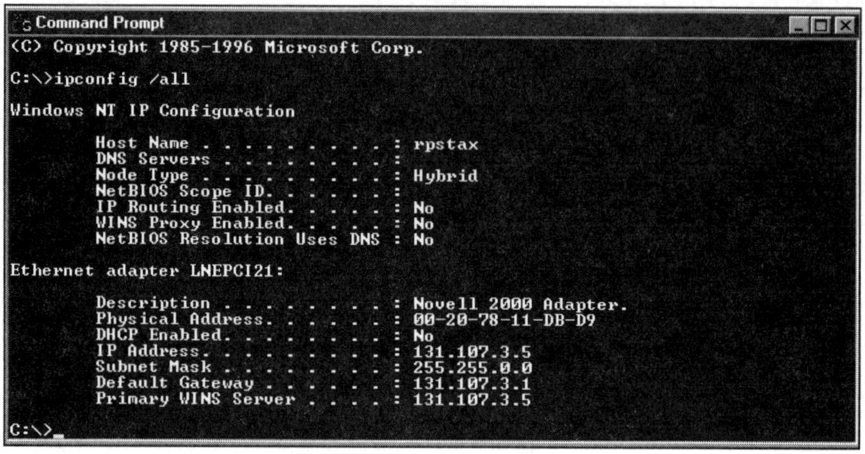

Figure 3-7   Example of IPCONFIG output

You can also manually release DHCP addresses through IPCONFIG by using the following command-line syntax:

IPCONFIG /release

Once you have released a machine's DHCP address, you must renew it by typing IPCONFIG /renew at the command line. Because you cannot release or renew DHCP addresses through Network Neighborhood, you must rely on the IPCONFIG utility.

Packet Internet Groper (PING)

This utility can be used to verify that TCP/IP is running, bound to the NIC, configured correctly, and communicating with the network. PING uses ICMP to send echo request and echo reply messages that determine the validity of an IP address. Echo requests work much in the same way that sonar operates. A signal is sent out to an object (in this case, another computer), which rebroadcasts the signal to the sender. The process of sending out a signal is known as pinging. You can ping either an IP address or a host name. By pinging the loopback address, 127.0.0.1, you can determine whether your workstation's TCP/IP services are functioning. By pinging a host on another subnet, you can determine whether the problem lies with your gateway or DNS server. Following is the correct syntax for a simple loopback ping:

ping 127.0.0.1

If your workstation's TCP/IP services are functioning properly, the workstation's response will look similar to the following:

Pinging 127.0.0.1 with 32 bytes of data:

Reply from 127.0.0.1: bytes=32 time<10ms TTL=32
Reply from 127.0.0.1: bytes=32 time<10ms TTL=32
Reply from 127.0.0.1: bytes=32 time<10ms TTL=32
Reply from 127.0.0.1: bytes=32 time<10ms TTL=32

If your TCP/IP services are not functioning correctly, the workstation will respond as follows:

Pinging 127.0.0.1 with 32 bytes of data:

Request timed out.
Request timed out.
Request timed out.
Request timed out.

You can ping any IP address on your network in the same manner. If the ping is successful, you will receive four reply messages as in the first response above. If the ping is not successful (because the IP address you entered is invalid or because the device belonging to that IP address is unreachable), you will see the second response.

You can use a variety of switches on the PING command line to tailor the kind of response you want, depending on the problem you are troubleshooting. Some of the common switches used with the PING utility are listed in Table 3-2 (note that all are in lowercase letters).

Table 3-2   Commonly Used Switches for the PING Utility

PING Switch Syntax	Function
ping –n [count] [IP address]	Specify number of packets to send
ping –w [timeout] [IP address]	Specify timeout (in milliseconds) for each packet to reply
ping –a [IP address]	Resolve IP address to its host name
ping –r [count] [IP address]	Record route for count hops
ping –i [TTL] [IP address]	Specify time to live for packet
ping –l [size] [IP address]	Send a specific buffer size

NETSTAT

This utility displays TCP/IP statistics and the status of the current TCP/IP connections. It also displays notice ports, which can signal whether services are using the correct ports. Because servers typically use a multitude of ports for their services, NETSTAT is especially useful for troubleshooting server systems. When you type NETSTAT at the command-line prompt, you will see something similar to the following response:

```
Proto    Local Address    Foreign Address    State
TCP      rpstax:1025      localhost:1033     ESTABLISHED
TCP      rpstax:1033      localhost:1025     ESTABLISHED
```

The netstat -a command displays all current TCP and UDP connections from the issuing device to other devices on the network, as well as the source and destination service ports. You can use netstat -r to post a listing of the **routing table** on a given machine. These and other NETSTAT switches are shown in Table 3-3.

Table 3-3   Commonly Used Switches for the NETSTAT Utility

NETSTAT Switch Syntax	Function
netstat –a	Displays all connections and listening ports
netstat –e	Displays all Ethernet connections
netstat –p [protocol]	Displays connections for the protocol specified, either TCP or UDP
netstat –r	Displays contents of the routing table
netstat interval	Displays connection statistics continuously in intervals until you press control-C

NBTSTAT

The NBTSTAT command displays the current TCP/IP connections using NetBIOS over TCP/IP. It may help with NetBIOS name resolution problems. Use of this utility is declining as networking relies increasingly less on NetBIOS. If you do need to use it, Table 3-4 lists the helpful switches that come with the NetBIOS utility. Note that the switches are case-sensitive.

Table 3-4   NBTSTAT Command Options

NBTSTAT Switch Syntax	Function
nbtstat –a [remote name]	Lists the remote machine's name table given its name
nbtstat –a [IP address]	Lists the remote machine's name table given its IP address
nbtstat –n	Lists the local NetBIOS names
nbtstat –r	Lists names resolved by broadcast and via WINS
nbtstat –r	Reloads the remote cache name table

NSLOOKUP

This utility queries the DNS system and allows you to determine the status of a name server, its IP address (if you know its host name), or its host name (if you know its IP address). Along with the other TCP/IP utilities, NSLOOKUP is a powerful troubleshooting tool. Examples of the command include the following:

C:\nslookup microsoft.com
C:\nslookup 131.107.3.6

NSLOOKUP has numerous settings you can specify to customize its output. Most of the time, however, you will use the simple form of the command shown above.

TRACERT

The TRACERT utility uses ICMP to trace the path from your workstation to a specified destination IP address, identifying all the intermediate hops in between. It is useful for determining router or subnet connectivity problems. Following is an example of a TRACERT utility command and its response:

C:\tracert ntserver
1 <10ms <10ms <10 ms 131.107.3.6

Like the other TCP/IP diagnostics, TRACERT allows you to tailor the information in the response. Table 3-5 shows the switches you can use with the TRACERT utility.

Table 3-5   TRACERT Utility Switches

TRACERT Switch Syntax	Function
tracert –d [target_name]	Does not resolve addresses to host names
tracert –h [max. # of hops] [target_name]	Maximum number of hops to search for target
tracert –j [host-list] [target_name]	Loose source route along host-list
tracert –w [timeout] [target_name]	Maximum wait in milliseconds for each reply

ROUTE

Among other things, this utility displays the current routing table, which reveals the routes and number of **hops** your packets take to reach their destination hosts. (Routing and routing tables are discussed in Chapter 11.) ROUTE allows you to add, change, or delete routes and clear the routing table. In troubleshooting TCP/IP, you will probably use the ROUTE command only rarely, though you might use the ROUTE PRINT command. An example of its output is shown in Figure 3-8.

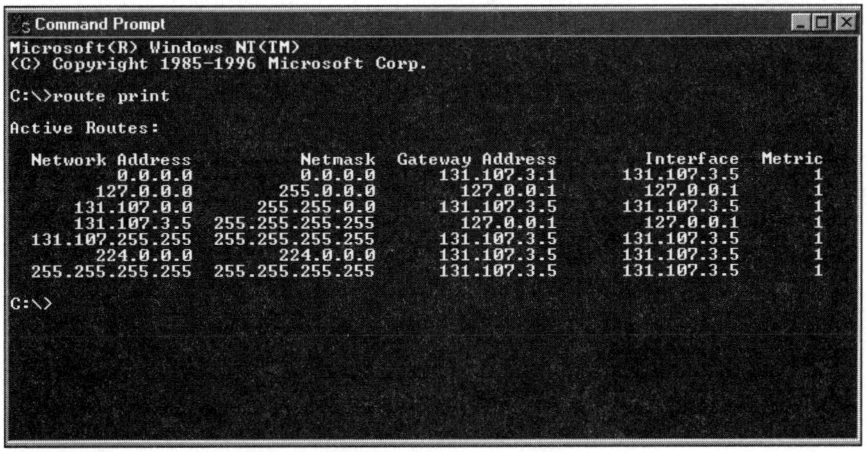

Figure 3-8   Example of ROUTE PRINT command output

CHAPTER SUMMARY

- To communicate with one another, computers use commonly accepted languages, known as network protocols. You should already be familiar with the seven-layer Open Systems Interconnection (OSI) model, which standardizes levels of service and types of interaction for network computers. Microsoft identifies three networking components that correspond roughly to layers of this model: network adapter drivers, transport protocols, and application/file system drivers.

- NetBIOS Enhanced User Interface (NetBEUI) is an efficient, fast Transport-layer protocol originally designed for networks running LAN Manager or Windows for Workgroups. It can support as many as 254 connections and requires no configuration. It does not contain Network-layer or addressing information and therefore cannot be routed. Because it is not routable, NetBEUI is a poor choice for large LANs or WANs.

- NWLink is a routable Transport-layer protocol that is required for communication with NetWare clients and servers. It is automatically bound to the NIC when you install Windows NT server and may require configuration, depending on which of its services your network uses. Because it contains Network-layer and addressing information, NWLink is a routable protocol, suitable for LANs with multiple segments or WANs.

- TCP/IP is not really a single protocol, but rather a suite of protocols, commonly known as the TCP/IP Internet Protocol Suite. This versatile and reliable protocol is used on many types of networks, including the Internet. TCP/IP is automatically bound to the server's NIC when you install Windows NT Server 4.0 and, in fact, is selected as the default protocol. It may require significant configuration, however, before the server can use it to communicate with clients running TCP/IP.

- The finer points of TCP/IP are beyond the scope of this book. Nevertheless, you should at least become familiar with the syntax of IP addresses—four octets separated by periods—and be able to translate the octets into binary form. Every computer or device on a network must have a unique IP address to communicate using TCP/IP. Networks are typically assigned groups of IP addresses that can be divided into three classes: A, B, and C. Some IP addresses are reserved for special networking functions. Subnetting allows you to separate network segments within an organization. If a network connects to the Internet, in addition to having a group of unique IP addresses, it must have a valid domain name. IP addresses and domain names are obtained from the current Internet naming authority, InterNIC.

- The Data Link Control (DLC) protocol provides interoperability with IBM mainframe and midrange computers, such as the AS/400, and direct connectivity for Hewlett-Packard JetDirect printers. It is not automatically installed when you install Windows NT; once installed, however, DLC requires no configuration. Because it is a highly specialized protocol, it should be avoided in favor of TCP/IP if possible.

- The AppleTalk protocol is used exclusively to communicate with Apple Macintosh computers. It is not automatically bound to the server's NIC during the installation process, but can be added through Network Neighborhood properties. AppleTalk requires some further configuration before the Windows NT server can communicate with Macintosh clients on the network.

- The process for installing and configuring network protocols in Windows NT is the same for all protocols. As a general rule, to lower network overhead and improve system performance, you should install only the protocols you truly need. To install a protocol, choose Add from the Protocols tab of the Network Neighborhood properties dialog box. NetBEUI and DLC do not require configuration after they are installed. NWLink, AppleTalk, and TCP/IP will require configuration.

- Protocol bindings are the connections between network interfaces, protocols, and services installed on a Windows NT computer. Windows NT servers can have one or all protocols running (or bound) at the same time, thereby allowing you to access Windows NT hosts, Novell NetWare hosts, and other third-party hosts simultaneously. Once a protocol is installed, it will bind itself to the server's NIC(s) and services. You can modify these bindings through the Bindings tab in the Network Neighborhood Properties dialog box.

- To troubleshoot network protocol problems, you should first identify the extent of the problem. Is the entire network affected? A group of clients? Only one client? NetBEUI is a difficult protocol to troubleshoot because it does not contain addressing information, but rather floods the network with requests in a broadcast manner. Solving problems with NetBEUI is best accomplished with a protocol analyzer such as Microsoft's Network Monitor or Network Associate's Net X-Ray. Most problems with NWLink will occur due to incorrect configuration. Check the internal network numbers, network adapter bindings, and frame types for errors. Protocol analyzers can also help diagnose NWLink problems, and they are the only option if you are using IPX/SPX to carry NetBIOS services between LAN segments.

- Troubleshooting TCP/IP is somewhat easier, because TCP/IP involves point-to-point communication between devices on the network and comes with a number of diagnostic utilities. Examples of these utilities are PING, IPCONFIG, NETSTAT, NBTSTAT, ROUTE, TRACERT, and ARP. You should be familiar with and practice using TCP/IP's diagnostic tools with their various switches. They can help you track down network problems in a matter of minutes and do not require any additional software or hardware, such as a protocol analyzer.

KEY TERMS

- **acknowledgment (ACK) messages** — Message sent by the receiver to acknowledge the receipt of a data packet.

- **Adapter Card Drivers layer** — One of the five layers of the Microsoft Networking model. Roughly equivalent to the Physical layer of the OSI model. Handles formatting of data for physical access to the network adapter card and the network wire.

- **Address Resolution Protocol (ARP)** — A protocol in the TCP/IP suite that obtains the MAC (physical) address of a host, matches it to an IP address, and stores this information in the ARP cache.

- **AppleTalk** — Protocol used to connect Apple computers to a Windows NT network.

- **Application/File System Drivers layer** — One of the five layers of the Microsoft Networking model. Roughly equivalent to the Application and Presentation layers of the OSI model. Holds the two application programming interfaces.

- **Application layer** — One of the four layers of the TCP/IP model, or stack. Roughly equivalent to the Application and Presentation layers of the OSI model. Allows applications access to the network.

- **application programming interface (API)** — A set of programmed routines that operates at the Application layer of the OSI model.

- **ARPAnet** — A network of U.S. Department of Defense and university computers that preceded the Internet.

- **binding** — Assigning protocols to function with a network computer or network service.

- **checksum** — A method used to determine whether data have been transmitted correctly.

- **connection-oriented** — Term used to describe a protocol that guarantees delivery of data packets in the proper sequence.

- **connectionless** — Term used to describe a protocol that does not guarantee delivery of data packets in the proper sequence.

- **Data Link Control (DLC)** — Protocol used to connect to IBM mainframe and midrange computers and to Hewlett-Packard JetDirect network printers.

- **firewall** — A device used to isolate a network and prevent external intrusion.

- **gateway** — A device or program that connects computers with dissimilar platforms.

- **hop** — A point during data transmission in which the data packet passes through a router.

- **Internet Control Message Protocol (ICMP)** — A protocol in the TCP/IP suite that notifies the sender if something goes wrong during data transmission and packets remain unsent.

- **Internet layer** — One of the four layers of the TCP/IP model, or stack. Roughly equivalent to the Network layer of the OSI model. Holds protocols concerned with routing messages and host address resolution.

- **Internet Protocol (IP)** — An unreliable, connectionless protocol in the TCP/IP suite that does not guarantee delivery of data. Provides addressing information for TCP/IP transmission.

- **Internetwork Packet Exchange/Sequenced Packet Exchange (IPX/SPX)** — Novell's native network protocol.

- **InterNIC** — The Internet authority organization that, among other things, controls the distribution of IP addresses.

- **IP address** — A unique number assigned to a computer in the TCP/IP addressing scheme. Takes the form of a 32-bit number broken up into four 8-bit fields separated by periods, with each field numbered from 0 to 255. An example might be 131.127.3.22.

- **IPCONFIG** — A command-prompt utility used to show TCP/IP configuration details for a host.

- **IP header** — The means by which the Internet Protocol (IP) provides information about how and where data should be delivered. A maximum of 20 octets long, the IP header contains a number of fields, such as packet destination address and Time to Live.

- **media access control (MAC) address** — Physical address of a network interface card that is hard-coded to the device by the manufacturer.

- **multiple protocol binding** — The Windows NT Server feature that allows you to use one or all available protocols on a single adapter card.

- **NBTSTAT** — A command prompt utility used to display the current TCP/IP connections using NetBIOS over TCP/IP. May help resolve name resolution problems.

- **NetBIOS Enhanced User Interface (NetBEUI)** — Simple, nonroutable protocol that can be used on small LANs of as many as 200 clients with Microsoft operating systems.

- **NETSTAT** — A command-prompt utility used to display TCP/IP connections and statistics.

- **Network Driver Interface Specification (NDIS) boundary layer** — One of the five layers of the Microsoft Networking model. Roughly equivalent to the Data Link layer of the OSI model. Provides interfaces between the protocols and the Adapter Card Drivers layer.

- **network interface card (NIC)** — The card that connects the server or client to the network cabling. Also called a network adapter.

- **Network Interface layer** — One of the four layers of the TCP/IP model, or stack. Roughly equivalent to the Data Link and Physical layers of the OSI model. Handles the formatting of data and transmission to the network wire.

- **network protocols** — The language or rules used by computers to communicate on a network to ensure that data are transmitted intact, in sequence, and without error.

- **NSLOOKUP** — A TCP/IP utility that queries the DNS system to determine the status of a name server, its IP address and host name.

- **NWLink** — Microsoft's implementation of Novell's native IPX/SPX protocol. Required for communication with NetWare clients and servers.

- **octet** — One of the four 8-bit fields in an IP address.

- **Open Systems Interconnection (OSI) model** — A seven-layer model that standardizes levels of service and types of interaction for network computers.

- **Packet Internet Groper (PING)** — A command-prompt utility that helps in diagnosing TCP/IP connection problems.

- **ping** — The process of sending out a test signal using the PING utility.

- **protocol binding** — The connections between network interfaces, protocols, and services installed on a Windows NT computer.

- **protocols** — See *network protocols*.

- **Protocols layer** — One of the five layers of Microsoft's Networking model. Roughly equivalent to the Transport and Network layers of the OSI model. Contains protocols responsible for translating data so that other operating systems can understand them.

- **routable** — The characteristic that allows protocols to be recognized and passed on by a router.

- **ROUTE** — A command-prompt utility that, among other things, displays the current routing table showing the routes and number of hops that a packet takes to reach a specific destination.

- **router** — A device that connects more than one network segment and intelligently transfers data between segments.

- **routing** — The process of forwarding data packets from a source computer on one network segment to a destination computer on another network segment.

- **routing table** — A table that provides information to a router about which paths to take in transferring data.

- **subnet** — A section of a larger network, as logically defined through TCP/IP configurations.

- **subnet mask** — When translated into binary, a number that is used to determine whether data can be sent to a particular network address.

- **subprotocols** — See *TCP/IP core protocols*.

- **TCP/IP core protocols** — Protocols in the TCP/IP suite concerned with providing communications between hosts on a network.

3

- **TCP/IP suite** — A widely used suite of protocols capable of connecting multiple networks with varying architectures. TCP/IP is the de facto protocol of the Internet.

- **Time To Live (TTL)** — The time allotted for the delivery of a data packet. The default TTL on the Internet is 32 seconds.

- **TRACERT** — A command-prompt utility used to display the route that TCP/IP packets take through a network.

- **Transmission Control Protocol (TCP)** — A connection-oriented protocol that guarantees delivery of data packets in the proper sequence. It is the most widely used protocol.

- **Transport Driver Interface (TDI) boundary layer** — One of the five layers of Microsoft's Networking model. Roughly equivalent to the Session layer of the OSI model. Handles requests to and from the lower Protocol layer and provides session services.

- **Transport layer** — One of the four layers of the TCP/IP model, or stack. Roughly equivalent to the Session and Transport layers of the OSI model.

- **transport protocols** — Networking protocols that operate at the Transport layer of the OSI Model. Transport protocols include NWLink, NetBEUI, DLC, AppleTalk, and TCP/IP.

- **User Datagram Protocol (UDP)** — A connectionless-oriented protocol in the TCP/IP suite that offers unreliable delivery of data packets with low overhead.

REVIEW QUESTIONS

1. Windows NT can have only one protocol running at any one time. True or False?

2. Five networking layers roughly correspond to the seven levels in the OSI model. What are they?

3. Which of the five protocols discussed in this chapter are routable? Which are not?

4. PPP and SLIP are Transport-layer TCP/IP protocols. True or False?

5. NWLink (IPX/SPX) allows you to assign duplicate addresses to clients on a network. True or False?

6. What method does TCP use to determine whether data were transmitted correctly?

7. Describe the difference between connection-oriented and connectionless protocols.

8. The AppleTalk protocol is bound to the server's network interface card when you install Windows NT Server. True or False?

9. 00688A2C is an example of a valid IPX/SPX internal network number. True or False?

10. What is the purpose of ICMP?

    a. resolving host names to IP addresses

    b. sending multicast messages to groups of Internet hosts

    c. diagnosing and sending messages about delivery errors

    d. resolving IP addresses to hardware addresses

11. The purpose of ARP is to resolve MAC addresses to IP addresses. True or False?

12. What is the advantage of using Dynamic Host Configuration Protocol (DHCP) on a TCP/IP-based network?

13. An IP address contains two types of information, _____ and _____ information.

14. Convert the following to decimal notation:

    01110011.11000011.00010001.00000110

    11000000.10000011.00111001.01001000

    10110101.11001000.10000000.01100101

15. Convert the following to binary numbers:

    131.107.15.7

    124.100.155.201

    215.254.17.139

16. Which of the following are valid IP addresses?

    a. 121.15.65.115

    b. 127.0.010

    c. 192.276.142.115

    d. 131.0.331.5.6

17. PING is a utility used to troubleshoot which protocol?

    a. NetBEUI

    b. TCP/IP

    c. NWLink (IPX/SPX)

    d. DLC

18. If a host has an IP address of 198.177.10.23, what class of TCP/IP network is it on?

    a. A

    b. B

    c. C

    d. D

19. Why might you need to configure NWLink after you install it?

20. NetBEUI problems are best tracked down using a protocol analyzer. True or False?

21. You can ping the local host (127.0.0.1) and other hosts on your local subnet, but you cannot ping across the router to other subnets. What is the likely cause of the problem?

    a. The default mask is incorrect.

    b. The default gateway's IP address is incorrect.

    c. The DNS server's address is incorrect.

    d. PING packets are broadcast so they cannot cross the router.

22. Which utility displays TCP/IP statistics?

    a. ARP

    b. PING

    c. IPCONFIG

    d. NETSTAT

23. The NWLink protocol is installed automatically when Windows NT Server is installed. True or False?

24. Which of the following protocols can be used to connect to an IBM mainframe?

    a. DLC

    b. TCP/IP

    c. NWLink (IPX/SPX)

    d. IBMPC

25. List five questions that you should ask yourself when troubleshooting a network problem.

Hands-on Projects

For some or all of these projects you will need a Windows NT Server, the Windows NT Server 4.0 installation CD, and a watch with a second hand.

Project 3-1

In this project, you will install TCP/IP on your server and measure its effect on your server's performance. You will need a watch with a second hand to complete this project.

1. Install and configure TCP/IP protocol on your server, following the steps outlined in the chapter.

2. Shut down the server and turn off the power.

3. Restart your server, noting the minute and second you turn the power on. Watch the boot-up sequence and note the exact time when the Begin Logon dialog box appears. How much time passed between powering up and the appearance of this dialog box?

4. Click **Start**, point to **Programs**, point to **Administrative Tools (Common)**, then click **Windows NT Diagnostics**. Click the **Memory tab**. Use the information in this tab to complete the "Without Additional Protocols" column in Table 3-6.

Table 3-6   Memory tab settings

Value	Without Additional Protocols	With Additional Protocols
Handles		
Threads		
Processes		
Physical memory available		
File cache		
Kernel memory total		
Kernel memory paged		
Nonpaged		

PROJECT 3-2

This project builds on the information you gathered in Project 3-1. You will install multiple protocols (in addition to TCP/IP, which you installed in Project 3-1) and measure their effect on your server's performance. You will need a watch with a second hand to complete this project.

1. Install the following protocols using the procedure outlined in this chapter: NetBEUI, NWLink, DLC, Connectivity to Macintosh.

2. Shut down the server and turn off the power.

3. Restart your server, noting the minute and second you turn the power on. Watch the boot-up sequence and note the exact time when the Begin Logon box appears. How much time passed between powering up and the appearance of this box? Compare this time with the time you wrote down in Project 3-1. Why do the two times differ?

4. Click **Start**, point to **Programs**, point to **Administrative Tools (Common)**, then click **Windows NT Diagnostics**. Click the **Memory tab**. Use the information in this tab to complete the With Additional Protocols column in Table 3-6. Explain why some of these entries differ from the entries in the Without Additional Protocols column.

PROJECT 3-3

In this project you will have an opportunity to work with one of the TCP/IP troubleshooting utilities, IPCONFIG.

1. Click **Start**, click **Programs**, then click the **MS-DOS icon**. The Command Prompt window opens.

2. At the command prompt, type **IPCONFIG /?**, then press **Enter**.

3. Note the alternatives shown on the screen that are available when you use the IPCONFIG command.

4. At the command prompt, type **IPCONFIG /all**, then press **Enter**.

5. The information presented on the screen will be helpful in subsequent projects. Note that this information includes your computer's IP address.

6. What is the adapter address? Why would you need to know this information?

7. Close the Command Prompt window.

PROJECT 3-4

In this project you will have an opportunity to work with another TCP/IP troubleshooting utility, PING.

1. Click **Start**, click **Programs**, then click the **MS-DOS icon**. The Command Prompt window opens.

2. At the command prompt, type **PING 127.0.0.1**, then press **Enter**.

3. What results do you see? Why would pinging this IP address be useful?

4. Obtain the IP address of your lab partner's computer. At the command prompt, type **PING** followed by a **single space** and the **IP address** of your partner's computer.

5. What results do you see? Why would pinging your partner's computer be useful?

6. Close the Command Prompt window.

PROJECT 3-5

In this project you will have an opportunity to work with another TCP/IP troubleshooting utility, NBTSTAT.

1. Click **Start**, click **Programs**, then click the **MS-DOS icon**. The Command Prompt window opens.

2. At the command prompt, type **NBSTAT**. (Do not include the period.) A list of choices appears.

3. Obtain the IP address of your lab partner's computer and use the NBTSTAT command with that number (for example, **NBSTAT –a 155.155.155.0**).

4. What results do you see?

5. Follow the same procedures outlined in Steps 2–3, but use the selections in Table 3-7 in place of the "-a". For each selection, answer the related questions in the Question column.

Table 3-7   NBSTAT Switches

Selection	Question
-A	How does the returned information differ from what you received when you used the –a selection?
-c	What information is returned? Why is it useful?
-n	What information is returned? Why is it useful?
-r	What information is returned? Why is it useful?
-S	What information is returned? Why is it useful?
-s	What information is returned? Why is it useful?

6. At the command prompt, type **NBSTAT** followed by a **single space** and **-R**.

7. What message is returned? Why would this command be useful?

CASE PROJECTS

1. The EZ Buy Realty Company is a medium-sized real estate company located in a single office building. The company has approximately 40 computers that are all medium-speed 486 PCs, with 16–32 MB of RAM and hard drives in the 300–500 MB range. These computers all run Windows 95. The broker who owns the office has been reading articles about how networking can improve productivity in the workplace. He has decided to connect the PCs in the office to form a network. Neither he nor the agents in the office have much computer knowledge, so they have asked you for help. The owner wants a system that is inexpensive and easy to administer, but does not want to implement Internet connectivity at this time. Each agent wants full and exclusive control over who can access files on his or her computer. You have completed the wiring and installation of required peripheral devices. You now need to set up the networking protocol. Write a short report (three to five paragraphs) explaining what network configuration you would recommend, which protocol(s) you would use, and why.

2. EZ Buy Realty's network has been up and running for several months. The broker has been satisfied with the way you met his original requirements. Now he has decided to make some changes. The agents and other personnel in the office have been struggling with the peer-to-peer network that you implemented because of its decentralized file control scheme and dwindling drive space on their workstations. Some problems have also arisen with sensitive client files being read or accidentally deleted from an agent's hard drive. The broker has read a little about client/server computing and the Windows NT operating system. He would like you to implement this solution in his office. You have decided to install a server with Windows NT Server 4.0 and implement a single domain model. All important and sensitive files will be placed on the server, freeing up drive space on the users' computers. Windows 95 will still run on the rest of the office's computers. The broker is warming up to the idea of connecting to the Internet, but remains unsure that he is ready to take that step. Write a short report (three to five paragraphs) explaining what changes you would make to the protocols you implemented in Case 1 and why.

3. Because of EZ Buy Realty's revolutionary commission structure, business has been so good that the company has grown to 15 local offices. The owner has obtained a venture-capital investment that will allow the firm to grow nationally. Initial plans call for opening 15 offices across the western United States within the next three months. An additional expansion of another 30 offices located across the rest of the nation is scheduled for this time next year. Because of your previous excellent advice, you have been contacted by EZ's principals to set up a network configuration that will enable

the main office to track pending real estate transactions at all of its offices. The company has learned about the importance of standardization from you. The owner would like to implement an enterprise network providing connectivity between each of the company's offices. Write a short report (three to five paragraphs) explaining your recommendations in terms of an operating system, communications protocols, and other matters that you believe are important.

WINDOWS NT CORE AND OPTIONAL SERVICES

As a Microsoft systems engineer, you are expected to have a thorough knowledge of Windows NT and its related services. In this chapter you will learn to identify Windows NT's core and optional services. You will also learn how to use these services to solve a variety of networking problems. Finally, you will install and configure all of the core services and many of the optional services.

A **core service** is one that is shipped with Windows NT and installed in a typical Windows NT environment. Such services include Computer Browser Service, Dynamic Host Configuration Protocol (DHCP), Windows Internet Naming Service (WINS), Domain Naming Service Server, and directory replication. Most **optional services** are included in the package of Windows NT BackOffice products, or are considered part of the BackOffice family of products. (Products not included in the BackOffice package generally require a separate licensing fee.) The list of BackOffice products includes Microsoft SQL Server, Exchange Server, SNA Server, System Management Server, Transaction Server, Proxy Server, Site Server, and Commercial Internet Systems. Other optional services include Microsoft Internet Information Server, FrontPage 98, Internet Explorer 4.0, Index Server, NNTP Server, SMTP Server, and NetShow.

AFTER READING THIS CHAPTER AND COMPLETING THE EXERCISES YOU WILL BE ABLE TO:

- Distinguish between core and optional services
- Install and configure Windows NT Browser Service
- Install and configure Windows Internet Naming Service (WINS)
- Install and configure Domain Naming Service (DNS)
- Install and configure Dynamic Host Configuration Protocol (DHCP)
- Describe some Windows NT optional services

WINDOWS NT CORE SERVICES

In the following sections you will learn the purposes of the various core services and the procedures for installing them. Those services presented first are those you are most likely to encounter in a typical Windows NT environment.

When installing Windows NT, you can choose to install the core services at the same time. Alternatively, you can install them later, after Windows NT is already operating. In most cases installing these services as part of the overall Windows NT installation simply involves selecting the appropriate check box. Installation at a later time is somewhat more complex and will be demonstrated in this chapter.

COMPUTER BROWSER SERVICE

The **Computer Browser Service** is used to create a centralized list of available network resources. The computer responsible for maintaining this database is called the **domain master browser**. The list of available resources (the **browse list**) is distributed to specially assigned computers known as browser computers. Network users can access the browse list to locate the resources they need.

Computers on an NT domain are classified into five categories in relation to the Computer Browser Service:

- **Master browser:** This computer maintains a database (or browse list) of available resources on the domain or workgroup and distributes it to the backup browsers.

- **Preferred master browser:** When this Windows NT server or workstation is turned on, it designates itself as the master browser if no other master browser is present on the network. If another computer is already serving as the master browser, then the preferred master browser sends a broadcast message that forces an election. (The election process is explained later in this chapter.)

- **Backup browser:** This computer receives a copy of the network resource list from the master browser and distributes it to the browser clients upon request.

- **Potential browser:** This computer can maintain a network resource list, but will not take this step unless specifically instructed to do so by a master browser.

- **Nonbrowser:** This computer—typically a client computer—does not maintain a network resource list. If a computer is already overloaded, consider making it a nonbrowser, so that browser or master browser duties will not be added to its list of responsibilities.

Only one master browser can exist for any workgroup or domain at any given time. You determine whether a computer has the potential to become a master browser or a backup browser through manual configuration.

Whether a Windows NT computer has the ability to become a browser depends upon settings in the registry located at \HKEY_LOCAL_MACHINE\SYSTEM\CurrentControlSet\ Services\Browser\Parameters\MaintainServerList. The values for the MaintainServerList parameter are explained in Table 4-1.

Table 4-1 MaintainServerList parameter

Value	Description
Yes	This computer will become a browser server. At startup, it will attempt to contact the master browser to obtain a current browse list. If the master browser cannot be found, the computer will force one to be elected. This computer will either be elected as the master browser or will become a backup browser. "Yes" is the default value for Windows NT domain controller computers.
No	This computer is disabled as a browser and will never become a master or backup browser.
Auto	This computer, known as a potential browser, may or may not become a browser server, depending on the number of currently active browsers. It will be notified by the master browser as to whether it should become a backup browser. "Auto" is the default value for Windows NT Workstation and Windows NT Server (non-domain controller) computers.

Any Windows NT server or workstation can be configured as a preferred master browser. Preferred master browsers have an advantage in elections, as explained later. To configure a computer as a preferred master browser, you set the following Registry parameter value to "True":

\HKEY_LOCAL_MACHINE\SYSTEM\CurrentControlSet\Services\Browser\ Parameters\ IsDomainMaster.

Distributing the Browse List

The browse list is distributed as follows:

1. A network computer is turned on and announces its presence to the master browser. This step happens regardless of whether the computer has shared resources to advertise. Whether or not a user logs in has no effect on the computer's browser status.

2. A user attempts to locate an available network resource by typing "net view" in the Run dialog box, by opening the Windows NT Explorer Connect Network Drive dialog box, or by clicking the "Network Neighborhood" icon to display the flashlight icon. The client computer then issues a "QueryBrowser Servers" broadcast, which asks the master browser for a list of backup browsers.

3. The client requests a list of available network resources from the backup browser.

4. The backup browser responds to the client request by sending a list of domains, workgroups, and servers local to the client's domain or workgroup.

5. The user at the client workstation selects a local server, domain, or workgroup. The user then selects the appropriate server and searches for the desired resource to establish a session in which to access that resource.

After a computer initially announces itself to the master browser, it continues to announce itself once every minute. If the computer remains running, the announcement time is extended to once every 12 minutes. If the master browser does not hear from this client for three announcement periods (36 minutes), it removes the computer from the browse list.

Backup browsers contact the master browser every 15 minutes to obtain an updated browse list, as well as a list of workgroups and domains. Each backup browser caches these lists and returns the browse list to any clients from which it receives a browse request. Periodically the master browser announces itself to the backup browsers via a broadcast. When backup browsers receive this announcement, they refresh their designation of the master browser name.

Determining the Master Browser

As mentioned earlier, whether the designated preferred master browser becomes the master browser may be determined through an **election**, which ensures that only one master browser exists in each domain or workgroup. As the network administrator, you have the ability to "fix the election." The election process is triggered when any of the following events occurs:

- A network client cannot locate the master browser.

- A backup browser attempts to update its network resource list but cannot locate the master browser.

- A second computer configured as a preferred master browser is turned on.

Whether a computer "wins" election and becomes the master browser depends upon the criteria given in Table 4-2.

Table 4-2   Master browser election criteria

Level	Criteria	Priority Order
First	Computer operating system	Windows NT Server, Windows NT Workstation, Windows 95
Second	Operating system version	NT 4.0, NT 3.51, NT 3.1, Windows 95, Windows for Workgroups
Third	Role in domain environment	Already a master browser? A backup browser?

If a computer is the primary domain controller, then it automatically wins election as the domain's master browser. When all other criteria are equal, a preferred master browser will win the election and become the master browser. In a domain environment, if the primary domain controller is configured as a nonbrowser, then another machine designated as a preferred master browser will win the election. When the election process reaches a "tie," where competing computers are involved in a "contested election," the criteria in Table 4-2 become important. For example, if two computers—one running Windows NT Server 4.0 and one running Windows NT Server 3.51—were "tied," the election process would end with the computer using the Windows NT Server 4.0 operating system winning the election. In general, a computer running the most recent version of an operating system will prevail over a computer using an older version. Where different operating systems are involved, NT Server prevails over NT Workstation, which in turn prevails over Windows 95. At the bottom of this stack is Windows for Workgroups.

An election is initiated when any computer on the network broadcasts a special packet, called an election packet, to all browsers on the network. This election packet contains that computer's criteria value. Upon receiving the election packet, a browser examines it and compares the requesting computer's status with its own election criteria. If the receiving browser has a higher priority than the issuer of the election packet, then the browser issues its own election packet and enters an "election in progress" state. This process will continue until a master browser is elected, based on which computer has the highest-ranking criteria value.

The number of available browsers in a network depends upon whether a workgroup or domain environment is involved. The number of browsers in a workgroup depends upon the number of computers. Table 4–3 identifies the number of browsers in a workgroup.

Table 4-3   Number of browser computers

Number of Computers in Domain or Workgroup	Number of Master Browsers	Number of Backup Browsers
1	1	0
2-31	1	1
32-63	1	2
64-95	1	3
96+	1	3

A backup browser will be added as the number of computers in the workgroup increases (as outlined in Table 4–3). A single domain can contain no more than one domain master browser and three backup browsers. This limitation may slow browser performance in larger domains, unless you either increase the backup browser server's performance (by adding RAM or installing a faster processor), or break up the domain into smaller domains.

Keep in mind that the Computer Browser Service does not always provide up-to-date information about resource availability. Suppose, for example, that at 12:01 a computer broadcasts its presence on the network. The master browser receives this notification and adds the computer to its list of computers on the network. At 12:02 the computer's power is disconnected suddenly, without giving the user time to shut it down normally. If it had been shut down normally, it would have broadcast an announcement causing the master browser to remove it from the list. Because normal shutdown did not occur, the master browser receives no such announcement. Instead, the computer simply fails to broadcast as scheduled at 12:13 and 12:25. At 12:36, the backup browser requests and obtains an updated resource list from the master browser. At 12:37, the master browser, after not receiving a broadcast from the computer for three consecutive times, removes the computer from the resource list. Until 12:52, when the backup browser receives an updated resource list, the computer will incorrectly appear as an available resource on its resource list.

Thus a resource may appear on the Network Neighborhood screen but not be truly unavailable. Conversely, when a resource does *not* appear on the Network Neighborhood screen, do not assume that it is inaccessible. This point is important when troubleshooting a network problem. To confirm the availability (or nonavailability) of any resource, use the Run dialog box to enter the resource's UNC path.

DYNAMIC HOST CONFIGURATION PROTOCOL

Dynamic Host Configuration Protocol (DHCP) is a network protocol that enables a DHCP server to automatically assign an IP address to an individual computer's TCP/IP stack. DHCP assigns a number automatically, based on a defined range of numbers (called a **scope**) assigned to a network. The process works as follows: A client boots up and sends out a request for an IP address. In return, a DHCP server offers an IP address that has not yet been assigned from its database. The IP address is leased to the client for a predefined period.

In more technical terms, DHCP functions in the following way:

1. A user turns on a DHCP client computer.

2. The client sends a DHCP Request packet.

3. All DHCP servers that have valid available IP addressing information send offers to the client.

4. The client accepts the first offer it receives from a DHCP server, sending a DHCP Acknowledgment packet in response.

5. The server assigns an IP number according to the range of IP addresses defined in the DHCP scope on the server.

Using DHCP to assign IP addresses has a number of benefits:

- It provides centralized management of IP address distribution.

- It reduces the amount of administrative time required to distribute IP addresses to host computers and configure those IP addresses.

- It reduces the likelihood of errors when configuring host computers.

Because DHCP provides IP addresses only when it receives requests from client host computers, it can use a smaller number of IP addresses, limiting access to this resource to those computers actually needing IP addresses. Computers that are shut down do not need IP addresses. Servers designated to provide DHCP service must have a static IP address (as opposed to one that is assigned when needed and relinquished when no longer needed.)

To install Microsoft DHCP on a Windows NT Server 4.0:

1. Log on as an administrator.

2. Click the **Start button**, point to **Settings**, click **Control Panel**, click the **Network icon**, then click the **Services tab** on the Network dialog box.

3. Click **Add**. The Select Network Service dialog box opens, as shown in Figure 4-1.

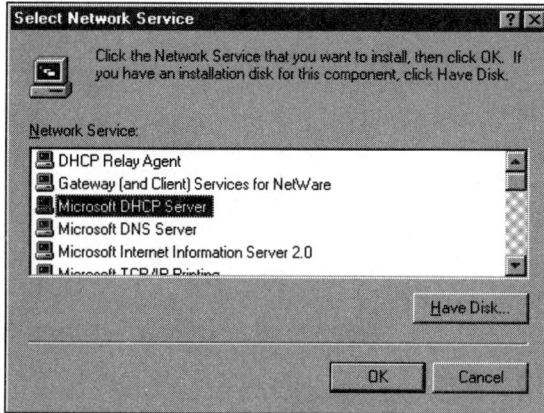

Figure 4-1   Select Network Service dialog box

4. Select **Microsoft DHCP Server** and click **OK**. The Windows NT Setup dialog box opens, as shown in Figure 4-2.

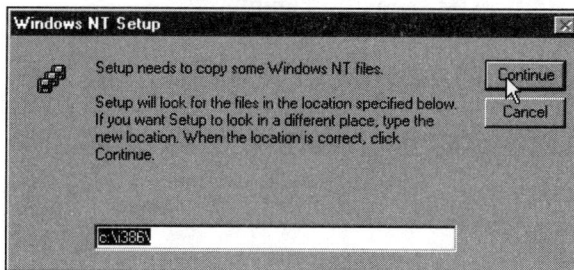

Figure 4-2   Windows NT Setup dialog box

5. Type the correct path for the Windows NT installation files. (These files are usually located on the I386 directory on the installation CD-ROM).

6. Click **Continue**, then click **OK**.

7. Click **Close**, then click **Yes** to reboot.

Next, you must configure DHCP Server. This service is configured using DHCP Manager, which is installed after the installation of DHCP. To configure DHCP Server:

1. Log on to the server as an administrator.

2. Click the **Start button**, point to **Programs**, click **Administrative Tools (Common)**, then click **DHCP Manager**. The DHCP Manager window opens, as shown in Figure 4–3.

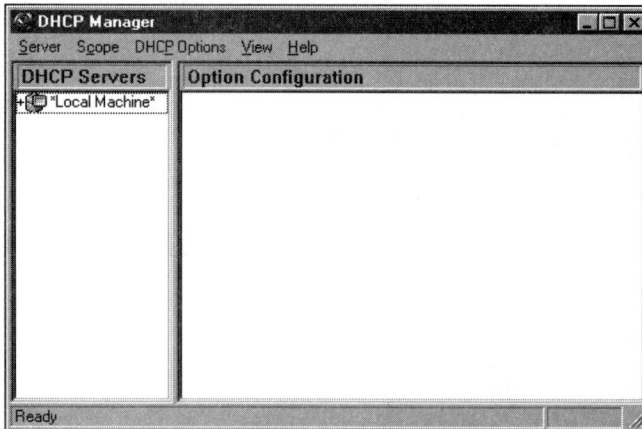

Figure 4-3   DHCP Manager window

3. Double-click **Local Machine** in the left-hand pane.

4. Click **Scope** on the menu bar, then click **Create** in the drop-down menu. The Create Scope dialog box opens, as shown in Figure 4-4.

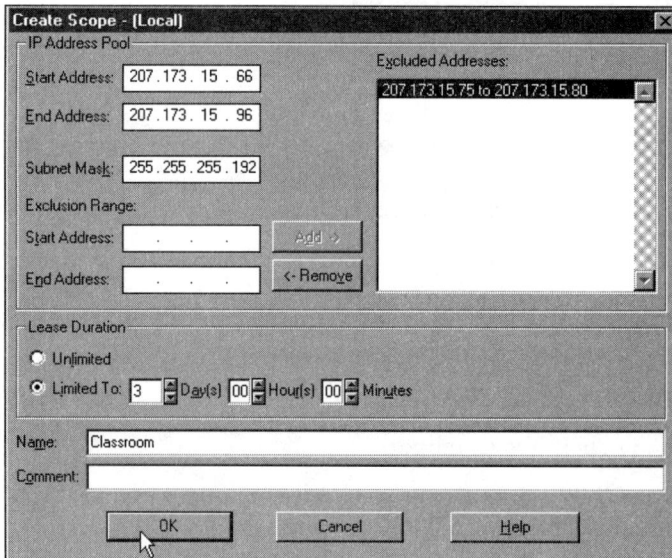

Figure 4-4   Create Scope dialog box

5. The Create Scope dialog box shown in the figure was configured to provide a variety of available IP addresses, ranging from 207.173.15.66 to 207.173.15.96. It was also configured to exclude addresses from 207.173.15.75 to 207.173.15.80. Thus two ranges of addresses are available: 207.173.15.66 through 207.173.15.74, and 207.173.15.81 through 207.173.15.96.

6. Click **OK**, then click **Yes**.

7. Click **OK**. DHCP Server is now installed.

It is possible to send additional configuration information to DHCP clients. Such information might include the IP addresses of the domain name server, Windows Internet Naming Server (WINS), or the default gateway. To send such information from within the DHCP Manager window, click DHCP Options on the menu bar, and then click Global. The DHCP Options: Global dialog box will open, as shown in Figure 4-5.

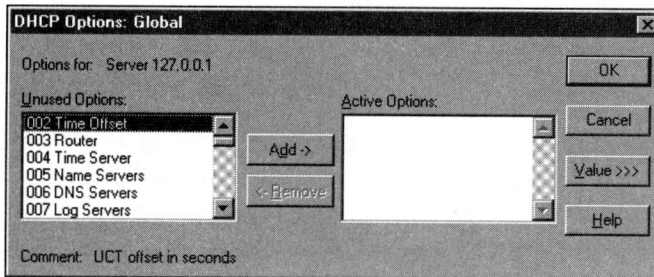

4

Figure 4-5   DHCP Options: Global dialog box

More than 50 configurable options appear in the DHCP Options: Global dialog box. A detailed discussion of these options lies beyond the scope of this book—and beyond the scope of the objectives for the Microsoft 70-68 Certification Exam relating to Windows NT in the Enterprise. Additional information about these configurable options is available in the Windows NT Server 4.0 Resource Kit and at Microsoft's Web site located at *http://www.microsoft.com/*.

WINDOWS INTERNET NAMING SERVICE (WINS)

Windows Internet Naming Service (WINS) enables a Windows NT computer to function as a TCP/IP-based NetBIOS name server. It enables client computers to resolve NetBIOS computer names of other network computers to their IP address. To understand WINS architecture you need to know something about NetBIOS.

NetBIOS is designed to free applications (and their programming developers) from having to understand the details of the network, including error recovery. A NetBIOS call takes the form of a network control block (NCB), identifying, among other things, a message location and the name of a destination host. NetBIOS provides the data format for transmission.

NetBIOS provides two communications modes: session and datagram. Session mode is a connection-oriented communication, in which two computers establish a connection for a "conversation." It provides reliable communication where delivery of data is assured by providing error detection and recovery. In contrast, datagram mode is "connectionless." Each message is sent independently. Reliability of data delivery is on a "best effort" basis and is not assured. With the datagram mode, error detection and recovery are the responsibility of the application; the transmission protocol does not provide these features. Datagram mode supports the broadcast of a message to every computer on the LAN.

NetBIOS names are used to identify resources on the LAN, such as computers, printers, routers, and other network-addressable devices. A NetBIOS name may be used only once within a network. These names are registered dynamically when computers boot up, services start, or users log on. With Windows NT Server services, the user or administrator specifies the first 15 characters of a NetBIOS name. The 16th character (the suffix) of the NetBIOS name (00–FF hex) is used to indicate a resource type.

Name resolution in a NetBIOS network is generally broadcast-based and is handled in a relatively straightforward manner. When a computer or other node configured with a NetBIOS name powers up on the network, it broadcasts a name registration request. This signal is sent to all nodes on the local network. If no objections are received after the request is made, the device configured with the NetBIOS name assumes that it has permission to use the name and issues a name overwrite demand. If the name is already in use, a negative name registration response datagram is sent by the node holding this name. In this case, the requesting node does not have permission to use the name.

A broadcast-based name resolution system has three major disadvantages. First, nodes may interact with one another within a broadcast area but cannot interoperate across routers in a routed network. Second, such a system generates high broadcast traffic, a use of significant network bandwidth that can impact network speed. Third, every node within the broadcast area must examine each broadcast datagram. This additional overhead consumes resources on every node.

Using NetBIOS with TCP/IP resolves the network problems associated with unroutable broadcast-based protocols such as NetBEUI. With NetBEUI, the goal is to map a computer's NetBIOS name with its MAC address on the computer's network card. Selecting TCP/IP merely adds another layer of resolution.

Table 4-4 provides information about two hypothetical computers on a LAN. When Jupiter wants to set up a connection-oriented session with Saturn, where TCP/IP is the protocol, Jupiter must first ascertain Saturn's IP address. This process is commonly known as NetBIOS name resolution. Once the remote computer's NetBIOS name has been matched (or resolved) to an IP address, network communications can be established with TCP/IP.

Table 4-4　Examples of Name Layering

Description	Computer A	Computer B
NetBIOS Name	Jupiter	Saturn
MAC Address	00-40-04-54-2E-EC	00-50-54-32-1E-EC
IP Address	151.103.16.203	151.103.16.204

Two strategies are commonly employed to perform NetBIOS name resolution in a TCP/IP environment. The first method uses a static database configured in a text file, known as an LMHOSTS file. This document's function is to identify a NetBIOS computer name and the

IP address associated with it. An example of the contents of a typical LMHOSTS file is shown below:

102.54.94.97	rhino	#PRE #DOM:networking	#net group's DC
102.54.94.102	"appname	\0x14"	#special app server
102.54.94.123	popular	#PRE	#source server
102.54.94.117	localsrv	#PRE	#needed for the include

Use of an LMHOSTS file to perform NetBIOS name resolution does have one problem: Every time a server is added or removed from the network, the LMHOSTS file on *each* individual computer on the network must be manually updated.

WINS provides a second solution designed to eliminate the network traffic associated with broadcasts used to resolve NetBIOS names to IP addresses. It works through a dynamic database that automatically keeps track of computers' IP addresses. WINS has two system components: the WINS client and the WINS server.

A **WINS client** is configured to direct the client to the IP address of one or more Windows Internet Naming Service servers. When the Windows Internet Naming Service client goes online, it communicates directly with a Windows Internet Naming Service server to register its NetBIOS computer name and IP address. If the Windows Internet Naming Service server already has a registered computer with that name, it rejects the new registration attempt. When a Windows Internet Naming Service client needs to resolve a computer name to an IP address, it sends a request to the Windows Internet Naming Service server for the IP address of the client it wishes to contact.

A **WINS server** maintains a dynamic database that maps the IP addresses of WINS clients to their computer names. A WINS client requests the IP address directly from the WINS server. Such a server needs a static IP address and cannot be a DHCP client.

Installing a WINS server offers the following immediate benefits:

- It eliminates the need to maintain LMHOSTS files.

- It reduces broadcast traffic on the network.

- It provides a dynamic, up-to-date database of computers and their IP addresses.

- It complements DHCP on the network. When using DHCP by itself, you still must maintain an LMHOSTS file. Maintenance of this file is complicated by the fact that computers frequently change their IP addresses when an existing IP address lease expires.

- It provides a tool for determining if duplicate computer names are accidentally configured.

WINS can be installed at the same time that TCP/IP is installed on a Windows NT server. If TCP/IP is already installed, you must install WINS as follows:

1. Log on as an administrator.

2. Click the **Start button**, point to **Settings**, click **Control Panel**, double-click the **Network icon**, click the **Services tab** on the Network dialog box, then click **Add**. The Select Network Services dialog box opens.

3. Select **Microsoft WINS Server**, then click **OK**. The Windows NT Setup dialog box opens.

4. Type the correct path for the Windows NT installation files. (These files are usually located on the I386 directory on the installation CD-ROM).

5. Click **Continue**, click **OK** to close the Network Properties dialog box, then click **Yes** to reboot the server. You must now configure the WINS service.

6. Log on to the server as an administrator.

7. Click **Programs**, click **Administrative Tools (Common)**, then click **WINS Manager**. The WINS Manager window opens, as shown in Figure 4-6.

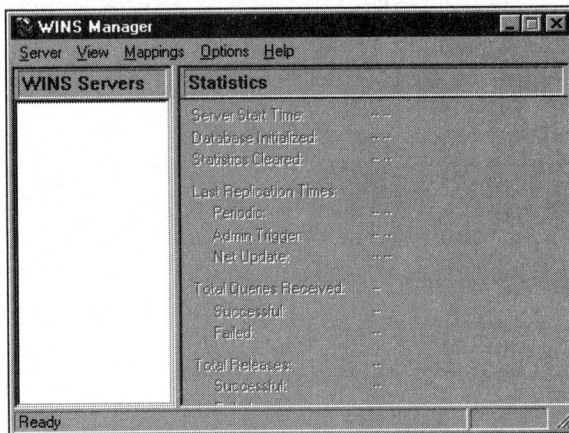

Figure 4-6   WINS Manager window

8. Click **Server** on the menu bar, then click **Configuration** on the drop-down menu. The WINS Server Configuration dialog box opens, as shown in Figure 4-7.

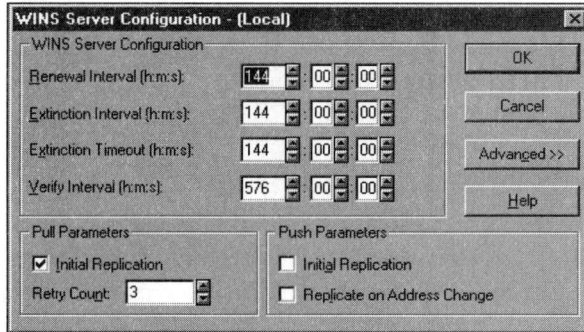

Figure 4-7   WINS Server Configuration dialog box

9. Click **Advanced** to enlarge the WINS Server Configuration dialog box to include the advanced WINS server configuration settings. Some of the basic configuration options are described in Table 4-5.

Table 4-5   WINS Server Configuration options

Configuration Option	Description
Renewal Interval	Specifies how often a client must reregister its name. The default is five hours.
Extinction Interval	Specifies the interval between when an entry is marked as released and when it is marked as extinct. Default is four times the renewal interval.
Extension Timeout	Identifies the interval between when an entry is marked as extinct and when the entry is finally scavenged from the database.
Verify Interval	Specifies the time interval after which the WINS server must verify that the old names it does not own are still active. The default is 20 times the extinction interval.
Initial Replication (Pull Parameters)	Enables the WINS server to pull new WINS database entries from its partners (i.e., other WINS servers).
Retry Count	Counts the number of times the WINS server attempts to contact a partner from which to pull the WINS database entries.
Initial Replication (Push Parameters)	Allows the WINS server to notify its partners of the status of its WINS database when the system is initialized.
Replicate on Address Change	Allows the WINS server to notify its partners of its WINS database status when a name registration changes.

WINS servers are designed to communicate with one another and to fully replicate their databases. This setup ensures that the name registered with one WINS server will eventually be replicated to all other WINS servers within the network.

DIRECTORY REPLICATION

Windows NT uses **directory replication** to maintain identical copies of specified files and directories on different computers. Changes made to files on one computer are automatically replicated on other computers configured to receive the changes. Replication requires a Windows NT server that will act as the export server. The import servers can consist of other Windows NT servers, Windows NT workstations, or OS/2 LAN Manager version 2.x servers. Windows 95 computers, however, cannot play this role. As its name implies, an export server is the server that provides information. An import server receives information from the export server.

To configure an export server:

1. In the User Manager window, create a user named REPL and specify a password, if desired. Remove the check from the **"User must change password at next logon" check box**. Click the **Groups** button at the bottom of the New User dialog box. If you plan to provide replication services between servers on the domain, this user must also be a member of the Administrators global group. Click **OK**, then click **Add** to create this account on the domain. Close the New User dialog box and verify that the user REPL has been added to User Manager.

2. In the User Manager dialog box, select the **Replicator** local group, click **Policies** on the menu bar, then click **User Rights** on the drop-down menu. The User Rights Policy dialog box opens.

3. Click **OK**, then close the User Manager window. Next you will configure the directory replication service.

4. Click the **Start button**, click **Settings**, click **Control Panel**, double-click **Services**, click **Directory Replicator Service**, then click **Startup**. The Service dialog box appears, as shown in Figure 4-8.

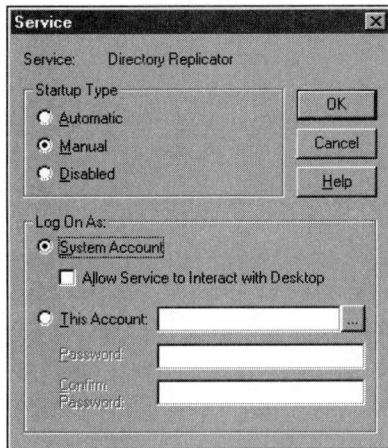

Figure 4-8   Service dialog box

5. Click the **Automatic option button**, click the **This Account option button**, then click the **ellipsis button next to the This Account text box**. The Add User dialog box opens.

6. Select the **REPL account**, click **Add**, then click **OK**.

7. Type the password for the replication account, then click **OK**. The Control Panel responds with a message such as "The account DOMAIN\REPL has been granted the Log On As A Service right and added to the Replicator local group."

8. Click **OK**, then click **Close** to close the Service dialog box.

9. Click **Programs**, click **Administrative Tools (Common)**, click **Server Manager**, click the **Export Server**, then click **Computer and Properties**. The Properties dialog box opens.

10. Click the **Replication button**. The Directory Replication dialog box opens, as shown in Figure 4-9.

11. Click the **Export Directories option button**, verify that the default path winntroot\SYSTEM32\REPL\EXPORT appears on the "From Path" text box, then click **Add**. The Select Domain dialog box opens.

12. Specify the name of a domain where files and directories are to be replicated. (The files will be replicated to every Windows NT computer in that domain that is configured for import replication.) Click **OK**. Next you will specify which directories on the replication server will be replicated.

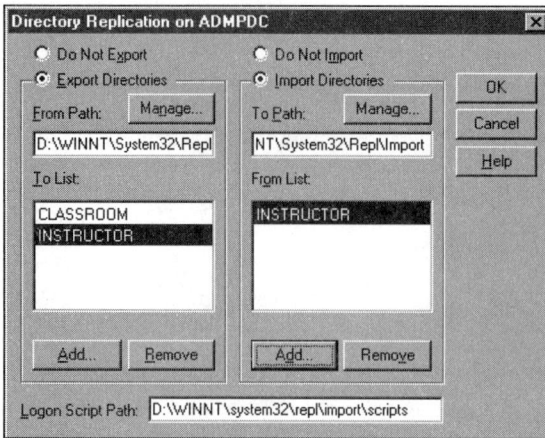

Figure 4-9   Directory Replication dialog box

13. Click **Manage**. By default, the Server Manager exports the Scripts directory that contains user logon scripts. Click the **Add button**. The Add Sub-Directory dialog box opens, as shown in Figure 4–10.

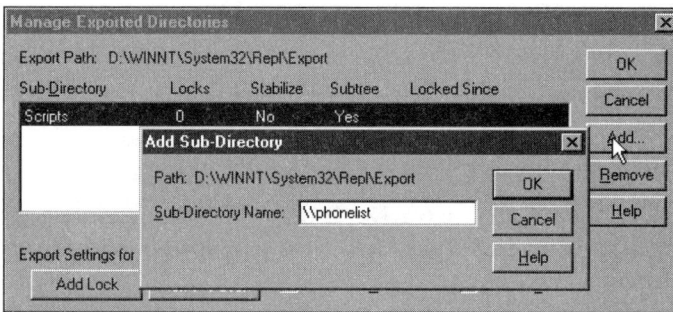

Figure 4-10   Add Sub-Directory dialog box

14. Specify an additional subdirectory, if necessary, and then click **OK**.

15. When all applicable options have been selected, click **OK** to close the Directory Replication dialog box. Windows NT responds with the message "Attempting to Start the Directory Replication service on <computername>."

Now that you have configured the server to act as a replication export server, thereby distributing files from the specified directories, you can use a similar procedure to configure the server as an import server.

To configure an import server:

1. Log on as an administrator.

2. Click the **Start button**, point to **Settings**, click **Control Panel**, double-click the **Services icon**, click the **Services tab**, click **Directory Replicator**, then click **Startup**.

3. Click the **Automatic option button**, click the **This Account Option button**, then click **Add User**.

4. Select the replication account created on the export server (REPL). If this account is not available on the import server, you must create the account with the same account characteristics. Click **Add**.

5. Type the password for the replication account, click **OK**, then click **OK** a second time. The Server Manager opens.

6. In the Server Manager window, select the server designated to act as an import server, then click **Computer and Properties**. The Properties dialog box opens.

7. Click **Replication**. The Directory Replication dialog box opens.

8. Click **Import directories**. Verify that the default path (winntroot\SYSTEM32\ REPL\IMPORT) appears on the "To Path" text box, then click **Add**.

9. Specify the name of the domain or computer to act as the export server, then click **Manage**. The Manage Import Directories dialog box opens.

10. Click **Add** to specify the location of import directories. Click **OK** twice, and then exit Server Manager.

When properly implemented, replication features provide a powerful file-maintenance tool and enable the load to be balanced across the enterprise network. Replication reduces file maintenance because updating files can be performed automatically. It relieves server loading by making the same files available on a number of servers.

DOMAIN NAMING SERVICE (DNS) SERVER

The **Domain Naming Service (DNS)** is the database that computers on the Internet use to look up one another's addresses. Understanding the DNS Server service provided by Windows NT is easier if you understand how the DNS relates to the Internet. The DNS is a distributed database—a much more useful tool than a static text file listing everyone on the Internet. A static file would not only be unmanageably large, but would also be consistently out of date (as a standard telephone book is). With DNS, when a site needs to add or remove computers, it simply updates its portion of the database; after a short period these changes are replicated across the Internet.

When you reference a computer by its fully qualified domain name (such as www.course.com) your computer system performs an address record DNS query. The nearest domain name server checks its memory cache for that address. If it finds the answer there, the server returns the address. Otherwise it determines which name servers on the Internet would know the answer, and then asks them. This activity goes on behind the scenes so that you can use easy-to-remember names like "www.course.com" rather than numeric names such as 198.112.168.244.

Many commercial and educational entities have host names in a subdomain of the .com or .edu domains. Examples of subdomains within the .com domain include microsoft.com and course.com. When you install Microsoft DNS Server services, you must create a zone in which this server will maintain its host names list. The DNS server can be set up to have multiple domains. It stores information in this zone, including host names and their associated IP addresses.

An alternative approach, developed for Windows networks and designed to lessen the administrative burden associated with manually maintaining this database, is to configure the DNS server to access a WINS server to resolve host names. As host names on a Windows NT network are generally the same as NetBIOS names, configuring your DNS server to take advantage of the WINS server's dynamic updating of NetBIOS names and associated IP addresses makes a great deal of sense.

The following steps outline the process for installing and configuring Microsoft DNS Server. First, you must install DNS Server. Next, you must configure the zone. Finally, you must configure clients on the network to use the DNS server for host name/IP address resolution. DNS client configuration is not covered on the Enterprise test, but is covered in the 70-73 exam for Windows NT Workstation.

To install and configure DNS Server:

1. Log on as an administrator.

2. Click the **Start button**, point to **Settings**, click **Control Panel**, double-click the **Network icon**, click the **Services tab** on the Network dialog box, then click **Add**. The Select Network Services dialog box opens.

3. Click **"Microsoft DNS Server"**, then click **OK**. The Windows NT Setup dialog box opens.

4. Type the correct path for the Windows NT installation files. (These files are usually located on the I386 directory on the installation CD-ROM.)

5. Click **Continue**.

6. Close the Network dialog box. Click **Yes** to reboot the server.

Now that DNS Server is installed, you are ready to configure it. To configure DNS:

1. Log on as an administrator.

2. Click the **Start button**, point to **Programs**, click **Administrative Tools (Common)**, then click **DNS Manager**. The DNS Manager window opens.

3. Click **DNS** on the menu bar, then click **New Server** on the drop-down menu. The Add DNS Server dialog box opens, as shown in Figure 4-11.

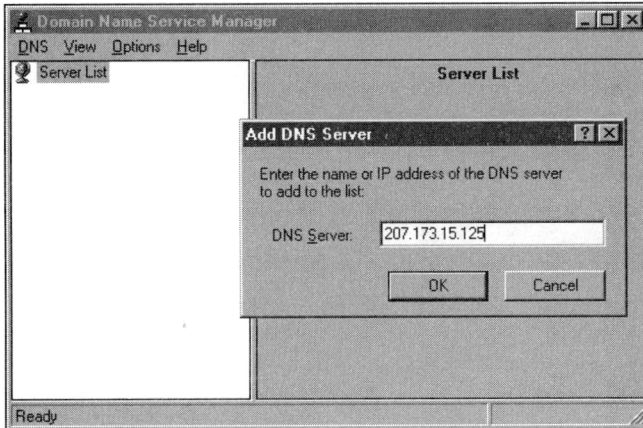

Figure 4-11   Add DNS Server dialog box

4. Type the **IP address or name** for your DNS Server, then click **OK**. The server appears in the Domain Name Service Manager window, as shown in Figure 4–12.

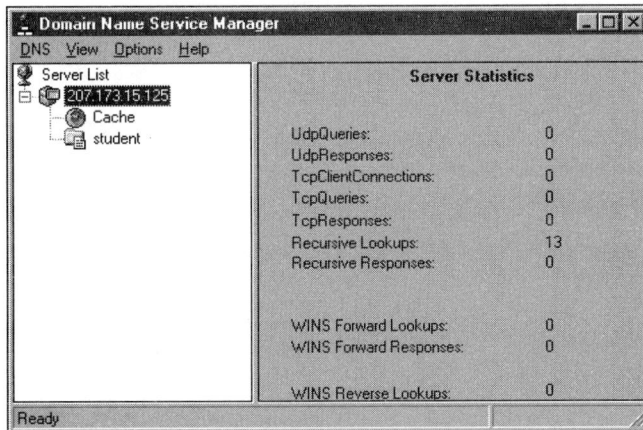

Figure 4-12   Domain Name Service Manager after adding DNS server

5. Right-click the **server's IP address**, then click **Refresh** in the shortcut menu.

6. Right-click the **server's IP address** again, then click **New Zone** in the shortcut menu. The first Creating new zone dialog box opens, as shown in Figure 4–13.

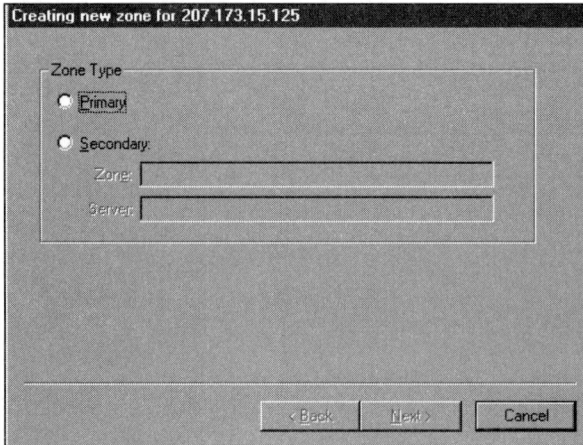

Figure 4-13   The first Creating new zone dialog box

7. Click the **Primary option button**, then click **Next**. The second Creating new zone dialog box opens, as shown in Figure 4-14.

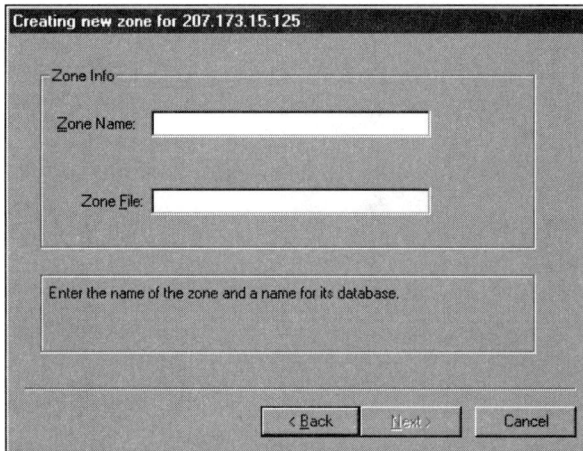

Figure 4-14   The second Creating new zone dialog box

8. Type the **Internet domain name** that this DNS server will manage in the Zone Name text box. Click on the **Zone File text box**. This action automatically creates a filename where the DNS server will store the host name and IP address for the domain. By default the name of this file is the domain name followed by a .dns extension. Click **Next**.

9. Click **Finish**. The new zone appears in the Domain Name Service Manager window, under the server, as shown in Figure 4-15. Next, you will manually add new hosts to the DNS database.

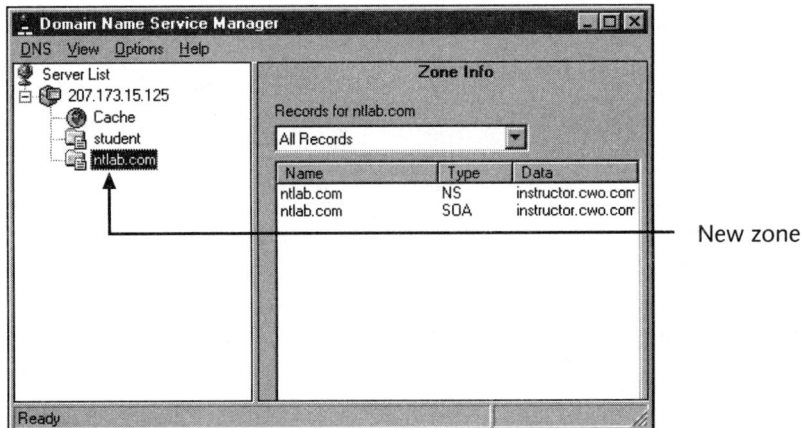

Figure 4-15   Domain Name Service Manager window

10. Right-click the **new zone**, then click **New Host** in the shortcut menu. The New Host dialog box opens, as shown in Figure 4–16.

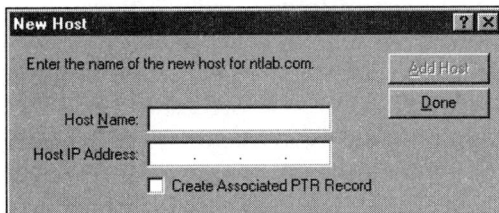

Figure 4-16   New Host dialog box

11. Enter the **host's name** and **IP address**, then click **Add Host**.

12. Repeat Steps 10 and 11 for each computer host you want to add to the DNS database. Click **Done** when you have finished adding entries into the DNS database and exit from DNS Manager.

As mentioned earlier, from an administrative standpoint it is wise to set up DNS Server to take advantage of the WINS Lookup feature for host name resolution.

To configure the DNS server to use WINS for host name resolution:

1. From the DNS Manager window, double-click the **IP address** of the DNS server to be configured.

2. Right-click the zone for which you want to configure a WINS lookup, then click **Properties** in the shortcut menu. The Zones Properties dialog box opens.

3. Click the **WINS Lookup tab**, check the **Use WINS Resolution check box**, enter the **IP address** of the WINS server, click **Add**, then click **OK**.

WINDOWS NT OPTIONAL SERVICES

The information that follows about Windows NT optional services is not detailed. Rather, it is designed to give you a general overview of the product and its capabilities. Each of these optional services are part of the Microsoft BackOffice suite of products. All of them, with the exception of Internet Information Server, require a separate licensing fee.

Installation and configuration of most BackOffice products require training that is beyond the scope of this book. Hence, we will cover products such as Internet Information Server, Proxy Server, SNA Server, SMS Server, and Exchange Server in general terms only. Each of these products has its own Microsoft certification exam. Students interested in obtaining a level of certification competency in those products are encouraged to investigate Microsoft's training and certification Web site at *www.microsoft.com/mcp*.

PROXY SERVER

Proxy Server allows a company to access the Internet, while providing security for the internal network. It does not require TCP/IP to be running on the client computer. By sharing a single, secure gateway, Microsoft Proxy Server eliminates the need to share one dedicated machine for the Internet among multiple users or to run multiple Internet lines into the organization so as to provide each desktop with its own connection. Proxy Server supports popular network protocols, including IPX/SPX and TCP/IP, and can be integrated with the Windows NT Server platform and Microsoft Internet Information Server. In addition, it enables a company to access applications on the Internet. Microsoft Proxy Server supports a wide range of applications and protocols, including RealAudio and VDOLive (which are used for streaming audio and video), LDAP and SMTP (which are mail transport protocols), IRC and Microsoft SQL Server.

Caching stores frequently accessed Internet data on a LAN, where users can reach this information as quickly as they access other information on the local network. This strategy helps reduce network traffic and congestion to and from the Internet. The Auto Dial tool in Microsoft Proxy Server automatically connects to an Internet service provider (ISP) whenever a user needs information not already stored in the local cache. When the desired information has been retrieved from the ISP and stored, Auto Dial disconnects from the ISP.

The network administrator can designate who can access the Internet, which services can be used, and who can establish additional credentials for logging on. The administrator can set specific dialing hours or days of the week, or prevent access to certain sites altogether.

INTERNET INFORMATION SERVER

Internet Information Server is a file service that enables a Windows NT 4.0 server to become a robust and secure vehicle for publishing information. The content of published information can be almost anything, from an internal company newsletter to company legacy data. This service is tightly integrated into Windows NT 4.0 Server. Users of Internet Information Server can take advantage of its many security features and performance capabilities, creating high-performance, robust server-based Web applications.

Internet Information Server comes with full search and database access capabilities. Full site searches are achieved with Index Server 2.0 (described below). Database access is accomplished via the Internet Database Connector (IDC), a component used to send queries to Open Database Connectivity (ODBC)-compliant databases, such as Microsoft Access, Microsoft SQL Server, or Oracle databases. Also included in the Internet Information Server package is the Key Manager, a tool for installing Secure Socket Layer (SSL) keys.

INDEX SERVER

Index Server is a search engine integrated into Internet Information Server that provides users with access to documents on a Web site. It allows users to perform full-text searches and retrieve information in a variety of formats with their Web browser. Index Server includes support for searching HTML, text, and Microsoft Office documents in their original format and in seven languages.

When Index Server is initially installed and started, it builds an index of all virtual roots and subdirectories on the Web server. The site administrator can choose directories and file types that should not be indexed. The content index is updated automatically whenever a file is added, deleted, or changed on the server, so users always have access to up-to-date information.

CERTIFICATE SERVER AND TRANSACTION SERVER

Certificate Server enables an organization to manage the issuance, renewal, and termination of SSL certificates without using the services of a third-party certificate issuer.

Developers use Transaction Server to deploy scaleable server applications built from Microsoft ActiveX components. Transaction Server automatically provides transaction support to applications running on the server, providing a reliable failure isolation and recovery mechanism.

COMMERCE SERVER

Commerce Server (formerly known as Merchant Server) allows you to create secure, shopping-cart applications for the Internet. In addition, you can develop sales promotions based on real-time information. Commerce Server also features a built-in order-processing pipeline that enables you to process orders online. It also supports VeriFone POS Internet-based payment processing and other third-party payment systems for secure credit card transactions. Commerce Server can be integrated with the Microsoft BackOffice family of server software and any ODBC-compliant relational database management system, including UNIX-based systems. Included with this product is Starter Stores, an off-the-shelf application designed to provide a framework for simple Web-based businesses. Starter Stores can be adapted to meet business needs or used as a learning tool. It includes built-in order-processing components that handle transaction details, such as inventory, tax, shipping, and payment processing.

CHAPTER SUMMARY

- A core service is one that is shipped with Windows NT and installed in the typical Windows NT environment. These services include Computer Browser Service, Dynamic Host Configuration Protocol Server (DHCP), Windows Internet Naming Service (WINS), Domain Naming Service (DNS) Server, and directory replication. Implementation of each of these services generally involves two stages: installation and configuration.

- The Computer Browser Service is used to create a centralized list of available network resources. The computer responsible for maintaining this list of available resources is called the master browser. The backup browser receives a copy of the network resource list (the browse list) from the master browser and distributes it to browser clients upon request. Network users can, in turn, use the browse list to locate resources. When a preferred master browser is turned on, it designates itself as the master browser if no other master browser exists on the network. If another computer already serves as the master browser, then the preferred master browser sends a broadcast message that forces an election.

- DHCP is a network protocol that enables a DHCP server to automatically assign an IP address to an individual computer's TCP/IP stack. It assigns a number automatically based on a defined range of numbers (called a scope) given to a network.

- WINS enables a Windows NT computer to function as a TCP/IP-based NetBIOS name server. Using this service, client computers can resolve NetBIOS computer names of other network computers to their IP addresses.

- Directory replication allows Windows NT to maintain identical copies of specified files and directories on different computers. This strategy ensures that changes made to files on one computer are automatically replicated to other computers configured to receive the changes.

- DNS is the database that computers on the Internet use to look up one another's addresses.

- An optional service is one that is included in the package of Windows NT BackOffice products. The list of BackOffice products includes Microsoft SQL Server, Exchange Server, SNA Server, System Management Server, Transaction Server, Microsoft Proxy Server, Site Server, and Commercial Internet System. In addition, a number of products, while not part of the official BackOffice suite, are considered optional services. (Microsoft imposes a separate licensing fee for these BackOffice products and views them as separate software products.)

- Microsoft Proxy Server allows a company to access the Internet, while providing security for the internal network, and does not require TCP/IP to be running on the client computer. It offers support for a wide range of applications and protocols, including those with live, streaming audio and video. Internet Information Server is a file service that enables a Windows NT 4.0 server to become a robust and secure vehicle for publishing information. Index Server is a search engine integrated into Internet Information Server that enables users to access documents on the Web. Certificate Server allows an organization to manage the issuance, renewal, and termination of Secure Socket Layer (SSL) certificates without using the services of a third-party certificate issuer. Commerce Server allows you to create secure shopping-cart applications for the Internet. In addition, you can develop sales promotions based on real-time information with this option.

KEY TERMS

4

- **backup browser** — A computer that receives a copy of the browse list from the master browser and distributes it to the browser clients upon request.

- **browse list** — The list of available resources distributed to specially assigned computers known as browser computers.

- **Certificate Server** — An optional Windows NT service that enables an organization to manage the issuance, renewal, and termination of Secure Socket Layer (SSL) certificates without using the services of a third-party certificate issuer.

- **Commerce Server** — An optional Windows NT service (formerly known as Merchant Server) that allows users to create secure, shopping-cart applications for the Internet, develop sales promotions based on real-time information, and process orders online.

- **Computer Browser Service** — A core Windows NT service that creates a centralized list of available network resources.

- **core service** — A service that is shipped with Windows NT and installed in the typical Windows NT environment. These services include Computer Browser Service, Dynamic Host Configuration Protocol Server (DHCP), Windows Internet Naming Service (WINS), Domain Naming Service (DNS) Server, and directory replication.

- **directory replication** — A core Windows NT service that maintains identical copies of specified files and directories on different computers. Changes made to files on one computer are automatically replicated to other computers configured to receive the changes.

- **Domain Naming Service (DNS)** — The database used by computers on the Internet to look up one another's addresses. Installed as a core Windows NT service.

- **Dynamic Host Configuration Protocol (DHCP)** — A network protocol that enables a DHCP server to automatically assign an IP address to an individual computer's TCP/IP stack.

- **election** — The process that ensures that only one master browser exists in each domain or workgroup. An election is triggered when a network client cannot locate a master browser, a backup browser attempts to update its browse list but cannot locate a master browser, or a second computer configured as a preferred master browser is turned on.

- **Index Server** — A search engine integrated into Internet Information Server that provides users with access to documents on the Web site.

- **Internet Information Server** — An optional Windows NT file service that enables a Windows NT 4.0 server to become a robust and secure vehicle for publishing information.

- **master browser** — The computer that maintains a database (or browse list) of available resources on the domain or workgroup; it distributes this list to the backup browsers.

- **nonbrowser** — A computer (typically a client computer) that does not maintain a network resource list.

- **optional service** — A service that is included in the Windows NT BackOffice suite. The list of BackOffice products includes Microsoft SQL Server, Exchange Server, SNA Server, System Management Server, Transaction Server, Proxy Server, Site Server, and Commercial Internet Systems. In addition, a number of products, while not part of the BackOffice family, are considered optional services.

- **potential browser** — A computer that can maintain a network resource list, but will not take this step unless specifically instructed to do so by a master browser.

- **preferred master browser** — A NT Windows server or workstation that designates itself as the master browser if no other master browser exists on the network. If another computer already serves as the master browser, the preferred master browser sends a broadcast message that forces an election.

- **Proxy Server** — An optional Windows NT service that allows a company to access the Internet, while providing security for the internal network, and does not require TCP/IP to be running on the client computer.

- **scope** — The range of numbers assigned to a network that DHCP uses when assigning IP addresses to an individual computer within that network.

- **Windows Internet Naming Service (WINS)** — A Windows NT feature that enables client computers to resolve NetBIOS computer names of other network computers to their IP addresses by providing a dynamic database that automatically keeps track of IP addresses. WINS has 2 parts: **WINS server**, a server component which maintains the database, and **WINS client**, which seeks this information from the server component.

REVIEW QUESTIONS

1. A Windows NT server on the Olympic domain is presently acting as the primary domain controller. It is also likely be a backup browser. True or False?

2. In an election, which of the following is likely to prevail as the master browser?

   a. a Windows NT server running version 3.51

   b. a Windows NT workstation running version 4.0

   c. a computer using Windows 95

   d. a computer using Windows for Workgroups

3. When a ————————— browser comes online, it calls for an election.

4. How many backup browsers will a workgroup of 65 computers have?

    a. 5

    b. 3

    c. 1

    d. 2

5. What is the maximum number of backup browsers in a domain?

    a. 1

    b. 2

    c. 3

    d. no limit

6. What is the maximum amount of time between when a computer is turned off and when it will disappear from the Network Neighborhood as an available shared resource?

    a. 3 days

    b. 51 minutes

    c. 14 minutes

    d. 1 hour

7. The "C" in DHCP stands for:

    a. connection

    b. configuration

    c. co-originated

    d. collective

8. Session mode is defined as a(n) ————————— communication.

    a. connectionless

    b. connection-oriented

    c. closed

    d. open

9. An LMHOSTS file is:

    a. a static database

    b. a dynamic database

    c. not available on Windows NT servers

    d. a locally monitored system file

10. WINS is used to provide resolution between:

   a. a computer's name and its IP address

   b. a computer's name and its MAC address

   c. a computer's IP address and its MAC address

   d. a list of computers on the network together with the type of operating system

11. What protocol(s) do you need to configure WINS?

   a. DLC

   b. NetBEUI

   c. TCP/IP

   d. IPX/SPX

12. Where can you place files in a Windows NT server configured as a primary domain controller so that they will be available for distribution to clients that log on to that server?

   a. \Winnt\system32\repl\import\scripts directory

   b. \Winnt\system32\repl\export\scripts directory

   c. root directory

   d. base directory of the replication service

13. The user account established for directory replication must be a member of which group?

   a. Administration

   b. Backup Operators

   c. Replication

   d. Guest

14. DNS Server service is used to:

   a. link NetBIOS names to their MAC addresses

   b. link NetBIOS names to their IP addresses

   c. link fully qualified domain names to their IP addresses

   d. link fully qualified domain names to their MAC addresses

15. A DNS server has a ———————— database.

   a. static

   b. dynamic

   c. rational

   d. molded

HANDS-ON PROJECTS

For some or all of these projects you will need a working NT 4.0 Server on a TCP/IP network. Also on this network, you will need another Windows NT Server running Replication services.

4

PROJECT 4-1

In this project you will configure your Windows NT server to be a preferred master browser. You'll start by finding the Regedit.exe file, then you'll change the registry setting to configure your server as a preferred master browser.

1. Click the **Start button**, point to **Find**, then click **Files or Folders**. The Find dialog box opens.
2. Type **REGEDT32.EXE** in the Named text box.
3. Use the Look in list arrow to select the partition where your NT system files are located, then click **Find Now**.
4. Double-click the **REGEDT32.EXE file** to open the registry editing utility.
5. Click **Options** on the menu bar, and then click **Read-only mode**. This will prevent you from making accidental changes.
6. Expand the registry as follows:

    ```
    \HKEY_LOCAL_MACHINE
        \SYSTEM
                \CurrentControlSet
                        \Services
                                \Browser
                                        \Parameters
    ```

7. Double-click the **MaintainServerList icon** in the right window.
8. Click **Options** on the menu bar, then click **Read-only mode** to turn off read-only mode.
9. Type **Yes** in the Value data text box, then click **OK**. Your machine is now configured as a preferred master browser.

PROJECT 4-2

In this project you will install and configure WINS on your computer. You will modify the Renewal Interval and the Retry Count.

1. Click **Start**, point to **Settings**, click **Control Panel**, double-click the **Network icon,** then click the **Services tab**, if necessary.

2. In the Services tab of the Network dialog box, click **Add**, select **Windows Internet Naming Service Server service** from the list of available services and then click **OK**. The Windows NT Setup dialog box opens, prompting you to enter the location of the files. (The default is the location from which you installed Windows NT.)

3. Enter the correct location of the files, and then click **OK**.

4. Reboot your server when prompted.

5. After rebooting your system, logon with Administrator privileges.

6. Click **Start**, click **Run,** type **WINSADMN** in the Open text box, and then click **OK**. The **Windows Internet Naming Service Manager window** opens.

7. In WINS Manager, click **Server** on the menu bar, then click **Configuration**.

8. Set the Renewal Interval to 8 hours, and set the Retry Count to 5. Why would you set the renewal interval to 8 hours?

PROJECT 4-3

In this project you will configure your server to act as both an export server and an import server. This project assumes that you have created a user account on the domain named REPL. If you have not created this account, do so now using User Manager, making sure that it is established with the characteristics defined in the "Directory Replication" section.

1. Click **Start**, point to **Programs** and then click **Windows NT Explorer**.

2. In the Windows NT Explorer window, navigate to the \winnt\system32\repl\export subdirectory.

3. Create a subdirectory in the \winnt\system32\repl\export subdirectory titled "phonebook."

4. Use a text editor to create a short text file with your name and the name of a few relatives and friends. Include their phone numbers. Save the text file in the \phonebook directory.

5. Click **Start**, point to **Settings**, click **Control Panel,** then double-click the **Services icon**. The Services dialog box opens.

6. Select the **Directory Replicator** service, then click **Startup**.

7. In the section labeled "Logon as," click the **This Account option button,** and then click the **ellipsis (…) button** located to the right of the text box. The Select User dialog box opens.

8. In the list of users, select the **Repl user** you created earlier, then click **OK** twice.

9. On the Services tab, click **Start** to start replication services, then click **Close**.

10. Click **Start**, point to **Programs**, point to **Administrative Tools (Common)** and then click **Server Manager**.

11. Select your server, click **Computer** on the menu bar, then click **Properties**.

12. Click **Replication**.

13. For both the Import and Export sections enable replication using the appropriate option buttons. This should export the phonebook subdirectory you created in Step 3 to all import servers in the domain. Close the Server Manager window.

14. Wait 10 minutes, then confirm that the file has been replicated into your import directory.

4

Project 4-4

In this project you will configure your server to provide Domain Naming Service Server service. You will identify the zone name as student.com and identify the IP address as 207.173.15.100.

1. Click **Start**, point to **Settings**, click **Control Panel**, double-click the **Network icon,** then click the **Services tab**, if necessary.

2. In the Services tab of the Network dialog box, click **Add**, select **Microsoft DNS service** from the list of available services and then click **OK**. The Windows NT Setup dialog box opens, prompting you to enter the location of the files. (The default is the location from which you installed Windows NT.)

3. Enter the correct location of the files, and then click **OK**.

4. After restarting your server, log on with Administrative rights.

5. Open the **Domain Naming Service Manager window**, click **Domain Naming Service** on the drop-down menu, then click **New Server**. The Add Domain Naming Service Server dialog box opens.

6. Type the IP address of your server, then click **OK**.

7. Select the IP address of your Domain Naming Service server.

8. Click **Domain Naming Service** on the menu bar, then click **New Zone**. The Creating New Zone dialog box opens.

9. Click the **Primary option button**, then click **Next**.

10. Type **STUDENT**, then click the **zone file text box**. The filename student.Domain Naming Service appears.

11. Click **Next**, and then click **Finish**.

CASE PROJECTS

1. You have been retained by Associated Airlines, a large commercial airline, to help manage three maintenance centers located in Los Angeles, Houston, and New York. All three centers have been experiencing slow network speeds during the day. It appears that each center's spare parts database is being replicated from that site's central server to the other two sites' central servers every 15 minutes. When you asked how critical this up-to-date information is, you were informed that it is important to know the parts available at the other sites in case one site needs an emergency part. Management informs you that it could "live with information that was no older than one day in accuracy." Some Associated employees, however, have said that such old information will cause problems. Summarize the issues involved and suggest corrective action to resolve the problem in a manner acceptable to most users.

2. Beneficial Construction Company has retained your services to design a Windows NT enterprise network. Beneficial has four branch locations. It wants a centralized management scheme, in which user access is controlled at one location in the company's headquarters. Each branch location should maintain local resources. The company's management wants to minimize the amount of network traffic between the branches. The Information Services Manager wants to implement a single WINS server at the corporate headquarters. Write a brief report (three to five paragraphs) for the IS Manager, explaining this arrangement's impact on traffic between the locations. Express your concerns and describe some possible solutions.

3. You are employed by Astro Products as a network engineer. Astro has a Windows NT enterprise network connecting its 10 remote locations. The Chief Information Officer has asked you whether it makes sense to implement DNS Server to supplement the existing WINS service. Summarize the benefits associated with DNS implementation. What problems may be encountered in its implementation?

4. One server on your Windows NT network is providing slow access time for users running a client/server application that uses Microsoft SQL Server. It's your job to improve this server's response time. Identify the core and optional services that may be operating on this server. Explain how to determine whether each service is installed and running properly, and describe how you might prevent these services from consuming server resources.

REMOTE ACCESS SERVICE (RAS)

In this chapter you will learn about Windows NT Server 4.0's Remote Access Service (RAS). This service is the primary means by which remote clients are granted access to a server (and ultimately a network) by using modem-type connections as a substitute for a network interface card. RAS is as simple as dialing up a BBS or ISP, or as complicated as connecting two networks together to support high-speed, high-security, fully routed communications.

This chapter introduces you to RAS through a lengthy discussion of its installation and configuration. It also describes RAS use, connection, establishment, and troubleshooting.

AFTER READING THIS CHAPTER AND COMPLETING THE EXERCISES YOU WILL BE ABLE TO:

- Explain Remote Access Service (RAS)
- Discuss connection types
- Discuss protocols supported by RAS
- Explain RAS name resolution
- Install and configure RAS
- Manage RAS with Remote Access Admin
- Explain the telephony features of RAS
- Configure dial-up networking
- Discuss callback security
- Understand other RAS connection features, including direct cable connect, X.25, and scripts

REMOTE ACCESS SERVICE IN THE ENTERPRISE

Windows NT **Remote Access Service (RAS)** is used to connect remote or mobile workers to a central office network. By implementing RAS, you can expand the extent of your network beyond the walls of your office. Traveling or telecommuting users can connect to the office LAN via direct secure dial-up connections or secure channels over the Internet. RAS is Windows NT's primary means of interacting with other networks and computers outside its immediate network media connections.

RAS uses **modems** (and similar communication devices) and standard communication lines just as if they were network interface cards. In fact, once a RAS session is established, the operating system cannot differentiate between a NIC connection and a RAS connection to the same network. A client connnected via RAS can do everything that a client connected directly to the network can do. The only difference between a NIC and a RAS connection is speed: A NIC connection is much faster (usually 10–100 MB per second or faster) than a RAS connection (usually only 28.8–128 Kb per second).

Windows NT Server 4.0's RAS offers several important features (each of which will be discussed in greater detail later in this chapter): support for 256 simultaneous connections, gateway capabilities, routing capabilities, and multiple levels and types of communication security.

CONNECTION TYPES

Windows NT Server 4.0's RAS supports three types of communication or connection media right out of the box:

- PSTN (Public Switch Telephone Networks)—standard telephone lines, sometimes called POTS (for Plain Old Telephone Service)
- Integrated Services Digital Network (ISDN)
- X.25 packet switching networks

Public Switch Telephone Networks (PSTN) is the technical term for the standard analog telephone that you use to communicate by voice with other people. Computers can establish a communication link by using a modem to transform their digital signals into analog signals, which can then be transferred over an analog line. PSTN is most often employed when establishing a RAS connection for a traveling user (who needs to connect to the network via the closest available telephone line). Otherwise, the speeds offered over PSTN (28.8–56 Kb per second) are too slow for some network activities.

Integrated Services Digital Network (ISDN) is a dial-up digital telephone service that provides a much faster transmission rate than standard telephone lines (typically 64–128 Kb per second). The standard ISDN connection consists of three separate data channels—two B channels, which provide a data communications rate of 64 Kb per second, and a single D channel, which establishes and maintains the connection. ISDN can be configured to use both B channels together, producing a transmission rate as high as 128 Kb per second. To achieve these high transmission rates, both the client and the server must use ISDN. Instead of modems, ISDN uses an **ISDN adapter card** (sometimes referred to as an **ISDN modem**).

Like ISDN, **X.25** packet switching networks require special communication hardware devices. In addition to an X.25 adapter card at both the remote client and the RAS server, they require a packet assembler/disassembler (PAD) at both locations.

PROTOCOLS SUPPORTED BY RAS

5

RAS supports two types of protocols—transport (or LAN protocols) and connection (or WAN protocols). You need one of each to establish a RAS connection over a communication media link. The WAN protocol creates the pathway between the two communication devices. The LAN protocol carries the network communications over that pathway, just as if the link were an ordinary segment of network cable.

TRANSPORT PROTOCOLS

RAS supports Windows NT's three default LAN (or transport) protocols—NetBEUI, TCP/IP, and IPX/SPX. It does not support either DLC or AppleTalk. (For details on these protocols, see Chapter 3.)

RAS clients can access resources on the network via the RAS server, as long as that server has routing enabled for the protocol in use over the RAS connection. If such routing is not enabled, the RAS client is limited to the resources available on the RAS server. Both the TCP/IP and IPX/SPX protocols offer true routing support. Because NetBEUI is not routable, however, Windows NT uses the NetBIOS Gateway protocol to allow users to access NetBIOS-enabled applications over the NetBEUI protocol.

CONNECTION PROTOCOLS

RAS supports two main WAN (or connection) protocols (PPP and SLIP), plus several variances of PPP (including PPTP and MPPP). WAN protocols are used to establish the communications pathway between two remote systems, over either standard communication lines (PSTN, ISDN, X.25) or the Internet. The following sections describe these WAN protocols.

Point-to-Point Protocol (PPP)

The current RAS and Internet connection protocol standard is **Point-to-Point Protocol (PPP)**. Microsoft highly encourages users to employ PPP for all RAS connections to maximize compatibility with both current and planned client/server hardware and software options. Your company's implementation of PPP via RAS enables you to either connect to, or accept connections from, any other PPP-compliant system.

Some PPP hosts require you to enter special commands or an activation script after establishing the initial RAS connection so as to switch the communication into PPP framing mode. This requirement is typically seen on older BBS systems and some Unix-hosted

Internet Service Providers (ISPs), for example. In contrast, Windows NT RAS allows you to use a post-connection script. You can also launch a terminal window to switch the host into PPP mode manually.

Standards for all remote access protocols are set by the Internet Engineering Task Force (IETF) and other technical standards organizations, which are charged with maximizing compatibility across platforms. The standards established by these organizations are published on the Internet in the form of Requests for Comments (RFCs). Windows NT Server 4.0's RAS PPP supports the following RFCs:

- RFC 1549: PPP in HDLC Framing
- RFC 1552: The PPP Internetwork Packet Exchange Control Protocol (IPXCP)
- RFC 1334: PPP Authentication Protocols
- RFC 1332: The PPP Internet Protocol Control Protocol (IPCP)
- RFC 1661: Link Control Protocol (LCP)
- RFC 1717: PPP Multilink Protocol

Point-to-Point Tunneling Protocol (PPTP)

Point-to-Point Tunneling Protocol (PPTP) is a variation of PPP that allows you to establish a secure network communications link (between a client and server) over the Internet. PPTP creates a RAS pathway or pipeline over the Internet and "tunnels" (that is, sends through the new pathway or pipeline) the LAN protocol (NetBEUI, IPX/SPX, or TCP/IP). All PPTP communications are fully encrypted, making PPTP communications more secure than those involving local network media segments. You can use PPTP to create virtual private networks (VPNs) by simply harnessing the inexpensive connections (such as modems and the Internet) often already used by the existing network. An RFC has not been released for PPTP.

PPP Multilink Protocol

The **PPP Multilink protocol**, another variation of PPP, can combine two or more physical connections into a single logical pathway. Hence, as many as 32 connections can serve as a single, larger, aggregated communication connection. All of the connections combined using Multilink, however, must be of the same type (PSTN, ISDN, or X.25).

Multilink is incompatible with the callback security feature of Windows NT RAS. Callback can store only a single telephone number, while multilink requires the use of several such numbers.

RFC 1717 defines the Multilink protocol. Microsoft's implementation, however, differs from the recommended standard for this protocol.

Microsoft RAS Protocol (Asynchronous NetBEUI)

Clients that do not support PPP (such as Windows NT 3.1, Windows for Workgroups, MS-DOS, and LAN Manager) may use the proprietary **Microsoft RAS Protocol** (also called **Asynchronous NetBEUI**). Once a communication link has been established, the RAS server acts as a gateway to provide network access via LAN protocols (NetBEUI, TCP/IP, or IPX/SPX). This protocol is not defined by an Internet RFC; rather, it is a proprietary protocol developed by Microsoft.

NetBIOS Gateway

NetBIOS Gateway is a backward-compatible connection protocol used by older versions of Windows NT, Windows for Workgroups, and LAN Manager to establish a RAS link. The RAS server translates communications between the client and the TCP/IP or IPX/SPX network resources as necessary. This connection method grants clients access to network-hosted resources without requiring them to host TCP/IP or IPX/SPX protocols. The NetBIOS Gateway protocol is not defined by an Internet RFC; rather, it is a proprietary protocol developed by Microsoft.

Serial Line Internet Protocol (SLIP)

Serial Line Internet Protocol (SLIP) was one of the first communication protocols developed to enable TCP/IP communications over RAS links. It has since been replaced by PPP on most systems. Windows NT Server 4.0, however, supports SLIP for dialing into a Unix system as a client. Note that the reverse operation is not allowed—that is, SLIP cannot accept inbound calls on a Windows NT Server 4.0 RAS server. Unlike PPP, SLIP has some disadvantages: It does not support dynamic addressing (DHCP), it supports only TCP/IP (not IPX/SPX or NetBEUI), and it does not provide encryption of any kind.

The following RFCs apply to SLIP:

- RFC 1144: Compressing TCP/IP Headers for Low-Speed Serial Links
- RFC 1055: A Nonstandard for Transmission of IP Datagrams over Serial Lines: SLIP

RAS NAME RESOLUTION

Name resolution over RAS does not differ from name resolution on standard networks. A RAS server can employ the four standard Windows NT methods for name resolution—Windows Internet Naming Service (WINS), broadcast name resolution, Domain Name System (DNS), and the HOSTS and LMHOSTS files. All operations performed on the RAS server use these four methods to resolve names and addresses.

RAS clients are automatically assigned the same WINS and DNS servers that are used by the RAS server to which they connect. In cases where the main network uses HOSTS or LMHOSTS files, these static resolution files can be placed on the client to speed name resolution and reduce traffic over the RAS link.

INSTALLING AND CONFIGURING RAS

The installation of RAS requires some preparation. First, you must install and configure all of the LAN protocols that will be used over a RAS link (such as TCP/IP, IPX/SPX, and/or NetBEUI). Next, you must install at least one communication device (such as a modem, ISDN adapter card, or X.25 adapter card). Note that you do not necessarily have to install the drivers for these devices before installing RAS. Instead, you can install these drivers during the RAS process, when prompted to do so. Whenever you install them, you must also indicate the device's communication port.

To install RAS, you will need the original installation CD-ROM, accessed via the network or a local CD-ROM. The RAS installation process makes use of the Service tab of the Select Network Service dialog box, shown in Figure 5-1.

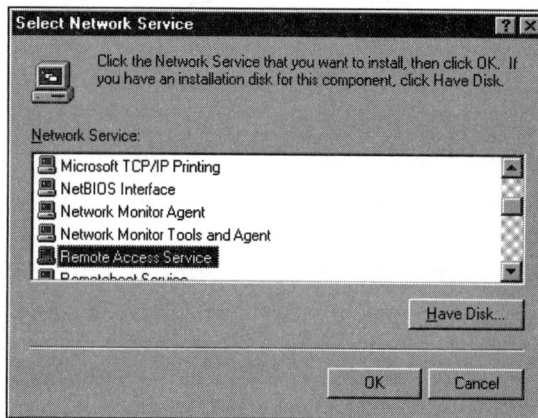

Figure 5-1   Select Network Service dialog box

You'll have a chance to actually install RAS in the Hands-On Projects found at the end of this chapter. For now, you need to know only the general procedure for installing RAS:

1. Install all necessary protocols on the RAS server.

2. Physically install or attach a modem.

3. Install RAS via the Services tab of the Network applet.

4. Install the drivers for the modem.

5. Define the modem by indicating which communications port to use.

6. Configure the RAS device for dial-in and/or dial-out access (as explained in the next section).

7. Configure the LAN protocols.

CONFIGURING RAS PORTS

As mentioned in the previous section, when installing RAS you need to configure a RAS device for dial access (notice that RAS refers to the device both by its device name and by its port definition). You accomplish this goal via the Configure button in the Remote Access Setup dialog box. You can make the port or device capable of dialing out only, receiving calls only, or dialing out and receiving calls. This setting determines whether RAS can initiate calls or listen for incoming calls over this device.

Keep in mind that a RAS device configured to receive calls cannot be used by any other application. RAS will lock the port to listen for inbound calls, thereby preventing other applications from using the port. Consequently, you need to plan your inbound and outbound connections carefully so that RAS doesn't interfere with other network applications.

CONFIGURING LAN PROTOCOLS

Another important step in RAS configuration is defining the LAN protocols to be used by both inbound and outbound calls. You configure RAS LAN protocols via the Network Configuration dialog box. The Network Configuration dialog box enables you to select the protocols to be used for dial-out connections. You set these properties in the Dial out Protocols section, located at the top of the dialog box (all other dial-out configurations are handled through the Dial Up Networking Phonebook entries, discussed later in this chapter).

In addition, you can use the first set of options in the Server Settings section of the Network Configuration dialog box to configure LAN protocols for inbound calls. Inbound RAS LAN protocols support only NetBEUI, TCP/IP, and IPX/SPX. Each protocol has its own settings, as explained in the following sections. You can select one, two, or all three of the protocols by checking the appropriate boxes.

Finally, the Network Configuration dialog box allows you to choose from several encryption options. These options are explained later in this chapter.

NetBEUI CONFIGURATION

When you select NetBEUI as an inbound RAS protocol, you must specify whether remote access will be granted to the entire network or to the local computer only. If you choose the first option, NetBEUI Gateway will grant remote client access to network-hosted resources. If you choose the second option, client access will be restricted to those resources hosted on the RAS server computer.

TCP/IP CONFIGURATION

When you select TCP/IP as an inbound RAS protocol, you must define several settings in the RAS Server TCP/IP Configuration dialog box, shown in Figure 5-2. In the top section of this dialog box, for example, you must decide whether to grant remote access to the entire network or to the local computer only. The first option allows RAS to act as a gateway; the second enables RAS to act like a firewall. Next, you must specify whether to use an existing

DHCP server to assign IP addresses to clients or to have the local RAS server make IP address assignments. If you choose the second option, you must also define a range (or pool) of available IP addresses; this scope can contain only IP addresses from the same subnet as that employed by the RAS server.

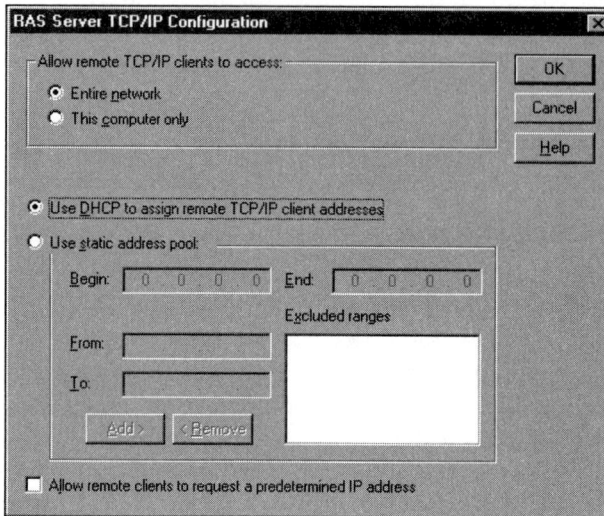

Figure 5-2   RAS Server TCP/IP Configuration dialog box

Finally, you can use the RAS Server TCP/IP Configuration dialog box to permit clients to select a predetermined IP address.

IPX/SPX CONFIGURATION

When you select IPX/SPX as an inbound RAS protocol, you must define several settings in the RAS Server IPX Configuration dialog box, shown in Figure 5-3. In the top section of this dialog box, for example, you must specify whether to grant remote access to the entire network or to the local computer only. Next, you must decide whether to automate the assignment of network numbers or to define a range of numbers that will be assigned to RAS clients.

RAS ENCRYPTION

The encryption settings, located at the bottom of the Network Configuration dialog box (shown in Figure 5-4), define the level of encryption RAS uses to authenticate users during inbound connections.

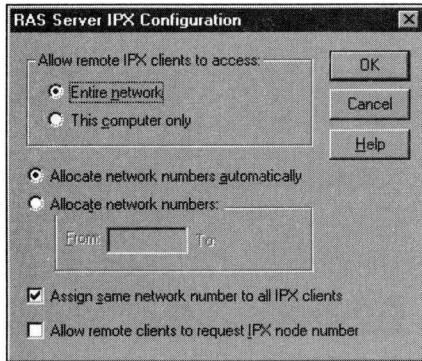

Figure 5-3   RAS Server IPX Configuration dialog box

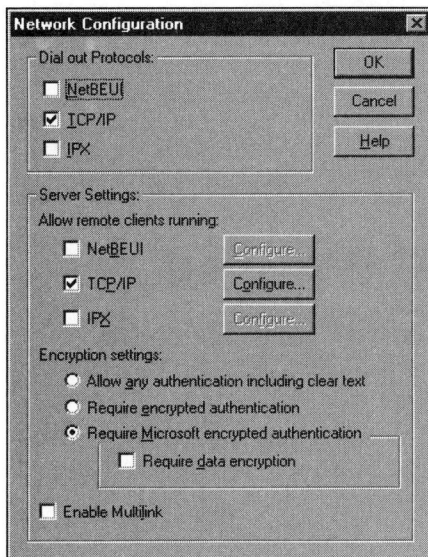

Figure 5-4   Network Configuration dialog box

The three encryption options are the same as those available through Dial-Up Networking Phonebook for outbound connections:

- *Allow any authentication, including clear text*—This setting uses no encryption. Names and passwords are transmitted as text. This option uses the Password Authentication Protocol (PAP), a clear text authentication protocol.

- *Require encrypted authentication*—This setting uses standard encryption methods to protect names and passwords transmitted over a communication link. It can use Challenge Authentication Handshake Protocol (CHAP), Shiva Password Authentication Protocol (SPAP), Data Encryption Standard (DES), or Microsoft Challenge Authentication Handshake Protocol (MS-CHAP).

- *Require Microsoft encrypted authentication*—This setting is the most secure selection and can be used only when both the server and client are Microsoft operating systems. It uses only Microsoft Challenge Authentication Handshake Protocol (MS-CHAP). With this option, you can choose to encrypt all data—a more secure option than encrypting just the initial authentication, as it forces the use of the RSA (Rivest-Shamir-Adleman) Data Security Incorporated RC4 algorithm. If data are not encrypted in both directions, the communications link is terminated.

SERVER SIDE MULTILINK

To use Multilink, both the client and the server must be configured to take advantage of this protocol. On a Windows NT RAS server, Multilink is enabled by checking the Enable Multilink check box in the Network Configuration dialog box.

MANAGING RAS WITH REMOTE ACCESS ADMIN

Remote Access Admin (RAA) is a Windows NT administration utility that gives you control over many aspects of a RAS server. To open the RAA window, click the Start button, point to Programs, point to Administrative Tools (Common), then click Remote Access Admin. The Remote Access Admin window is shown in Figure 5-5.

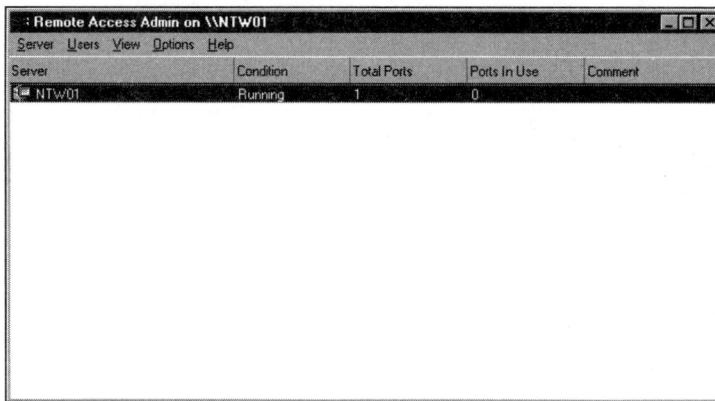

Figure 5-5 Remote Access Admin window

The RAA utility allows you to:

- Start and stop RAS on the server.
- Assign dial-in permissions to users.
- Configure callback security for users.
- Manually disconnect users from COM ports.
- View COM port status and statistics.
- Remotely manage other Windows NT computers that have RAS installed.

The RAA utility is automatically installed along with RAS. If you are working on a Windows NT workstation that does not have RAS installed, you can nevertheless manage RAS servers on the network via the Windows NT Server tools.

The Server menu of the RAA utility allows you to start, stop, or pause RAS. The Communication Ports command on the Server menu provides information about port status. The Users menu contains the two most useful commands—Permissions and Active Users. Permissions allows you to grant or deny RAS dial-up access to users and to assign callback security. (You'll learn more about callback security later this chapter.) Active Users allows you to view active RAS sessions, disconnect users, or send messages to users.

5

TELEPHONY

The **Telephony application programming interface (TAPI)** allows Windows NT to dial out and receive calls. It standardizes communication methods for a wide variety of applications, communication devices, and communication media types, thereby providing the computer with seamless access to public communication systems. TAPI was developed to facilitate the integration of third-party products into Windows NT, especially products serving areas in which Microsoft currently has no interest in development—such as PBX and other telephone control systems. After installing the proper drivers, you can use TAPI to control most modern telephone systems and communication devices, thereby automating the transmission and receipt of information over these communication media.

TAPI 2.0 provides the following benefits:

- It is consistent across current Microsoft operating systems, including Windows 95, Windows NT Server 4.0, and Windows NT Workstation 4.0.

- The native 32-bit process supports symmetrical multiprocessing, multithreaded applications, and preemptive multitasking.

- It can be incorporated into Windows 95 applications, which can then function without modification on Windows NT.

- It allows multiple applications to share a single communication device for both outbound and inbound calls.

For more information about TAPI, see the Microsoft Web site at *http://www.microsoft.com/win32dev/netwrk/wnetwrk.htm#TAPI.*

CONFIGURING DIAL-UP NETWORKING

The **Dial-Up Networking (DUN)** utility allows Windows NT clients to initiate outbound calls to other dial-up servers (whether Windows NT or other network operating systems). To open the Dial-Up Networking dialog box, click the Start button, point to Programs, point to Accessories, then click Dial-Up Networking. The Dial-Up Networking dialog box opens, as shown in Figure 5-6.

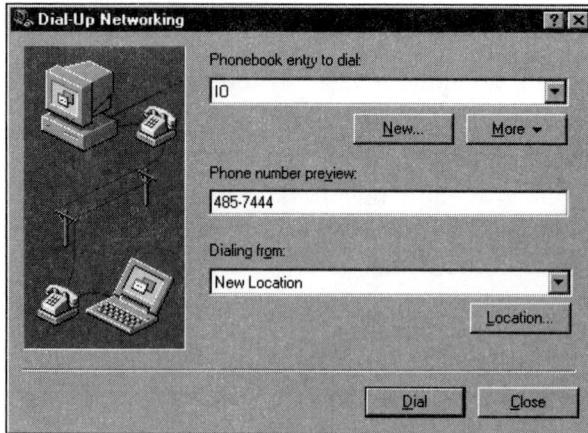

Figure 5-6   Dial-Up Networking dialog box

> **Note** The first time you select the Dial-Up Networking command, you will be prompted to provide the installation CD-ROM so as to install DUN.

DUN maintains a database, known as the phonebook, detailing the settings and connection features required to establish a communications link with a dial-up server. You can use DUN **phonebook entries** to connect to almost any kind of dial-up system. In addition to defining the connection to a remote system, DUN can control the placement of the call. Settings relating to how a call is placed are known as dialing properties.

You can access the Dialing Properties dialog box two ways:

- Double-click the Telephony icon in the Control Panel.
- Double-click the Modem icon in the Control Panel, then click Dialing Properties.

The Dialing Properties dialog box consists of two tabs—My Locations and Telephony Drivers. You use the My Locations tab (shown in Figure 5-7) to provide information about the location from which you are placing the call.

This information includes the following:

- The location from which you are dialing
- The area code and country from which you are dialing
- Numeric codes required to access outside lines
- Whether to use a calling card
- Whether to disable call waiting
- Whether to use tone or pulse dialing

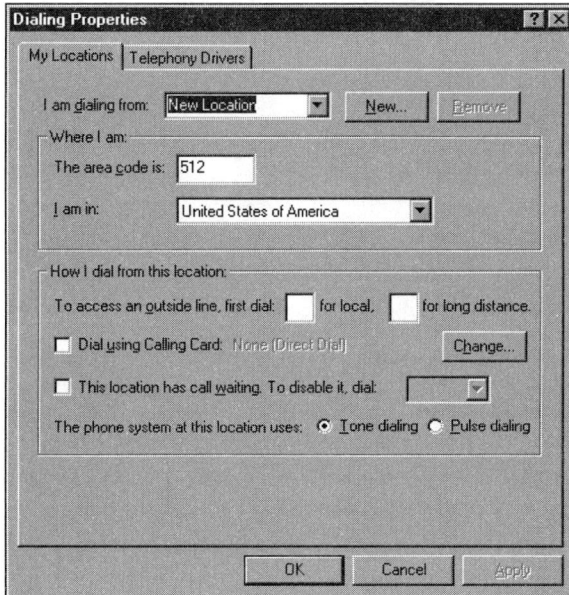

Figure 5-7   My Locations tab of the Dialing Properties dialog box

The Telephony Drivers tab (shown in Figure 5-8) is available only via the Telephony icon in the control panel. This tab lists the installed drivers used by Windows NT telephony, which were probably installed automatically during the installation of a modem. Two drivers almost always appear in the Telephony Drivers tab—the TAPI Kernel-Mode Service Provider and the Unimodem Service Provider. These drivers provide generic interface compatibility with a wide range of RAS modems.

To configure DUN to initiate outbound calls, you must first define a phonebook entry for the server you wish to contact. The details of creating such an entry are presented in the next few sections.

DEFINING PHONEBOOK ENTRIES

To begin defining a phonebook entry, click New in the Dial-Up Networking dialog box. Next, follow the steps presented in the New Phonebook Entry Wizard dialog boxes. As you'll see when you actually create a new phonebook entry in the Hands-On Projects at the end of this chapter, the wizard dialog boxes explain the entire process of defining such an entry. The New Phonebook Entry Wizard automatically configures many settings for a new phonebook entry. If you disable this wizard (by checking the "I know all about phonebook entries and would rather edit the properties directly" check box), you must configure every setting manually.

> The first time you open the Dial-Up Networking dialog box, you will be informed that no Phonebook entries exist and that you must create one.

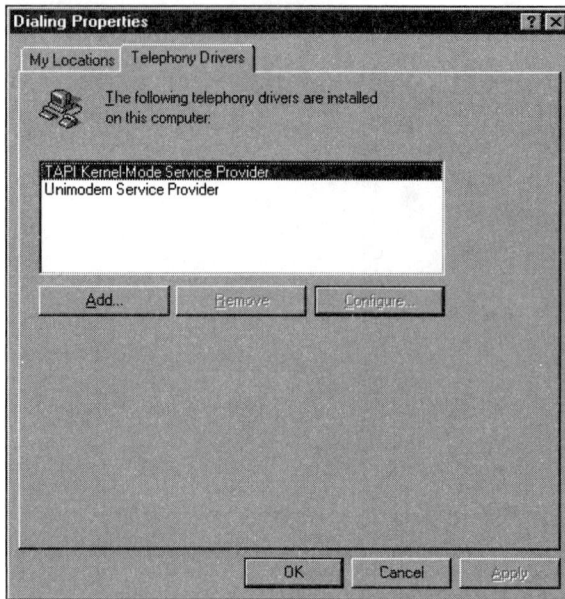

Figure 5-8 Telephony Drivers tab of the Dialing Properties dialog box

After creating a phonebook entry, you can edit its settings manually by opening the Dial-Up Networking dialog box, clicking the More list button, and selecting Edit entry and modem properties. The Edit Phonebook Entry dialog box opens; it has five tabs:

- Basic tab—This tab is where you define the phonebook entry name, add an explanatory comment, provide alternative telephone numbers, specify whether to use dialing properties, and specify which modem(s) to use.

- Server tab—This tab is where you specify the server type as PPP (Windows NT, Windows 95 Plus, or Internet), SLIP (Internet), Windows NT 3.51, or Windows for Workgroups 3.11. Depending on the server type, you may also need to indicate which network (LAN) protocol to use, define TCP/IP settings, enable software compression, and enable PPP LCP extensions. (LCP extensions are new features of PPP as defined by RFC 1570; they are not supported by all systems, however.)

- Script tab—This tab is where you specify whether to open a terminal window or to execute a script after connection to complete the logon process. (You will learn more about scripts later this chapter.)

- Security tab—This tab is where you select an encryption policy. The options presented here are almost identical to those used for inbound connections (explained earlier in this chapter). The only difference is the option of using the current username and password to establish a link with the remote server. If the name and password differ on the remote system, do not select this option. You can use the Unsave

Password button (at the bottom of the Security tab) to delete the phonebook entry's saved password; you can then reenter or change the logon information.

- X.25 tab—This tab is where you define X.25 settings (explained later in this chapter).

PHONEBOOK ENTRY TCP/IP SETTINGS

If you plan to use TCP/IP to establish a DUN connection with a remote server, you'll need to define several parameters. To define these parameters, open the Edit Phonebook Entry dialog box, click the Server tab, then click the TCP/IP Settings button. The PPP TCP/IP Settings dialog box opens, allowing you to make the following selections:

- Select a server-assigned IP address or a static IP address. (Subnet mask is always automatically assigned.)
- Select server-assigned name resolution servers or define specific ones for primary and secondary DNS and WINS servers.
- Use IP header compression.
- Use the default gateway of the remote network.

CLIENT SIDE MULTILINK

To use the Multilink protocol, both the client and the server must be configured properly. To enable Multilink on a Windows NT RAS client:

1. Click **Start**, point to **Programs**, point to **Accessories**, then click **Dial-Up Networking**. The Dial-up Networking window opens.
2. Click the **Phonebook entry to dial list arrow** and select the phonebook you want to edit.
3. Click **More**, then click **Edit entry and modem properties**. The Edit Phonebook Entry dialog box opens.
4. Click the **Dial using list arrow**, then select **Multiple Lines**.
5. Click **Configure**. The Multiple Line Configuration dialog box opens.
6. Select a modem or other communication device.
7. Click **Configure** to modify the speed and hardware features for the selected modem or device.
8. Repeat Steps 6–7 as necessary.
9. Use the **Phone numbers button** to add, remove, and rearrange telephone numbers.
10. Click **OK** in the Multiple Line Configuration dialog box to save your changes. You will return to the Edit Phonebook Entry dialog box.

11. Click **OK** in the Edit Phonebook Entry dialog box to save your changes.

12. Click **Close** to close the Dial-Up Networking dialog box.

After you have completed these steps, all of the defined devices will attempt to establish links to the dial-up host when the phonebook entry is dialed.

OTHER DUN CONFIGURATION OPTIONS

From the More menu of the Dial-Up Networking dialog box, you can access two other collections of configuration options—User Preferences and Logon Preferences. The User Preferences and Logon Preferences dialog boxes have similar tabs:

- Dialing—In the User Preferences dialog box, you use this tab to enable or disable autodial by location and to specify whether to reconnect if a link failure occurs. In both dialog boxes, you use this tab to set the number of redial attempts, the number of seconds between redial attempts, and the number of idle seconds before hangup.

- Callback—You use this tab to preset your client callback responses by refusing callbacks, asking to be prompted, or predefining callback numbers to give to the server.

- Appearance—You use this tab to enable or disable previewing of numbers, previewing of location, starting the dial-up networking monitor before dialing, showing connection progress, and other operations.

- Phonebook—You use this tab to define which phonebook DUN uses. Multiple phonebooks can exist, especially if several different users use this computer or if an organization-wide "approved" phonebook is provided.

CONFIGURING PPTP

To use PPTP to establish a secure network connection over the Internet, you need to have several items installed or available:

- The TCP/IP protocol

- RAS and DUN

- A PPP ISP account

PPTP is installed just like any other protocol—that is, via the Protocol tab of the Network applet. After installing it, you will be prompted for the number of VPN connections allowed (1–256). (Remember that Windows NT Server is limited to 256 RAS connections; thus, if this server will be used to connect to an ISP, you can have only 255 VPN connections.) Next, you need to add all capable VPN devices as RAS ports and configure them for inbound and/or outbound connections. Finally, you can set the encryption and protocol for each VPN device just as you did for standard RAS devices (modems), via the Remote Access Setup.

To restrict the server to use as a PPTP RAS server only, you can enable PPTP filtering on the TCP/IP protocol's Properties tab. This action will block all packets except PPTP packets received over the VPN devices. PING and TRACERT requests will be rejected, as will any other standard TCP/IP packets. You'll also need to enable IP forwarding to permit VPN/PPTP clients to access resources hosted on the network, rather than just resources on the RAS server.

Setting up clients to connect over PPTP is similar to configuring the server. The only difference is that you must now define two phonebook entries—one to connect to your ISP and a second to connect to the RAS PPTP server. The PPTP phonebook entry should use the RASPPTPM (VPN1) device.

An excellent guide to using PPTP with Windows NT is the article "Using PPTP on NT," by Tom Kellen, in the November 1997 issue of *NT Systems*. This article is available online at *http://www.ntsystems.com/db_area/archives/1997/9711/109c2.htm*.

5

CALLBACK SECURITY

To increase RAS security, you can use the **callback** feature, which first disconnects a client dialing the server and then calls the client back. Callback security is enabled on a per-user basis in the same dialog box in which dial-up access is granted (through either the Remote Access Admin or the Dialing button of a user account's Properties dialog box from User Manager for Domains).

The callback feature has three possible settings, only one of which actually enhances network security:

- No Call Back—This option represents the default setting, in which callback is disabled.

- Set by Caller—When the client initially connects, it is prompted for a callback number. This feature can enable the client to save on long-distance charges, but does not really increase security.

- Preset To:—This option defines a specific number that the server will use in an attempt to reconnect to the client. If the client is not present at this number, then no connection will be established. This choice is the only secure callback setting.

OTHER RAS FEATURES

Several other features of RAS are detailed in the following sections.

AUTODIAL

AutoDial enables the system to automatically reconnect to remote systems so as to retrieve previously accessed resources. Once a DUN phonebook entry is defined and used, the system keeps a record of all resources accessed over that connection. Whenever the same resource is requested by some other application or part of the system, the system reestablishes the DUN entry used to connect to that resource.

AutoDial works with TCP/IP and NetBEUI, but not with IPX/SPX. It is enabled by default. To obtain a list of known AutoDial addresses, simply execute the command "rasautou –s" from a Command Prompt. You can disable AutoDial through the Dialing tab by clicking More and then clicking User Preferences in the pop-up menu.

RAS LOGGING

To troubleshoot RAS, you can activate the logging feature. Two Windows NT logging systems record data about RAS events—modemlog.txt and device.log. The modemlog.txt is enabled through the Advanced Connections Settings area of a modem's Properties from the Modems applet. This log file, which is stored in the root directory of Windows NT, records the communications with the modem that occur during call placement and setup. The device.log file must be enabled via the registry. In the \HKEY_LOCAL_MACHINE\SYSTEM\ CurrentControlSet\Services\RasMan\Parameters key, the "Logging" value should be set to 1 to enable recording. This log file is stored in the \WINNT\System32\Ras\ directory.

The Event Viewer's system log also records some RAS-related events. For example, it monitors the system when auditing is enabled to record logon failures.

NULL-MODEM CABLE

A network connection over a null-modem cable can be established with RAS. This feature enables you to transfer files and perform other communication activities between two computers that are in close proximity without requiring a modem or a network interface card. Simply install the null-modem cable via the Modems applet, then enable it as a RAS port device.

SINGLE COMMON PROTOCOL

Even though RAS supports several LAN and WAN protocols, only a single LAN and a single WAN protocol are used over any particular RAS connection. Typically, PPP will serve as the WAN protocol. Only the first LAN protocol that the client/server have in common, however, will be used. Consequently, it is important to change the binding order on the client so that the desired protocol will be bound more closely to the RAS device than any other protocols.

DUN MONITOR

After the establishment of a RAS connection, the DUN Monitor can be used to view the status of that link. The Status tab (shown in Figure 5-9) displays information about each RAS connection, including device statistics, transfer statistics, and error statistics.

The Summary tab lists the active and inactive devices as well as the connection duration. The Preferences tab allows you to specify which events will cause system beeps and how the DUN Monitor should be displayed. Many users find the system beeps annoying, so you will probably want to turn them off.

RESTARTABLE FILE COPY

NT RAS automatically retransmits files whose transfers become interrupted by a connection failure. This retransmission feature applies only to file transmissions initiated using My Computer, Windows NT Explorer, or Network Neighborhood.

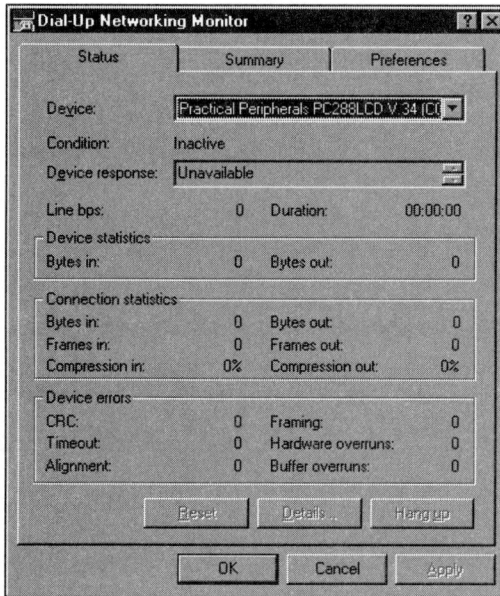

Figure 5-9   Status tab of the Dial-Up Networking Monitor dialog box

X.25 SUPPORT

To configure X.25 support, use the X.25 tab of the Edit Phonebook Entry dialog box. X.25 networks can be used to provide network communications through asynchronous packet assemblers/dissemblers (PADs, which are special X.25 connection hardware) or direct connections. X.25 connections support all standard features of RAS, except for callback. The configuration settings are explained in Table 5-1.

Table 5-1   Edit Phonebook Entry dialog box tabs

Tab	Description
Network	Used to select the X.25 network provider or PAD type
Address	Used to define the X.25 address
User data	Typically left blank, but used if additional information is required for logon
Facilities	Typically left blank, but used to define additional connection parameters, such as reverse charging

TERMINALS AND SCRIPTS

If your ISP requires more information than a simple name and password, you must use either a terminal window or a logon script to establish a connection. (You can select such a terminal window or a logon script via the Script tab of the Edit Phonebook Entry dialog box.) A terminal window is a plain-text, character-only interface with a remote system (that is, a dial-up server, typically a Unix server at an ISP, similar to Telnet). In this type of connection, your keystrokes are delivered to the remote system as if you were physically present at that system. Although a terminal window is useful for troubleshooting or gaining access to shell accounts, it requires you to type in the same connection information each time you want to establish a RAS connection.

A logon script can automate this process for you. Windows NT's RAS comes with several predefined logon script files that you can edit to satisfy your ISP's specific demands. To edit a logon script, open the Edit Phonebook Entry dialog box, click the Script tab, click the drop-down list, select the script you want to edit, then click OK. Scripts are stored in the \WINNT\System32\Ras\ directory, and typically have the extension .INF or .SCP. Details about how to edit and customize a predefined script are included in the script itself.

ROUTING AND REMOTE ACCESS SERVICE (RRAS)

Routing and Remote Access Service (RRAS) is an update to the RAS service for Windows NT Server 4.0. The update adds greater flexibility, extensibility, and reliability to the existing RAS and MPR services and will eventually replace those services. Some important features of RRAS are as follows:

- A unified and integrated service for routing and remote access
- The ability to provide 256 simultaneous remote access connections, 48 demand dial interfaces, and 16 LAN interfaces
- A full set of routing protocols for IP and IPX, including RIPv2 for IP and Bay Network's OSPF
- A remotable GUI with command-line operation and scripting support
- APIs for third-party product integration
- Demand-dial routing
- Server-to-server PPTP to provide more secure VPNs
- Support for Remote Authentication Dial-In User Service (RADIUS) clients
- Router configuration load and save capability
- Packet filtering and integration with Proxy Server 2.0

RRAS is available for free to owners of Windows NT Server 4.0. For more information, visit Microsoft's Web site at *http://www.microsoft.com/communications/routing&ras.htm*.

CHAPTER SUMMARY

- Windows NT's Remote Access Service (RAS) is used to connect remote or mobile workers with the central office network. By applying RAS, the extent and reach of your network can expand beyond the walls of your office. Traveling or telecommuting users can connect to the office LAN via direct secure dial-up connections or secure channels over the Internet. RAS is NT's primary means of interacting with other networks and computers outside its immediate network media connections.

- RAS transforms standard communication links into network connections. In other words, it uses modems (and similar communication devices) and standard telephone lines (and other communication line types) just as if they were network interface cards. In fact, once a RAS session is established, the operating system cannot differentiate between a NIC connection and a RAS connection to the same network. Everything that a direct network-connected client can do, perform, and access, a RAS-connected client can also do, perform, and access. The only difference between a NIC and a RAS connection is that a NIC connection is much faster.

- Windows NT Server 4.0's RAS supports three communication or connection media types right out of the box—PSTN, ISDN, and X.25. These options give you the versatility to meet both your current needs and your future needs.

- RAS supports two types of protocols—transport (or LAN) protocols and connection (or WAN) protocols. One LAN protocol and one WAN protocol are required to establish a RAS connection over any type of communication media link. The WAN protocol creates the pathway between the two communication devices. The LAN protocol carries the network communications over that pathway just as if the link was an ordinary segment of network cable.

- RAS supports the three standard or default LAN protocols of Windows NT Server 4.0—NetBEUI, TCP/IP, and IPX/SPX. It does not support DLC or AppleTalk. Clients connecting to Windows NT over RAS can use any of these protocols to perform network communications.

- In addition, RAS supports two main WAN or connection protocols (PPP and SLIP) plus several varieties of PPP (such as PPTP and MPPP). WAN protocols establish the communications pathway between two remote systems, over either standard communication lines (PSTN, ISDN, X.25) or the Internet.

- The current RAS and Internet connection protocol standard is Point-to-Point Protocol (PPP). Microsoft encourages users to employ this protocol for all RAS connections so as to maximize their compatibility with both current and planned client/server hardware and software. Microsoft's implementation of PPP via RAS enables you to connect to or host connections from any other PPP-compliant system.

- Point-to-Point Tunneling Protocol (PPTP) is a variation of PPP that facilitates the establishment of a secure network communications link between a client and server over the Internet. Basically, PPTP creates a RAS pathway or pipeline over the Internet

5

and "tunnels" the LAN protocol (NetBEUI, IPX/SPX, or TCP/IP). All communications of PPTP are fully encrypted, making PPTP communications more secure than those carried on local network media segments. Companies can use PPTP to create virtual private networks (VPNs) simply by harnessing the inexpensive connections often already in use by their networks.

- PPP Multilink protocol is another variation of PPP that is supported by Windows NT Server 4.0. It offers the capability of aggregating two or more physical connections into a single logical pathway. As many as 32 PSTN, ISDN, or X.25 connections can be combined into a single, larger pipeline. All of the connections combined using Multilink must be of the same type.

- For clients that do not support PPP, the proprietary Microsoft RAS Protocol (also known as Asynchronous NetBEUI) can be used. For example, Windows NT version 3.1, Windows for Workgroups, MS-DOS, and LAN Manager clients can work with this connection protocol. Once a communication link has been established, the RAS server acts as a gateway to provide network access via LAN protocols (NetBEUI, TCP/IP, or IPX/SPX).

- NetBIOS Gateway is another backward-compatible connection protocol that older operating systems can use to establish a RAS link. Client computers running older versions of Windows NT, Windows for Workgroups, and LAN Manager, for example, can use this protocol. The RAS server translates communications between the client and the TCP/IP or IPX/SPX network resources as necessary. In this way, the connection method grants clients access to network-hosted resources without requiring them to host TCP/IP or IPX/SPX protocols.

- Serial Line Internet Protocol (SLIP) was an early communication protocol developed to enable TCP/IP communications over dial-up links. Although it has since been replaced by PPP on most systems, Windows NT Server 4.0 supports SLIP to a small extent. This protocol can be used only when dialing into a Unix system as a client. In other words, SLIP cannot accept inbound calls on a Windows NT Server 4.0 RAS server. Some disadvantages of SLIP are that it does not support dynamic addressing (DHCP), it supports only TCP/IP (not IPX/SPX or NetBEUI), and it does not provide encryption.

- Name resolution over RAS does not differ from name resolution on standard networks. A RAS server can access Windows NT's four standard methods for name resolution—Windows Internet Naming Service (WINS), broadcast name resolution, Domain Naming Service (DNS), and HOSTS and LMHOSTS files. All operations performed on the RAS server use these four methods to resolve names and addresses.

- The installation of RAS requires some preparation. All LAN protocols to be supported over RAS links (TCP/IP, IPX/SPX, and/or NetBEUI) must be installed and configured. It is also necessary to have at least one communication device (modem, ISDN adapter card, or X.25 adapter card) physically installed, although driver installation is not strictly necessary. If you do not install these drivers before launching RAS installation, you will be prompted during RAS installation to install the drivers for the communication device.

- The encryption settings (located at the bottom of the Network Configuration dialog box) define the level of encryption Windows NT RAS uses to authenticate users. Three selections are available (the same selections available through Dial-Up Networking Phonebook for outbound connections): accept any authentication, including clear text; accept only encrypted authentication; and accept only Microsoft-encrypted authentication.

- Windows NT RAS is supported by the RAS Telephony API (TAPI). This application programming interface provides a uniform method for applications, communication devices, and communication media types to work together to provide a RAS solution. In other words, the underlying structure enables Windows NT to dial out and receive calls over communication lines. TAPI was developed to facilitate integration of third-party products into Windows NT, especially those serving areas where Microsoft currently has no interest in development (such as PBX and other telephone control systems). TAPI can control nearly all modern telephone systems and communication devices (when the proper drivers are installed), enabling a computer to automate the process of using and interacting over the communication media. Thus TAPI gives a computer seamless access to public communication systems.

5

- Dial-Up Networking (DUN) is the outbound call initiation portion of RAS. It allows you to use a computer running Windows NT as a client to other dial-up servers. DUN operates by maintaining phonebook entries, which detail the settings and connection features required to establish a communications link with a remote system. These entries can be used to connect to nearly any kind of dial-up system. DUN can also control how a call is placed (a feature known as dialing properties).

- An additional level of security can be established by using the RAS callback feature. With this option, when a client dials into a server, that server hangs up the connection and then calls the client back. Callback security is enabled on a per-user basis in the same location where dial-up access is granted (through either Remote Access Admin or the Dialing button of a user account's Properties dialog box from User Manager for Domains).

- Other features of RAS include AutoDial, RAS logging, null-modem cable, single common protocol, DUN Monitor, and restartable file copy.

- If your ISP requires more information or command selection than a simple name and password, you will need either a terminal window or a logon script to establish a connection. You can select either of these options on the Script tab of the Edit Phonebook Entry dialog box. A terminal window is a plain-text, character interface with a remote system (similar to Telnet); it delivers your keystrokes to the remote system as if you were physically present at that system. A terminal window is useful for troubleshooting or gaining access to shell accounts, but having to type in the same connection information each time you want to make a RAS connection is time-consuming. A logon script can automate this process for you.

- Routing and Remote Access Service (RRAS) is an update to the RAS service for Windows NT Server 4.0. It adds greater flexibility, extensibility, and reliability to the existing RAS and MPR services and will eventually replace these services.

KEY TERMS

- **Asynchronous NetBEUI (Microsoft RAS Protocol)** — A protocol that enables clients that do not support PPP to establish communications with Windows NT.

- **AutoDial** — A feature of RAS that enables the system to automatically reconnect to remote systems to retrieve previously accessed resources.

- **Callback** — A feature of RAS in which the server disconnects clients and then calls them back to establish a communications link.

- **Dial-Up Networking (DUN)** — The outbound call initiation interface of RAS.

- **Integrated Services Digital Network (ISDN)** — A digital subscriber line that can be used for data or voice communications. When used for data, it can offer transmission rates as high as 128 Kb per second.

- **ISDN adapter card (ISDN modem)** — A communication device used to connect a computer to an ISDN line. Similar to but not the same as a modem.

- **modem (modulator/demodulator)** — A communications device that translates digital computer signals into analog signals for transmission over standard telephone lines.

- **NetBIOS Gateway** — A RAS service that provides access to resources for NetBIOS clients even though NetBIOS is not routable.

- **phonebook entry** — A collection of settings that define the parameters for establishing a RAS connection with a specific server or system.

- **Point-to-Point Protocol (PPP)** — The WAN protocol commonly used to establish network communication pathways over communication links.

- **Point-to-Point Tunneling Protocol (PPTP)** — A version of PPP that can establish secure communication pathways over the Internet.

- **PPP Multilink protocol** — A version of PPP that enables multiple physical connections to be aggregated into a single, larger communication pipeline.

- **PSTN (Public Switch Telephone Networks)** — Standard telephone lines, sometimes called POTS (Plain Old Telephone Service).

- **Remote Access Admin (RAA)** — The administration utility used to manage and observe the activity of RAS.

- **Remote Access Service (RAS)** — The service that adds remote network communication functionality to Windows NT.

- **Routing and Remote Access Service (RRAS)** — An update to Windows NT that combines routing and RAS into a single service, thus providing improved performance, security, and features.

- **Serial Line Internet Protocol (SLIP)** — An early protocol developed to establish communications over telephone lines; it has since been superceded by PPP.

- **Telephony application programming interface (TAPI)** — A standard interface between software, hardware, and communication media.

- **X.25** — A standard that defines packet-switching networks.

REVIEW QUESTIONS

1. If you do not have control over the operating system, protocol, methods of dial-up, or location of any of the remote clients that require access to your network via a RAS server, what is the highest level of security you can enforce without preventing a client from gaining access?

   a. allow any authentication, including clear text

   b. callback at a specified number

   c. Microsoft encrypted authentication

   d. require encrypted authentication

2. Which of the following statements are true for PPP but not true for SLIP? (Choose all that apply.)

   a. supports TCP/IP

   b. supports encrypted passwords

   c. supports dynamic address assignments

   d. can be used to connect to Unix systems

3. Which service is used to assign dial-up clients' IP addresses and other specific settings?

   a. WINS

   b. DNS

   c. DHCP

   d. RRAS

4. You can grant users permission to dial into a Windows NT RAS server through which utility? (Choose all that apply.)

   a. Modems applet

   b. User Manager for Domains

   c. Server Manager

   d. Remote Access Admin

5. A null-modem cable can be used for which of the following purposes? (Choose all that apply.)

   a. connect two computers

   b. route IPX

   c. maintain a PPTP link

   d. impersonate a RAS dial-up client

6. An ISDN line, three modem connections, and an X.25 link can all be aggregated into a single communications pipeline with PPP Multilink. True or False?

7. Which protocol is supported by Windows NT only when used to dial out to remote, non–Windows NT systems?

   a. PPP

   b. DLC

   c. NetBEUI

   d. SLIP

8. Which of the following methods of resolving domain or host names to IP addresses does Windows NT support for RAS clients? (Choose all that apply.)

   a. WINS

   b. DNS

   c. HOSTS file

   d. LMHOSTS file

9. Which LAN protocols can be used over RAS connections? (Choose all that apply.)

   a. NetBEUI

   b. AppleTalk

   c. IPX/SPX

   d. TCP/IP

10. Which level of RAS security also offers the option to encrypt all data as well as the authentication process?

    a. allow any authentication, including clear text

    b. call back at a specified number

    c. Microsoft encrypted authentication

    d. require encrypted authentication

11. Which callback setting actually offers an increase in security?

    a. disabled

    b. set by caller

    c. preset to

    d. all of the above

12. Which feature of Windows NT RAS allows traveling users to establish secure network connections over the Internet?

    a. PPTP

    b. SLIP

    c. AutoDial

    d. NetBIOS Gateway

13. Your RAS server has all three LAN protocols installed (TCP/IP, IPX/SPX, and NetBEUI), and a RAS client has only TCP/IP and NetBEUI installed. The client has NetBEUI bound at a higher priority on the dial-up adapter than TCP/IP. When a RAS connection is established, which LAN protocol will be used?

   a. TCP/IP

   b. IPX/SPX

   c. NetBEUI

   d. all of the above

14. You are working from home using your notebook computer. Before lunch, you read a Word document that resided on the file server at the office LAN. You hang up your connection and go to lunch. After lunch, you decide to make corrections to the document, so you launch Word and select the document name from the "last used" list in the File menu. What happens?

   a. You are refused access because the file does not reside locally.

   b. A copy of the document is pulled from the dial-up adapter's memory cache.

   c. AutoDial reconnects and retrieves the document.

   d. A document with the closest name on your local hard drive is opened.

15. Where can you find information about RAS devices that will be useful for troubleshooting? (Choose all that apply.)

   a. Devices applet

   b. device.log

   c. Windows NT Diagnostics

   d. modemlog.txt

16. A RAS connection between a Windows NT Workstation client and a Windows NT Server host grants the client the same ability to interact with the network as any other normally attached client. True or False?

17. Which encryption schemes or methods does RAS use for authentication? (Choose all that apply.)

   a. PAP

   b. MS-CHAP

   c. SPAP

   d. DES

18. Which media can RAS use to establish network links? (Choose all that apply.)

   a. ISDN

   b. X.25

   c. semaphore

   d. PSTN

19. Which LAN protocol for inbound RAS clients requires the least amount of configuration?

    a. TCP/IP

    b. IPX/SPX

    c. NetBEUI

20. When a TCP/IP RAS client connects, which configuration setting is always set to match that of the host RAS server?

    a. IP address

    b. subnet mask

    c. DNS server

    d. WINS server

21. If your network does not host dynamic name resolution, where should the HOSTS and LMHOSTS files be located to maximize performance for RAS client name resolution?

    a. network PDC

    b. RAS server

    c. network BDC

    d. RAS client

22. Dialing properties can be used to define and set which RAS connection-related parameters? (Choose all that apply.)

    a. credit card calls

    b. access to outside lines

    c. connection speed

    d. Multilink

23. Where are X.25 settings configured?

    a. the X.25 tab of a phonebook entry

    b. the X.25 tab of the Dialing Properties dialog box

    c. the X.25 PAD applet

    d. the X.25 command on the Devices menu of Remote Access Admin

24. Which service or feature of RAS enables clients to access TCP/IP or IPX/SPX network resources without having either of these protocols installed?

    a. Asynchronous NetBEUI

    b. DLC

    c. SLIP

    d. NetBIOS Gateway

25. For a RAS client to use PPTP to connect to a properly configured Windows NT server, two DUN phonebook entries are required. True or False?

HANDS-ON PROJECTS

For some or all of these projects you will need a Windows NT 4.0 server with NetBEUI installed.

PROJECT 5-1

In this project you will install a modem to be used by RAS. You do not need a modem physically attached to the computer.

1. Click the **Start button**, point to **Settings**, then click **Control Panel**.
2. Double-click the **Modems icon**. The Modems Properties dialog box opens.
3. Check the **"Do not detect my modem, I'll select it from a list" check box**, then click **Next**.
4. In the Manufacturers list box, select **Standard Modem Types**.
5. In the Models list box, select **Standard 28800 bps modem**, then click **Next**. The next page of the Install New Modem dialog box opens.
6. Select a free COM port, then click **Next**.
7. Click **Finish** to complete the modem installation.
8. If this modem is the first one installed on this computer, you will be prompted for dialing properties information. You need to provide only your area code. Click **OK** to close the Dialing Properties dialog box and return to the Modems Properties applet.
9. The new modem should appear in the list of installed devices on the Modem Properties dialog box.
10. Click **Close** to close the Modem Properties dialog box.

PROJECT 5-2

In this project, you will install RAS. This project requires a modem to be preinstalled. The modem does not need to be physically present; a fictitious modem as installed in Project 5-1 will suffice. It also requires that NetBEUI be present.

1. Click the **Start button**, point to **Settings**, click **Control Panel**, then double-click the **Network icon**. The Network dialog box opens.
2. Click the **Services tab**, then click **Add**. The Select Network Service dialog box opens.
3. In the Network Service list, click **Remote Access Service**, then click **OK**. The Windows NT Setup dialog box opens.
4. Type the correct path for the Windows NT installation files. (These files are usually located on the I386 directory on the installation CD-ROM.)

5. Click **Continue**. The Add RAS Device dialog box opens, as shown in Figure 5-10.

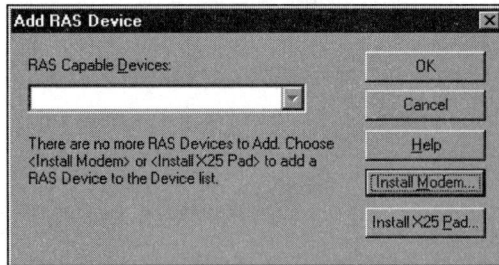

Figure 5-10   Add RAS Device dialog box

6. In the RAS Capable Devices list, select the modem or port over which you wish to enable RAS access, then click **OK**. The Remote Access Setup dialog box opens.

7. Verify that the modem or port you selected appears in the Port list.

8. Select a port or modem, then click **Configure**. The Configure Port Usage dialog box opens, as shown in Figure 5-11.

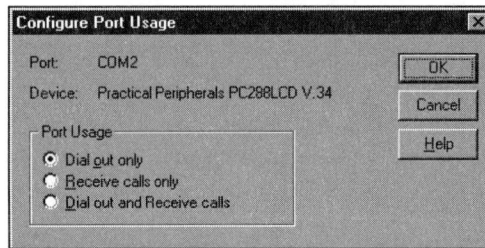

Figure 5-11   Configure Port Usage dialog box

9. Click the **Dial out and Receive calls option button**, then click **OK**. You will return to the Remote Access Setup dialog box. Do not close or exit the Remote Access Setup dialog box; you will need to use it in the next project.

PROJECT 5-3

Having installed RAS in the previous project, you are now ready to configure the network protocols. In this project, you will configure two types of protocols: the protocols used by this server when making outbound calls, and the protocols used by inbound clients when calling this server.

1. Verify that the Remote Access Setup dialog box is open, then click **Network**. The Network Configuration dialog box opens, as shown in Figure 5-12.

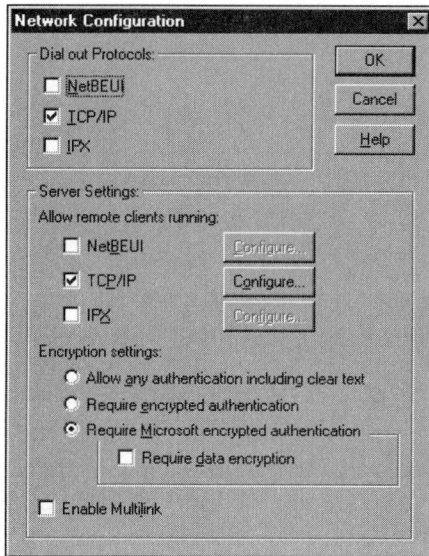

Figure 5-12   Network Configuration dialog box

2. Enable NetBEUI as an outbound protocol by checking its check box under the Dial out Protocols heading.

3. Enable NetBEUI as an inbound protocol by checking its check box under the Server Protocols heading. Disable all other protocols.

4. Click the **Configure button** beside NetBEUI, under Server Protocols. The RAS Server NetBEUI Configuration dialog box opens, as shown in Figure 5-13.

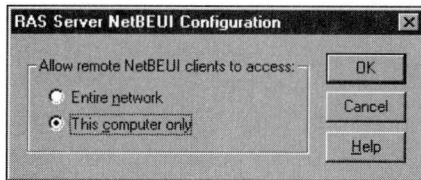

Figure 5-13   RAS Server NetBEUI Configuration dialog box

5. Click the **Entire network option button**, then click **OK**. You return to the Network Configuration dialog box.

6. Click **OK** to return to the Remote Access Setup dialog box.

7. Click **Continue** to close the Remote Access Setup dialog box.

8. Click **Close** to close the Network applet. When prompted, click Yes to restart the computer.

PROJECT 5-4

In this project you will create a DUN phonebook entry. You will start by opening Dial-up Networking, and then define the specifics for a DUN phonebook entry.

1. Click the **Start button**, point to **Programs**, point to **Accessories**, then click **Dial-Up Networking**.

2. If this occasion is the first time you have accessed DUN, you will be prompted for the Windows NT installation CD-ROM. Place it in the CD-ROM drive, then type the correct path for the Windows NT installation files. (These files are usually located on the I386 directory on the installation CD.) Click **OK** to allow the wizard to install the DUN files.

3. If this session is the first time you have accessed DUN, a message will appear indicating that the phonebook is empty. Click **OK** to open the New Phonebook Entry Wizard (shown in Figure 5-14), and skip to Step 5.

4. If this session is not the first time you have accessed DUN, the DUN Dialog box will appear. Click the **New button**. The New Phonebook Entry Wizard opens, as shown in Figure 5-14.

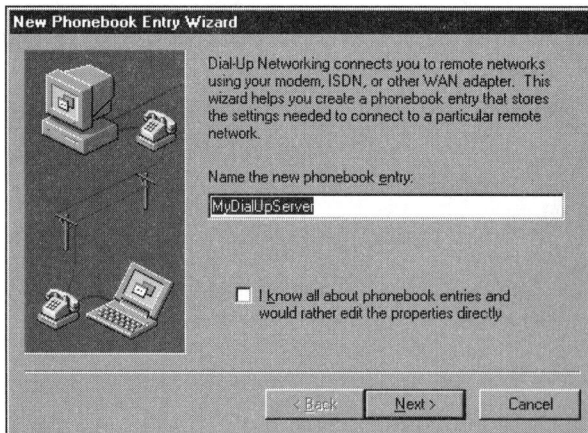

Figure 5-14   New Phonebook Entry Wizard

5. In the Name the new phonebook entry: text box, type **RAS-Test**, then click **Next**. The Server dialog box opens, as shown in Figure 5-15.

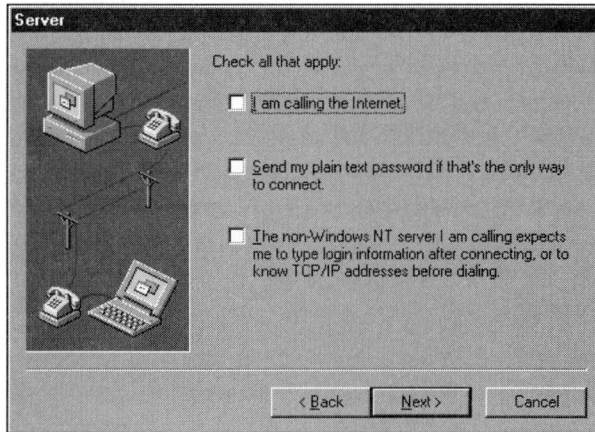

Figure 5-15   Server dialog box

6. Select all of the check boxes in the Server dialog box, then click **Next**. If only a single modem is installed on this computer, the Phone Number dialog box opens (as shown in Figure 5-16) and you can skip to Step 8. If more than one modem is installed, the Modem or Adapter dialog box opens.

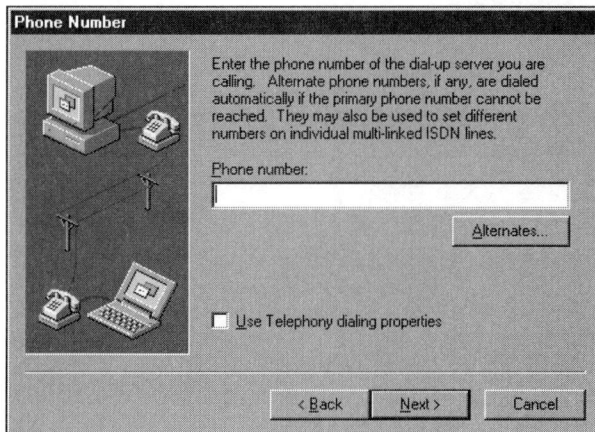

Figure 5-16   Phone Number dialog box

7. In the Modem or Adapter dialog box, select a modem for this entry, then click **Next** to open the Phone Number dialog box.

8. In the Phone number text box of the Phone Number dialog box, type the phone number of the remote server, then click **Next**. The Serial Line Protocol dialog box opens, as shown in Figure 5-17.

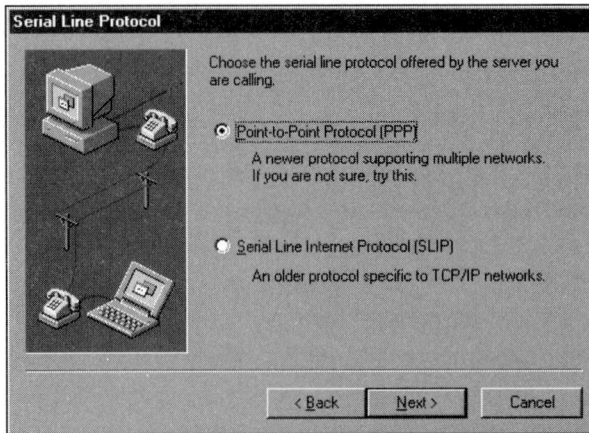

Figure 5-17   Serial Line Protocol dialog box

> 9. Select **PPP**, then click **Next**. The Login Script dialog box opens, as shown in Figure 5-18.

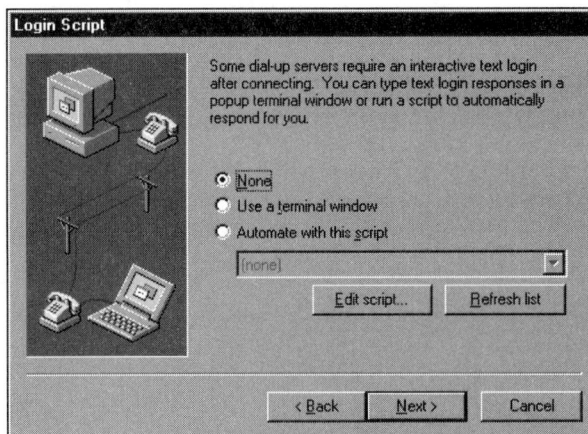

Figure 5-18   Login Script dialog box

> 10. Verify that the None option button is selected and that the other two option buttons (Use a terminal window and Automate with this script) are *not* selected; then click **Next**. The IP Address dialog box opens, as shown in Figure 5-19.

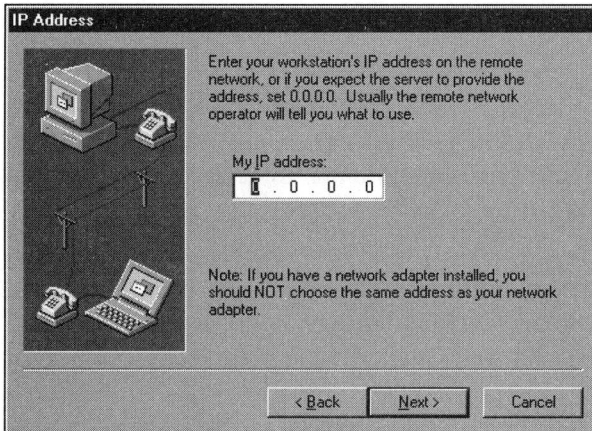

Figure 5-19   IP Address dialog box

11. Verify that the IP address is set to 0.0.0.0. This choice will ensure that the computer will be assigned an IP address when you connect to the dial-up server.

12. Click **Next**. The Name Server Addresses dialog box opens, as shown in Figure 5-20.

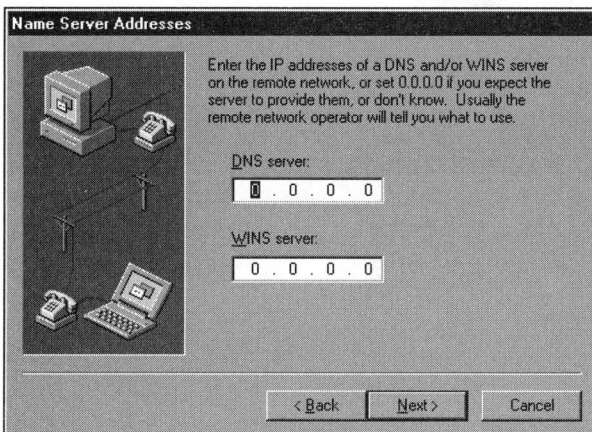

Figure 5-20   Name Server Addresses dialog box

13. If you know them, define the DNS and WINS server IP addresses; otherwise, leave them as 0.0.0.0. This choice will allow the dial-up server to define these IP addresses for your computer.

14. Click **Next**, then click **Finish** to complete the phonebook entry. You will return to the Dial-Up Networking dialog box.

15. Click the **Phonebook entry to dial list arrow** and verify that the new phonebook entry, named RAS-Test, appears in the list of available phonebook entries.

16. Click **Close** to exit DUN.

PROJECT 5-5

In this project, you will define the dialing properties for a computer. To complete this project, you need to have a modem installed on this computer (as described in Project 5-1). Dialing Properties are stored as My Locations. A My Location is simply the stored collection of settings used to dial DUN entries.

1. Click the **Start button**, point to **Settings**, click **Control Panel**, then double-click the **Modems icon**. The Modems applet dialog box opens.

2. Click **Dialing Properties**. The My Locations tab of the Dialing Properties dialog box opens, as shown in Figure 5-21.

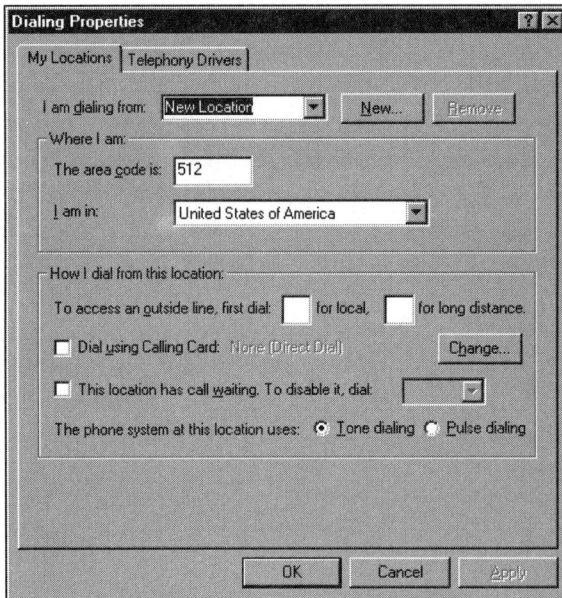

Figure 5-21 My Locations tab of the Dialing Properties dialog box

3. Click **New**. A message box appears, indicating that a new location was created.

4. Click **OK** to close this message box. Notice that the text box beside "I am dialing from" now has a name of New Location. If another location already had this name, the name field will have a number in parenthesis behind this name.

5. In the text box beside "I am dialing from," type **Traveling**.

6. In the The area code is: text box, type **714**.

7. In the To access an outside line, first dial: text box, type **9**.

8. In the For long distance text box, type **91010811**.

9. Check the **Dial using Calling Card check box** to enable calling card use.

10. Click **Change**. The Change Calling Card dialog box opens.

11. Click the **Calling Card to use list arrow**, then select your calling card.

12. In the Calling Card Number text box, type your **calling card number**, then click **OK**. You will return to the Dialing Properties dialog box.

13. Select the **This location has call waiting option**. To disable it, select the Dial checkbox, then select **★70** in the drop-down list.

14. Click **OK** to save this new My Location.

15. Close the Modem applet, and then close the Control Panel.

5

CASE PROJECTS

1. You have recently opened three new branch offices in Austin, San Antonio, and Houston. Your central office in Dallas houses the organization's LAN, where all sales and production information must be stored. Write a short report (four to five paragraphs) explaining how to enable the branch offices to connect to the Dallas network without incurring long-distance charges.

2. You don't have a network in your office, but you have two Windows NT computers, neither of which has a modem. You have a 10 MB file that you need to move from one computer to the other. Write a short report (four to five paragraphs) describing the least expensive and simplest way to accomplish this task.

3. To save on office space, you allow several users to telecommute from their homes. You want to provide security so that only those designated telecommuters can gain access to the office network over RAS. Write a short report (four to five paragraphs) describing your options.

4. Your office network is using a single modem connection to the Internet. By using a shareware proxy software, all 10 users can access the Web, FTP, and e-mail. Performance over this single link, however, is very poor. Write a short report (four to five paragraphs) explaining how you can improve bandwidth with the least expense.

5. One traveling sales representative needs access to specific product documentation while on the road. Because these files are updated daily, she must dial into the office network to download the new versions. You have become concerned about security and think someone other than this sales representative has been dialing into the network. Write a short report (four to five paragraphs) explaining how you can increase security but still enable the traveling staff member to make RAS connections.

CONFIGURING AND PROTECTING HARD DISKS

In this chapter, you will learn how data redundancy, reliability, and recoverability allow you to protect the data stored on hard drives on enterprise networks. **Redundancy** is a state in which a second device stands ready to assume the duties of the primary device in the case of a failure. Redundancy can be implemented for hard drives, network connections, power supplies, servers, and almost any other network or server component. It allows you to remove points of failure in the network, thereby moving the network closer to the ideal of 100% availability.

AFTER READING THIS CHAPTER AND COMPLETING THE EXERCISES YOU WILL BE ABLE TO:

- Explain the implications of server failure in different environments
- Describe the various SCSI technologies
- Configure disk volumes
- Make a system fault-tolerant
- Back up enterprise servers
- Explain the importance of having an uninterruptable power supply

SERVER FAILURE IN DIFFERENT ENVIRONMENTS

As long as computer parts move, components will wear out, causing part of the network to fail. As an enterprise network engineer, you are charged with predicting and, when possible, preventing server failure; you must also revive, repair, and restore systems that do fail. In addition, you need to configure servers so that, even when a server fails, the end user does not notice it.

The most common causes of server failure are as follows:

- **Memory Errors** — an error in memory can produce a variety of negative results. When memory fails, values compute incorrectly, DLLs loaded into memory may become corrupt and act unpredictably, and data can be lost.

- **Hard Disk Failures** — a hard disk failure can cause loss of data on a much larger scale than that produced by memory errors. The loss of a critical drive can also make the operating system unusable or inaccessible.

- **System Hangs** — incompatible hardware and drivers can cause the system to lock up. In such a case, it is not possible to access the system to correct the problem.

- **Power Supply Problems** — if a power supply failure occurs, you will not be able to use your server.

> The predicted average time between installation of hardware and its failure is referred to as the device's **mean time between failures.** Many server hard drives are sold with a certification of this measurement. Some servers provide online monitoring tools that actually warn administrators that a disk may be ailing before a failure occurs. By measuring live drive parameters (such as temperature, disk rotation speed, and number of data access errors per unit of time), these can predict a failure before it happens. Failed drives are often covered under pre-failure warranties and can be replaced before they fail.

The importance attached to certain types of data varies from one business to the next. Some data, while critical, does not need to be available all of the time; what matters is that the business must never lose this information. In other situations, both the integrity and the availability of the data are critical. Table 6-1 classifies networks into three different types, based on the importance of data within the organization.

Table 6-1   The Importance of Data in Various Networks

Network Type	Description	Relevant Businesses
Data-Critical	Stores information that cannot be deleted or destroyed for any reason. Requires regular backups. These backups are often stored off-site for added protection. In some cases, the network manager will back up the data to read-only media, such as a CD-ROM or other optical storage, to ensure that the data are never overwritten.	Tax document storage company, Department of Motor Vehicles, Department of Corrections, medical records
High-Availability	Provides a high percentage of resource availability. Servers need to recover from faults quickly, either by rebooting or by continuing to operate in a slightly degraded mode until system maintenance can be performed. Not entirely fault-tolerant. Most enterprise PC servers fall into this category.	Businesses where immediate access to data by end users is top priority, such as telephone call-centers and customer support teams; when servers are unavailable, business can still be conducted, but is hampered
Business/Mission-critical	If the system became unavailable, the company would lose revenue, the ability to conduct business, or the respect of the community it serves, or would put lives at risk.	New York Stock Exchange, The GAP (clothing store), air traffic control

6

SCSI TECHNOLOGIES

The **Small Computer System Interface** (**SCSI**) standard was developed so that hard disks would have uniform specifications across the computer industry. Today, hard disks built according to this standard are almost universally used in network servers. SCSI hard disks are easy to install, configure, and upgrade, and they work well with dissimilar SCSI devices when chained together. The SCSI standard has gone though several revisions to reach its current level of performance.

SCSI-1 is an 8-bit I/O bus standard that was developed to attach intelligent controllers to a chain of storage devices. With all SCSI devices on the same bus, control signals could be sent simultaneously to all peripherals on that bus, allowing centralized synchronization of data flow. As is the case in any contention bus architecture, both ends of the cable must be terminated with a resistor to eliminate signal bounce. One device on the bus is the **host bus adapter** (**HBA**), which serves two functions: it controls the flow of data to each device on the bus, and it acts as the interface between the SCSI bus and the rest of the computer. Figure 6-1 illustrates how the host bus acts as both the bus controller, and the interface with the CPU.

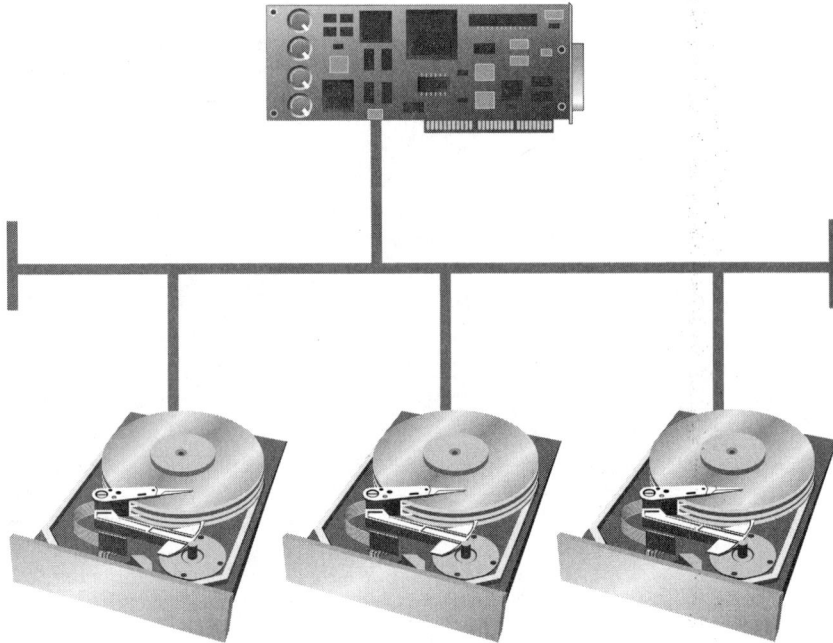

Figure 6-1   Host bus adapter

Because each SCSI disk has its own **internal logic board** that keeps track of cylinders, heads, and sectors, the HBA doesn't have to be concerned with tracking that data. As a result, the same bus can support many dissimilar SCSI devices, including hard disks, CD-ROM drives, tape drives, and DAT drives. When data are required from a SCSI device, the HBA negotiates the details of this data transfer with the drive's local logic board. While it may seem to take a lot of overhead, this negotiation process is actually quite efficient compared with the length of time it takes to read data from a spinning disk. The net result is an increase in performance. Under the SCSI-1 standard, data could be transferred at a maximum speed of 5 MB per second.

Because the SCSI-1 standard was so loosely defined, it did not result in wide-scale device interoperability. Instead, many device manufacturers sold only incompatible, proprietary hard disks, which ultimately proved unacceptable to consumers. SCSI-2, a more narrowly defined standard, was developed to eliminate many of these compatibility problems. Under the new standard, transfer rates remained the same, but interoperability was ensured.

A short time later, the revised Fast-SCSI-2 standard introduced a number of technical advances that doubled the speed of data transfer to 10 MB per second. Later, the Fast-Wide SCSI-2 standard followed the same parameters as SCSI-2, but widened the parallel bus to 16 bits, effectively doubling the transfer rate to 20 MB per second. This standard was stable and effective. Today, most mainstream servers that are two or more years old have Fast-Wide SCSI-2 disks.

One reason that both the Fast-SCSI-2 and Fast-Wide SCSI-2 standards are so popular relates to their interoperability. Because each SCSI device negotiates its own transfer rates during the Command Setup phase, it is perfectly acceptable to have Fast-SCSI-2 and Fast-Wide SCSI-2 devices on the same SCSI bus. Consequently, however, the Fast-Wide SCSI-2 bus, though capable of having as many as 15 SCSI disks connected, will be limited to 8 devices to ensure backward-compatibility with the non-wide variety. Most major server manufacturers, including Compaq, IBM, and Hewlett-Packard, have maintained this standard to protect their customers' investments in their server products.

> Before a standard for Fast-Wide SCSI-2 was released, some vendors referred to their implementations as SCSI-3. This nomenclature can prove confusing, as a true SCSI-3 standard now exists.

6

The definitive SCSI-3 standard, called Ultra-Wide SCSI, doubled the bus speed yet again to 40 MB per second. With a data channel of 32 bits, this standard takes advantage of the PCI buses common in most new Pentium servers. In some new disk array controller (DAC) implementations, Ultra-Wide SCSI nearly approaches the threshold where the transfer of data from the hard drive is no longer the slowest part of the data transfer process. At this point, an I/O bottleneck no longer exists, as data can be gathered from several SCSI drives fast enough keep copper data lines completely active. Once this threshold is reached, the only limitation is the speed with which electrons can travel through the copper lines on the system board. The next major advance in this process is **fiber channel**, which uses fiber-optic cables—instead of copper—to increase the speed and distance over which data can be effectively transferred.

CONFIGURING DISK VOLUMES

A Windows NT **volume** consists of one or more partitions on one or more hard disks that are spanned together as a single formatted entity and can be assigned a single drive letter. As you will see in the following sections, Windows NT Server 4.0 supports both volume sets and stripe sets. Each set has its own advantages and disadvantages, making the two types appropriate for different environments.

JBOD

JBOD (Just a Bunch of Disks) is a slang acronym used by some systems engineers. It refers to a volume configuration in which each hard disk is its own volume and receives its own drive letter. JBOD sets are easy to configure and manipulate. They can be backed up easily, and can isolate the impact of failure to a single volume. In highly unusual situations, it may even be practical to take a drive from a JBOD set and place it into another server to increase the availability of the data during a server failure or upgrade.

JBOD is the required standard on Windows NT workstations. It is not a practical solution in servers because of its inflexibility, lax performance, and fallibility. With each drive serving as its own volume, a single point of failure exists for each volume that could be exploited by a failing system. JBOD sets are not mirrored, and must be regularly backed up to protect against the inevitable disk failure. If the drive does fail, any data changed since the most recent usable backup are lost forever. Thus, JBOD is an unacceptable option in data-critical environments.

One general drawback of JBOD relates to the finite number of drive letters available to Windows NT. Windows NT can address only 26 drive letters (A–Z). Most computers have at least one floppy drive and a CD-ROM drive, which leaves only 24 letters available for assignment to hard drives. Using a JBOD configuration will use up the drive letters faster than other formats.

Another drawback of JBOD sets is that once a drive becomes full, any new data must be stored on another drive letter. This setup can be confusing for end users and sometimes wastes space, as several non-contiguous chunks of free space may exist. For this reason, many administrators choose to create a volume set, as explained in the next section.

CREATING A VOLUME SET

A **volume set** is any group of hard drives configured to act as a single volume. A volume set with a single drive letter can span multiple disks, making use of irregularly sized chunks of free space. If such a set is running out of space, the administrator can easily add another hard drive or partition to it, thereby expanding the volume set without affecting the data it contains. Figure 6-2 depicts a volume set that spans three physical disks.

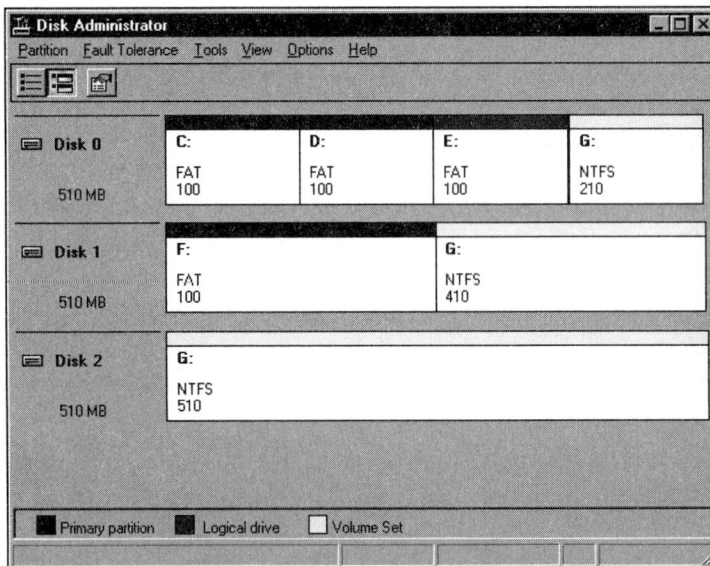

Figure 6-2   Volume set spanning three physical drives

> Because each volume set has its own drive letter and can include up to 32 areas of free space, it is possible to have as many as 25 volume sets, each with a total of 32 areas of free space.

You create a volume set in Windows NT using the **Disk Administrator** utility. (You can also use this utility to create, format and delete partitions, volume sets, stripe sets, mirror sets, and stripe sets with parity.) One benefit to using Disk Administrator to modify your disk configuration is that this utility warns you clearly of the possible consequences of every action you take. Even after you acknowledge a warning, no change you make becomes permanent until you choose the Commit Changes Now option or exit the utility. For example, when you first use Disk Administrator, a dialog box may appear asking if you want to write a signature on Disk 0 so that Disk Administrator can access the drive. You can click "Yes" to write a 32-bit unique identifier signature to the primary partition of the disk. If the disk is later used with a different controller or if its identity changes, Disk Administrator will nevertheless be able to recognize the disk and configure it.

6

Disk Administrator is a powerful utility that can easily wipe out an entire hard disk if used improperly. For this reason, a user must have administrative rights to access Disk Administrator.

To create a volume set:

1. Click **Start**, point to **Programs**, click **Administrative Tools (Common)**, then click **Disk Administrator**. The Disk Administrator window opens, as shown in Figure 6-3.

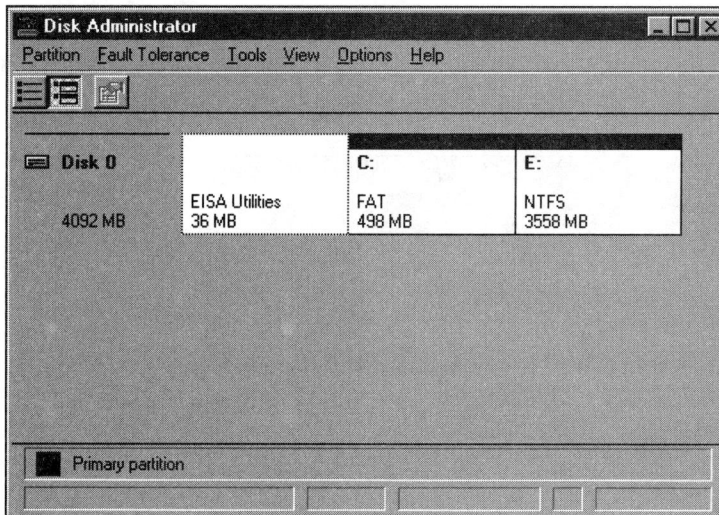

Figure 6-3   Disk Administrator window

2. Click the first area of free space you want to include in your volume set.

3. Hold down the **CTRL key**, then click the other areas of free space you want to include in your volume, one by one.

4. Click **Partition** on the menu bar, then click **Create Volume Set.** The Create Volume Set dialog box opens, allowing you to specify the total size for the volume set. By default, the dialog box displays the maximum amount of space available.

5. Accept the default value, then click **OK** to finish creating the volume set with its own assigned drive letter. Next, you need to save the configuration, and reboot the computer so that the disk subsystem will recognize the new partition. (If you attempted to exit the Disk Administrator before saving changes, Windows NT would prompt you to save changes first.)

6. Click **Yes** when asked if you want to commit your changes.

7. Reboot the computer when you are prompted.

Once you save your changes, Windows NT recommends that you update your Emergency Repair information using the RDISK.EXE utility.

Before you can use the new volume set, you must format it, using either a FAT or NTFS file system.

To format a volume set:

1. Click **Start**, point to **Programs**, click **Administrative Tools (Common)**, then click **Disk Administrator**.

2. Select the new volume set by clicking one of its parts.

3. Click **Tools** on the menu bar, then click **Format.** The Format dialog box appears, with the new volume's drive letter in the title bar. In Figure 6-4, the new drive letter is "G."

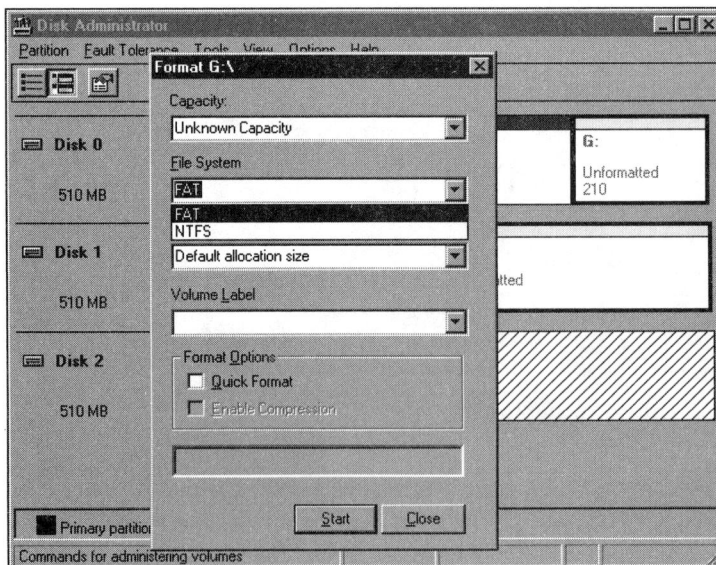

Figure 6-4   Format dialog box

If the Format option on the Tools menu appears gray, you either failed to save the configuration after creating the volume set or did not reboot the computer. Save the configuration, reboot the computer, then begin again with Step 1.

4. Click the **File System list arrow**, then select **NTFS**.

Because they provide data recovery features in the event of system failure, NTFS partitions are usually recommended.

5. Click the **Start button** to begin formatting the new volume set.

Although Windows NT supports both FAT and NTFS volume sets, NTFS is the better choice for several reasons. First, NTFS is more secure than FAT is. Second, you can extend a volume set (as explained in the next section) using other drives without additional formatting or data loss. Finally, because DOS and Windows 95 cannot access a volume set, one of FAT's main advantages (its provisions for dual booting) is not an option with volume sets.

EXTENDING A VOLUME SET

Sooner or later, a volume may begin to run out of space. Assuming you have chosen the NTFS file system, you can extend the volume set to include new areas of free space, without reformatting the volume set. You can continue to extend a volume set until it uses 32 noncontiguous spaces.

If one drive in a volume set fails, you may lose the information stored on all areas of the volume set. For every physical disk you add to your volume set, you increase the risk of losing the entire set and add another potential point of failure.

When you extend an existing NTFS volume set, you do not need to reformat the entire volume. Windows NT will format the newly added space as soon as the computer reboots. All data present on the volume set before the change will remain intact.

To extend an NTFS volume set:

1. Click **Start**, point to **Programs**, click **Administrative Tools (Common)**, then click **Disk Administrator**.

2. Select the first area of free space you want to add to the volume set.

3. Continue selecting additional areas of free space by holding down the **CTRL key** while you click the desired free spaces.

4. Continue holding down the CTRL key while you click the volume set to be expanded. At this point you should have highlighted every section to be added to the volume set, as well as the volume set itself.

5. Click **Partition** on the menu bar, then click **Extend Volume Set**. The Extend Volume Set dialog box opens, allowing you to specify the total expanded size for the volume set. By default, the dialog box displays the maximum amount of space available.

6. Type the desired size, then click **OK**.

7. Save your changes, exit Disk Administrator, then reboot your computer.

STRIPE SETS

A **stripe set** is a volume that spans multiple physical disks, writing data in blocks (or stripes) to each physical disk. A stripe set represents the lowest level of Redundant Array of Inexpensive Disks (RAID), and is also called RAID-0. Stripe sets write to more than one physical disk simultaneously and can improve data retrieval times by a significant margin.

Like a volume set, a stripe set combines from 2 to 32 areas of free space into a single logical drive. Unlike a volume set, however, this type of set writes data across all disks in the set, in 64 KB blocks on each disk. To coordinate this effort, the striped partitions on each disk must be of the same size and must all be created at the same time. Once created, a stripe set cannot be expanded or reduced without backing up the data, deleting, re-creating, and restoring it from backup.

To create a stripe set:

1. Click **Start**, point to **Programs**, click **Administrative Tools (Common)**, then click **Disk Administrator**.

2. Click one area of free space on a hard disk.

3. While holding down the **CTRL key**, click an area of free space on another hard drive.

4. Continue holding down the CTRL key and clicking areas of free space on other hard drives, until you have selected all areas to be included in the stripe set.

5. Click **Partition** on the menu bar, then click **Create Stripe Set**. The Create Stripe Set dialog box opens, allowing you to specify the total size for the stripe set. By default, the dialog box displays the maximum amount of space available.

6. Accept the default, then click **OK** to finish creating the stripe set. Next, you need to save changes to the disk configuration and reboot the computer.

7. Click **Partition** on the menu bar, then click **Commit Changes Now**.

8. When you are prompted to update the emergency repair information, click **OK** and allow the system to reboot. Before you can use the new stripe set, you need to format it.

9. Format the new stripe set by following the same steps you used to format a volume earlier in this chapter.

> Disk Administrator is also used to create and format partitions. This topic lies beyond the scope of this textbook.

DELETING STRIPE SETS OR VOLUME SETS

Because Windows NT volume sets and stripe sets are each accessed as single entities, they cannot be reduced in size. In addition, only volume sets can grow.

To delete a volume or stripe set:

1. Click **Start**, point to **Programs**, click **Administrative Tools (Common)**, then click **Disk Administrator**.

2. Select the volume or stripe set you want to delete.

3. Click **Partition** on the menu bar, then click **Delete**. A prompt appears, informing you that the action is irreversible once committed. Click **Yes** to commit your changes.

SHORTCOMINGS OF VOLUME SETS AND STRIPE SETS

One problem with volume sets and stripe sets in Windows NT is the increased likelihood of a drive error. Each physical drive in a volume or stripe set represents an additional potential point of failure for the whole volume. The failure of a single drive would cause all data from all parts of the volume set to be lost. Even a professional data recovery service may be able to retrieve only a limited amount of information from a failed set. Thus, when using volume sets and stripe sets, it is essential that the system engineer maintain good backups. If a failure were to occur, all server activity would immediately stop, and the server would crash. Such an occurrence can mean costly downtime in business-critical environments, as users must wait while data are restored from backup.

Another limitation of volume sets and stripe sets is their inability to enhance the performance of the most heavily accessed partition, the one that contains the operating system. Because Windows NT must be loaded and running to access a stripe set or volume set, neither the boot partition nor the Windows NT System files can reside on a stripe or volume set. If they did, the operating system could not boot, as the PC would have no software in RAM that would allow access to the set. In the next section, you learn about some hardware solutions that allow striping of the system and boot partitions.

FAULT TOLERANCE

The term **fault tolerance** refers to the ability of a system to respond to hardware failures without losing or corrupting data. Fault tolerance is generally achieved by adding redundant components or error correction mechanisms. As mentioned earlier, *redundancy* refers to the practice of having an extra piece of hardware, such as a hard drive or power supply, that can take over the functioning of a failed part when necessary. **Redundant Array of Independent Disks (RAID)** techniques allow sets of drives to be grouped together as a team to accomplish a single task. They provide the redundancy necessary for data protection and, in some cases, performance advantages. High-availability, business-critical, and mission-critical servers can take advantage of RAID technology in satisfying their specific availability needs.

Several levels of RAID exist, each of which was designed to serve a specific type of need. Those needs include combinations of faster data access on larger volume sets, fault tolerance, and availability. Understanding the various RAID implementations, including their costs, benefits, and drawbacks, help systems engineers determine the most cost-effective servers to purchase.

RAID can be implemented either through software (levels 0, 1, 4, and 5) or as a hardware add-on (all RAID levels). Software-based RAID solutions are less expensive to implement but have certain drawbacks (discussed later in this section). Hardware RAID does not have the same shortcomings but is more expensive to implement. Determining the correct type of RAID to implement is an important task for systems engineers.

RAID-0

RAID-0 uses striping to distribute data across multiple hard disks, with stripes being divided into contiguous pieces or blocks. By allowing data to be accessed on multiple disks simultaneously, striping balances the I/O load across the disks, yielding high-performance data transfers and fast access time. Windows NT supports software RAID-0 in the form of stripe sets. Despite its name, data striping is *not* redundant. The name RAID-0 is somewhat misleading, as it does not render or store any parity or backup information that would provide data redundancy in case of failure. Thus this technique uses less space and processor time than a solution that includes parity. RAID-0 should be used only for the purpose of improving system performance, because if one hard disk in an array fails, all data in the array will be lost. Recovery requires replacing the failed drive and restoring data to all drives from backup.

There can be significant downtime while restoring data from a backup, a situation that would not be acceptable in a business-critical or mission-critical environment. For networks that can afford the operating time lost to restore operations when a disk fails (such as in a high-availability environment), however, RAID-0 represents a higher-performance alternative to JBOD solutions. RAID-0 can be implemented through software or hardware.

The performance enhancement provided by RAID-0 may be adequate to prompt some systems engineers to consider its use in high-availability environments, as long as the stripe set is coupled with another form of data redundancy, such as server clustering. Because data-critical environments place the highest importance on data integrity, a RAID-0 implementation would not be the best choice in these networks due to its high risk of data loss.

RAID-1

The first redundant RAID level, RAID-1 is also known as **mirroring**. In RAID-1, data on one disk are duplicated onto another identical drive, providing a complete "live" backup of all data. If one disk fails, the other disk continues to work, so no interruption in service occurs.

Duplexing takes the redundancy aspects of mirroring a step further by adding a second disk controller. Because the system includes two drives and two controllers, there is no longer a single point of failure. In **disk duplexing**, a separate disk controller is used for each disk in a mirrored set. In the event of either a disk or controller failure, the server will remain available and usable, as the redundant component will take over the responsibilities of the failed component. Windows NT is capable of both disk mirroring and disk duplexing configurations as a part of the operating system.

To create a mirrored or duplexed partition in Windows NT:

1. Click **Start**, point to **Programs**, click **Administrative Tools (Common)**, then click **Disk Administrator**.

2. Hold the **CTRL key** down while you click both the original drive (or partition) and an area of unused space on another hard disk that is at least the same size as the original drive or partition.

3. Click **Fault Tolerance** on the menu bar, then click **Establish Mirror**. Notice that the mirror takes up exactly the same amount of space as the original drive, even if the mirror volume contains more space than actually needed. The rest of the unused space on the mirror is left as free space.

4. Save your changes, then exit Disk Administrator. Restart your computer when prompted.

5. After the server is restarted, the data from the original partition are now duplicated on the new mirrored partition, and any new data written to one partition will be simultaneously written to the other.

One key benefit of a mirror or duplex partition is that, unlike with other levels of RAID, you can use RAID-1 to protect both the boot and the system partitions. Mirroring does not improve performance, however, because even with duplexing, the net I/O request remains the same as that seen with one disk or controller.

Although it represents a proven and simple reliability technique, RAID-1 is more costly to use than higher levels of RAID due to its inclusion of duplicate components. Out of the total possible disk space from all disks combined, RAID-1 leaves only 50% for actual storage of data; the other 50% is reserved for a backup copy of the first half. Thus, if you need to upgrade your server by adding 9 gigabytes of disk space, you must actually purchase 18 gigabytes in a RAID-1 implementation. The greater expense makes RAID-1 a less preferred method of fault tolerance.

RAID-4 AND RAID-5

RAID levels 4 and 5 provide a method of data recovery and correction called parity. You can create stripe sets with parity, so that each stripe has one additional block reserved for data redundancy information. The data redundancy information is a checksum that allows reconstruction of the data in the event of damage. The term **parity** describes an algorithm that is used to regenerate lost stripes of data in case of a disk failure. Parity on a RAID volume is similar to the parity used on error-correcting memory chips. It allows data to be rebuilt on the fly, keeping the server in operation during a disk failure. Until the failed drive is replaced, performance will be degraded, but processing continues.

Windows NT software-based fault tolerance supports only RAID-5. While RAID-4 stores parity information on a single, dedicated parity drive, RAID-5 stripes the parity, along with stored data, across all disks in the stripe set. RAID-5 is also sometimes called striping with distributed parity, or distributed data-guarding. At least three partitions on three physical disks must be used to create a stripe set with parity.

To create a stripe set with parity:

1. Click **Start**, point to **Programs**, click **Administrative Tools (Common)**, then click **Disk Administrator**.

2. Hold the **CTRL key** down while you click three or more areas of unused space, one from each hard drive to be used in the set.

3. Click **Fault Tolerance** on the menu bar, then click **Create Stripe Set with Parity**. The Create Stripe Set with Parity dialog box opens, allowing you to specify the total size for the new partition. By default, the dialog box displays the maximum amount of space available.

4. Click **OK**. The newly created members of the stripe set with parity appear in green in the Disk Administrator window. In Figure 6-5, G:\ is the stripe set with parity.

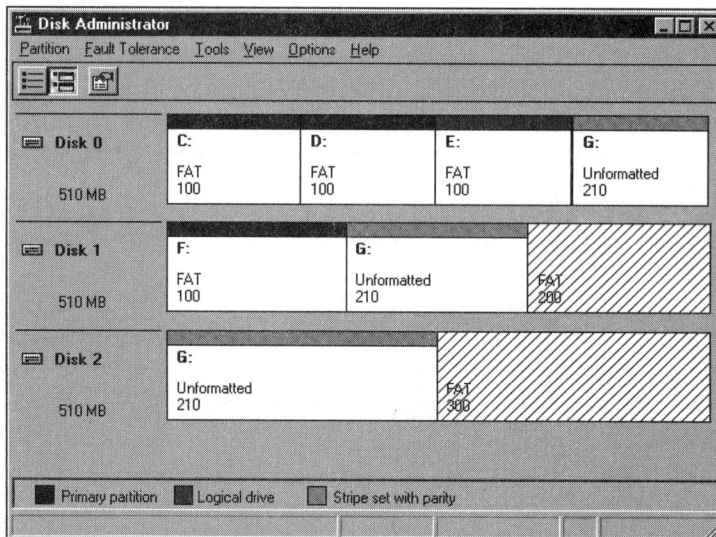

Figure 6-5   New stripe set with parity

5. Click **Partition** on the menu bar, then click **Commit Changes Now**.

6. Click **OK** to restart the computer.

HARDWARE RAID SOLUTIONS

While Windows NT software-based fault tolerance is easy to configure and manage, it can generate a great deal of processor overhead, especially on busy enterprise servers. Adding a RAID controller card can offload the required overhead to a secondary processor that is dedicated to this task. This offloading of the control of the RAID array frees the primary CPU to deal with operating system tasks, making its processing power go farther. The trade-off in this setup is cost.

BACKING UP ENTERPRISE SERVERS

6

Nothing could be more important in a data-critical environment than an effective, reliable server tape backup system. Not only is such a system important for recovery in case of system failures, but tape backups also provide:

- The ability to restore files that are accidentally (or intentionally) deleted by users.
- A "snapshot history" of your data that can be used for tracking activity (illegal or otherwise), or for audit purposes.
- "Clean" versions of files that were corrupted by a virus infection that went undetected for some time.
- Physical separation from the server site, in case of fire or natural disaster.

When planning an effective server backup strategy in an enterprise, you need to make many decisions. Some important backup-related questions are listed in Table 6-2.

Table 6-2   Important Backup Questions

Issue	Questions
Management	Should management of the backup be centralized or localized? If you have several major corporate offices, localized backups reduce the workload of the central server, although this strategy can create management difficulties as it entails additional work and more hardware.
Network Bandwidth	Will you back up over the network or directly at each server? Backing up large amounts of data over the network can dramatically slow network performance.
Time of Day	When should you schedule your backups? Is your network in use all night long? How will server backups affect users?
Type and Cost of Media	What media should you use for your backup? Some backup media, such as DAT and DLT tapes, are fairly inexpensive, but not as reliable as the more expensive optical media.

Windows NT Backup is a simple, effective utility for backing up small LAN servers, but is probably not be the best software choice for an enterprise. Nevertheless, it does provide an effective introduction to backup technology. Figure 6-6 illustrates the Windows NT Backup utility.

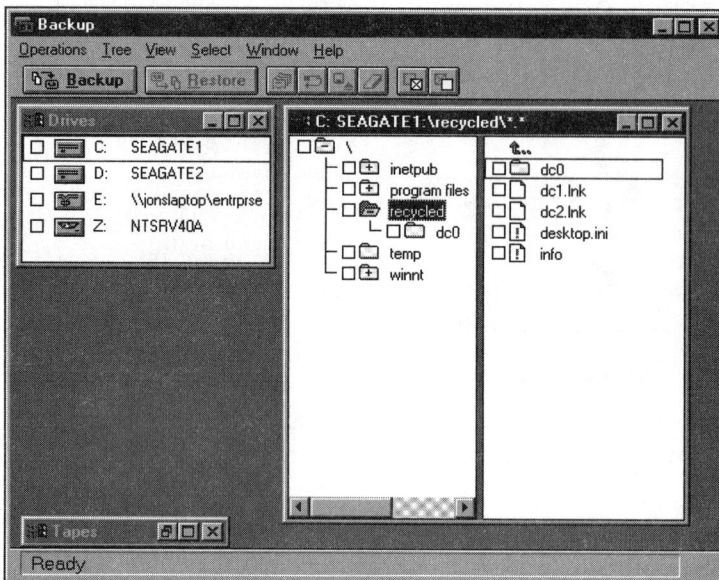

Figure 6-6   Windows NT Backup

Before you can use the Windows NT Backup utility, you must install a tape backup device that is compatible with Windows NT. The first time you start the utility, it will try to locate a tape backup device. Unlike the workstation or Windows 95 backup utility, Windows NT Backup will not allow you to back up to a local hard disk or network drive. The window will display all drives, including network-mapped drives and CD-ROM drives. Entire drives, folders, or individual files can be selected for backup. Data from network drives can be backed up just as easily as local drives, though such backups generate heavy network traffic.

You may need to back up different types of data at different intervals. Files that rarely change (such as shared or clip art files) don't need to be backed up as frequently as, for example, a folder of MS Word documents that contains a department's daily correspondence. Windows NT uses a file attribute, called the **archive bit**, to determine which files to back up and which ones not to back up. When a file is modified, the archive attribute is turned on, indicating that the file has changed since the last backup. Table 6-3 describes the various types of backups undertaken by the Windows NT Backup utility and their use of the archive bit.

Table 6-3   Types of Backups

Backup Type	Description
Full (Normal) Backup	All components selected in the backup window are backed up regardless of the archive attribute. All archive bits are cleared after backup.
Copy Backup	All selected components are backed up regardless of the archive attribute. The archive bit is not changed after backup.
Incremental Backup	All selected components with the archive bit turned on are backed up. The archive bit is cleared after backup.
Differential Backup	All selected components with the archive bit turned on are backed up. The archive bit is not changed after backup.
Daily Backup	All selected components that were modified on the current day, regardless of the archive bit, are backed up. The archive bit is not changed after backup.

UNINTERRUPTIBLE POWER SUPPLIES

Two types of power fluctuations can damage a server: long-term, low-grade fluctuations and short-term, intense fluctuations.

Persistent voltage levels above or below the specified standard can damage the circuitry, resulting in intermittent problems and eventual component failure. **Hotspots** are long-lasting voltage surges. They are rare and are usually caused by utility company failures. **Brownouts** are more common, often characterized by lights dimming for extended periods of time. They can occur when an electrical device nearby drains the common current to low levels. Although many computer power supplies are designed to adapt to abnormal input voltages, continual lows or highs will fatigue and eventually damage the power supply or internal components.

Unexpected changes in voltage, sometimes called **spikes or surges**, can be instantly devastating. Lightning bolt strikes, electrical circuit failures, and even static shocks from an ungrounded fingertip can overload circuits and damage delicate electronic components.

Power conditioning devices are designed to control incoming voltages and protect computer equipment from hotspots, brownouts, and spikes. They come in all shapes and sizes, from the simple surge suppressors commonly used on workstations to heavy-duty, battery-backed **uninterruptible power supplies (UPS)**.

In addition to maintaining full power when AC power fails, most new UPS units will monitor external power carefully to watch for irregular power flow and will absorb spikes without self-destructing. They will recondition power to an acceptable steadiness on the server's end, and even communicate directly with a server to send administrative alerts when a change in power conditions occurs. When planning an enterprise network, it is extremely important to choose a good UPS.

CHAPTER SUMMARY

- Redundancy is a state in which a second device stands ready to assume the duties of the primary device in the case of a failure. It allows you to remove potential points of failure in the network, thereby moving the network closer to the ideal of 100% availability. The most common reasons for server failure—which may damage data—are memory errors, hard disk failures, system hangs, and power supply problems. The importance attached to types of data varies from one business to the next. In data-critical environments, information cannot be deleted or destroyed for any reason. In high-availability environments, a high priority is placed on resource availability. In business/mission-critical environments, server unavailability could result in serious losses.

- The Small Computer System Interface (SCSI) standard was developed so that hard disks would have a uniform presentation across the computer industry. SCSI-1 is an 8-bit I/O bus standard that was developed to attach intelligent controllers to a chain of storage devices. It uses a host bus adapter (HBA), which controls the flow of data to each device on the bus and acts as the interface between the SCSI bus and the rest of the computer. SCSI-2 was developed to eliminate many of the compatibility problems associated with SCSI-1. The Fast-SCSI-2 standard introduced a number of technical advances that doubled the maximum data transfer rate to 10 MB per second. Fast-Wide SCSI-2 followed the same standard as SCSI-2, but widened the parallel bus to 16 bits, effectively doubling the transfer rate yet again to 20 MB per second. Most of today's mainstream servers that are two or more years old have Fast-Wide SCSI-2 disks. The definitive SCSI-3 standard, called Ultra-Wide SCSI, doubled the bus speed again to 40 MB per second.

- A Windows NT volume consists of one or more partitions on one or more hard disks that are spanned together as a single formatted entity and can be assigned a single drive letter. JBOD (Just a Bunch of Disks) is a volume configuration in which each hard disk is its own volume and receives its own drive letter. A volume set is a group of hard drives configured to act as a single volume. After you create a volume set, you must format it, using either a FAT or NTFS file system. You can extend a volume set to include new areas of free space without reformatting it. A stripe set is a volume that spans multiple physical disks, writing data in blocks (or stripes) to each physical disk. Volume sets and stripe sets have their own advantages and disadvantages, making them appropriate for different network situations.

- You can create, format, and delete volumes. To create a volume set in Windows NT, you use the Disk Administrator utility.

- The term "fault tolerance" refers to the ability of a system to respond to hardware failures without losing or corrupting data. Fault tolerance is generally achieved by adding redundant components or error correction mechanisms. Redundant Array of Independent Disks (RAID) techniques allow sets of drives to be grouped together as a team to accomplish a single task. These techniques provide the redundancy necessary for data protection and, in some cases, offer performance advantages. Several levels of RAID exist, each of which was designed to satisfy a specific type of need. RAID can be implemented either through software or hardware. Software-based RAID solutions are less expensive to implement but have certain drawbacks. Hardware RAID does not have the same shortcomings but is more expensive to implement.

- Nothing could be more important in a data-critical environment than an effective, reliable server tape backup system. It permits recovery in case of system failure and provides other advantages as well. When planning a server backup strategy in an enterprise, you must make many decisions regarding backup management, network bandwidth, backup schedules, and type and cost of the backup media. Windows NT Backup utility is a simple, effective utility for backing up small LAN servers, but is probably not the best software choice for an enterprise. It does, however, provide an effective introduction to backup technology.

- Two types of power fluctuations can damage a server. Persistent voltage levels above or below the specified standard can damage the circuitry, resulting in intermittent problems and eventual component failure. Unexpected changes in voltage, sometimes called spikes or surges, can be instantly devastating. Power conditioning devices are designed to control incoming voltages and protect computer equipment from power fluctuations. These devices come in all shapes and sizes, from the simple surge suppressors commonly used on workstations to heavy-duty, battery-backed uninterruptible power supplies (UPS). When planning an enterprise network, it is extremely important to choose a good UPS.

KEY TERMS

- **archive bit** — A file attribute used to determine which files will be backed up and which ones will not be backed up. When a file is modified, the archive attribute is turned on, indicating that the file has changed since the last backup.

- **brownouts** — Power fluctuations associated with lights dimming for extended periods of time. Brownouts can occur when an electrical device nearby drains the common current to low levels, or the needs of a geographic area cannot be met.

- **business/mission-critical** — Term used to describe a network in which business stops if the network goes down. Monetary losses can be measured during downtime.

- **data-critical** — Term used to describe a network in which servers store highly important information that absolutely cannot be lost.

- **Disk Administrator** — A Windows NT utility used to create, format, and delete partitions, volume sets, stripe sets, mirror sets, and stripe sets with parity.

- **disk duplexing** — The process in which a separate disk controller exists for each disk in a mirrored set.

- **fault tolerance** — The ability of a system to respond to hardware failures without losing or corrupting data.

- **fiber channel** — A data transfer method that uses fiber-optic cables instead of copper to increase the speed and distance over which data can be transferred.

- **high-availability** — Term used to describe a network that places the strongest focus on server uptime and performance.

- **host bus adapter (HBA)** — A device that controls the flow of data to each device on the bus, and acts as the interface between the SCSI bus and the rest of the computer.

- **hotspot** — Long-lasting voltage surge. Hotspots are rare and are usually caused by utility company failures.

- **internal logic board** — A device on a SCSI disk that keeps track of cylinders, heads, and sectors, so that the bus controller does not have to.

- **JBOD (Just a Bunch of Disks)** — A slang acronym used to refer to a volume configuration in which each hard disk is its own volume and receives its own drive letter.

- **mean time between failures** — The predicted average time between installation and failure of hardware.

- **mirroring** — The process by which data on one disk are duplicated onto an identical drive, providing a complete "live" backup of all data. If one disk fails, the other disk continues to work, and no interruption in service occurs.

- **parity** — Term used to describe an algorithm that is used to regenerate lost stripes of data in the event of a disk failure.

- **redundancy** — A state in which a second device is available to take over the duties of the primary device in case of failure.

- **Redundant Array of Independent Disks (RAID)** — Techniques used to group sets of drives so that they can perform a single task as a team. RAID techniques provide redundancy and, in some cases, performance advantages. Several levels of RAID exist, each of which is designed to satisfy a different need.

- **Small Computer System Interface (SCSI)** — A standard developed so that hard disks would have a uniform presentation across the computer industry. This standard has gone through several revisions.

- **spikes** — Sudden changes in voltage that can instantly destroy a server. Also called *surges*.

- **stripe set** — A data volume that spans multiple physical disks, writing data in blocks or stripes to each physical disk. Also called RAID-0, stripe sets write to more than one physical disk simultaneously and can improve data retrieval times by a significant margin.

- **uninterruptible power supply (UPS)** — A device that maintains full power when AC power fails, monitors external power for fluctuations, absorbs spikes, and reconditions power to an acceptable steadiness through the use of batteries or AC/DC-DC/AC converters.

- **volume** — One or more partitions on one or more hard disks that are spanned together as a single formatted entity and can be assigned a single drive letter.

- **volume/set** — Any group of hard drives configured to act as a single volume. A volume set with a single drive letter can span multiple disks, making use of irregularly sized chunks of free space.

R E V I E W   Q U E S T I O N S

1. Redundancy is a state in which:

   a. a second piece of hardware stands ready to take over for a failed device

   b. a second piece of hardware is used for load sharing to provide better performance

   c. a second piece of hardware can do both (a) and (b)

   d. none of the above

2. The most common reasons for a server to fail are (check all that apply):

   a. too many users

   b. memory errors

   c. drive failures

   d. power supply failures

3. The predicted average time between installation of a piece of hardware and its failure is called its ————————.

4. A data-critical network is one in which:

   a. stored information must be continually available

   b. data cannot be deleted or destroyed for any reason

   c. data must be available most of the time

   d. neither data nor servers have any particular requirement for availability

5. A mission-critical network is one in which:

   a. stored information must be continually available

   b. data cannot be deleted or destroyed for any reason

   c. data must be available most of the time

   d. neither data nor servers have any particular requirement for availability

6. A high-availability network is one in which:

   a. stored information must be continually available

   b. data cannot be deleted or destroyed for any reason

   c. neither data nor servers have any particular requirement for availability

   d. none of the above

7. If a business-critical network were to fail (select all that apply):

   a. the company would lose money

   b. the company could not conduct business

   c. lives would be put at risk

   d. the company's reputation could be damaged

6

8. The SCSI standard was developed to ＿＿＿＿＿＿＿＿ hard disks across the computer industry.

9. SCSI is an acronym that stands for ＿＿＿＿＿＿＿＿ ＿＿＿＿＿＿＿＿ ＿＿＿＿＿＿＿＿ ＿＿＿＿＿＿＿＿.

10. SCSI-1 uses a(n) ＿＿＿＿＿＿＿＿ bit bus.

11. Which of the following functions does the host bus adapter perform? (Pick two.)

    a. It caches data that arrive when the device to which it is addressed is busy.

    b. It routes packets between devices, bypassing the CPU.

    c. It controls the flow of data to each device on the bus.

    d. It acts as the interface between the SCSI bus and the computer.

12. The internal logic board of a SCSI device keeps track of:

    a. the drive letter of the device

    b. free drive space on the device

    c. cylinders, heads, and sectors of the device

    d. all of the above

13. Under the SCSI-1 standard, a maximum of ＿＿＿＿＿＿＿＿ MB of data could be transferred per second.

14. Fast-SCSI-2 introduced a number of technical advances that brought the data transfer rate to ＿＿＿＿＿＿＿＿ MB per second.

15. Fast-SCSI-2 and Fast-Wide SCSI-2 are interchangeable. True or False?

16. Ultra-Wide SCSI features a ＿＿＿＿＿＿＿＿-bit bus capable of data transfers of ＿＿＿＿＿＿＿＿ MB per second.

17. A Windows NT volume can span:

    a. physical devices

    b. multiple partitions

    c. multiple hard disks

    d. all of the above

18. JBOD arrays and stripe sets are fault-tolerant. True or False?

19. Which of the following are true? (Pick all that apply.)

    a. A volume set can span multiple disks.

    b. A volume set can use irregularly sized chunks of free space.

    c. A volume set must use contiguous space on a single partition.

    d. A volume set is assigned one drive letter per partition.

20. Volume sets and stripe sets are configured using ＿＿＿＿＿＿＿＿.

21. If you are using NTFS, you can extend a volume set after it has been created. True or False?

22. In RAID-0, if a single drive fails, the remaining data will still be accessible because of its use of redundancy. True or False?

23. Which levels of RAID does Windows NT support without additional hardware? (Pick all that apply.)

    a. 0

    b. 1

    c. 2

    d. 4

    e. 5

24. Duplexing uses _____ hard drives and _____ controller cards to provide fewer single points of failure.

25. RAID-4 stores parity information:

    a. striped across multiple disks

    b. on a dedicated drive

    c. nowhere—RAID-4 does not use parity information

    d. on the emergency repair disk

    e. none of the above

HANDS-ON PROJECTS

For some or all of these projects, you will need a Windows NT Server with an unformatted hard drive.

> Keep in mind that any use of Disk Administrator carries with it the possibility of data loss. These projects should not be completed on a server in a production environment or on a server that holds critical data.

PROJECT 6-1

In this project, you will use Windows NT Backup to perform a complete backup.

    1. Click the **Start button**, click **Programs**, click **Administrative Tools (Common)**, then click **Backup**. The Backup window opens.

    2. Select the check boxes for each hard drive on your server. Do *not* check your CD-ROM drive, if you have one.

    3. Click **Backup** to initiate a complete backup of the selected drives.

PROJECT 6-2

In this project, you will make three partitions on your blank drive, leaving some free space.

1. Click the **Start button**, click **Programs**, click **Administrative Tools (Common)**, then click **Disk Administrator**. The Disk Administrator window opens.
2. Click the **blank drive** to highlight it.
3. Click **Partition** on the menu bar, then click **Create Volume Set**. The Create Volume Set dialog box opens, allowing you to specify the total size for the volume set. By default, the dialog box displays the maximum amount of space available.
4. Type a value that is approximately one-fourth the size of your hard drive.
5. With the partition still highlighted, click **Tools** on the menu bar, then click **Format**.
6. Select **NTFS** when prompted.
7. Repeat Steps 3 to 6 twice so that you have three NTFS partitions. Do not use the same value in Step 5, but try to average one-fourth of the hard drive for each partition.
8. Click **Partition** on the menu bar, then click **Commit Changes Now**.
9. Close Disk Administrator and reboot your computer to bring the NTFS partitions online.

PROJECT 6-3

In this project, you will create a volume set comprised of two partitions.

1. Click the **Start button**, click **Programs**, click **Administrative Tools (Common)**, then click **Disk Administrator**. The Disk Administrator window opens.
2. Press and hold the **CTRL key**, click a partition on your test drive, then click a second partition. Both partitions should be highlighted.
3. Click **Partition** on the menu bar, then click **Create Volume Set**. Disk Administrator displays the minimum and maximum sizes for the volume set, based on the areas of free space you have selected.
4. Type the size of the volume set that you want to create, then choose **OK**. (If you choose less than the maximum size, Disk Administrator divides the total size proportionately among the selected areas, then assigns a single drive letter to the collection of partitions that make up the volume set.)

PROJECT 6-4

In this project, you will extend the volume set you created in Project 6-3.

1. Click the **Start button**, click **Programs**, click **Administrative Tools (Common)**, then click **Disk Administrator**. The Disk Administrator window opens.

2. Press and hold the **CTRL key**, click on the volume set you created in Project 6-3, then click on any area marked "Free Space."

3. Click **Partition** on the menu bar, then click **Extend Volume Set**. The Extend Volume Set dialog box opens.

4. Type the size of the volume set that you want to create. For this project, choose the default (the maximum size based on the areas you have highlighted).

5. Click **OK**. You will return to the Disk Administrator.

6. Click **Partition** on the menu bar, then click **Commit Changes Now**.

7. When prompted, click **Yes** to restart your machine.

6

CASE PROJECTS

1. You are the senior engineer for Ellison Electrical, a family firm that has been operating in the same area for three generations. Your accountant has created a financial model that will take your estimates and compare them with actual costs. This process will demonstrate the accuracy of each contractor's forecasting and help your firm bid for future jobs more precisely. The model is stored on your server along with all of the forecasts. Now you want to do some long-term forecasting to show how, over the course of one, three, and five years, using this model has increased company profits. For the model to work, the data from every job must be available when the analysis is run. What are two options to ensure that these data will be accessible and accurate?

2. You work for *SLACK*, a trendy chain of clothing stores. The company consists of 48 stores in major metropolitan areas and a corporate headquarters in San Francisco. Each store is connected to the corporate headquarters with a point-to-point connection that feeds data from each store to a central database at the headquarter site. This database is used to forecast trends and predict the various run lengths for each piece of clothing made. The network is data-critical. Write a brief report (three to five paragraphs) explaining how you would transform this network into an appropriately fault-tolerant system while being conservative on costs.

3. You have been promoted to network manager at *SLACK*. Your first project is to take the central database described in the previous exercise and use it to set prices in all of *SLACK's* stores in real time, based on an expert system that has been developed in-house. The expert system takes sales data from each store and combines it with weather information taken from NOAA. It must remain operational whenever stores are open or your company cannot conduct business. Your predecessor set up the central database using mirroring—an acceptable solution in the past, when data came in consistently from the stores. Now, however, the constant transfer of data back and forth is creating I/O bottlenecks that management wants to remove. How can you improve the performance of the database server while being conservative on costs? Write a brief report (three to five paragraphs) explaining your ideas.

4. You are the network manager for Cycles, an electronic music label. Recently, a number of artists have been found in the Ozarks. The company would like to open an office there to handle logistics and recording for these musicians. The new site is central to all of the company's new artists, but is not located in a metropolitan area. Because most of the recording work is handled through your PCs and Macintosh computers, the owners are concerned that the location may present problems because of the large number of thunderstorms and frequent brownouts that occur there. What solution can you offer to protect against these potential problems?

MANAGING CLIENTS AND SERVERS

Large enterprise networks generally encompass many servers and a large number of clients. In this chapter you will learn how to configure a Windows NT server for various types of client computers, including Windows NT Workstation, Windows 95, DOS, OS/2, and Macintosh clients. You will also learn how to use client-based server administration tools to simplify the task of administering large enterprise networks.

AFTER READING THIS CHAPTER AND COMPLETING THE EXERCISES YOU WILL BE ABLE TO:

- Discuss the role of clients in the client/server model
- Discuss the role of client/server applications in business
- Explain how to connect a variety of clients to Windows NT Server 4.0
- Discuss the tools and resources useful during a client rollout
- Use the Windows NT Network Client Administrator Utility
- Install Services for Macintosh and describe the support tools provided with it
- Administer remote servers and other network resources

CLIENTS AND THE CLIENT/SERVER MODEL

In Chapter 1, you reviewed the role of the client in the client/server model. Clients were originally designed to simply request information from servers. The modern client is more complicated, however, performing tasks that were once assigned exclusively to servers. Indeed, as operating systems have evolved and improved, both client and server computers have become remarkably complex—in some cases, in fact, it is difficult to distinguish between a client and a server. Some clients, including those running Windows NT Workstation, even use the client/server model for internal communication. For example, you can map a drive to a shared resource on the local workstation, from the local workstation. As software developers try to simplify the delivery of information to users' fingertips, the distinction between clients and servers will likely blur even more. But the distinction must always remain at some level, if computers on a network are to cooperate effectively as a distributed computing network.

Keeping in mind the evolving nature of the modern client, a **client** may be defined as a stand-alone computer that has been integrated into a network so that it may access information from a server. Windows NT includes a number of possible client types, such as computers running Windows NT Workstation, Windows 95, Windows 3.x, and even DOS.

This large mix of potential client types has complicated Microsoft's job of supporting and improving its operating systems, as they all are composed of different code and components. Windows NT is Microsoft's **shared base code operating system**, an operating system that can act as both a network operating system (NOS) and a desktop operating system (OS). Thus the code making up the base operating system is the same for both Windows NT Server and Windows NT Workstation. The settings in each operating system's registry, however, differ greatly. Windows NT Server is designed to perform best when serving information to remote computers on a LAN; in contrast, Windows NT Workstation places the highest priority on applications that run at the local computer. It may be tempting to consider Windows NT Server to be a more powerful operating system, but it is really only a more powerful *network* operating system because of its design.

You can illustrate the differences between Windows NT Server and Windows NT Workstation by conducting a simple experiment. Set up a print queue for a DLC or TCP/IP printer on a computer running Windows NT Server, then set up an identical print queue on a computer running Windows NT Workstation. Print a test page from a Windows 95 computer twice. The first time the Windows 95 computer should be served by the Windows NT Server machine, and the second time by the Windows NT Workstation machine. Notice that Windows NT Server responds significantly more quickly than Windows NT Workstation.

CLIENT/SERVER APPLICATIONS AND BUSINESS SOLUTIONS

The client/server model is popular in the business world because it gives decision-makers quick and relatively easy access to critical data. The development of client/server applications has made critical data even more accessible. A **client/server application** is an application in which the interface (or front end) is on the client machine and the processing (or back end) is on the server. This division of labor allows for more complex applications and for improved sharing of data. Microsoft tools—such as Access, SQL Server, Visual Basic, and Visual InterDev—make programming client/server applications almost as easy as composing a spreadsheet in Microsoft Excel. Rather than spending a fortune to have programmers develop a customized solution, businesses can simply put easy-to-use tools in the hands of end users. The end users can then develop their own ways of organizing data into profitable information.

7

Consider the example of a computer support help desk. In the past, help desk managers had to rely on expensive call logging software. Today, they can create their own call logs from simpler, customized tools. The process is as follows: First, a network administrator must set up the back end, where the data will be stored and processed using SQL Server, determine the rights to be granted to end users, and create a database and tables with fields for caller information, the problem description, and so on. The help desk manager then creates a Microsoft Access database with tables linked to those on the SQL server, using **open database connectivity** (**ODBC**). (ODBC establishes a connection between Access and SQL Server for the passing and manipulating of data.) Using Microsoft Access, the help desk personnel can then customize their interface to the SQL tables and create customized call logging software that best suits their needs; the data on the back end remains standardized so that it can be used by everyone in the department.

> For more information on SQL, consider enrolling in an SQL Server course. You can use SQL 6.5 Administration as an elective toward an MCSE certification.

CONNECTING TO WINDOWS NT SERVER 4.0

A client computer needs three components to connect to and communicate with Windows NT Server 4.0: client software, a compatible transport protocol, and a software driver for the NIC. Many network connectivity problems result from a failure of one of these three components.

Client software is discussed in the following section. The transport protocols supported by Windows NT (covered in Chapter 3) include NetBEUI, IPX/SPX, and TCP/IP. The AppleTalk protocol is also supported by Windows NT, but only when accompanied by Services for Macintosh. Services for Macintosh will be discussed later in this chapter. A compatible software driver for most mainstream network interface controllers is included on the Windows NT compact disk. These drivers function with adapter cards included in the Microsoft Hardware Compatibility List (HCL).

CLIENT SOFTWARE

To simplify the task of gathering information from dissimilar networks, both Windows NT and Windows 95 include client software for many different types of network servers. Because a computer running Windows NT Server can also act as a workstation, the client software must be installed to support any kind of communication with other servers. For example, if a Windows NT server needs to communicate with a NetWare server, the Windows NT server would have to have *client* software for NetWare installed. While the Microsoft client software is a relatively "bare bones" program, it is easy to configure and is as stable and reliable as the operating system itself. Third parties also offer client software with additional features, but their programs do not necessarily match the stability and reliability of the client software provided by Microsoft. Microsoft considers Novell's client software, Client 32, to be a third-party application to Windows NT; consequently, the company does not provide support for it. Fortunately, Novell provides support for all of its products, including Client 32. If you need help with Client 32, see the NetWare software documentation.

Client for Microsoft Networks includes support for the browser service, and is required to permit file sharing in both workgroup environments and Windows NT domains. Combined with file and printer sharing for Microsoft networks, Windows 95 and NT Workstation can act as both clients and servers on Microsoft networks.

Microsoft client software consists of two parts: a network driver and a redirector. The **network driver** is the component that actually packages network information and sends it out onto the network. The **redirector** runs at a higher level, intercepting software requests for data from network drives, converting the requests into network I/O requests, and passing them on to the network driver to be packaged.

CLIENT, SERVER, AND GATEWAY SERVICES FOR NETWARE

Server Services for NetWare, which is included in Windows NT Server, is a service that allows a NetWare client to log onto a Windows NT server as easily as if it were a NetWare server. Server Services for NetWare allows an administrator to perform a quick, easy, and nearly seamless migration from NetWare to Windows NT. When you install Client Services for NetWare on a Windows NT server, Server Services is automatically installed.

Gateway Services for NetWare (GSNW) could be considered the opposite of Server Services for NetWare, in that it allows Microsoft clients to access resources on a NetWare server. The Microsoft clients need not have a NetWare client installed. When using GSNW, the Windows NT server maps a drive letter to a NetWare volume and then reshares the new folder with its own Microsoft clients, thereby serving as a gateway to the NetWare environment. The cleverness of this connection lies in its use of only one NetWare client access license. In addition, this scheme eliminates the need for additional networking components on the client, which in turn decreases the client's memory requirements. Server performance is degraded, however, when more than one user uses the gateway.

Connectivity with NetWare is discussed in detail in Chapter 10.

MS-DOS Clients

Included with the Windows NT CD-ROM are two clients for MS-DOS: Network Client 3.0 for MS-DOS, and LanMan 2.2c. LanMan 2.2c works with both DOS and OS/2 clients. Client 3.0 is useful because it can log onto a domain, run logon scripts, run Winsock applications, and use Remote Access Services to log in. Browsing of network resources is also supported, but *only* in a workgroup that includes a Windows NT computer or a Windows for Workgroups computer.

Microsoft LAN Manager was Microsoft's first network operating system. Windows NT uses some of the same basic concepts formed by LAN Manager, including the browser service.

7

Workgroups

Workgroups are Microsoft networks in which members share information by acting as both clients and servers. Members of a workgroup can use any combination of Windows for Workgroups, Windows NT Workstation, or Windows 95 as their operating system. In a Windows NT Workstation workgroup, a member cannot access shared resources without a valid user account. In Windows 95 and Windows for Workgroups workgroups, however, the shared resources are protected only by a password. For all of these operating systems, the client software is automatically installed as part of that operating system; you merely have to configure the workgroups to enable members to communicate with one another.

Clients in a Windows NT Domain

Special considerations apply to clients in an enterprise environment. For example, each Windows NT client must maintain a computer account in the Windows NT domain. (You create such an account via the Server Manager utility.) Before logging on for the first time, users must create a user account, thereby establishing a user name and password. (You will learn how to create a user account in Chapter 8). For Windows 95 clients, only a user account is required. It is important to remember this distinction: Windows NT clients need a computer account *and* a user account on the domain, while Windows 95 clients need only a user account.

User Manager and Server Manager are installed automatically on all Windows NT servers, and these utilities are included in the client-based server management tools.

Domain Logon Scripts

When a user logs on to a domain, the client runs a **logon script**, or a file of sequentially executed commands. Logon scripts can contain just about any commands that can be executed from the command prompt in Windows NT. They can include several parameters that can be used only at logon. Figure 7-1 shows an example of a logon script.

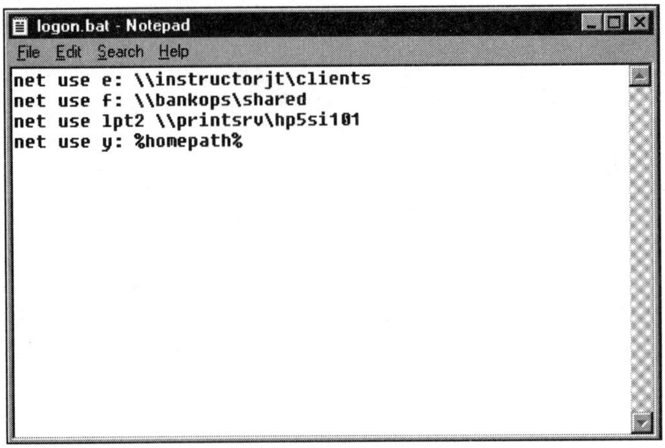

```
logon.bat - Notepad
File  Edit  Search  Help
net use e: \\instructorjt\clients
net use f: \\bankops\shared
net use lpt2 \\printsrv\hp5si101
net use y: %homepath%
```

Figure 7-1   Example of a Windows NT logon script

Logon scripts are commonly used for the following purposes:

- Mapping standard drive letters to network shares at logon
- Redirecting printer (LPT) ports to network printers
- Synchronizing the workstation clock with the server clock
- Running workstation auditing software for automated asset management
- Loading additional client software, such as that used with Microsoft Systems Management Server
- Issuing logon announcements, such as notices of system outages, security warnings, virus alerts, and so on

Logon scripts should be saved in the winnt\system32\repl\import\scripts folder. On the PDC, the contents of the import directory should be copied to the export directory, and directory replication configured to distribute logon scripts to other domain controllers. When a user logs on, the specified logon script is loaded from the import directory on the domain controller that provided the logon authentication. If the logon script has not been exported, it will not run from a BDC. Figure 7-2 shows the User Environment Profile dialog box in which the logon script is set.

You can specify a logon script for each user account. For example, to specify the file named LOGON.BAT as a logon script for a particular user account:

1. Log on to the Windows NT server with an account that has administrative rights.
2. Click the **Start button**, point to **Programs**, point to **Administrative Tools (Common)**, then click **User Manager for Domains**. The User Manager for Domains window opens.
3. Select the user account for which you want to specify a logon script, then click **Profile**. The User Environment Profile dialog box opens.

4. In the Logon Script Name text box, type the name of the logon script file: **LOGON.BAT.** You do not have to specify the path (in the User Profile Path text box), as long as the script is in the default location (winnt\system32\repl\import\scripts).

5. Click **OK** to close the User Environment Profile dialog box. Click **OK** again to close the User Properties dialog box. Finally, close User Manager for Domains.

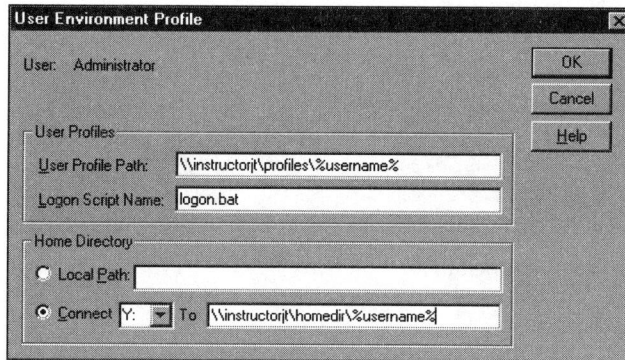

Figure 7-2   User Environment Profile dialog box

CLIENT ROLLOUTS

In an enterprise **client rollout**, a large number of client workstations are installed and configured simultaneously. Anyone can individually load a few workstations in a small network. When the rollout numbers reach the hundreds or thousands, however, the task becomes considerably more difficult. A number of ways to manage the process exist, as do a number of tools and methods to simplify the installation process. These tools and methods include outsourcing, hard drive duplication, and batch installation.

The first of these options, **outsourcing**, simply means hiring someone else to do the job. Outsourcing is often the preferred option for large companies that lack the facilities to configure huge numbers of clients. For these companies, the most cost-effective solution may be to delegate the task of client configuration to a company that does have the necessary facilities. Value-added resellers (VARs) sometimes offer predelivery configuration services to their customers as an enticement to earn their continued business. Having a large number of systems preconfigured by a VAR can save a great deal of work in the implementation of a large client rollout. Sometimes entire local area networks—including printers, servers, and clients—are loaded, configured, and tested in-house before they leave the warehouse. For companies whose business does not focus on computers and technology, outsourcing to a VAR can save much time and money.

For operating systems that don't require a unique security identifier code (or SID), the second option, hard drive duplication, automates a client rollout quickly and comprehensively. (Microsoft does not recommend disk duplication for Windows NT, as explained below.)

Many hardware and software methods are available for duplicating hard drives. Software methods that have gained popularity in recent years include approaches that create exact copies of a disk, sometimes referred to as **disk images**. A number of software products allow you to save compressed disk images on one hard disk and then download them onto several other hard drives simultaneously. Because these programs broadcast the same information to multiple machines all at once, they conserve network bandwidth and server performance. As a result, you can configure 10 workstations as quickly as you configure only one. The process of disk duplication is illustrated in Figure 7–3.

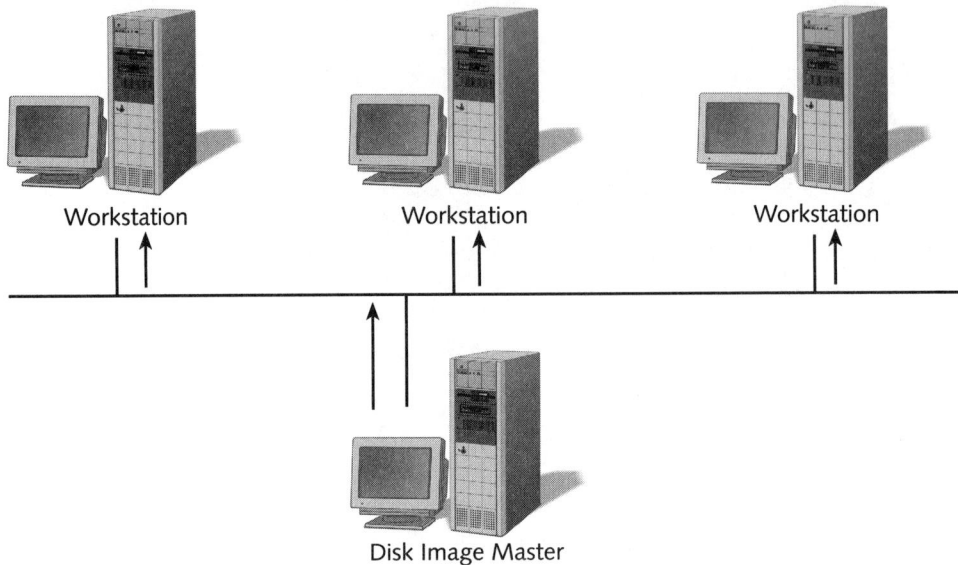

Figure 7-3   Duplicating hard drives from a single master image

> ⚠ **Caution**
> Although hard drive duplication is widely used today, Microsoft will not support it. The company does not recommend this approach, because unpredictable results may occur. Do not attempt to use this method on Windows NT, because SID duplication may occur, rendering two or more PCs inoperable on your network.

One problem with using disk images is that network damage is compounded when errors occur. Because the same image loads on several PCs at once, a single error—either in the original image or in the transmitted image—will affect more than one client. Sometimes these errors go undetected until months after the rollout, when hundreds of clients suddenly crash. The problems generated can be more costly than the time saved in setup.

During installation, Windows NT generates the unique code sequence called a security identifier (SID). The SID is a trusted value, and one critical to many processes in Windows NT architecture and domains. If the entire hard disk is duplicated, then the SID value is duplicated along with it. This creation of identical SIDs can cause workstations and servers on a network to crash suddenly, for no readily apparent reason. The fact that the SID is not actually generated until near the end of the installation process makes it possible for you to work around this potential problem by making an image (or clone) of the workstation halfway through the setup process, when Setup reboots the workstation. All workstations created from that image will boot to the middle of installation their first time. Once these "half-cloned" systems boot, you only have to perform the last half of the installation process individually, to ensure a unique SID for each machine.

Another tool you can use during client rollouts is batch installation, a process in which the installation is scripted to ensure that each workstation receives the same setup. Because this method uses boot disks and automated response files, batch installations of Microsoft client computers are quick, efficient, and accurate. This process uses a boot disk that has the files required to connect to the network and launch setup. The setup process takes advantage of response files that provide the information you would normally enter yourself during a manual installation. Thus a batch installation—Microsoft's recommended method of client installation—can take place virtually unattended.

WINDOWS NT NETWORK CLIENT ADMINISTRATOR

The Network Client Administrator utility helps to automate the process of sharing client installation files, creating Windows 95 installation boot disks, and sharing server administration tools.

> **Note** Although computers running Windows NT Workstation are the preferred clients for the Windows NT Server operating system, the Windows NT Workstation installation files are *not* included with the Windows NT Server CD-ROM, as they are with the Windows 95 CD-ROM. With both Windows 95 and Windows NT Workstation, you are responsible for ensuring that you have an operating system license as well as a client access license for the server. Installing software without a license is considered piracy and carries the risk of severe penalties—both operationally, due to the disruptive nature of a software audit and monetarily, due to the fines assessed.

You can use Network Client Administrator to perform the following functions:

- Copy and share the Windows 95 installation files
- Make a customized network boot disk to simplify client installation
- Make a client software installation disk set (DOS, OS/2, and Windows for Workgroups 3.11)
- Make an installation disk for 32-bit TCP/IP for Windows for Workgroups 3.11
- Copy and share the client-based server administration tools

These functions are explained in the following section.

CREATING A NETWORK INSTALLATION STARTUP DISK

An **installation startup disk**, when used for batch installation, lets administrators automate the installation process for Windows NT Server, Windows NT Workstation, Windows 95, Windows for Workgroups version 3.11, or Microsoft Network Client for MS-DOS version 3.0. During the installation process, the disk you create performs certain tasks automatically: It starts the computer and Microsoft Network Client 3.0, connects to the server containing the installation files, and initiates the installation process. These actions are accomplished through an automated batch process, as described above, that allows the installation to continue virtually unattended.

> Windows NT boot disks cannot be used as installation startup disks.

To create a network installation startup disk for Windows 95 or Microsoft Client 3.0:

1. Make a bootable floppy disk using the Format /s or the SYS command on a Windows 95 or DOS workstation.

2. Click the **Start button**, point to **Programs**, point to **Administrative Tools (Common)**, then click **Network Client Administrator**. The Network Client Administrator window opens.

3. Click the **Make a Network Installation Startup Disk option button**, then click **Continue**. The Share Network Client Installation Files dialog box opens.

4. Click the **Copy Files to a New Directory, and then Share option button**. Your dialog box should match Figure 7-4.

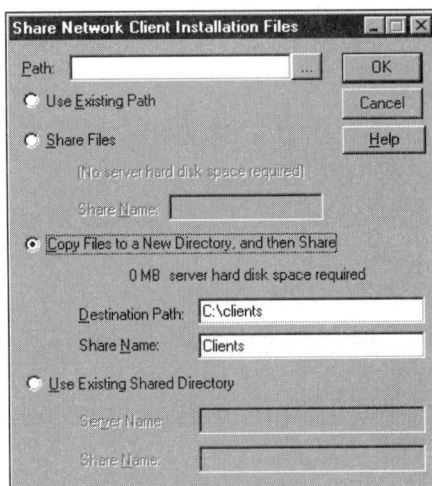

Figure 7-4   Share Network Client Installation Files dialog box

5. Enter the path to the Client files and then click **OK**. For example, if you are accessing these files from your CD-ROM, you might type **D:CLIENTS**.

6. Type the location of the installation CD-ROM, then click **OK**. Once the files are copied from the CD-ROM to your hard drive, you will be prompted to choose a floppy disk type for the boot disk.

7. Choose the correct floppy drive, network client, and network card for your system, then click **OK**. The Network Startup Disk Configuration dialog box opens, showing the name of the client that will be installed and the network adapter that will be used.

8. In the Computer Name text box, type a unique name on your network. In the User Name text box, type the name of your administrator account. In the Domain text box, type your domain name. In the Network Protocol text box, select an appropriate protocol (one used by both the client and server), such as TCP/IP. If you are using the DHCP Server service, select the Enable Automatic DHCP Configuration check box. In the Default Gateway text box, accept the default 0.0.0.0. When you are finished, your dialog box should resemble Figure 7-5.

7

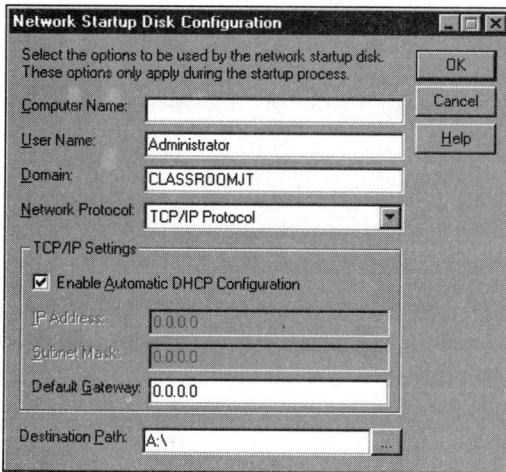

Figure 7-5   Network Startup Disk Configuration dialog box

> Because every computer name on your network must be unique, be sure to use a different computer name for each client boot disk you create.

9. Click **OK** to close the Network Startup Disk Configuration dialog box. The Confirm Network Disk Configuration dialog box appears, describing the components you selected in creating the boot disk (see Figure 7-6).

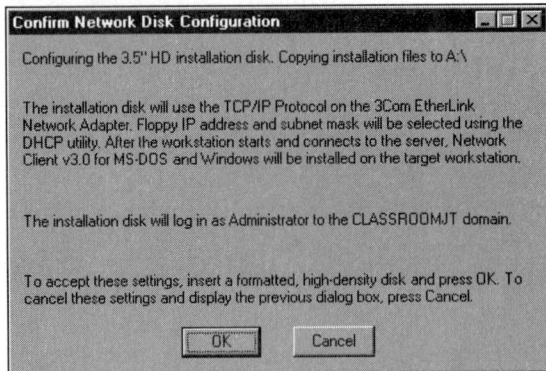

Figure 7-6   Confirm Network Disk Configuration dialog box

    10. Click **OK** if the settings are correct. Click **Cancel** to go back and change
           something.

    11. If you did not make the bootable floppy disk in Step 1, Client Administrator will
           warn you that you need to do so.

Client Administrator generates the files and copies them onto the floppy disk. After creating
the disk, you may see a dialog box with a list of steps or warnings that you need to resolve
before setting up the new workstation. These steps and warnings may include the following:

- Make sure you have sufficient permission to access this shared directory. Contact
  your system administrator about changing privilege levels.

- Be sure to enter a unique computer name on the startup disk for each machine
  being configured over the network.

- Network client installation files have not been copied to a suitable floppy disk.
  Copy the files from their temporary path to a formatted, high-density system disk
  and verify that the disk fits the target workstation's drive A.

- There is not enough memory to run Setup when installing either Windows for
  Workgroups or the Network Client for MS-DOS over the network. Modify the
  boot floppy's CONFIG.SYS file to use extended memory—for example, use
  EMM386.EXE.

- The network adapter card was configured using default settings. Verify that the
  default settings are the settings that should be used and modify them if necessary.

You may need to take additional steps to ensure that the boot disk works properly. For example, if the client is a laptop that requires specific card service drivers to be loaded before the
NIC can be detected, you will have to load the card services manually. Use the information
in Table 7-1 to determine your storage needs for the various clients included on the
Windows NT Server CD-ROM.

Table 7-1   Storage by Client Type

Description	Directory	Size
RAS for MS-DOS	\RAS	2.5 MB
Network Client for MS-DOS	\MSCLIENT	4 MB
LAN Manager for MS OS/2	\LANMAN.OS2	3.5 MB
LAN Manager for MS-DOS	\LANMAN	3.5 MB
Client-based network administration tools for Windows NT	\Srvtools\winnt	11 MB
Client-based network administration tools for Windows 95	\Srvtools\win95	2.5 MB
TCP/IP-32 for Windows for Workgroups	\TCP32WFW	2.5 MB
Windows 95	\WIN95	33 MB

The installation files for Windows NT Workstation and Windows for Workgroups are not included on the installation CD-ROM. To use a network installation startup disk to install Windows NT Server, Windows NT Workstation, or Windows for Workgroups, you should add the appropriate directories (under the Clients directory) to the installation files. Table 7-2 lists the directories you need to create and indicates the amount of disk space that these files will occupy.

Table 7-2   Network Installation Startup Disk Directories

Directory	Size
\Clients\Wfw\Netsetup	23 MB
\Clients\Winnt\Netsetup	22 MB
\Clients\Winnt.srv\netsetup	61 MB

> **Note** You can use startup disks to install Windows NT only on x86 or Pentium computers. You cannot use them on Alpha, MIPS, or Power PC computers; these computers require installation from the CD-ROM.

CREATING AN INSTALLATION DISK SET

You can create an **installation disk set** when you need to connect workstations that already have an operating system to the Windows NT network. The following steps outline the process for creating an installation disk set containing the installation files for Microsoft Network Client for MS-DOS, LAN Manager for MS-DOS, LAN Manager for MS OS/2, RAS for MS-DOS, or TCP/IP-32 for Windows for Workgroups. The resulting set of disks does not include a boot disk capable of logging you into the network. These disks can, however, be used to install Microsoft client software on an already-configured operating system.

In addition to connecting these workstations to the network, you can install RAS for MS-DOS or TCP/IP-32 for Windows for Workgroups by creating a connection to the network share containing the installation files, and then installing the software over the network.

To make an installation disk set:

1. Click the **Start button**, point to **Programs**, point to **Administrative Tools (Common)**, then click **Network Client Administrator**. The Network Client Administrator window opens.

2. Click the **Make Installation Disk Set option button**, then click **Continue**. The Share Network Client dialog box opens, verifying that your client installation files have already been shared.

3. Review your parameters to make sure they are correct, then click **OK**. The Make Installation Disk Set window appears with the available clients listed in the box.

4. Select your preferred client in the Make Installation Disks dialog box, then verify the destination drive letter.

5. Select the **Format Disks check box**. This action will format the floppy disks before files are copied to them, thereby verifying the integrity of the floppy disk.

> **Note**
> Windows NT Workstation is not included in the Network Client or Service list, because client software is already included as part of the Windows NT Workstation operating system. Workstation installation files are not even included on the installation CD-ROM, as they are for Windows 95.

6. Insert a blank floppy disk and then click **OK**. The Network Client Administrator formats your floppy disks and copies the necessary files to them.

COPYING CLIENT-BASED NETWORK ADMINISTRATION TOOLS

Client-based network administration tools comprise domain server management tools that can be run from a workstation that is a member of the domain. They can be shared from the CD-ROM, or copied to a server drive and then shared. Among other things (a more complete discussion of these tools is contained at the end of this chapter), these tools allow you to:

- Administer users and groups
- Administer servers
- Work with WINS and DHCP
- Set replication properties
- Edit policies
- Administer RAS

To share the installation files for the client-based network administration tools on the Windows NT Server compact disc:

1. Click the **Start button**, point to **Programs**, point to **Administrative Tools (Common)**, then click **Network Client Administrator**. The Network Client Administrator window opens.

2. Click the **Copy Client-based Network Administration Tools option button**, then click **Continue**. The Share Client-based Administration Tools dialog box opens.

3. Click the **Share Files option button**, then, in the Path text box, type the path to the srvtools directory on the installation CD (usually **\clients\srvtools**).

4. In the Share Name text box, type a unique name for the share. Your dialog box should resemble Figure 7-7.

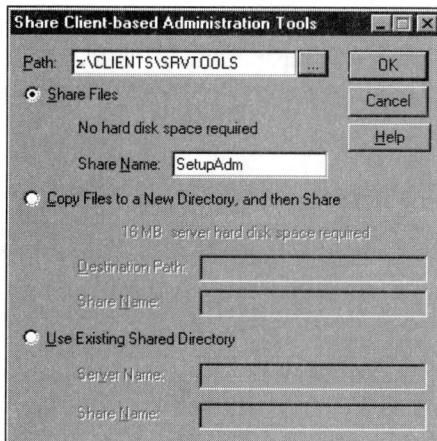

Figure 7-7   Share Client-based Administration Tools dialog box

5. Click **OK** to return to the Network Client Administrator window.

This set of steps requires you to leave the installation CD-ROM in the server so as to share the files on it. If you would rather not leave this compact disc in the server, you can copy the installation files for the client-based network administration tools to a new directory on a network-server hard disk, and then share the files. To follow this course, click the Use Existing Shared Directory option button in the Network Client Administrator. The files will be placed in an already-created share.

> **Note** Client-based network administration tools allow you to provide administrative support for Windows NT, LAN Manager for MS OS/2, or LAN Manager for UNIX servers from a computer running Windows 95, Windows NT Workstation, or Windows NT Server.

VIEWING REMOTEBOOT CLIENT INFORMATION

The **Remoteboot service** is a Windows NT Server feature that starts MS-DOS and Microsoft Windows computers over the network. Rather than running from a local hard disk, the operating system runs from the server. The benefit of this service is that it makes it easy to change the configuration for all remoteboot clients. The downside is that this option increases network traffic and creates a potential single point of failure (the server that holds the operating system files for all remoteboot clients).

Remoteboot clients are becoming relatively rare today, partly because they are incompatible with many mainstream application packages as a result of the design of the Remoteboot service. For more information on how to install the Remoteboot service, see the detailed summary in Microsoft's Windows NT Server 4.0 Resource Kit.

DETERMINING THE TYPE OF DISK YOU NEED TO CREATE

Different types of clients require different levels of preparation or installation before networking can begin. These various needs can result in some confusion. Table 7-3 shows disk requirements for each operating system.

Table 7-3   Disk Requirements by Operating System

Description	Installation Startup Disk	Installation Disk Set
Windows NT Server	X	
Windows NT Workstation	X	
Windows 95	X	
Network Client for MS-DOS	X	X
TCP/IP-32 for Windows for Workgroups		X
LAN Manager for MS-DOS		X
LAN Manager for MS OS/2		X
RAS for MS-DOS		X

SERVICES FOR MACINTOSH

In addition to offering the client support options described earlier in this chapter, Windows NT can also support Macintosh clients. These clients pose a distinct communication challenge. The Macintosh file system, naming conventions, protocols, and frame types are vastly different from those used by Windows NT. Fortunately, a Windows NT server can act as a fully functional AppleShare file server. This capability provides common ground for Macintosh clients and Microsoft clients for data sharing. A Windows NT server can also act as an AppleTalk router and as a Macintosh print server.

There is no coded limit to the number of Macintosh clients that can connect to a Windows NT server simultaneously. In Microsoft's testing labs, more than 1000 Macintosh clients were simultaneously connected to a single Windows NT server. Even a high-performance Macintosh file server would have struggled under such a load, but Windows NT performed well.

Because of the vast differences between Macintosh and PC computers, the most practical method of sharing data is to rely on a common file server that can provide the necessary translation between the two systems. Windows NT functions extremely well as an **AppleShare file server**, appearing to Macintosh clients as though it were a standard AppleShare server. One key to this performance is that one of the core systems of an AppleShare file server, the AppleTalk Filing Protocol, actually runs as a multithreaded process in the Windows NT Executive. Not only can it take advantage of multiple processors, but it does so with high system priority, producing a lightning-fast response. The result is high-performance connectivity for two completely dissimilar network types.

In addition to acting as a file server, Windows NT can act as a print server to both Macintosh and PC clients. Macintosh computers normally communicate with their printers in PostScript format. Windows NT supports PostScript printer drivers, making it possible for PCs to print to Apple LaserWriter printers on the AppleTalk network. Another powerful feature is Windows NT's ability to translate PostScript print requests from Macintosh clients into bitmap images, and then send them to non-PostScript printers in the Microsoft network. Macintosh clients can print to any printer installed on the Windows NT server.

When a Windows NT server is used to bridge two AppleTalk networks, it becomes an AppleTalk router—that is, the server passes AppleTalk traffic between the two networks as if it were a router. As long as Services for Macintosh are installed, Windows NT will function fully as an AppleTalk router and will appear to the Macintosh clients to be a Macintosh server.

To install Services for Macintosh:

1. Open the **Start menu**, point to **Settings**, then click **Control Panel**.

2. Double-click the **Network icon**, then click the **Services tab**.

3. Click **Add**, select **Services for Macintosh** from the list of available services, and then click **OK**.

4. When you are prompted for the location of the Windows NT Install files, enter the location of the installation CD-ROM, then click **Continue**. Setup will then install Services for Macintosh. Use configuration settings that are appropriate to your network and click **OK**.

5. After the files are copied, you will need to restart your Windows NT server. When prompted to restart your computer, click **Yes**.

When you add Services for Macintosh, the AppleTalk protocol is installed as well. In addition, a new icon called MacFile appears in the Control Panel. You can use this icon (or the MacFile menu in Server Manager) to configure the Services for Macintosh server. You can also use the MacFile menu in File Manager or Server Manager to configure Macintosh-accessible volumes. Once you have created a Macintosh-accessible volume, the folder can also be shared with Microsoft clients using Windows NT Explorer.

ADMINISTERING REMOTE SERVERS AND OTHER NETWORK RESOURCES

Using Windows NT Server, you can administer other servers within your domain as if you were local to those machines. This feature can prove very convenient in an enterprise network, as you do not have to be physically present at the server to administer it. As a result, a single administrator can manage servers in geographically disparate locations, without having to spend the time or money to travel from one server to another.

What Components you are able to administer depends wholly on what type of machine you have available to you as not all utilities are available for all platforms.

REMOTE ADMINISTRATION FROM A WINDOWS 95 WORKSTATION

As mentioned previously, several tools are available to help with the process of remote administration. To install these utilities, you need to download the file NEXUS.EXE from Microsoft's ftp site at *ftp://ftp.microsoft.com/Softlib/MSLFILES/*. NEXUS, which is also part of Windows 95 Service Pack 1, contains versions of Server Manager, User Manager for Domains, and Event Viewer that can be used from a Windows 95 machine. These versions of the utilities offer the same functionality as their Windows NT counterparts, but run on any Windows 95 machine. The following steps assume that you have NEXUS.EXE in C:\NEXUS.

To install the remote administration server tools in Windows 95, follow these steps:

1. Open **Windows Explorer**, navigate to **C:\NEXUS**, then double-click **NEXUS.EXE** to extract the files.
2. Click the **Start button**, point to **Settings**, click **Control Panel**, then double-click the **Add/Remove Programs icon**. The Add/Remove Program dialog box opens.
3. Click the **Windows Setup tab**, then click **Have Disk**.
4. In the Install From Disk text box, specify **C:\NEXUS** (which contains the Srvtools.inf file) and then click **OK**.
5. Click **Install**.

Once installed, the Nexus tools enable you to exert a good deal of control over your domain. With Event Viewer, you can diagnose server problems or check a server's status by monitoring events that occur on a specific server. Server Manager allows you to see what files are in use on a given server and lets you start and stop services remotely. User Manager for Domains enables you to manage accounts remotely. With User Manager for Domains, you can create, edit, and remove user accounts and groups as well as edit system policies.

REMOTE ADMINISTRATION FROM A WINDOWS NT WORKSTATION

When performing administration functions from a Windows NT Workstation computer, you have more options than with Windows 95. You can use Server Manager, User Manager for

Domains, and Event Viewer, just as you can with Windows 95, but you are also able to take advantage of several other utilities that give you more control over your Windows NT domain.

Windows NT Workstation comes with many of the same tools that are available with Windows NT Server. These tools include all of the tools that you are able to use on Windows 95, but also include DHCP Administrator, WINS Administrator, RAS Administrator, the System Policy Editor, Print Manager, and Remoteboot Manager.

DHCP Administrator allows you to manage DHCP leases and the DHCP database for a specific server. Using this utility, you can terminate a DHCP lease, browse the DHCP database, or perform any other task that you would normally carry out on the server using this tool. WINS Administrator allows you to work with the WINS database on the various servers in your domain. You can even initiate scavenging of the database without going to the server itself. RAS Administrator lets you manage RAS connections; you can see which computer is connected to which port at any given time and review information about each session. With the System Policy Editor, you can edit system policies that will be applied to users logging on to your domain. Remoteboot Manager allows you to manage remoteboot characteristics.

Windows NT Workstation provides some other options for domain management. For example, it allows you to manage shares remotely. You can create or delete a share and assign rights using several methods. You can use the Administration Wizard by selecting "Managing File and Folder Access" or you can employ SHAREUI from the Windows NT Resource Kit. SHAREUI is a graphical tool that serves the same function as the file and folder access portion of the Administration wizard. You can also use Explorer for share management.

Using Print Manager, you can oversee printer functions, including the creation of new ports and new print devices. When using this utility to manage the printing characteristics of a remote printer, however, a few limitations come into play. First, you cannot create a NetWare printer that is shared through the gateway service; this task must be carried out on a local level. Second, when creating a printer on a remote server, Print Manager cannot select a printer unless it is physically connected to that remote server. Attempting to connect to a printer that is not physically attached will result in an error message.

If you are running Routing and Remote Access Service on your servers, you can use MPRADMIN and ROUTMON to administer both RRAS and legacy RAS services.

> **Caution** Do not attempt to administer RRAS from your Windows NT workstation if you are running traditional RAS services. The DLLs needed for the RRAS tools are not compatible with the older service.

The Windows NT Resource Kit also contains a remote command line utility (RCMD.EXE) that allows you to enter a command line locally and have it execute as if it were entered on the remote server itself. Thus you can remotely perform any function that can normally be done from the command line. This option is especially helpful for gathering information while troubleshooting.

ADMINISTRATION FROM A WEB BROWSER

It is possible to administer Windows NT Server from any machine with a supported Web browser using Web Administration tools from the Windows NT Resource Kit. This software can be installed on any Windows NT Server 4.0 server that is running Microsoft Internet Information Server version 2.0 or later. It enables the server to display Web pages that include forms through which you administer that server.

To use the Web browser tools, you must first install them on the server. Then you need only a computer equipped with a connection to your network, a Web browser (such as Microsoft Internet Explorer), and an administrator account on the domain.

Table 7-4 illustrates the activities you can perform using the Web browser tools.

Table 7-4   Administrative Capabilities Available via Web Browser Tools

Web Browser Tool	Administrative Capabilities
Account Management	▪ Create and delete user accounts (including FPNW user accounts) ▪ View and change user information (properties) ▪ Change user passwords ▪ Disable user accounts ▪ Create and remove groups ▪ Add users to and remove them from groups ▪ Add workstations to the domain
Share Management	▪ View shares for all installed file services (Microsoft-, Macintosh-, and NetWare-compatible file services) ▪ Change permissions on shares ▪ Create new shares for all installed file services
Session Management	▪ View current sessions ▪ Terminate one or all sessions ▪ Send a message to the current users of the server
Server Management	▪ Shut down (reboot) the server ▪ Change services/driver configuration ▪ View System, Application, and Security Log events ▪ Carry out a server configuration data dump
Printer Management	▪ List print queues and jobs in each queue ▪ Pause a queue or a specific print job ▪ Flush a queue or a specific print job

You manage security for the Web browser tools either through Windows NT challenge and response or through SSL. In environments requiring more security, you might consider using both methods simultaneously.

CHAPTER SUMMARY

- Large enterprise environments, by definition, contain multiple servers and many clients. A client is most easily envisioned as a stand-alone computer that has been integrated into a network so that it may access information from a server. As operating systems have evolved and improved, client and server computers have become remarkably complex, making it more difficult to distinguish between clients and servers. Windows NT is Microsoft's shared-code operating system, which means that it can act as both a network operating system, and a desktop operating system. In the business world, client/server applications are gaining popularity because they allow end users to develop their own methods for organizing data into profitable information.

- For a client computer to connect to and communicate with Windows NT Server 4.0, it must have client software, a compatible transport protocol, and a software driver for the NIC. Most network connectivity problems result from a failure in one of these three components.

- To simplify the process of gathering information from dissimilar networks, both Windows NT and Windows 95 include client and service software for many different types of network servers. Windows NT Server includes Server Services for NetWare, which allows NetWare clients to log onto a Windows NT server as if it were a NetWare server. Gateway Services for NetWare (GSNW) allow Microsoft clients to access resources on a NetWare server without installing a NetWare client. Using GSNW, the Windows NT server maps a drive letter to a NetWare volume, and then reshares the new folder with its own Microsoft clients.

- The Windows NT installation CD-ROM includes two clients for MS-DOS: Network Client 3.0 for MS-DOS, and LanMan 2.2c.

- Workgroups are Microsoft networks whose members can act as both clients and servers. In a Windows NT Workstation workgroup, a valid user account must be used to access shared resources. In Windows 95 and Windows for Workgroups groups, the shared resources are protected with only a password.

- With a domain logon, a client can access all necessary resources on many different servers through a single logon. Unique to domain logons is the ability to run a logon script, or a batch file of commands to be executed when a user logs onto the domain. Logon scripts can contain virtually any command that can be executed from the command prompt in Windows NT; they may also include certain parameters that can be used only at logon.

- In an enterprise client rollout, large numbers of client workstations are installed and configured simultaneously. Outsourcing can be a cost-effective option for companies that don't have the facilities to prepare a massive client rollout. Hard drive duplication can simplify the process, but brings the risk of wide-scale disaster if the same bug is unwittingly copied to thousands of clients. Batch response files and boot disks are Microsoft's preferred method of client installation.

7

- The Client Administrator tool helps to automate the process of sharing client installation files, creating Windows 95 installation boot disks, and sharing server administration tools.

- The Remoteboot service is a Windows NT Server feature that starts MS-DOS and Microsoft Windows computers over the network. Rather than running from a local hard disk, the operating system runs from the server.

- The Macintosh file system, naming conventions, protocols, and frame types are vastly different from those used by Windows NT. A computer running Windows NT Server can act as a fully functional AppleShare file server, however, providing common ground for Macintosh clients and Microsoft clients to share data. Windows NT Server can also act as an AppleTalk router and as a Macintosh print server.

- Servers can also be administered remotely from Windows 95 machines, Windows NT workstations, and, if Web administration tools are installed on the server, any machine with a compatible browser.

KEY TERMS

- **base code operating systems** — Multiple operating systems that utilize the same basic code to form their structure. Windows NT Server and Windows NT Workstation fall into this category.

- **client** — A stand-alone computer that has been integrated into a network so that it may access information from a server.

- **client-based network administration tools** — Utilities that can be executed on a workstation and are used to administer one or more servers.

- **client rollout** — The process of loading and configuring software on multiple computers simultaneously.

- **client/server application** — An application with components that execute both locally and at the server.

- **Gateway Services for NetWare** — A Windows NT Server service used to provide access to NetWare resources without having additional software on each client.

- **installation disk set** — A set of disks that contains all software, files, and settings needed to access a Windows NT server.

- **logon script** — A list of commands that execute when the user logs on to the network.

- **network driver** — Software that facilitates communication between the operating system and the network card.

- **open database connectivity (ODBC)** — A protocol used for providing access to multiple data sources using a common language.

- **outsourcing** — The act of hiring an outside firm to conduct some element of your business. Generally outsourcing is done to alleviate manpower shortages.

- **redirector** — Software that intercepts software requests for data from network drives, converts them into network I/O requests, and passes the I/O requests to the network driver to be packaged.

- **Remoteboot** — A Windows NT Server feature that starts MS-DOS and Microsoft Windows computers over the network.

- **Server Services for NetWare** — A service that allows a NetWare client to log on to a Windows NT Server as if it were a NetWare Server.

- **workgroup** — A collection of computers that work together, each acting as both a client and a server to the other group members.

REVIEW QUESTIONS

1. Before a Windows NT client can access a resource, it must be made a(n) _____ of the domain.

2. Windows NT can act as:

   a. a desktop operating system

   b. a network operating system

   c. both a desktop operating system and a network operating system

   d. Neither a desktop operating system nor a network operating system

3. Windows NT Workstation places the highest execution priority on _____ .

4. Windows NT supports the following transport protocols (choose all that apply):

   a. TCP/IP

   b. AppleTalk

   c. IPX/SPX

   d. NetBEUI

   e. DECNet

5. Windows NT Server uses _____ software to communicate with other servers.

6. Gateway Services for NetWare is installed by default in a standard Windows NT installation. True or False?

7. Using Gateway Services for NetWare eliminates the client's need for a _____ .

8. Microsoft Client for Windows 95 is composed of two parts:

   a. a gateway and a redirector

   b. a network driver and gateway

   c. a network driver and redirector

   d. a file and print sharing service and a network driver

9. Microsoft provides software for the following clients with Windows NT (choose all that apply):

   a. Banyan Vines

   b. Macintosh

   c. MS-DOS

   d. OS/2

   e. All client software must be downloaded.

10. Logon scripts can contain (choose all that apply):

    a. batch files and DOS executables

    b. anything that can be executed from a command line

    c. any executable

    d. none of the above

11. Microsoft's recommended mass rollout procedure is:

    a. batch installation with response files

    b. hard drive duplication

    c. outsourcing

    d. GHOST.EXE or Image Blaster

12. Client administrator can be used to (choose all that apply):

    a. Make an installation disk for 32-bit TCP/IP for WFW 3.11.

    b. Make a customized network boot disk for Windows NT Workstation and Windows 95.

    c. Make a client software installation disk set (DOS, OS/2, and Windows for Workgroups 3.11).

    d. Copy and share the client-based server administration tools.

13. When using Client Administrator to create boot disks, all software required for laptops is included. True or False?

14. Startup disks to install Windows NT can be made for the following hardware platforms (choose all that apply):

    a. Intel

    b. Alpha

    c. MIPS

    d. Power PC

15. Client-based network administration tools enable you to have administrative support for (choose all that apply):

    a. Windows NT

    b. LAN Manager for MS OS/2

    c. LAN Manager for UNIX

    d. NetWare 3.12 and earlier

16. The Remoteboot service can be installed using the Client Administrator. True or False?

17. Using Windows NT Services for Macintosh, a Windows NT Server can act as (choose all that apply):

    a. an AppleShare file server

    b. an AppleTalk router

    c. a PostScript printer

    d. a Macintosh client

18. The AppleTalk filing protocol runs (choose all that apply):

    a. only when required

    b. in the Windows NT Executive

    c. as a service

    d. as a multithreaded process

19. Using Services for Macintosh, a Macintosh client can print to a PCL printer. True or False?

20. Once a Macintosh-accessible volume has been created, the folder can be shared with Microsoft clients using _____.

21. On a Windows 95 machine, you can use the following tools for remote administration of a Windows NT server in your domain (choose all that apply):

    a. Server Manager

    b. User Manager for Domains

    c. WINS Administrator

    d. RAS Administrator

22. On a Windows NT machine, you can use the following tools for remote administration of a Windows NT server in your domain (choose all that apply):

    a. Server Manager

    b. User Manager for Domains

    c. WINS Administrator

    d. RAS Administrator

23. Using Print Manager on a Windows NT workstation to remotely manage a Windows NT server, you can perform any tasks that you could carry out locally on that server. True or False?

24. It is not possible to manage shares on a Windows NT server remotely. True or False?

25. The Web administration tools in the Windows NT Resource Kit enable you to perform the following administrative tasks from a computer with a supported Web browser (choose all that apply):

  a. Change user passwords.

  b. Create and delete user accounts (including FPNW user accounts).

  c. View shares for all installed file services (Microsoft-, Macintosh-, and NetWare-compatible file services).

  d. Shut down (reboot) a server.

  e. Change services/driver configuration.

HANDS-ON PROJECTS

For some or all of these projects, you will need a Windows 95 workstation that is either running SP1 or that has the file NEXUS.EXE available on Microsoft's FTP site; and a Windows NT server with an NTFS volume running a compatible network protocol with the workstation (TCP/IP is recommended). A Macintosh would also be helpful but is not necessary.

PROJECT 7-1

In this project you will install server tools on a computer running Windows 95. Note that the file containing the server tools can be found on the Windows NT Server installation CD. However in this project you will download the file so that you can become familiar with Microsoft's FTP site.

  1. Download **NEXUS.EXE** from *ftp://ftp.microsoft.com/Softlib/MSLFILES/* to an empty folder on your hard drive.

  2. From within Windows Explorer, double-click **NEXUS.EXE** to extract the files.

  3. On a Windows 95 machine, click the **Start button**, point to **Settings**, click **Control Panel**, then double-click the **Add/Remove Programs icon**. The Add/Remove Programs dialog box opens.

  4. Click the **Windows Setup tab**, then click **Have Disk**.

  5. In the Install from disk text box, specify the folder containing **Srvtools.inf**.

  6. Click **Install**. The tools will be installed, and Windows NT Server Tools will be added to your Program Groups. You will need to reboot your computer before using these tools.

  7. Reboot the computer.

PROJECT 7-2

In this project you will install Gateway Services for NetWare.

1. Click the **Start button**, point to **Settings**, click **Control Panel**, then double-click the **Network icon**. The Network dialog box opens.
2. Click the **Services tab**.
3. Click **OK**.
4. In the Services list, select **Gateway (and Client) Services for NetWare**, then click **Continue**. The Windows NT Setup dialog box opens.
5. In the text box, type the path to the Windows NT installation CD-ROM, then click **OK**. The necessary files are copied to your computer.
6. Click **Close**. When you are prompted to restart your machine, click **Yes**.

7

PROJECT 7-3

In this project you will use Server Manager to stop and then start a service on a remote Windows NT server. You can use Server Manager from another Windows NT server, a Windows NT workstation, or a Windows 95 machine that has the server tools installed. For any of these to work, you will need network access to the server and sufficient administrative privileges to effect the change.

1. If you are using a Windows NT Server, click the **Start button**, point to **Programs**, point to **Administrative Tools (Common)**, then click **Server Manager**. If you are using Windows 95, you must first install the server tools as described in Project 7-1. After these tools are installed in Windows 95, click the **Start button**, point to **Programs**, point to **Windows NT Server Tools**, then click **Server Manager**. On a Windows NT Workstation, these tools are installed from the Windows NT Server CD-ROM. After these tools are installed on a Windows NT Workstation, click the **Start button**, point to **Programs**, point to **Administrative Tools (Common)**, then click **Server Manager**.
2. In the Available Servers list, select a server.
3. Click **Computer** on the menu bar, then click **Services**. The Services dialog box opens.
4. In the Services list, select the **Licensing service**, then click **Stop**. The service stops.
5. Click **Start** in the Services dialog box to restart the service and return to your previous state.

If you had stopped the Net Logon or Server service, you would not be able to restart it remotely, as they are required for this remote administration.

PROJECT 7-4

In this project you will install Services for Macintosh, which will allow you to use Macintosh clients on your Windows NT network and enable your Windows NT Server to function as an AppleTalk router. Your shared volume must be on an NTFS partition.

1. Click the **Start button**, point to **Settings**, click **Control Panel**, then double-click the **Network icon**. The Network dialog box opens.

2. Click the **Services tab**, then click **Add**. The Add Services dialog box opens.

3. In the Network Service list, select **Services for Macintosh**, then click **OK**. The Setup dialog box opens.

4. In the File Path text box, type the path to the Windows NT server distribution files, then click **Continue**. The files are copied to your server.

5. In the Network dialog box, click **Close**.

6. The AppleTalk Protocol Properties dialog box appears. You can use this dialog box to select a new zone, a different network, or to enable AppleTalk routing. In the zones section, click **Add**.

7. In the Add Zone box, type **Printers**, then click **OK**. You have now added an AppleTalk zone called Printers.

8. Click the **Routing tab**. Select the **Enable Routing check box** if necessary. Also select the **Use these routers to seed the network check box**, and then enter the appropriate router. (Routing is discussed in Chapter 11.)

9. Click **OK**.

10. Restart your computer when prompted to do so.

CASE PROJECTS

1. You are the network administrator for the advertising firm Sterling-Gibson. You need to add the publishing division to your company's network so that the publishing division can exchange files with the accounting and finance departments and access the high-speed PCL laser printer. The publishing division consists of 45 Macintosh computers on an Ethernet network. The rest of the network consists of Windows 95 and Windows NT workstations on a separate Ethernet network served by three Windows NT Server 4.0 servers. Write a short report (three to six paragraphs) describing a solution that is fast and simple to implement and does not require additional hardware.

2. You have volunteered your time to the Makepeace Foundation, which helps domestic violence victims deal with the psychological aspects of their past. Makepeace has 18 offices across the state, each of which has its own LAN running Windows NT. The LANs are not interconnected, and not all of them offer RAS access. You plan to undertake a network audit of these sites. To assist in this endeavor, you are preparing a notebook computer to be used as a traveling administrator's workstation. Write a brief report (three to five paragraphs) explaining how you would configure it.

3. Your employer, GKK CardWorks, is planning to open a medium-sized office in Los Angeles. The office will initially house 100 employees. Because your current computers are all relatively old, you decide to buy all new PCs and use Windows NT Workstation for these new machines. As is so often the case, you have very little time to accomplish the rollout. Instead, you will have to spend most of your energies on the networking side of the project. Write a short report (three to five paragraphs) explaining two different ways in which you can accomplish this rollout. In your report, describe the benefits and drawbacks of each method.

7

4. You are the network manager for NV—eNterprise Ventures. Your company has announced plans to merge with the competing firm of Ellis/Adams. NV's network is all Windows NT, while the Ellis/Adams network is all Novell. The long-term plan is to migrate Ellis/Adams to Windows NT. In the meantime, however, the two networks need to exchange files. In addition, you need to give the Windows NT clients access to resources on the Novell servers. Write a brief report (two to four paragraphs) explaining the best way to accomplish your goals.

MANAGING USER AND GROUP ACCOUNTS

While user and group management is fairly easy in a single-domain environment, it is more challenging in an enterprise network. This chapter will introduce you to the basics of user and group management. You will also learn about the structure of the built-in users and groups, their roles in the network, and account policy administration.

AFTER READING THIS CHAPTER AND COMPLETING THE EXERCISES YOU WILL BE ABLE TO:

- Describe the built-in user accounts included with Windows NT and create new user accounts

- Describe the built-in groups included with Windows NT and create new group accounts

- Explain issues related to account policies

- Implement user and group account auditing

WINDOWS NT USER ACCOUNTS

To successfully access a network and its resources, you need a user account. Thus, user accounts represent the first line of defense when it comes to network security. As you will see in this chapter, however, you can make a network even more secure by requiring passwords and, in some cases, by requiring that those passwords be unique. In addition, you can set a minimum password length, set logon time parameters, and restrict the stations from which a user can log on to the network.

Each user account on a Windows NT server is granted some level of access within the domain. When a user account (or user) is created, it is assigned a **Security Identifier (SID)**. A SID is an alphanumeric identifier that is referenced whenever the user requests a resource. The SID assigned to a user is unique within a domain. All user account settings, including permissions, are linked to the SID, rather than the user name. This setup enables you to rename a user account without losing its configuration.

Because each account is linked to its SID, deleting an account eliminates its SID as well. Even if you recreate a user account exactly (using the same user name, password, group memberships, and so on), the account will receive a new SID and you must reestablish all permissions.

As you learned in Chapter 2, account information is stored in the **Security Access Manager (SAM)** database, which is located in the Registry at HKEY_LOCAL_MACHINE\sam. For a local account, this information is stored in the local Registry on the computer. For a network account, this information is stored in the SAM database in the Registry of the primary domain controller (PDC) and distributed to all backup domain controllers (BDCs).

BUILT-IN USER ACCOUNTS

Installing Windows NT automatically creates two accounts: Guest and Administrator. These **built-in accounts** can be managed and used just like any other accounts. They can be renamed, assigned passwords, assigned logon restrictions, or even disabled. They cannot, however, be deleted. If you try to delete one, you will receive the message shown in Figure 8-1.

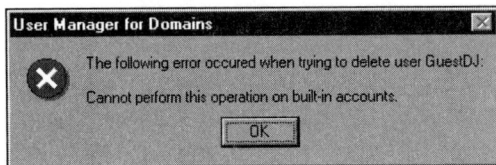

Figure 8-1   Results of trying to delete built-in accounts

The Guest account provides the lowest level of access for a user and is automatically granted membership to a global group, Domain Guests (described later in this chapter). By default, this account is disabled on both Windows NT Workstation and Windows NT Server computers so as to decrease the chance of someone using it to access the network. If you plan to use this account, it is highly recommended that you assign a password to it. To provide a slightly higher level of security, you could also rename the Guest account. It is usually best to leave this account alone, however, and provide users who require minimal access—such as visitors who need to print a document or temporary employees—with a separate account.

The Administrator account lies at the opposite end of the security spectrum from the Guest account. It is granted the highest level of security, having access to everything on the network. This account is the first one you will use after installing Windows NT. In fact, the installation is not complete until the Administrator logs on. During the installation process, you need to provide a password for the Administrator account.

In many networks, the Administrator account is used to perform most domain functions, from adding users to assigning rights. With this concept in mind, and the knowledge that every hacker in the world is familiar with the Administrator account in Windows NT, you may find it safest to rename or disable this account.

Like all other Windows NT user accounts, the Administrator account can be renamed by opening User Manager for Domains, selecting the user, clicking User on the menu bar, then clicking Rename. You can then use the Rename dialog box, shown in Figure 8-2, to change the Administrator user name.

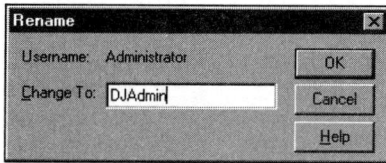

Figure 8-2 Rename dialog box

Microsoft recommends renaming or disabling the Administrator account *after* you have created other accounts. The most secure option is to disable the Administrator account and then assign another user the same rights. By including the new user in the Administrators and Domain Admins groups, you grant it the same access to the computer and the domain as the Administrator.

ESTABLISHING NEW USER ACCOUNTS

On a Windows NT Workstation, user and group accounts are created using the User Manager. On a Windows NT Server, they are created using a variation of this program called User Manager for Domains. To open User Manager for Domains, click the Start button, point to Programs, click Administrative Tools (Common) then click User Manager for Domains. The User Manager for Domains window is shown in Figure 8-3, with the domain name (in this case, "WORKGROUP") appearing in the title bar.

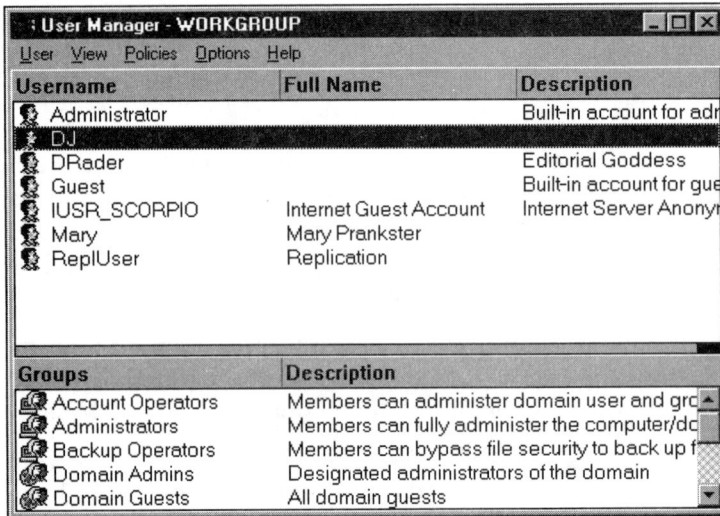

Figure 8-3   User Manager for Domains window

As you can see, the User Manager for Domains window offers five menu options: User, View, Policies, Options, and Help. The User menu allows you to add, copy, delete, or rename user and group accounts. In addition, this menu enables you to view the properties for a user or group, select a group of users, or select another domain to view. In the Hands-on Projects at the end of this chapter, you will have the chance to add and manage a user account using the options in the User menu.

The View menu allows you to sort user accounts by either full name or user name, and to refresh the list of users. (You can also refresh the list by pressing F5.) The Policies menu allows you to establish account policies, assign user rights, audit particular events through the Event Viewer, and manage trust relationships for the domain. The Options menu enables you to specify basic options for the User Manager for Domains, such as connection speed, whether to request confirmation of events, and whether to save settings when you exit User Manager for Domains. Finally, the Help menu provides access to the help file for the User Manager for Domains.

WINDOWS NT GROUP ACCOUNTS

Like most network operating systems, Windows NT uses groups to simplify network administration. Strictly speaking, a **group account** is a logical collection of users that are assigned access rights and permissions. Each user in the group is granted the same access rights and permissions as the rest of the group. Grouping users together into group accounts, and then assigning access levels to the group as a whole, prevents the network administrator from having to assign access rights individually. As with user accounts, installing Windows NT automatically creates some groups, which are then managed through the User Manager for

Domains. Windows NT groups fall into three categories: global, local, and system. To fully understand the distinction between global and local groups, you must be familiar with trusts (discussed in Chapter 2). Remember that global groups can contain only users, while local groups can contain both users and groups.

GLOBAL GROUPS

A **global group** is a group of users that are granted access to the domain. Three global groups are installed by default: Domain Admins, Domain Users, and Domain Guests.

The Domain Admins global group has the network access that its name implies—that is, full access to administer the domain. This access includes the ability to create, delete, and modify users and groups in the domain. By default, the Domain Admins global group is a member of the Administrators local group. Only one user is added to this group automatically—the Administrator. By default, the global group Domain Admins is added to the local Administrators group on every Windows NT machine in the domain. As a result, members of the Domain Admins group can control access on any computer in the domain. Only Administrators are able to modify the Domain Admins group.

The Domain Users global group provides user-level access to all members of the domain. Members of this group are granted access to log on to the domain and rights to use resources in the domain, but are not permitted to manage those resources. When a domain user is created, it is placed in this group by default. When the Domain Users group is added to the Users group on a workstation (for example, when the workstation becomes a member of the domain), all members of the group are granted user-level access to the system. Only Administrators and members of the Account Operators group are able to modify the Domain Users group.

The Domain Guests global group allows its members minimal access to the domain. By default, it contains the Guest account. Members of this group can do very little. Most often, this group is used to assign very-low-level access on a case-by-case basis. Again, only Administrators and members of the Account Operators group are able to modify this group.

LOCAL GROUPS

Local groups provide access to local resources on a particular machine. Even if users have access to the domain, they cannot use the resources on a particular computer unless they are members of that computer's local group. A user can be a member of a local group as an individual or as part of a global group. One key difference between local groups and global groups is that local groups can contain both users and global groups. In fact, trust relationships are established by adding global groups to local groups.

Eight local groups are created automatically when the operating system is installed. These groups perform specific functions, as discussed in the following sections.

8

User Rights

Before you can work with local groups, you need to understand the concept of user rights. **User rights** allow a particular user to perform a function, such as logging on to the server locally or backing up and restoring data. Two types of user rights exist: regular rights and advanced rights. The default local groups—and by extension the global groups—are granted certain user rights, depending on the function of the particular group.

To assign user rights, open the User Manager for Domains, click Policies on the menu bar, then click User Rights. The User Rights Policy dialog box, shown in Figure 8-4, provides the necessary options.

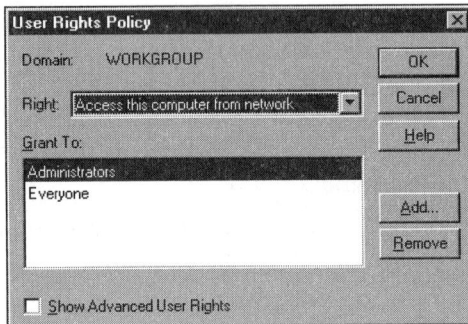

Figure 8-4   The User Rights Policy dialog box

Table 8-1 lists the regular user and advanced user rights that can be assigned to a group.

Table 8-1   Regular and Advanced User Rights for Windows NT Server

Regular User Rights	Advanced User Rights
Access this computer from network	Act as a part of the operating system
Add workstations to domain	Bypass traverse checking
Back up files and directories	Create a pagefile
Change the system time	Create a token object
Force shutdown from a remote system	Create permanent shared objects
Load and unload device drivers	Debug programs
Log on locally	Generate security audits
Manage auditing and security log	Increase quotas
Restore files and directories	Increase scheduling priority
Shut down the system	Load and unload device drivers
Take ownership of files or other objects	Lock pages in memory
	Log on as a batch job
	Log on as a service
	Modify firmware environment values

Table 8-1   Regular and Advanced User Rights for Windows NT Server (continued)

Regular User Rights	Advanced User Rights
	Profile single process
	Profile system performance
	Receive unsolicited device input
	Replace a process level token

Now that you are familiar with the concept of user rights, you are ready to learn about the various built-in local groups.

Built-in Local Groups

The first of the built-in local groups, the Administrators group, is the most powerful group in that it enables users to fully administer the local computer. By default, the Administrator user and the Domain Admins group are members of this group (though both can be removed). Note, however, that members of this group are not automatically granted access to every file on the computer, as takes place with other operating systems. If the Administrators group is specifically not granted access to a file, members of that group lose the ability to assign permissions or otherwise administer the file. You can, however, maneuver around this restriction. Members of the Administrators group retain the ability to modify the ownership of a file; by making themselves owners, they can modify the file and its permissions.

> Although the Administrators group is all-powerful, not even a member of this group can delete built-in groups.

Another built-in local group, the Users group, is afforded relatively few rights on the server. Members of this group can create local groups and manage the local groups they create. However, unless they have access to User Manager for Domains (which requires the Log on locally user right), they have no way to create or manage groups.

As you might imagine, the Guests local group has the lowest level of access to the server. Its members are granted no access at the server console. This group is most often used for occasional or one-time logons, though the Guest user is automatically made a member of this group.

The Server Operators local group is second only to the Administrators group in terms of its level of access. Members of this group can perform all functions relating to managing the domain's servers. For example, they can create, manage, and delete printer and network shares; back up and restore files; format a server's hard drive; lock and unlock servers; change the server's clock; shut down the server; and log on to the domain from the server console.

The Print Operators local group is granted access to manage printer shares on the network. Its rights include creating, managing, and deleting printer shares, as well as logging on from the server and shutting down the server.

As its name implies, the Backup Operators local group enables its members to back up and restore files and directories on a server. Like Print Operators, Backup Operators can log on at the server and shut down the server.

The Account Operators local group is able to manage most user and group accounts in a domain. Its members can add and fully manage (modify or delete) new user and group accounts, and partially manage the default users and groups. Account Operators cannot modify the following groups or accounts: the Administrators group, the Domain Admins group, the Account Operators group, the Backup Operators group, the Print Operators group, the Server Operators group, or any Administrator account. They can, however, add computers to the domain, log on at the server, and shut down the server.

The Replicator local group is a specialized group that forms part of the directory replication service (discussed in Chapter 6). Normal user accounts should not be included in this group, which should include only the account that is used by the Replicator to log on to the domain controller and to the other servers in the domain.

Table 8-2 summarizes the user rights that are assigned to each of the built-in local groups by default. If a particular user right is not listed in the table, it is not assigned to any group by default.

Table 8-2   The User Rights of the Built-in Local Groups

User Right	Admini-strators	Users	Guests	Server Operators	Print Operators	Backup Operators	Account Operators	Repli-cator	Every-one
Access this computer from Network	X								X
Back up files and directories	X			X		X			
Bypass traverse checking									X
Change the system time	X			X					
Create a pagefile	X								
Debug programs	X								
Force shutdown from a remote system	X			X					

Table 8-2   The User Rights of the Built-in Local Groups (continued)

User Right	Admini-strators	Users	Guests	Server Operators	Print Operators	Backup Operators	Account Operators	Repli-cator	Every-one
Increase quotas	X								
Increase scheduling priority	X								
Load and unload device drivers	X								
Log on as a service								X	
Log on locally	X			X	X	X	X		
Manage auditing and security log	X								
Modify firmware environment values	X								
Profile single process	X								
Profile system performance	X								
Restore files and directories	X			X		X			
Shut down the system	X			X	X	X	X		
Take ownership of files or other objects	X								

SYSTEM GROUPS

The Windows NT architecture includes four special **system groups**: Everyone, Interactive, Network, and Creator Owner. You cannot modify these groups or change their names.

Likewise, you cannot manually add or delete users from them. On the other hand, you can assign rights to the Everyone, Interactive, and Network groups.

The Everyone group is just that—everyone. Unlike in NetWare environments, however, the Windows NT Everyone group includes only users logged on to the server. When users log off, they are automatically removed from the group. Note that, by default, this group is granted full access to resources.

All new users have access to all resources by default. To limit access to resources, you must revoke the rights assigned to the Everyone group. Thus, it's important to remember that the Everyone group exists, and that its members will have full access to all resources until you restrict their rights.

The Everyone group represents a combination of the Interactive and Network groups. The Interactive group includes all users that are logged on to a server locally. Naturally, this group includes only one user at a time. The Network group, as you might expect, includes all users that are logged on to the server across the network.

The last of the four default system groups, the Creator Owner group, grants full access to a resource to its creator. While members of the Everyone group can be restricted to read-only access to a particular file or directory, the members of Creator Owner group enjoy full access to that resource. A unique Creator Owner group exists for each resource, including only the user who created the resource or a user who has taken ownership of the resource.

MANAGING ACCOUNT POLICIES

Armed with a working knowledge of the default users and groups in Windows NT, you are almost ready to add your own users. First, however, you need to consider a number of issues. For example, what is your password policy? Does a naming convention for users already exist, or will you create one? What are, or will be, the rules for the naming convention? Will you create Windows NT user profiles (covered in Chapter 9)? If so, how extensive will they be? Where will each user's home directories reside—on the server or on the user's local drive?

You establish many of these **account policies** for a domain through the Account Policy dialog box, shown in Figure 8-5. To open the Account Policy dialog box, open User Manager for Domains, click Policy on the menu bar, then click Account.

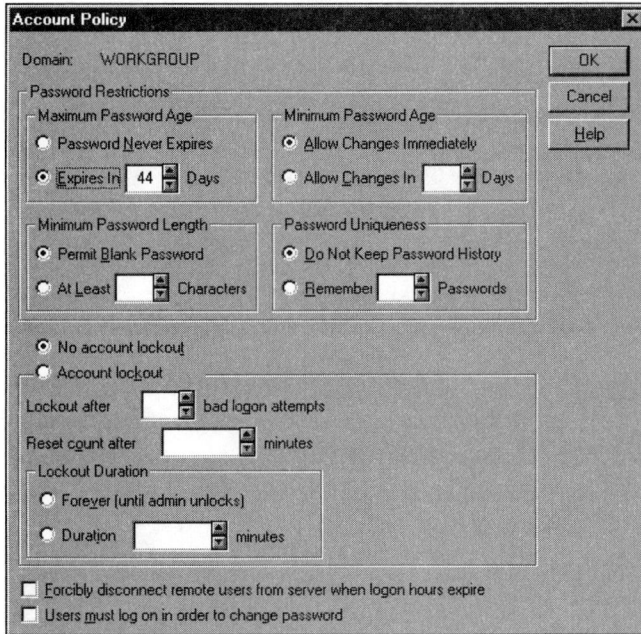

Figure 8-5   Account Policy dialog box

The following sections explain the most important issues pertaining to managing accounts.

Password Policies

The password policies you establish for a domain can make or break the system's security. Before adding users to your domain, you should take some time to formulate your password policies. You will need to consider several issues. Most importantly, who will be allowed to manage—that is, modify—the password?

When you initially create a user account, you have three options regarding password control: User Must Change Password at Next Logon, User Cannot Change Password, and Password Never Expires. Each of these are represented as a check box in the New User dialog box, shown in Figure 8-6. (The fourth checkbox, Account Disabled, will be discussed in the section "Other Account Considerations" later in this chapter.)

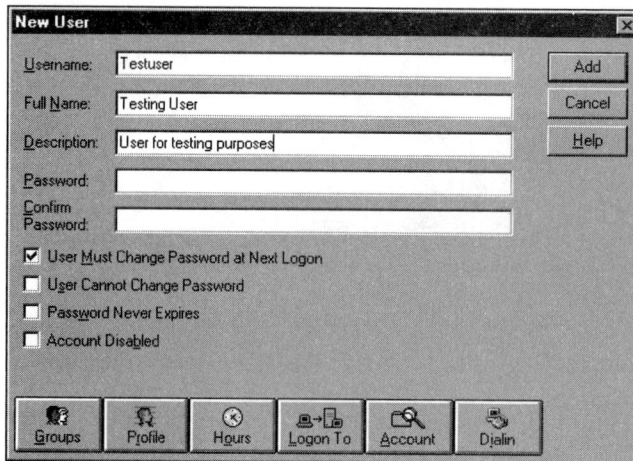

Figure 8-6   Password options in the New User dialog box

When you create a new user, by default the User Must Change Password at Next Logon box is checked. This option requires the new user to choose a new password when logging on for the first time. Thus an administrator can assign a dummy password to a user account when it is created, and the user can protect his or her privacy by changing that password when logging on for the first time.

The User Cannot Change Password option should be selected for user accounts assigned to temporary employees or accounts used by automated programs, such as backup managers, that need to log on to the network.

The Password Never Expires option overrides the forced password change settings (discussed later in this chapter). This option should be used only in exceptional cases, as it is generally a good idea to force periodic password changes on all accounts. This approach ensures that, if by some chance a hacker has figured out a user's password, the password would be valid for only a specific number of days. When the user changes his or her password, the hacker would be locked out again.

Windows NT passwords are case-sensitive and can include numbers. These features can protect a network from dictionary attack programs, which attempt to gain access to a network by using lists of words found in the dictionary. Appending even a single digit to the end of a password protects the network from dictionary attacks because, for every conceivable password, ten possible variations would exist. The number of possible combinations grows exponentially when capital letters are used throughout the password (hEllO, for example).

The following list summarizes the various ways to enhance password security on the network:

- Append a number to the end of a password.
- Require users to include capital letters in their passwords.
- Require passwords to be changed periodically. The default period of time is 44 days. The accepted industry standard is 45 to 60 days.

- Require users to log on to change their passwords. If a user fails to change his or her password in time, this option (found at the bottom of the Account Policy dialog box) locks the user out of the domain. After a user's password has expired, only the Administrator can change it.

- Set a minimum password length. Six characters is the default and is an accepted industry standard. Establishing a minimum length makes it more difficult for an unauthorized user to guess a password, because it is far more difficult to guess a six-letter password than a three-letter password.

- Require unique passwords. When this approach is used, a user cannot switch back and forth between two words. Instead, the user must provide a new password every time the password is changed.

Naming Conventions

In addition to developing a password policy, you should establish your naming conventions before adding users and group to a network. In the Windows NT environment, user names can be up to 20 characters long and are not case-sensitive. The particular naming convention you employ depends on the type of network involved and the number of users.

A user name should easily identify a user. In addition, each user name should be unique within the domain. Some naming conventions can satisfy these needs initially, on a small network, but may work over time, as the network expands to accommodate more users. For example, assigning a user's first, last, and middle initial as a user name would give user names that were unidentifiable for anyone except the person who originally established them. Some smaller organizations use the first-name, last-initial naming convention (for example, DAVIDJ). This strategy may suffice at first, but as the company grows and more people are hired, the chances of more than one person having the same first name and last initial increase. The network administrator would then have to decide whether to add the second letter of a user's last name, or possibly the second and third letter.

Generally, for larger organizations, a combination of the full last name and the first initial works best (either DJOHNSON or JOHNSOND). This convention decreases the chances of having two people in the same domain with the same potential logon name. Keep in mind, however, that you may occasionally have to make exceptions for extremely common names, such as Smith or Lee. Nevertheless, taking the time to plan your naming convention before you begin adding users will limit the number of exceptions needed.

Home Directories

A user's **home directory** is generally a location on a centralized file server that is used to store the user's data. A home directory can be located on a local computer, but for backup and security reasons, it is usually best to place home directories on a central file server. If the home directory resides on an NTFS volume, it can be secured so that only the user and the Administrator have access to the data. Company managers often prefer to place their files on a home directory, because these files can be backed up regularly and are totally secure—even more so than on a local hard drive.

To specify the location for a home directory:

1. Open the User Properties dialog box by double-clicking on an existing user. Alternatively, you can open the New User dialog box by selecting **New** from the User menu.

2. Click the **Profile button**. The User Environment Profile dialog box opens.

3. Click the **Connect option button**, then click the **Connect list arrow** and select the drive to which you want to assign the home directory.

4. In the To text box, type the UNC for the server and share where you want the home directory to reside. Figure 8-7 shows a home directory assigned to the W drive, on the Server1 server, drive C:, the Homedirs share.

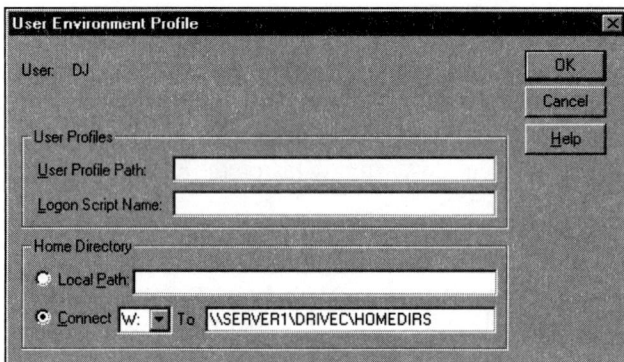

Figure 8-7   Specifying a home directory's location

OTHER ACCOUNT CONSIDERATIONS

There are other, no less important considerations when establishing user account policies. Some of these issues include the following:

- **User profiles**— If user profiles (discussed in detail in Chapter 9) are being used on the network, their location and role should be defined early in the user creation process. By doing so, you will save yourself the administration headache of having to apply a user profile to a number of users that already exist.

- **Logon hours**—You can greatly enhance security by specifying the exact hours that a user can log on to the network. This approach ensures that accounts for users who work during the day are not available at night or on weekends, when most hackers strike. In addition, the user can be forcibly disconnected from the domain after logon hours have expired by checking the box at the bottom of the Account Policy window.

- **Station restrictions**—Windows NT allows you to limit the stations from which a user can log on to the network. In a network that employs a firewall to restrict access to the Internet, the station ID is often used to develop access lists. Limiting the stations from which users can log on prevents them from circumventing the access restrictions.

- **Account lockout**—Windows NT allows you to disable an account for a specified amount of time if that user unsuccessfully attempts to log on too often. For example, you could specify that if a user account is denied access three times in a row, the account would become inaccessible for the next two hours. This strategy could prevent someone from repeatedly trying to guess a user's password.

- **Disabling, deleting, or renaming accounts**—Windows NT allows you to disable, rename (maintaining the same security settings), or delete an account. These options come into play when someone leaves the company. It is often a good idea to rename the account assigned to an employee's replacement. Remember that once you delete an account, it cannot be recovered.

By establishing guidelines for each of these areas, you will increase your network's security. Clearly thought-out policies save everyone time and prevent problems in the long run.

AUDITING SECURITY EVENTS

The Event Viewer is used to track events on a Windows NT computer. By default, the Event Viewer, which is accessible from the Start Menu under Programs/Administrative Tools (Common), tracks system and application events on the System Log and Application Log. It can also be configured to track security events such as failed logon attempts and changes in security policy.

To configure the Event Viewer to track—or audit—these types of events, open the User Manager for Domains, click Policy in the menu bar, then click Audit. The Audit Policy dialog box opens, as shown in Figure 8-8. Here you can choose to audit a list of security events.

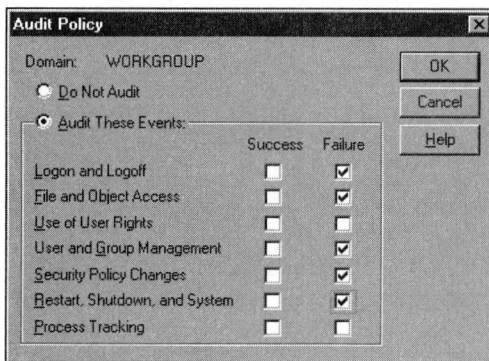

Figure 8-8   Audit Policy dialog box

Table 8-3 describes the security events listed in the Audit Policy dialog box. Note that, for each event, you can track both successes and failures.

Table 8-3   Event Viewer Options in the Audit Policy Dialog Box

Event	Description
Logon and Logoff	Tracks logons and logoffs for the server, the domain, and network connections
File and Object Access	Tracks user access of files, directories, and printers to provide general tracking of these types of access; this option must be enabled before specific users and groups can be tracked, a type of auditing that is performed at the resource level.
Use of User Rights	Tracks when a user right, such as setting the system clock or loading a device driver, is invoked
User and Group Management	Tracks user and group management, including creation, modification, or deletion of accounts
Security Policy Changes	Tracks changes to user rights or account policy settings
Restart, Shutdown, and System	Logs restart, shutdown, and system events, and tracks information on which specific user initiated a particular event
Process Tracking	Tracks process-related events, such as starting an application or indirectly accessing an object

Keep in mind that the more events you choose to track, the more resources the network will consume, and the harder it will be to interpret the data you collect. For this reason, it is generally a good idea to track as few events as possible.

CHAPTER SUMMARY

- User accounts in Windows NT are required to gain access to the network. When you create a user, Windows NT assigns a Security Identifier (SID) that is referenced whenever the user requests a resource. Each user's SID is unique. Deleting a user account eliminates its SID as well. Even if a user is later recreated with all the same characteristics, a different SID will be assigned.

- Windows NT has two types of users, local and network. Local user accounts are granted access to log on to the workstation itself, while network accounts are only able to access the system across the network. All user account information is maintained in a database called the Security Access Manager (SAM). Depending on the type of account, information for the user is stored in either the SAM in the Registry on the local machine or the SAM located on the primary domain controller.

- When Windows NT is installed, two built-in user accounts are created automatically—Guest and Administrator. The Guest account, which is disabled by default, is granted very limited access to the system; in contrast, the Administrator is granted full access.

Neither the Guest nor the Administrator account can be deleted from a Windows NT computer, but both can be disabled or renamed. For security purposes, Microsoft recommends renaming or disabling the Administrator account after other accounts have been created, Account management—including creation, deletion, and modification of users and groups—on Windows NT Server computers is handled through the User Manager for Domains.

- A group account comprises a logical collection of user accounts. Placing users together into group accounts, then assigning access levels to the group, prevents the network administrator from having to assign access rights on an individual basis. Windows NT includes three types of group accounts: global, local, and system.

- Global groups can contain only global users (members of the domain) and are used to perform domain functions. When you install Windows NT, three built-in global groups are automatically created: Domain Admins, Domain Users, and Domain Guests. Each of these groups is granted specific access to the domain.

- Local groups can contain both users and groups and are used in interdomain trust relationships. They provide access to the resources of a specific computer. User rights are assigned to local groups to allow them to perform certain functions on the computer, such as log on locally or back up files and directories. Eight local groups are created automatically during installation, each of which is allowed to perform specific functions on the computer. For example, the Server Operators group is allowed to back up and restore files, log on locally, and shut down and restart the server; in contrast, the Users group is allowed only basic access to the server's resources.

- The four system groups are special in that they are populated automatically and cannot be modified. Groups like Everyone can, however, be assigned permissions on the server. In fact, the Everyone group is assigned full access to all resources by default.

- It is very important to establish solid account policies before adding users and groups to a Windows NT network. Such policies govern issues such as passwords, naming conventions, home directories, and logon hours.

- It is possible to monitor, or audit, changes to the system by using the Event Viewer. To enable event auditing, use the Audit Policy dialog box. To conserve network resources, you should track as few events as possible.

KEY TERMS

- **account policies** — A set of rules that govern user account settings, such as password length.

- **built-in accounts** — User and group accounts that are automatically created upon installation of Windows NT.

- **global group** — A group of users that is granted access to a domain.

- **group account** — A logical collection of users that are assigned access rights and permissions. Each user in the group receives the same access rights and permissions as the rest of the group.

- **home directory** — A location on a server or local hard drive used to store user data.

- **local group** — A set of related users that are granted access to resources on a particular computer.

- **Security Access Manager (SAM)** — The database on Windows NT computers in which all user settings are maintained.

- **Security Identifier (SID)** — The unique number assigned to each user account that is referenced when a resource is requested to verify that user's access rights.

- **system group** — A special group of users that is populated automatically by the server.

- **user rights** — Permissions assigned to a group of users to allow them to perform specific functions on the server, such as backing up files and directories.

REVIEW QUESTIONS

1. Which of the following types of groups are managed by the administrator? (Select all that apply.)

   a. local

   b. system

   c. global

   d. domain

2. It is possible to lock a user account if it has been repeatedly denied access to the domain due to invalid passwords. True or False?

3. After you have installed Windows NT and created users, you should rename the _____ account.

4. The System Operators group is second only to the Administrators group in terms of its level of access. True or False?

5. Which of the following is not an option when setting password specifications for a new user?

   a. User Must Change Password at First Logon

   b. User Cannot Change Password

   c. Password Never Expires

   d. User Must Change Password at Next Logon

6. On a Windows NT server, user and group accounts are managed via the _____.

7. Which of the following local groups cannot shut down the server?

   a. Replicator

   b. Backup Operators

   c. Administrators

   d. Print Operators

8. The Guest account is the first account used after the installation of the operating system. True or False?

9. User rights are assigned to _____ groups.

10. Which of the following user rights is assigned to the Replicator group?

    a. back up files and directories

    b. log on as a service

    c. log on locally

    d. change the system's time

11. To enable event auditing, open the User Manger for Domains, click _____ on the menu bar, then click _____.

12. Which of the following are considerations for password policies? (Select all that apply.)

    a. use capitalization and numbers

    b. require periodic password changes

    c. require unique passwords

    d. set a minimum password length

13. The users and groups that are created automatically when Windows NT is installed cannot be deleted. True or False?

14. Which of the following is not a system group?

    a. Interactive

    b. Users

    c. Everyone

    d. Creator Owner

15. _____ groups are used to establish trust relationships between domains.

16. The Users groups is automatically granted access to log on to the server locally. True or False?

17. The Event Viewer can be configured to track user events on the _____ log.

    a. Application

    b. System

    c. Security

    d. User

18. To assign a user's home directory, click the _____ button in the User Properties or New User window.

19. A user's SID can be reassigned if the user is recreated with exactly the same characteristics as the original account. True or False?

20. All user account information is stored in the registry in the _____ database.

21. The Administrator user is automatically a member of both the Administrators and Domain Admins groups. True or False?

22. Which of the following are automatically recorded in the Event Viewer?

    a. changes to the system security policy

    b. user-initiated system restarts

    c. unsuccessful logon attempts

    d. no user events

23. Along with Administrators and Backup Operators, which built-in group has access rights to back up files and directories?

24. Which of the following statements does not accurately describe passwords in Windows NT?

    a. Multiple users in a domain can have the same password.

    b. Passwords can have a maximum length of 8 characters.

    c. Passwords are case-sensitive.

    d. Passwords can include numbers.

25. A user's home directory must reside on a server. True or False?

HANDS-ON PROJECTS

These Hands-on Projects focus on adding users and groups and changing user rights and password policies. For all the projects, you will need access to a Primary Domain Controller running Windows NT Server 4.0.

PROJECT 8-1

In this project you will view the configuration of the built-in users and groups and familiarize yourself with User Manager for Domains.

1. Click the **Start button**, point to **Programs**, point to **Administrative Tools (Common)**, then click **User Manager for Domains**. The User Manager for Domains window opens. In the Username column of the upper pane, click **Administrator**.

2. Click **User** in the menu bar, then click **Properties**. The User Properties dialog box opens. Note that the actual password for this user is not displayed in the Password or Confirm Password text boxes; instead you see only a line of asterisks. To protect the user's privacy, passwords are always represented by 14 asterisks in User Manager for Domains. Also, by default, the Password Never Expires option is checked for the Administrator user.

3. Click the **Groups button** to view group information for the user. The Group Memberships dialog box opens, as shown in Figure 8-9. The Member of list box indicates the groups to which the Administrator user belongs: the Administrators local group, the Domain Admins global group, and the Domain Users global group.

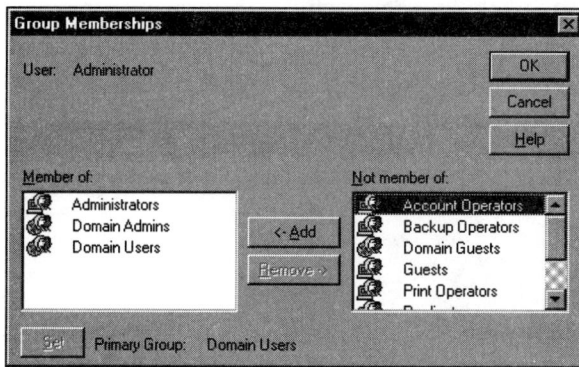

Figure 8-9   Group Memberships dialog box

4. Click **OK** twice to return to the User Manager for Domains.

5. In the Username column of the upper pane, click the **Guest** user and press **Enter**. The User Properties dialog box opens. Note that the Guest user is disabled by default. In addition, this user cannot change passwords, and the password never expires.

6. Click the **Groups button**. The Group Memberships dialog box opens. Notice that the Guest user is a member of only the Domain Guests group.

7. Press **OK** twice to return to User Manager for Domains.

8. In the Groups column of the bottom pane, click **Domain Users**, and then press **Enter**. Note that all users except Guest are members of this group.

9. Click **Cancel** to return to the User Manager for Domains.

10. Repeat Steps 8 and 9 to view the members of the Domain Admins, Domain Guests, and Users groups.

PROJECT 8-2

In this project you will add two users to the domain.

1. Click **User** in the menu bar, then click **New User**. The New User dialog box opens, as shown in Figure 8-10.

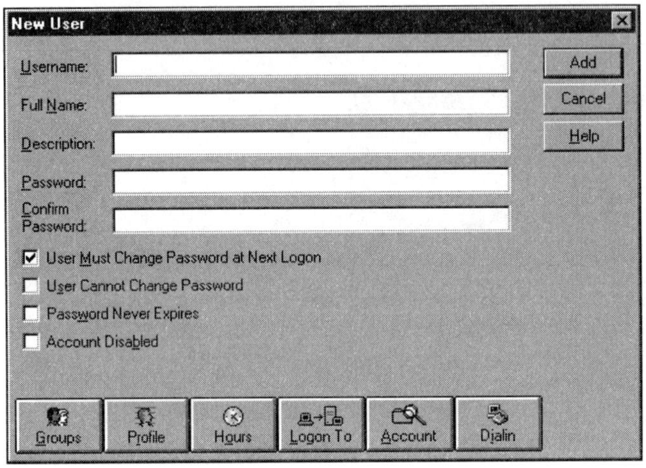

Figure 8-10   New User dialog box

2. In the appropriate boxes, type the username **(TSINNOTT)**, full name **(Thomas Sinnott)**, and password **(hello)**. Type the password again in the Confirm Password box. Remember that passwords are case-sensitive and that the password confirmation must match the password exactly.

3. Click **Add** to add the user to the domain. Note that the New User dialog box remains active. The next user account will be used only by guests.

4. Type **Visitor** for the Username, and **visitor** (all lowercase) for the password. Type **visitor** again (all lowercase) in the Confirm Password textbox.

5. Deselect the **User Must Change Password at Next Logon checkbox**, then verify that the User Cannot Change Password and Password Never Expires checkboxes are deselected.

6. Click **Add** to add the user to the domain.

7. Click the **Close button** in the title bar to close the New User dialog box.

PROJECT 8-3

In this project you will add a local group to the server. You will then use this group in Project 8-4.

1. Click **User** in the menu bar, then click **New Local Group**. The New Local Group dialog box appears.

2. In the Group Name text box, type **Administrative Testing.** In the Description text box type **Administrative Testing Users.** Your New Local Group dialog box should match Figure 8-11.

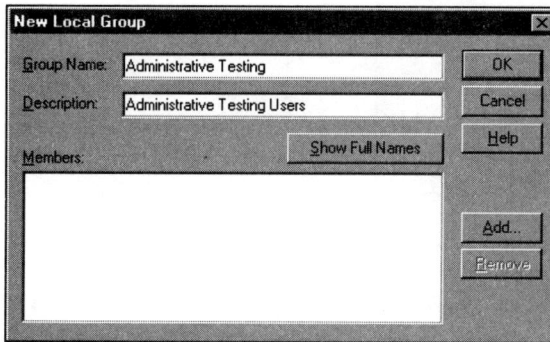

Figure 8-11   Creating a new local group

3. Click **OK** to add the group to the domain.

PROJECT 8-4

In this project you will add one of the users you created in Project 8-2 to the Administrative Testing group you created in Project 8-3. You will then grant the group full access to the server by changing its user rights.

1. In the Groups column of the bottom pane, click **Administrative Testing**, and then press **Enter**. The Local Group Properties dialog box opens.

2. Click **Add**. The Add Users and Groups dialog box opens, as shown in Figure 8-12. The Names: list box shows all available users and global groups.

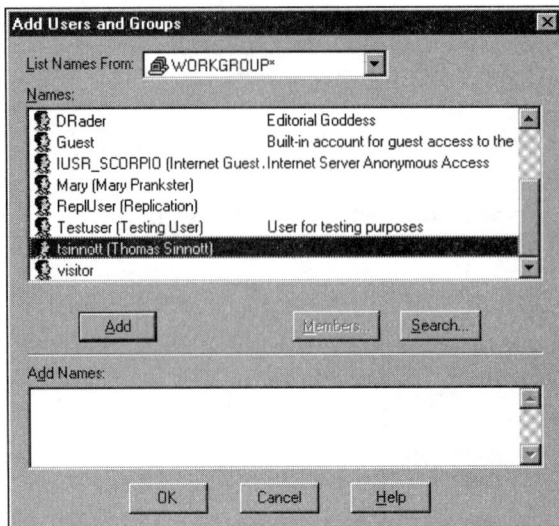

Figure 8-12   Add Users and Groups dialog box

3. In the Names list, click **tsinnott (Thomas Sinnott)**, and then click **Add**.

4. Click **OK** twice to return to the User Manager for Domains. Now that you have added the user to the group, you will change the group's user rights.

5. Click Policies in the menu bar, then click **User Rights**. The User Rights Policy dialog box opens.

6. Click the Right: list arrow to display a list of available rights, click **Log on locally**, then click **Add**. The Add Users and Groups dialog box opens. Note that this dialog box closely resembles the Add Users and Groups dialog box you saw when you added TSINNOTT to the Administrative Testing group earlier.

7. From the Names list, click **Administrative Testing**, then click **Add**. The group is added to the Add Names: pane of the window.

8. Click **OK** to return to the User Rights Policy window.

9. Repeat Steps 6-8 to give the user the **Manage auditing and security log** right.

10. Click **OK** to return to the User Manager for Domains. In the remaining steps you will change the groups membership for the Visitor user.

11. In the User Name column at the top of the pane, click **Visitor**, then press **Enter**. The User Properties dialog box opens.

12. Click the **Groups** button.

13. In the Not member of: list, click **Domain Guests**, then click **<-Add**.

14. In the Member of: list, click **Domain Guests**, then click **Set**. This choice will make Domain Guests the primary group for the Visitor user.

15. In the Member of: list, click **Domain Users**, then click **Remove->**.

16. Click **OK** twice to return to the User Manager for Domains.

PROJECT 8-5

In this project you will change the standard password policies for all users in the domain.

1. Click **Policies** in the menu bar, then click **Account.** The Account Policy dialog box opens, as shown in Figure 8-13.

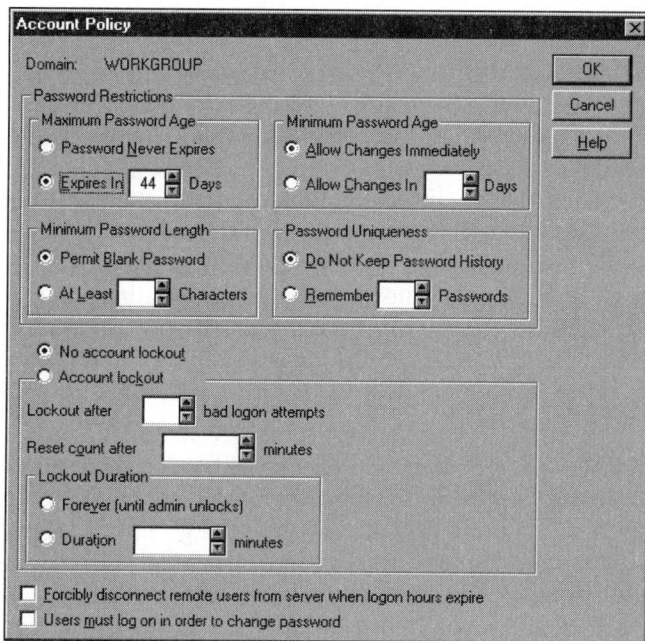

Figure 8-13   Account Policy dialog box

2. Under Maximum Password Age, change the number of days in which the password expires to **60**.

3. Under Minimum Password Length, select the **At Least option button**, then type **6** in the At Least text box. This choice dictates that a password must be at least six characters long.

4. Under Password Uniqueness, click the **Remember option button**, then type **10** in the Remember text box. This choice ensures that Windows NT will not allow any of the 10 most recently used passwords to be reused.

5. Select the **Account lockout** option button, then adjust the settings as follows:

   - Lockout after 3 bad logon attempts.
   - Reset count after 60 minutes.
   - Duration 60 minutes.

6. Select the two check boxes (**Forcibly disconnect remote users from server when logon hours expire** and **Users must log on in order to change password**) at the bottom of the dialog box.

7. Click **OK** to return to the User Manager for Domains.

8. Click **User** in the menu bar, then click **Exit** to close the User Manager for Domains.

CASE PROJECTS

1. Your small accounting firm recently installed a Windows NT network. The company currently has only 25 employees, but it looks as though you will be merging with another company of comparable size, effectively doubling the size of your network. The other company has stand-alone PCs, but no network at this time. When you installed your NT server, you assigned user names according to people's nicknames (Jimbo and Buffy, for example). You also allowed users to choose their own passwords and did not ever require them to change those passwords. As your network grows, however, the need for easy identification is becoming clearer, and security must be increased. Write a brief report explaining how to provide a better naming convention and password policy for your small but growing company.

2. As your company has grown, it has become increasingly difficult to centrally administer your network user and group accounts. The Director of Information Technology has decided to hire regional IS administrators to handle user and group management for each region's domains. Write a brief report (three to five paragraphs) explaining how to provide the regional administrators access to manage users and groups, without giving Administrator privileges to these groups.

3. Your company encompasses 15 sites with more than 800 workstations. It has three domains spread evenly across all 15 sites (five sites per domain). In recent months, some concern has arisen that unauthorized personnel are attempting to access sensitive information by guessing passwords in the Accounting domain. Write a brief report (three to five paragraphs) outlining an auditing policy for your company that will allow you to determine if such attempts are taking place. List the steps necessary to implement your policy.

CREATING AND MANAGING USER PROFILES AND SYSTEM POLICIES

Both Windows 95 and Windows NT enable individual users to configure their computers' settings. While this option is valuable to the user, it can create an administrative nightmare. In an effort to provide standard settings for the operating system environment, Microsoft provides user profiles and system policies. In this chapter you will learn about these profiles and policies, their roles in the Enterprise computing environment, and their implementation.

AFTER READING THIS CHAPTER AND COMPLETING THE EXERCISES YOU WILL BE ABLE TO:

- Configure and manage user profiles
- Configure and manage system policies
- Understand the implications of using Profiles and Policies together

CONFIGURING AND MANAGING USER PROFILES

A **user profile** is a collection of files that define the Windows NT configuration (including environment settings, mouse pointers, and desktop preferences). User profiles are loaded into the Registry when a user logs on to a computer. Three types of profiles exist in Windows NT: local, roaming, or mandatory. A **local user profile** is specific to a computer—that is, it defines the user's settings for the computer on which the profile was created. A **roaming profile** is stored on a network-shared directory and can be accessed from any networked computer, thereby providing the user with the same settings on any Windows NT computer on the network. A **mandatory profile** is a roaming profile that has been locked; thus the user cannot change the environment and desktop preferences. With a mandatory profile, no matter what changes the user makes, the environment and desktop revert back to the settings specified in the profile when the system shuts down or the user logs off. This option helps simplify systems administration in situations in which a group of people require a common interface and standard configuration.

Windows NT's three default profile structures are shown in Figure 9-1: Administrator, All Users, and Default User. The Administrator profile is used only by the Administrator user; the All Users profile applies to any user who logs on to a computer. When a user logs on to a computer for the first time, a directory is created for that account in the \\<*systemroot*>*Profiles* directory. The contents of the Default User directory are then copied into the new directory to create the user's profile.

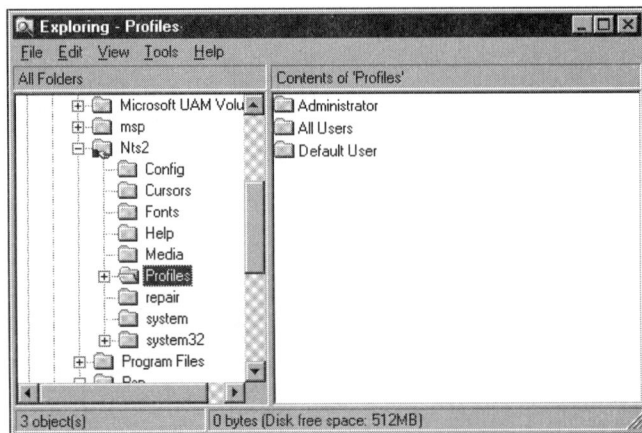

Figure 9-1 Defaults profile structures

In a Windows NT environment, a user profile consists of a Windows NT Registry hive and a set of profile directories. As you've learned, the Registry is a database that stores settings for user and computer configurations. For roaming profiles to function, portions of the Registry (that is, the HKEY_CURRENT_USER hive) must be saved as files that can be loaded when the user logs on. The hive is saved in the **NTUSER.DAT file** and is loaded when a user with a roaming profile logs on.

The NTUSER.DAT file holds settings that maintain network connections, control panel configurations that are unique to the user (such as the desktop color and mouse), and specific application settings. As shown in Figure 9-2, a number of profile directories store information such as shortcut links, desktop icons, and startup applications. The contents of each of these directories are discussed later in this chapter.

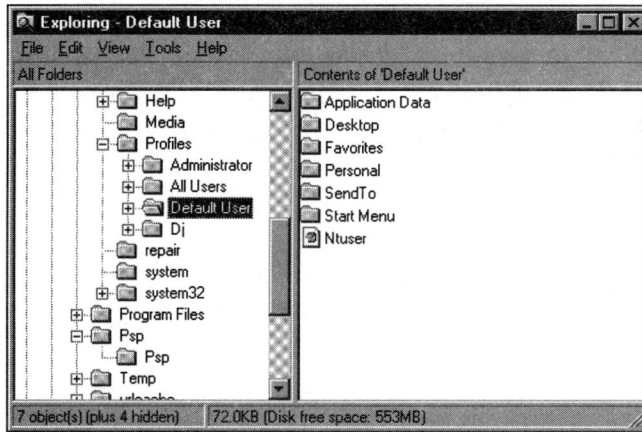

Figure 9-2   Profile directories for the Default User profile

When a user logs on to a computer, a log file (NTUSER.DAT.LOG) is created to which profile changes are made. When the user logs off, the changes are applied to the profile. The HKEY_CURRENT_USER hive that makes up the NTUSER.DAT file contains a number of settings that can be modified from either the Policy Editor or the Registry Editor. Using the Registry editor to make changes to a hive is a complicated and potentially risky maneuver, however, and should be performed only by experienced administrators and only after a backup has been made.

The folders present in a user profile depend on the changes the user has made. As you can see in Figure 9-3, the profile for a new user who has made no changes contains very few folders.

A user's profile can contain the following folders:

- **Application Data**—Pointers to specific applications; this folder is generally modified during the installation process for applications.

- **Desktop**—Files, shortcuts, and other items on the user's desktop.

- **Favorites**—Shortcuts to favorite locations or programs.

- **NetHood**—Shortcuts to Network Neighborhood items.

- **Personal**—Location where user documents are stored by default.

- **PrintHood**—Shortcuts to printer folders.

- **Recent**—Shortcuts to most recent documents or other items used.

- **SendTo**—Shortcuts to document storage locations (such as My Briefcase, or 3 ½ Floppy (A))

- **Start Menu**—Shortcuts to program items located on the Start menu.

- **Templates**—Shortcuts to templates.

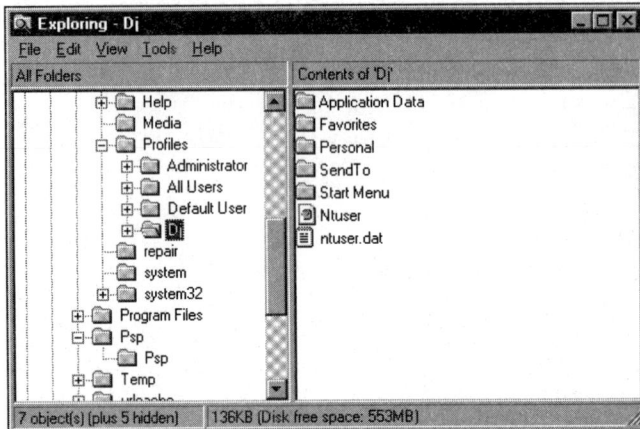

Figure 9-3   User profile with very few folders

As an administrator, you can copy an existing user profile so that another user can use it. Copying user profiles ensures that all users receive the same profile settings. Because the NTUSER.DAT file is a "system read–only" file, however, you cannot use Windows NT Explorer to copy user profiles. Instead, you must work with the System applet in the Control Panel, as described in the following steps. To copy a user profile:

1. Click the **Start button**, point to **Settings**, click **Control Panel**, double-click the **System icon**, then click the **User Profiles tab**. The User Profiles tab of the System Properties dialog box, as shown in Figure 9-4, appears. This dialog box includes a list of users with existing profiles.

2. Click **Copy To**. The Copy To dialog box opens.

3. Click **Browse**, then select the directory to which you wish to copy the profile.

4. Click **OK** to return to the Copy To dialog box. Next, you need to identify the user who will be permitted to use this profile.

5. Click **Change**. The Choose User dialog box opens, as shown in Figure 9-5.

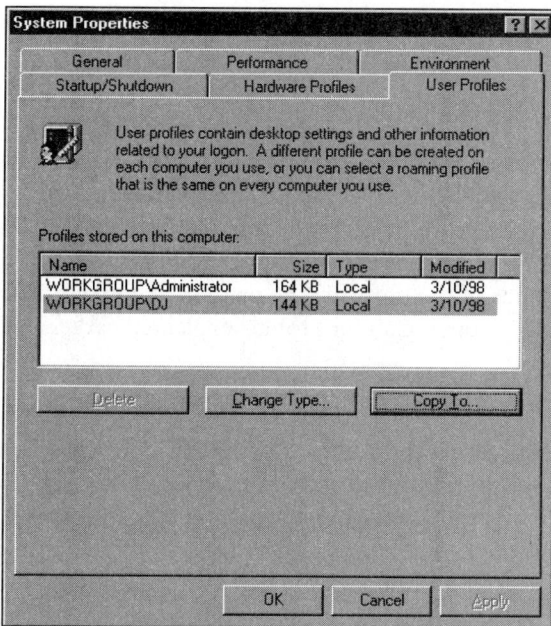

Figure 9-4   User Profiles tab of the System Properties dialog box

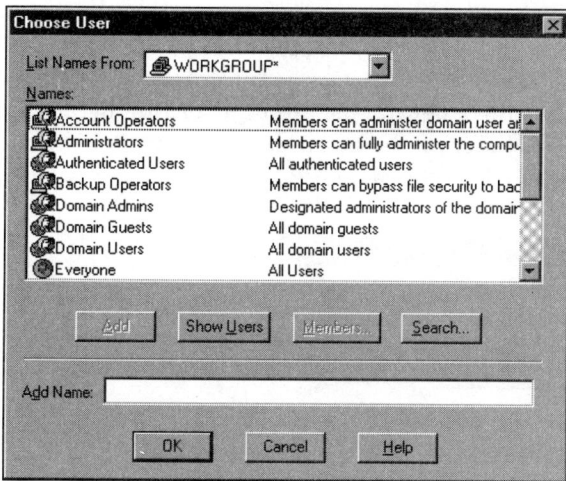

Figure 9-5   Choose User dialog box

6. By default, the list contains only groups. Click **Show Users** to add users to the Names list box.

7. In the Names: list box, click **Guest**, then click **Add**. Guest is added to the Add Name: section of the dialog box.

8. Click **OK** to close the Choose User dialog box.

9. Click **OK** to close the Copy To dialog box.

10. Click **OK** to close the System Properties dialog box.

You can make user profiles as uniform as possible by creating a local or domain-wide Default User profile, which individual users can then customize. Changes made to the local Default User profile folder affect only new users who log on to the local computer. The domain-wide Default User profile applies to all new domain users when they log on to a Windows NT workstation or server that is a member of the domain. The process of copying a profile to the Default User profile resembles that for copying a user profile, explained earlier in this section.

ROAMING PROFILES

Roaming profiles, which are stored in a central location on the domain, are available to domain users regardless of which computer on the domain they log on to. They allow a user to customize the system and desktop settings and then have those customizations travel with the user from one computer to another—the user does not have to reconfigure the settings on each new computer. When a user logs on to any Windows NT computer, the user's settings are retained and applied to the configuration of the computer, regardless of whether it is the same computer that the user used last.

Creating a roaming user profile is a straightforward process. First, copy the profile to be used as a roaming profile to a network-shared directory on any server, using the steps outlined in the previous section. Then, open User Manager for Domains, click User Properties to open the User Environment dialog box, and identify the user profile path as the shared directory on the server. This action automatically designates the profile as a roaming profile. Figure 9-6 shows the user profile path for the DJ user on the Taurus server. Figure 9-7 shows settings for the same profile in the User Profiles tab of the System Properties dialog box.

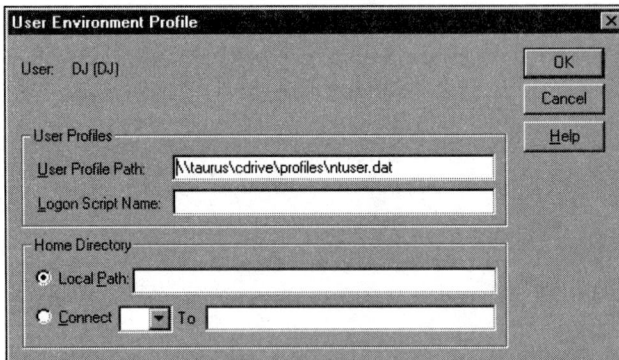

Figure 9-6   Roaming profile path defined in the User Environment Profile dialog box

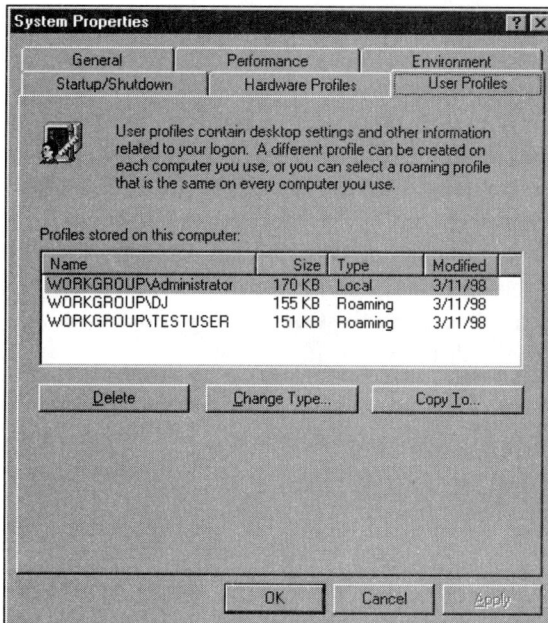

Figure 9-7   Roaming profile settings in the User Profiles tab of the System Properties
dialog box

MANDATORY USER PROFILES

As explained earlier, mandatory user profiles are assigned to the user, who cannot permanently change them. This restriction eases the administration requirements for large networks, where maintaining a certain level of consistency is essential.

To change an existing user profile to a mandatory user profile, simply change the extension on the NTUSER file from ".DAT" to ".MAN." (The NTUSER.DAT file appears in the root of the user's profile directory.) Changing the filename to NTUSER.MAN marks the profile as read-only, and any changes that the user makes will not be retained when the user logs off.

If a user's profile is changed to a mandatory profile while the user is logged on, the user's copy of the profile will overwrite those changes when the user logs off. Such a modification should be made only when the user is not logged on.

> **Caution** Before changing filenames in Windows NT Explorer, make sure that all files and filename extensions are displayed. You can then review the new file extension to check it for errors.

CONFIGURING AND MANAGING SYSTEM POLICIES

A **system policy** is a set of Registry settings that define the computer resources available to a group of users or an individual. They define the desktop environment that a system administrator needs to control. The desktop settings in user profiles, as well as logon and network access settings, are stored in the computer's Registry database. The system policy for users overwrites the settings in the current user area of the Registry, while the system policy for computers overwrites the current local machine area of the Registry. This setup allows administrators to control both user environments and computer environments for users and groups. You can manage system policies via the **System Policy Editor**, which appears in the Start menu under Administrative Tools (Common).

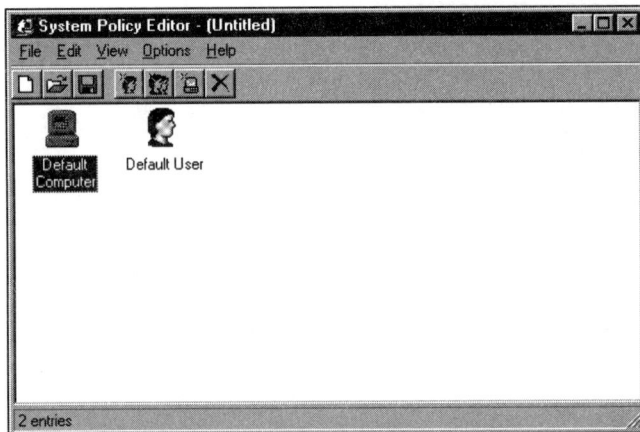

Figure 9-8   System Policy Editor

Figure 9-8 shows the System Policy Editor when it has been set to create a new policy. Policy modifications made with this tool result in the following changes to the local computer's Registry settings:

- Default User settings, such as desktop settings, modify the HKEY_CURRENT_USER Registry hive (the hive that defines the content of the user profile when a user logs on to the computer).

- Network access and logon settings for Default Computer in the System Policy Editor modify the HKEY_LOCAL_MACHINE key in the Registry.

A **user policy** is a collection of Registry settings that restrict a user's access to programs and network options. Like user profiles, user policies can be used to enforce a particular configuration of the user's working environment. Windows NT includes two types of user policies: one that applies to a specific user, and the Default User policy, which applies to all users and is created concurrently with the overall policy file. Administrators can modify the Default User policy, including overall user restrictions or establishing specific restrictions for certain individual users. From that point on, when users log on to the domain, if no specific user policy exists, the Default User policy will apply.

A **group policy** is a system policy that applies to all members of a specified group, except those members who have their own individual policies. Group policies should be used in situations where multiple users require the same settings. From an administrative standpoint, creating one group policy—rather than establishing multiple identical user policies—is a more efficient option.

A **computer policy** is a group of settings that are specific to a local workstation and apply to all users on that workstation. Windows NT includes two types of computer policies: those that apply to a specific computer, and the Default Computer policy, which applies to all computers. Like the Default User policy, the Default Computer policy is created simultaneously with the system policy file. The default policy applies only if a computer does not have a specific policy. As with the Default User policy, only administrators can modify computer policies.

System policies allow an administrator to control user work environments and actions and to enforce system configurations. These policies, however, provide administrators with considerably more options than are available with mandatory user profiles. For example, system policies can be used as security devices that limit access to network resources, restrict the use of specific administrative tools, and specifically define which applications users can access.

As mentioned earlier, system policies can be applied to users, groups, or computers. Consequently, they can be broadly applied to all domain users and computers or selectively applied to individual users, groups, and computers. After creating a system policy file, you should save it in the Net Logon share on each domain controller. When a user logs on to the domain, Windows NT retrieves the system policy file from the Net Logon share on the domain controller that authenticates the user's logon.

Because a system policy is invoked at logon by the domain controller authenticating the user, it is important to have accurate policies on all domain controllers. Rather than manually copying the policies to each domain controller to effect a change, you can take advantage of directory replication. When instituting a policy change, however, you should always verify that replication is working properly. By default, Windows NT computers check for a policy file in the Net Logon share of the validating domain controller. If directory replication to a domain controller fails and a Windows NT-based workstation does not find a policy file on that server, no policy will be applied and the existing settings will remain in force.

CREATING AND CONFIGURING A SYSTEM POLICY FILE

As noted earlier, you use the System Policy Editor to create a system policy file. Before beginning the following steps, which describe how to establish such a file, make sure you are logged on as an administrator. As you proceed through the exercise, you will notice that every check box in the System Policy Editor offers three options: grayed out, clear, or checked. An option that is grayed out means the current configuration setting for the local computer will be retained. If an option is cleared, the setting will be applied only if no current registry setting for the option currently exists. An option that is checked will be applied to the local computer.

To create and configure a Windows NT system policy file:

1. Log on as a system administrator.

2. Open the **System Policy Editor**.

3. Click **File**, then click **New Policy**. The Default Computer and Default User icons appear (review Figure 9-8).

4. Double-click on the **Default Computer icon**. The Default Computer Properties dialog box opens, as shown in Figure 9-9. To view or customize a particular policy's settings, you can click on the + sign next to that setting.

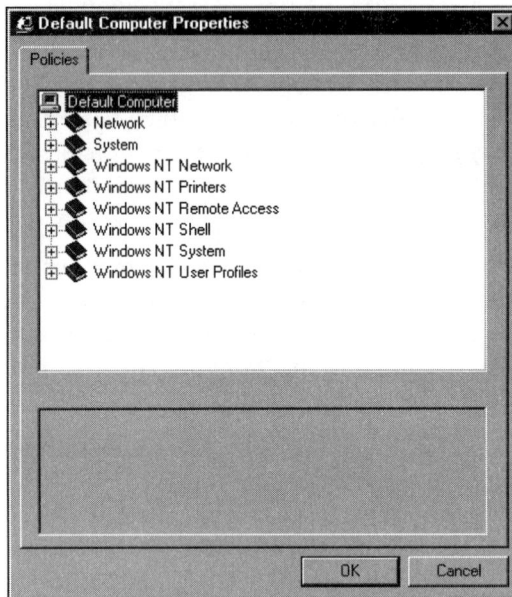

Figure 9-9   Default Computer Properties dialog box

5. Click the **+** next to Windows NT System, then the **+** next to Logon. A list of options that can be modified appears.

6. Click the **Logon banner check box** to display a check. Your dialog box should now match Figure 9-10.

7. In the Caption text box, type **Warning:** and in the Text text box type **This machine is property of Joe's Discount Accounting Services. Unauthorized use is prohibited**. From this point forward, when the system policy is invoked at logon, the logon banner message will appear.

8. Click **OK** to return to the System Policy Editor.

9. Double-click the **Default user icon**. The Default User Properties dialog box opens, as shown in Figure 9-11.

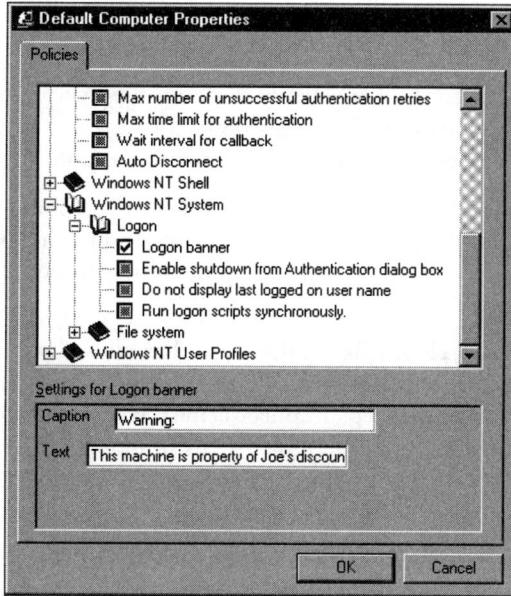

Figure 9-10   Modifying the Logon banner for the Default Computer policy

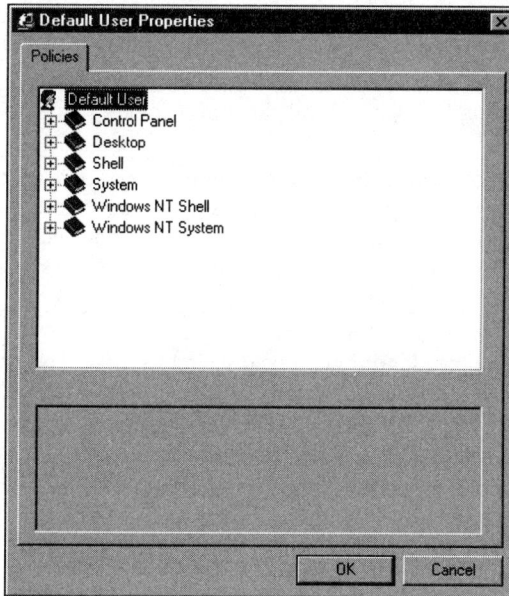

Figure 9-11   Default User Properties dialog box

10. Click the **+** next to Desktop. Click the **check box** next to Color scheme to display a check.

11. Select a scheme in the Settings for Color Scheme window, then click **OK** to close the Default User Properties dialog box. From this point forward, the same color scheme for the desktop will be produced for all users when the policy is invoked.

12. To establish system policies for a specific group, click **Edit** on the menu bar, then click **Add Group** on the Edit menu. Enter the group's name and click **OK**. Once the group is added, you can modify its settings using the same procedure employed in the previous steps.

13. To save the modified policy file, click **File** on the menu bar, click **Save As**, then save the document as the **NTCONFIG.POL file** in the Net Logon file of the domain controller (\winnt\system32\repl\import\scripts). If directory replication is configured on the domain, place the NTCONFIG.POL file in the export directory (winnt\system32\repl\export\scripts).

Tables 9-1 and 9-2 outline the settings available to the Default User and Default Computer system policies. Table 9-1 outlines the settings available under the Default User policy.

Table 9-1   Default User Settings

Setting Category	Explanation
Control Panel	Items included in this category relate to user activity in the Display option in the Control Panel. You can restrict user access to the Display option here.
Desktop	You can designate a background wallpaper and color scheme for the desktop.
Shell	Customization of desktop folders and restriction of what appears on the desktop are configurable options. You can also limit access to the Run, Find, and Shut Down commands. To create custom folders, you can enter paths to program items, desktop icons, startup items, Network Neighborhood items, and so on.
System	Windows NT Registry Editor (Regedt32.exe) and Windows 95 Registry Editor (Regedit.exe) can (and should) be disabled so that users cannot edit the Registry files. If you decide to provide a list of Windows-based applications available for users, any application not in the list will be unavailable.
Windows NT System	When Parse Autoexec.bat is selected, Windows NT reads the environment variables from this file and merges them with the user's environment variables.

Table 9-2 outlines the settings available under the Default Computer policy.

Table 9-2   Default Computer Settings

Setting Category	Explanation
Network	You can update system policies remotely instead of updating from the NTCONFIG.POL file on domain controllers. You can identify a path to a different policy file, thereby enabling manual updating of the policy file in a location other than the server location.
System	The Simple Network Management Protocol (SNMP) configuration can be changed by adding or removing communities, managers, and public community traps. This icon also enables you to configure the system to specify the contents of the Run and Run once entries, which are used to identify the applications that should run at startup.
Windows NT Network	You can automatically create hidden drive shares for workstation and server shares.
Windows NT Printers	For print servers, the print spooler browse process (that periodically sends information to other print servers) can be disabled. You can also set the print scheduler priority and specify a notification beep if error conditions occur at a remote printer.
Windows NT Remote Access	The maximum number for unsuccessful authentication retries and a maximum time limit for authentication can be set for users working from a remote access server. You can also configure the time interval between callback attempts and a time limit for automatic disconnection from the server.
Windows NT User Profiles	This configuration option is available for environmental options associated with Windows NT user profiles. Options include the ability to delete cached copies of roaming profiles and the ability to automatically detect slow network connections.
Windows NT Shell	This selection mirrors the Windows NT shell configurable settings in the Default User policy.
Windows NT System	This selection mirrors the Windows NT system configurable settings in the Default User policy.

System Policies Application Order

Under some circumstances, the user profiles and system policies associated with a specific user, group, or computer may conflict. Use the following rules to resolve any conflict:

- An individual user policy takes precedence over a user profile.

- If a user does not have an individual user policy, and the user is a member of a group that has a group policy, then the group policy applies as though it were a user policy. If a user policy does exist, however, it takes precedence over the group policy.

- If a user does not have an individual user policy, then the default user policy is applied to the user.

- An individual computer policy takes precedence over any user profile or policy.

- If the user logs on to a computer that does not have an individual computer policy, then the default computer policy is applied and its settings take precedence over any user profile or policy.

USING THE SYSTEM POLICY EDITOR TO EDIT THE REGISTRY

The System Policy Editor can also be used to change the Windows NT registry settings on the local computer. Selecting Open Registry from the File menu of the System Policy Editor will save changes made directly to the registry when the system Policy Editor is closed or File/Save is selected. To make changes to the Windows NT registry settings on a remote computer, you can use the Connect command on the System Policy Editor File menu. For example, a help desk technician can use this strategy to connect to a computer and correct settings that a user mistakenly modified.

> The System Policy Editor is designed to manage Registry settings for the entire domain. Use the Open Registry mode only in exceptional circumstances.

USER PROFILES AND SYSTEM POLICIES: USING ONE OR BOTH

The decision of whether to use system policies or user profiles to control a user's settings is often a matter of preference. In larger Windows NT environments, system policies are often the better alternative. These types of policies give an administrator greater control over a user's environmental settings than mandatory user profiles do. Remember, if the user profile and a system policy conflict, the settings in the system policy will take precedence. Make sure, however, that the user profile is complementary to—and not in conflict with—system policies.

CHAPTER SUMMARY

- A user profile is a collection of files that are loaded into the Registry when a user logs on; these files define the user's working environment. Three types of profiles exist: local profiles (which pertain only to that computer), roaming profiles (which provide consistent configuration settings as a user moves from computer to computer), and mandatory profiles (which also provide consistent configuration settings, but do not enable the user to save any configuration changes). The heart of any user profile is the NTUSER.DAT file, which contains the HKEY_CURRENT_USER hive of the Registry.

- Windows NT provides three built-in profiles: Administrator, Default User, and All Users. As its name implies, the All Users profile configures settings for all users that log on to a computer. The Default User profile serves as the basis for profiles that are created when new users log on to the computer. The Administrator profile is used only by the administrator.

■ System policies are similar to profiles in that they configure the user's environment. These profiles are defined not only for particular users, however, but also for groups or computers. You manage system policies through the System Policy Editor, which is part of Administrative Tools (Common) menu.

■ Profiles and policies can be configured to complement one another in controlling specific settings for users, groups, and computers.

KEY TERMS

■ **computer policy** — A collection of Registry settings that specifically define the operating environment for a specific workstation.

■ **group policy** — A collection of Registry settings that define the operating environment for a specific group of users.

■ **local user profile** — A profile that controls the settings for a user on a specific computer.

■ **mandatory profile** — A roaming profile that cannot be modified by the user.

■ **NTCONFIG.POL file** — The system policy file that contains settings for users, groups, and Windows NT computers; it is placed on a network-shared folder so that system policies can be uniformly or selectively enforced across the domain.

■ **NTUSER.DAT file** — The user profile file that contains the settings that maintain network connections, Control Panel configurations that are unique to the user (such as the desktop color and mouse), and specific application settings.

■ **roaming profile** — A user profile stored on a network-shared directory that can be accessed from any networked computer.

■ **system policy** — A collection of Registry settings that defines the domain resources that are available to a group of users or an individual user.

■ **System Policy Editor** — A utility that allows the administrator to manage the user desktop by changing the Default User settings and to manage the logon and network settings by changing the Default Computer settings.

■ **user policy** — A collection of Registry settings that define the operating environment for a user logged on to the domain.

■ **user profile** — A collection of files that define the Windows NT configuration for a specific user, including the user's environment and preference settings.

9

REVIEW QUESTIONS

1. In a Windows NT environment, when is a user profile created?

   a. each time a user logs on to a computer

   b. the first time a user logs on to a computer

   c. when a user account is added with User Manager for Domains

   d. when an administrator elects to have a user profile created for a designated user

2. Which of the following is not a type of user profile?

   a. roaming

   b. stationary

   c. local

   d. mandatory

3. Where is a roaming user profile stored?

   a. in the workstation's local profile directory

   b. on a network-shared directory that can be accessed from any networked computer

   c. in the local computer's cached profile directory

   d. in the user's public directory

4. Which file contains the user's environmental preferences in a Windows NT user profile?

   a. CONFIG.SYS

   b. USERCONFIG.SYS

   c. NTDATA.POL

   d. NTUSER.DAT

5. In a Windows NT environment, a user profile consists of (pick two):

   a. a Windows NT Registry hive

   b. a close linked Registry impute file

   c. a set of profile directories

   d. a list of configurable options

6. A mandatory profile is:

   a. a system developed to facilitate the maintenance of profiles

   b. a profile freely configurable by the user

   c. a roaming profile that cannot be modified by the user

   d. a set of files that contains information relative to the user's directory access

7. Roaming user profiles:

   a. are carried by users on floppy disks and inserted into their A: drive every time they log on to a computer

   b. are not valid unless the user logs on to a Windows 95 configured computer on a Windows NT network

   c. allow users to customize their system and desktop settings and have those customizations travel with them from one computer to another

   d. are unavailable unless the user has administrative privileges

8. The NTUSER.DAT file maps to which Registry key?

   a. HKEY_CURRENT_USER

   b. HKEY_CURRENT_COMPUTER

   c. HKEY_LOCAL_MACHINE

   d. HKEY_NETWORK_MACHINE

9. To create a mandatory user profile, you must:

   a. change the extension of the NTUSER.DAT file from .DAT to .MAN

   b. declare the user profile mandatory in the system Registry

   c. create a mandatory profile and replace the user's local user profile with the new mandatory profile

   d. in User Manager for Domains, check the mandatory check box in the Profiles dialog box

10. The NTUSER.DAT file is (choose all that apply):

   a. a read-only file

   b. accessible only to users having administrative rights

   c. a system file

   d. used only when a new user logs on to the network

11. To copy Windows NT user profiles from one directory to another:

   a. use the Copy to dialog box located in the User profile tab of the System icon on the Control Panel

   b. use Windows NT Explorer

   c. copy user profile directories and files by utilizing the copy command from the MS-DOS command prompt

   d. Drag and drop the user profile folders and files from the directory tree structure to the My Computer icon

12. A user will not be allowed into the domain if the associated mandatory profile is unavailable. True or False?

13. Which of the following Windows NT utilities are used to manage user profiles? (Choose all that apply.)

    a. Event Viewer

    b. System Applet on the Control Panel

    c. Server Manager

    d. User Manager for Domains

14. Every user has the ability to define system policies. True or False?

15. System policies provide greater control over the user's environment than mandatory user profiles. True or False?

16. Which tool is used to establish system policies?

    a. User Manager for Domains

    b. Server Manager

    c. Policy Manager

    d. System Policy Editor

17. In which directory must system policy files be stored?

    a. the NETLOGON directory of the PDC only

    b. the SYSTEM32 directory of all domain controllers

    c. the WINNT directory of the PDC only

    d. the NETLOGON directory of all domain controllers

18. The Default Computer policy is created at the same time that the installation process for Windows NT is completed on a server. True or False?

19. System policies cannot be created for:

    a. computers

    b. users

    c. domains

    d. groups

20. Where a user's mandatory profile and a system policy conflict, the configuration content of the mandatory profile will override the system policy. True or False?

HANDS-ON PROJECTS

For some or all of these projects you will need one Windows NT server that is configured as a primary domain controller and one Windows NT workstation that is a member of the domain.

PROJECT 9-1

In this project you will configure user profiles for a number of users. You will also test the effects of creating roaming profiles and mandatory profiles.

1. In Windows NT Explorer on the Windows NT server, create a directory called **Test Profiles** on the root of the drive. Right-click on the new directory, then click **Sharing** in the shortcut menu. Name this share **Profiles**.

2. Click the **Start button**, point to **Programs**, point to **Administrative Tools (Common)**, then click **User Manager for Domains**.

3. Create three new users with the following configurations:
   - Student1, password=testing, not required to change password at next logon, Administrators group, Profile path = \\<servername>\profiles\%username%
   - Student2, password=testing, not required to change password at next logon, Backup Operators group, Profile path = \\<servername>\profiles\%username%
   - Student3, password=testing, not required to change password at next logon, no new groups, Profile path = \\<servername>\profiles\%username%

4. Create a new group on the domain called **Students**. Make each of the new users a member of the Students group. Grant the Students group the right to log on locally to the Windows NT server through the User Rights option of the Policies menu.

5. Return to Explorer and use the Permissions option in the Sharing dialog box to grant the Students group full control to the Profiles directory.

6. Log off of the server.

7. Log on to the workstation as each of the Student users.

8. Make specific changes to the desktop, changing color schemes and desktop shortcuts. Record the changes you make in Table 9-3.

Table 9-3   Desktop Changes

User	Desktop Colors	Shortcuts
Student1		
Student2		
Student3		

9. When you have completed logging on, changing settings, and logging off for each student user at the workstation, return to the server. Log on as an **administrator**, open **Explorer**, then go to the **Profiles directory**. Note that a folder has been created for each new user.

10. Click the **Start button**, point to **Programs**, then click **Command Prompt**.

11. Change to the **Profiles directory**.

12. Change to the **Student3 directory**. Change the extension on the **NTUSER.DAT** file in this directory by typing **REN NTUSER.DAT NTUSER.MAN**.

13. Return to the workstation and log on as **Student3**. Change part of the color scheme again and log off. Immediately log back on as **Student3**. Note that the color scheme change has reverted back to the original setting.

14. Log off of the workstation, return to the server, and logon as Student3. Notice that the original color scheme has followed you to the server.

PROJECT 9-2

In this and subsequent projects you will create system policies for Windows NT Workstation and the users you created in Project 9-1. These activities will teach you how to use the System Policy Editor to establish computer policies, group policies, and user policies. In this project, you will create a default computer and default user profile.

1. Log on to the server as **Student1**. (This account has administrative privileges.)

2. Click the **Start button**, point to **Programs**, point to **Administrative Tools (Common)**, then click **System Policy Editor**.

3. Click **File** on the menu bar, then click **New Policy**. The Default Computer and Default User icons appear.

4. Save the policy file by selecting **Save as** from the File menu. Place the file in the **NETLOGON share** (\winnt\system32\repl\import\scripts) with the filename **NTCONFIG.POL**.

5. Open the User Manager for Domains, and remove the Policies path for each of the users created in Project 9-1.

PROJECT 9-3

In this project you will create a system policy for each of the users you created in Project 9-1 (Student1, Student2, and Student3). When making changes to the policies, be sure that the settings and files requested are available on the workstation. For example, if changing the color scheme to Blue Days 256, ensure that it is available on the workstation before making the change.

1. Make sure that the System Policy Editor is open.
2. Click **Edit** on the menu bar, then click **Add User**.
3. Identify the new user as **Student1**, then click **OK**. Next, create user system policies for Student2 and Student3.
4. Double-click the **icon for Student2**. Make several policy changes, such as dictating a specific color scheme (under the Desktop option) and removing the Run command from the Start menu (under Shell/Restrictions). Write down the changes you made for this user on a separate sheet of paper so that you can review the status of these changes when you log on as Student2.
5. Repeat Step 4 for Student3, making different policy changes and recording those changes for later comparison.
6. When you have completed these changes, resave the policy file.
7. Log on to the workstation as **Student2**. Verify that the changes you made to the Student2 user system policy have taken effect. Note the results of these changes.
8. Follow the same procedure outlined in Step 7 for Student3.

PROJECT 9-4

In this project you will create a system policy for the Students group.

1. Log on as the **Administrator**.
2. Open **User Manager for Domains**.
3. Remove **Student1** from the Students group.
4. Open **System Policy Editor**.
5. Open the policy you saved in the previous project.
6. In the Edit drop-down menu, select **Add Group**. Identify the new group as **Students**.
7. Double-click on the group **Students**. Using your property sheet, change the group policy so that it differs from all the individual student user system policies.
8. Save the system policy file.

9

9. Log on as **Student2**.

10. Verify that the changes you made to the group policy have taken effect.

PROJECT 9-5

In this project you will create a system policy for the workstation computer.

1. Log on to the server as **Student1**.

2. Open **System Policy Editor**, then open the policy file you saved in the previous project.

3. In the Edit drop-down menu, select **Add Computer**. Identify the new computer as the workstation computer. If you do not know the computer's NetBIOS name, click the browse button and select the computer from the list that appears.

4. Double-click on the new computer's icon. Pick a single modification that has not been previously chosen for either a user or group system policy.

5. Save the system policy file.

6. Log on to the workstation as **Student1**. Verify that the changes you made to the computer policy have taken effect.

CASE PROJECTS

1. Your company's help desk team consists of 10 people on shift schedules, who share six computers running Windows NT Workstation. People often sit at the same computer, but not necessarily. Users have requested that they be able to log on to any of the workstations and have their normal desktop configuration available. Each user has enough experience to modify his or her individual settings. Write two to three paragraphs explaining how you could accomplish this goal.

2. A new manager has taken over the help desk team described in the previous project. He wants to limit his team members' ability to change their settings and would rather have all workstations identical. Write two to three paragraphs describing how you could accomplish this change.

3. You have been asked to develop a network for a business with 50 employees. To conserve resources, the business operates on a shift basis, with many of the employees sharing job duties. As an example, Mary and John share the same job duties, which involve the management of accounts receivable. Both need access to the same software programs and the same data files. Both share the same computer. Write a brief description (two to three paragraphs) of the workstation configuration that would best suit this network.

INTEROPERABILITY WITH NETWARE SERVERS

Making your Windows NT network interoperable with NetWare systems will probably be among the most difficult tasks you will face as a system administrator. While you will encounter only a few general questions about NetWare connectivity on the Microsoft Enterprise exam, this subject is important for systems administrators because of the large number of NetWare networks in operation today. In Chapter 3, you learned about the NWLink protocol, which provides the common language between Windows NT and NetWare. In this chapter you will learn about the Windows NT services that make connectivity to NetWare resources as transparent as possible to users.

AFTER READING THIS CHAPTER AND COMPLETING THE EXERCISES YOU WILL BE ABLE TO:

- Discuss and implement Microsoft services for NetWare
- Discuss and implement Gateway Services for NetWare
- Use Migration Tool for NetWare
- Implement File and Print Services for NetWare
- Implement Directory Services Manager for NetWare

MICROSOFT SERVICES FOR NETWARE

If you plan to connect to NetWare networks, in addition to installing the NWLink (IPX/SPX) protocol, you must install at least one of Microsoft's services for NetWare connectivity. Microsoft offers four services for exchanging resources between NetWare and Windows NT network operating systems. Two of these services—Gateway Services for NetWare (GSNW) and Migration Tool for NetWare—relate to integrating a Novell system into a Windows NT network; they are included in the Windows NT Server 4.0 package. The other two services—File and Print Services for NetWare (FPNW) and Directory Services Manager for NetWare (DSMN)—deal with integrating Windows NT into a Novell network; they are available as add-on software.

Gateway Services for NetWare (GSNW) enables a Windows NT server to access NetWare file and print resources directly and acts as a gateway for other Microsoft clients, enabling them to access the NetWare resources. **Migration Tool for NetWare** allows users and groups, along with their associated rights and permissions, to be recreated on (or migrated to) Windows NT servers. **File and Print Services for NetWare** (FPNW) allows NetWare clients to access resources on a Windows NT server without the use of any additional NetWare client software. **Directory Services Manager for NetWare** (DSMN) enables the Windows NT server to manage NetWare users and groups.

GATEWAY SERVICES FOR NETWARE (GSNW)

GSNW allows Microsoft clients (running Windows 3.1, Windows for Workgroups, Windows 95, Windows NT Workstation, or Windows NT Server) to access NetWare resources through a Microsoft server, without the use of separate client software on the Microsoft client.

GSNW provides access to NetWare resources in two ways:

- It allows the Windows NT server in which GSNW is installed to access NetWare file and print resources directly as a client. This direct access is made possible by Client Services for NetWare (CSNW), which is automatically installed along with GSNW on the Windows NT server.

- It allows a Windows NT server to act as a gateway for Microsoft clients, allowing them to access NetWare resources. A **gateway** translates protocols, thereby enabling computers running different protocols to communicate with one another.

You install GSNW as a network service through the Control Panel of a Windows NT server. After installing GSNW, you must then configure the access point for each NetWare server by creating Windows NT shares and assigning appropriate permissions for access from Microsoft clients. (You'll configure a Novell server later in this chapter.) Figure 10-1 shows Windows NT Server being used as a gateway to NetWare resources. (In the Figure "SMB" and "NCP" refer to interprocess communication protocols.)

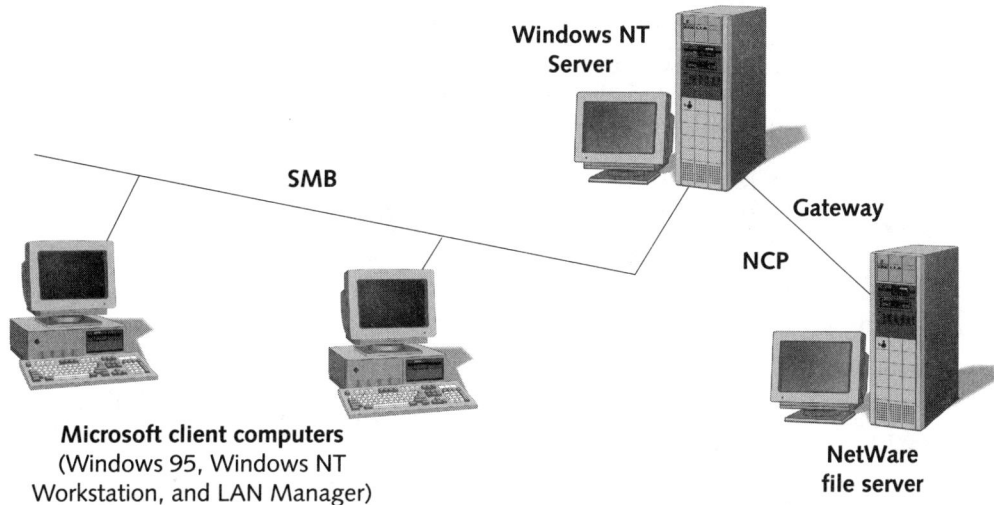

Figure 10-1   Windows NT Server being used as a gateway to NetWare resources

One advantage of GSNW is that it doesn't require the system administrator to configure each Microsoft client so as to give it access to NetWare resources. Another advantage of GSNW relates to the number of licensed NetWare users permitted. Only the Windows NT server actually connects to the NetWare server, so the number of licensed NetWare users doesn't really matter. That is, as many users as required can access resources on the NetWare server, via a single Windows NT server connection, without incurring licensing violations.

Although the single connection provides a benefit regarding licensing issues, it is also the cause of GSNW's chief disadvantage: the potential for a bottleneck as more clients connect to the server. Ideally, GSNW should be used only to obtain occasional access to NetWare resources.

If large-scale access to NetWare resources is required, consider installing CSNW (or other client software) on each client computer that requires access to NetWare resources. Alternatively, you could consider migrating the entire network to Windows NT.

CONFIGURING GATEWAY SERVICES FOR NETWARE (GSNW)

If you haven't installed the NWLink protocol, Windows NT Server will automatically install it when you install GSNW. At the same time, Windows NT Server automatically installs CSNW.

Windows NT Workstation includes only CSNW, and not GSNW.

To install GSNW, perform the following steps:

1. Click **Start**, point to **Settings**, click **Control Panel,** double-click the **Network** icon, click the **Services tab in the Network dialog box**, then click **Add.** The Select Network Service dialog box opens.

2. In the Network Service list, click **Gateway (and Client) Services for NetWare**, then click **OK.** The Windows NT Setup dialog box opens.

3. In the Windows NT Setup text box, type the correct path for the Windows NT installation files. (These files are usually located on the I386 directory on the installation CD-ROM.)

4. Click Continue.

5. The Network dialog box opens, as shown in Figure 10-2, indicating that GSNW has been installed as a service.

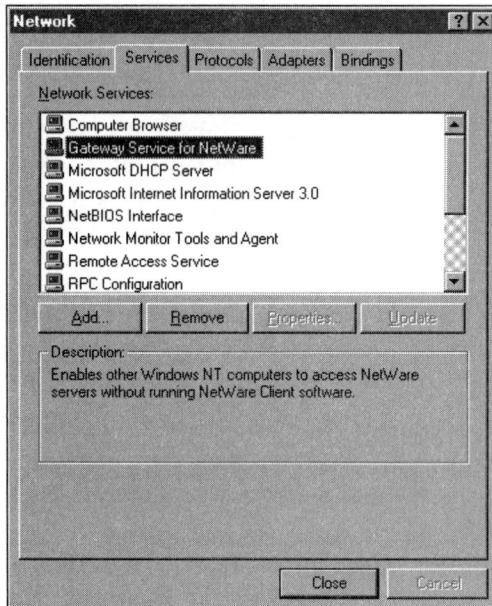

Figure 10-2 Network dialog box with GSNW installed

6. Click **Close**.

7. Click **Yes** when you are asked if you want to restart the computer.

Now that you've installed GSNW, you must configure it. The first step in configuring GSNW is to create at least one user account and a group account on the NetWare server to which you want to connect. To configure GSNW:

1. Log onto the NetWare server with Supervisor rights.

2. Create a user account(s) that has the necessary rights to the resources you want to access.

3. Create a group account named "NTGATEWAY" that also has the necessary rights to the resources you want to access.

4. Add the user account to the "NTGATEWAY" group.

5. On the Windows NT server, Click **Start**, point to **Settings**, then click **Control Panel**. The Control Panel now contains an icon labeled GSNW, as shown in Figure 10-3.

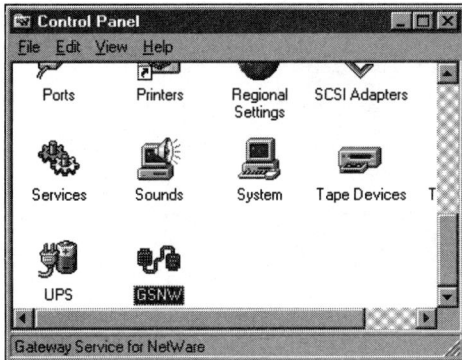

Figure 10-3   GSNW icon added to the Control Panel

6. Double-click the **GSNW** icon. The Gateway Service for NetWare dialog box opens, as shown in Figure 10-4.

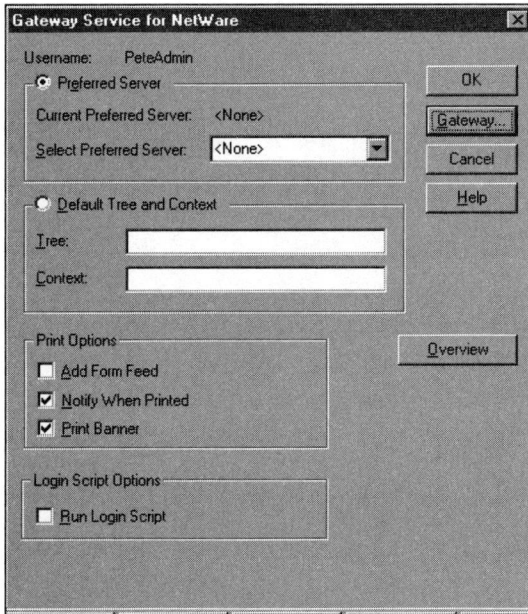

Figure 10-4   Gateway Service for NetWare dialog box

7. Click **Gateway**. The Configure Gateway dialog box opens, as shown in Figure 10-5.

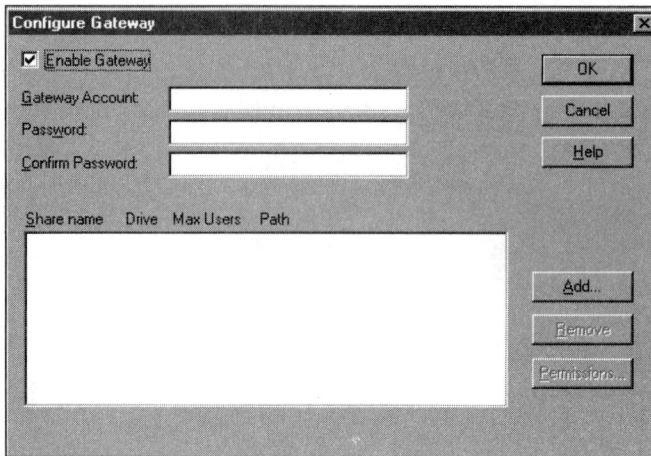

Figure 10-5   Configure Gateway dialog box

8. In the Gateway Account text box, type the name of the user account you created on the NetWare server.

9. In the Password text box, type the account's password, then type the password again in the Confirm Password dialog box.

10. Click the **Add button**. The New Share dialog box opens.

11. In the Share Name text box, type a name for the directory you want to share.

12. In the Network Path text box, type the UNC name for the directory you want to share.

13. Click the **Use Drive list arrow**, then select a drive letter in the Windows NT server that will be associated with the shared directory on the NetWare server. (The default letter is "Z.") You will use this drive letter to access NetWare files from the server.

14. Verify that "10" appears in the Allow Users spin box. This number specifies that no more than 10 simultaneous connections can be made to the shared directory. At this point, your dialog box should resemble Figure 10-6. (Figure 10-6 assumes that you are sharing the "Payroll" subdirectory of the "Employee" directory on a NetWare server named "NW2.")

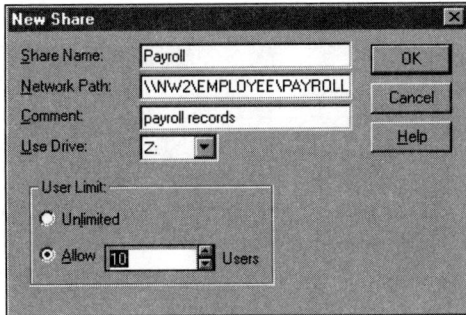

Figure 10-6   New Share dialog box

15. Click **OK**, then click **OK** again to close the Configure Gateway dialog box.

16. Log off, then log on again so that your changes can take effect.

> You can create a NetWare share only by following the preceding steps. You cannot use My Computer or Explorer, as you would when creating Windows NT shares.

Next, you need to set permissions for the shares you've created through the GSNW applet in the Control Panel. To set permissions for the shares you've created:

1. On the Windows NT server, click **Start**, point to **Settings**, click **Control Panel**, then double-click the **GSNW icon**. The Gateway Services for NetWare dialog box opens.

2. Click the **Gateway button**. The Configure Gateway dialog box opens.

3. In the Share name list box, select the permissions you want to change, and then click **Permissions**. The Permissions dialog box opens.

4. Set permissions (such as read-only) for the selected share. When you are finished, click **OK**.

NETWARE FILE ATTRIBUTES

When assigning permissions, you may have noticed differences in the file permissions available between the two platforms. GSNW does not support the following NetWare Attributes: RW (Read-Write), S (Shareable), T (Transactional), P (Purge), Ra (Read-Audit), Wa (Write-Audit), and Ci (Copy Inhibit). When copying files from a Microsoft client to a NetWare server by means of GSNW, only the Ro, A, Sy, and H file attributes are preserved. Table 10-1 compares the file attributes available in Windows NT with their equivalents under NetWare when a NetWare file is opened through GSNW.

Table 10-1   File Attributes in Windows NT and NetWare:

Windows NT File Attributes	NetWare File Attributes
A (Archive)	A (Archive)
S (System)	Sy (System)
H (Hidden)	H (Hidden)
R (Read-Only)	Ro (Delete Inhibit), Ri (Rename Inhibit)

ACCESSING NETWARE PRINT RESOURCES

In addition to sharing file resources using the NetWare services available on Windows NT, you can access NetWare printers. You can reach these printer resources via the Add Printer applet found in the Start menu under Settings.

To attach a NetWare printer to a Windows NT server running GSNW:

1. Click **Start**, point to **Settings**, click **Control Panel**, then double-click the **Add Printer icon**. The Add Printer Wizard dialog box opens.

2. Select the **Network Printer Server** option button, then click **Next**. The Connect to Printer dialog box opens, as shown in Figure 10-7. In the list box, you see two icons: NetWare or Compatible Network and Microsoft Windows Network. These trees can be expanded just like Windows Network trees.

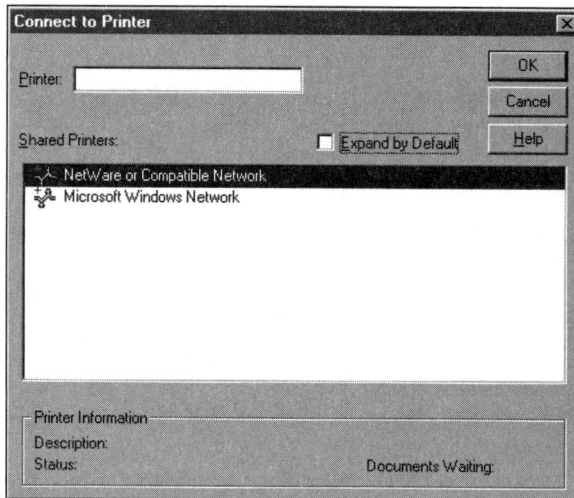

Figure 10-7   Connect to Printer dialog box

3. Double-click **NetWare or Compatible Network** to expand the NetWare tree.

4. Double-click the NetWare server that runs the print queue, select the printer, then click **OK**.

MIGRATION TOOL FOR NETWARE

The Migration Tool for NetWare transfers users, groups, folders, and files from NetWare file servers to computers running Windows NT Server. (The Windows NT servers involved must be primary domain controllers or backup domain controllers.) The Migration Tool preserves most user account information, including account restrictions and administrative rights and user and group names. It also allows you to select the files and folders to transfer, specify the location to which they should be transferred, and preserve their effective rights. In addition, you can conduct trial migrations to preview the result of your settings. Finally, the Migration Tool allows you to generate comprehensive **log files** that detail every change made during the migration (trial or actual).

If folders and files are transferred to a volume formatted to use the Windows NT file system (NTFS), then file and folder security is preserved as well. Migrations can be performed from the server to which information is being migrated or from a remote computer running Windows NT Server or Windows NT Workstation. To run the Migration Tool from a remote Windows NT workstation, you must first copy the files from a computer running Windows NT Server. To copy the Migration Tool to a Windows NT workstation, copy the NWCONV.EXE, NWCONV.HLP, LOGVIEW.EXE, and LOGVIEW.HLP files from a Windows NT server's *systemroot*\SYSTEM32 folder; place these copied files in the Windows NT workstation's *systemroot*\SYSTEM32 folder. To run the Migration Tool and to access NetWare servers, the computer performing the migration must use the NWLink transport protocol and either GSNW or CSNW. Figure 10-8 illustrates the migration process.

10

Users and groups are migrated to the domain controller.

The domain controller replicates users and groups to the domain's backup controllers.

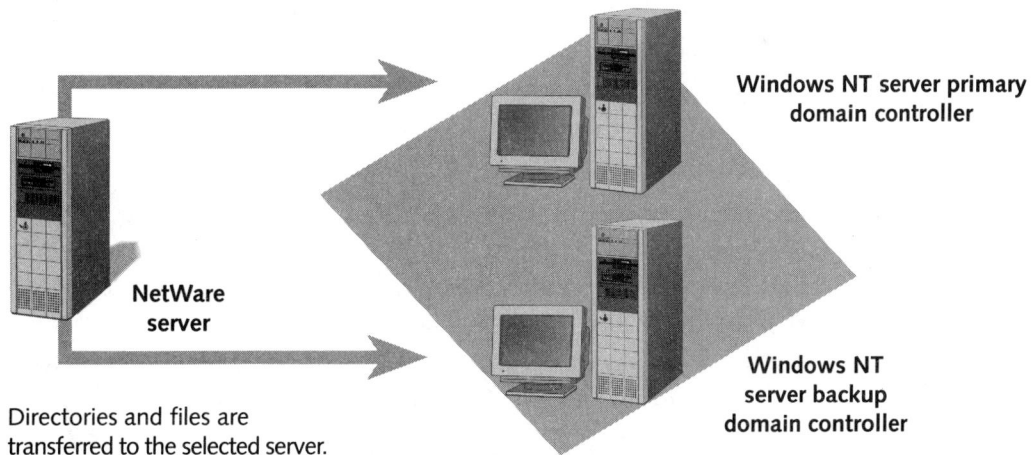

Windows NT server primary domain controller

NetWare server

Windows NT server backup domain controller

Directories and files are transferred to the selected server.

Figure 10-8 Migrating from NetWare to Windows NT

Before beginning a migration between two servers, it is very important that all users close all files and log off the servers involved.

To start Migration Tool for NetWare:

1. Click the **Start button**, then click **Run**.

2. In the Open text box, type **NWCONV.EXE**, then click **OK**. If you are starting the Migration Tool for the first time, the Select Servers for Migration dialog box opens (as shown in Figure 10-9), prompting you to choose the servers to which you want to migrate.

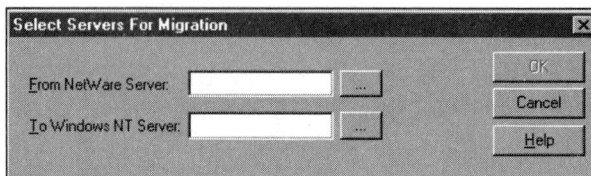

Figure 10-9   Select Servers for Migration dialog box

3. In the From NetWare Server text box, type the name of the server from which you want to migrate users or resources. Alternatively, you can click the browse button (the button with three dots, to the right of the From NetWare Server text box) and select the NetWare server.

4. In the To Windows NT Server text box, type the name of the server to which you want to migrate users or resources. Alternatively, you can click the browse button (the button with three dots, to the right of the To Windows NT Server text box) and select the Windows NT server.

5. Click **OK**. You return to the Migration Tool for NetWare dialog box (shown in Figure 10-10), where you face several choices. First, you can use the File Options and User Options command buttons to set specific transfer mechanics. You can click Start Migration to actually begin the migration process, or you can click Trial Migration to preview the results of the migration. In most cases, you should begin with a trial migration, during which the Migration Tool creates a set of log files that indicate how users, groups, and volumes will be transferred. After reviewing the log files, you can adjust the migration options as necessary.

6. Click **Trial Migration**. At the end of the trial migration, you will be asked if you want to review the logs. Click **Yes** to review them.

7. If necessary, click **User Options** or **File Options** to adjust settings, then click **Trial Migration** again until the log files show that the actual migration will proceed as planned.

8. Click **Start Migration** to perform the actual migration.

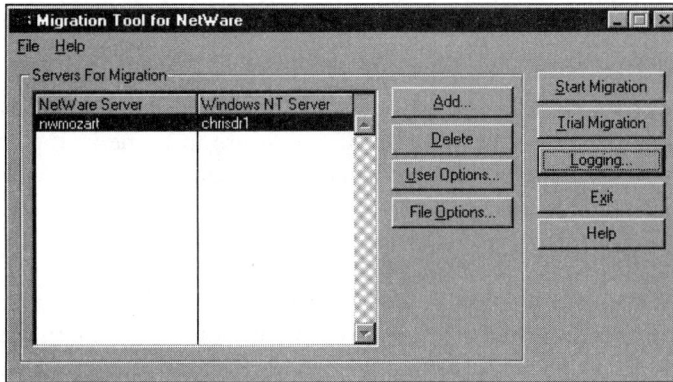

Figure 10-10   Migration Tool for NetWare dialog box

Passwords are encrypted on a NetWare server and therefore cannot be read or transferred by the Migration Tool. By default, all users must change their passwords the first time they log in, after the migration. You have several options for setting new passwords during the migration process:

- Assign a null password to all accounts so that users can log on without specifying a password.
- Make each user's password identical to his or her username.
- Assign the same password to all migrated accounts.
- Use a **mapping file**, which lists each account being migrated and specifies a new password for each account.

When user names being transferred are identical to the existing Windows NT usernames, the duplicate names are not migrated by default. You can, however, create a new account on the Windows NT server by adding a prefix to the current username.

If you choose to use a mapping file, you must specify this selection when setting your migration options. You can either use the Migration Tool to create the mapping file or create the file on your own using a text editor. Note, however, that a mapping file created with the Migration Tool is easier to manage, because it obtains the required section headings and the names of all user and group accounts from the NetWare server. Once the mapping file is created, you can edit the information manually using the text-editing tool of your choice. Although you can also revise the file via the User and Group Options dialog box, using a text-editing tool is faster.

To create a mapping file using the Migration Tool:

1. Click **Start**, then click **Run**.

2. In the Open text box, type **NWCONV.EXE**, then click **OK**. The Migration Tool for NetWare dialog box opens.

3. Click **Users**. The User and Groups Options dialog box opens.

4. Click **Create**. A dialog box opens, asking whether you want to edit the mapping file.

5. Click **Yes** to edit the file. The log file opens.

A mapping file consists of two discrete sections: one containing user information, and another containing group information. For each transferred user or group, a line in the appropriate section of the mapping file will contain the information needed to make the transfer. The format for users is as follows:

current_username, new_username, password

For example, if the NetWare user account is "jeff," and you want to rename the account to "jwilliams" and set the password to "niceguy," you would enter the following in the user section of the mapping file: jeff, jwilliams, niceguy. If you do not include a password, the account will be migrated with a null password. All transferred users, by default, must change their passwords at their first logon to a Windows NT server. If the username will not change during the migration, you would place the current username in both the first and second positions in the mapping file entry, as follows: jeff, jeff, niceguy.

Remember that passwords cannot exceed 14 characters and *are* case-sensitive in Windows NT. Usernames must be unique on the server and in the domain; they can be 20 characters or less.

The group section of the mapping file closely resembles the user section. The group entries have the following format:

current_groupname, new_groupname

If you do not want a NetWare group to be migrated, you must remove the relevant line from your mapping file.

When editing a mapping file, remember that Windows NT security information can be maintained only on an NTFS partition. If you attempt to transfer files to a FAT partition, all security information will be lost.

During the migration process, an account's NetWare rights are translated into the equivalent Windows NT permission. Table 10-2 describes the relationship between NetWare rights and Windows NT permissions.

Table 10-2   Relationship Between NetWare and Windows NT Rights and Permissions

NetWare Rights	Windows NT File Permissions
Supervisor (S)	Full Control (All)
Read (R)	Read (RX)
Write (W)	Change (RWXD)
Erase (E)	Change (RWXD)
Modify (M)	Change (RWXD)
Create (C)	No equivalent
File Scan (F)	No equivalent
Access Control (A)	Change Permissions (P)

FILE AND PRINT SERVICES FOR NETWARE (FPNW)

To replace NetWare servers with Windows NT servers, you must install Microsoft's File and Print Services for NetWare (FPNW). FPNW allows NetWare clients to access resources on the Windows NT server without making any software or configuration changes to the client. To the NetWare client, the Windows NT server looks just like a NetWare server.

FPNW is a separate product not included on the Windows NT Server installation disk. It acts as a **redirector**, which (as you may recall from Chapter 7) means that it intercepts software requests for resources, converts them into network I/O requests, and passes the I/O requests on to the network driver to be packaged. FPNW enables a Windows NT server to provide file and print services directly to NetWare client computers; the server appears just like any other NetWare 3.12 server to the NetWare clients.

DIRECTORY SERVICES MANAGER FOR NETWARE (DSMN)

Directory Services Manager for NetWare (DSMN) synchronizes user accounts between Windows NT Server domains and servers running Novell NetWare version 2.x, 3.x, or 4.x, operating in the bindery emulation mode. (The term **synchronization** refers to the process of maintaining an identical database on one or more servers. The term bindery refers to the NetWare equivalent of the Windows NT SAM database.) It allows you to administer user and group accounts (on both Windows NT and NetWare servers) from User Manager for Domains on a Windows NT computer. DSMN also allows a single user to access both NetWare and Windows NT resources using a single username and password. To accomplish this goal, it copies NetWare user and group account information to a Windows NT server and then propagates any changes to the accounts back to the NetWare servers.

10

DSMN does not allow resource sharing. To implement resource sharing, you must use either GSNW (on Windows NT servers) or CSNW (on Windows NT workstations). Novell also provides its own proprietary client redirectors for use on Microsoft clients.

CHAPTER SUMMARY

- The NWLink protocol provides a common language that allows Windows NT and NetWare servers to communicate with one another. In addition to offering NWLink, Windows NT Server provides services that allow you to combine the Windows NT network with a NetWare network. These services include Gateway Services for NetWare (GSNW), Migration Tool for NetWare, File and Print Services for NetWare (FPNW), and Directory Services Manager for NetWare (DSMN).

- GSNW enables a Windows NT server to access NetWare services directly and allows clients of that Windows NT server to use NetWare resources. GSNW's chief disadvantage is the potential for a bottleneck as a greater number of clients connect to the server. Ideally, GSNW should be used only to obtain occasional access to NetWare resources.

- The Migration Tool for NetWare allows you to transfer users and groups, along with their associated rights, plus files, directories, and volumes, from a NetWare server to a Windows NT server that is acting as a domain controller. If the partition on the Windows NT server is formatted for NTFS, security characteristics for the files, directories, and volumes will be translated to their Windows NT equivalents. Before conducting a complete migration, however, it is recommended that you run a trial migration as many times as necessary to ensure that the results will be satisfactory. User names and group names can be transferred to Windows NT or, if you prefer, they can be remapped to different values using a mapping file.

- FPNW allows NetWare clients to access resources on a Windows NT server without installing additional client software. Installing these services on a Windows NT server enables NetWare clients to access resources on the server without making any software or configuration changes to the client. To the NetWare client, the Windows NT server looks just like a NetWare 3.12 server.

- DSMN enables NetWare users and groups to be managed from the Windows NT server. It synchronizes user accounts between Windows NT Server domains and servers running Novell NetWare version 2.x, 3.x, or 4.x (operating in the bindery emulation mode). DSMN allows you to centrally administer user and group accounts on both Windows NT and NetWare servers from the User Manager for Domains tool on a Windows NT computer. In addition, it provides single user account and password access to both Windows NT and NetWare resources to which the accounts have access. To accomplish this goal, DSMN copies NetWare user and group account information to a Windows NT server and then propagates any changes to the accounts back to the NetWare servers.

KEY TERMS

- **bindery** — NetWare's equivalent to the SAM (Security Accounts Manager) database; it keeps track of NetWare users and privileges. The Migration Tool for NetWare converts bindery information to SAM information.

- **Directory Services Manager for NetWare (DSMN)** — A Windows NT service that enables the management of NetWare users and groups from the Windows NT server.

- **File and Print Services for NetWare (FPNW)** — A Windows NT service that allows NetWare clients to access resources on a Windows NT server without installing any additional client software.

- **gateway** — A software component that facilitates the translation of different protocols and allows computers running different protocols to communicate with one another.

- **Gateway Services for NetWare (GSNW)** — A Windows NT service that enables a Windows NT server to access NetWare file and print resources directly and acts as a gateway for other Microsoft clients, allowing them to access the NetWare resources.

- **log file** — A file generated by a software program that tracks processes performed by the software.

- **mapping file** — A file that shows how NetWare users and groups are migrated to Windows NT servers; it is primarily used to assign NetWare passwords to migrated accounts.

- **Migration Tool for NetWare** — A Windows NT utility that allows users and groups, along with their associated rights and permissions, to be recreated on (or migrated to) Windows NT servers.

- **redirector** — Software that intercepts I/O requests for network resources and directs them to the proper server.

- **synchronization** — The process of maintaining an identical database, such as the user and groups database, on one or more servers.

REVIEW QUESTIONS

1. NWLink must be installed before installing GSNW. True or False?

2. To use print resources on a NetWare server, which component(s) must be installed on a Windows NT server?
   a. NWLink and CSNW
   b. NWLink and GSNW
   c. none; you can connect to NetWare servers automatically

3. If the Migration Tool for NetWare encounters usernames on the NetWare server that match existing usernames in the existing Windows NT domain, what will it do by default?
   a. Replace the existing Windows NT user account information with incoming NetWare user account information.
   b. Give the administrator the option to overwrite existing account information or prevent the information from being transferred.
   c. Ignore or not transfer any duplicate account information.
   d. Transfer the account and add a prefix to the duplicate user account.

4. What must be present on a Windows NT server if NetWare clients are to access a client/server application on the Windows NT server?
   a. Gateway Services for NetWare
   b. Migration Tool for NetWare
   c. NWLink protocol
   d. File and Print Services for NetWare

5. What must be present on a Windows NT server if NetWare clients are to access a database file on the Windows NT server?

    a. Gateway Services for NetWare

    b. Migration Tool for NetWare

    c. NWLink protocol

    d. File and Print Services for NetWare

6. For the Migration Tool to work properly, GSNW must be present on the Windows NT server to which you will migrate accounts. True or False?

7. Before the Migration Tool can transfer security information from a NetWare server, what protocol system and file must be present on the Windows NT server?

    a. NetBEUI and FAT

    b. TCP/IP and NTFS

    c. NWLink and FAT

    d. NWLink and NTFS

8. GSNW allows NetWare clients to access Windows NT file and print resources. True or False?

9. A gateway is a software component that _____ different protocols.

10. One advantage of GSNW is that it allows an unlimited number of clients to access NetWare resources without performance penalties. True or False?

11. Before a Windows NT server with GSNW installed can act as a NetWare client, you must also install Client Services for NetWare (CSNW). True or False?

12. When you install GSNW on a Windows NT server, you must also configure special accounts on the NetWare server for the Windows NT server to access. True or False?

13. A mapping file is necessary to transfer passwords for user accounts from a NetWare server to a Windows NT server. True or False?

14. Account information can be transferred with the Migration Tool to any Windows NT server. True or False?

15. The name of the program that starts the Migration Tool is _____.

16. It is not necessary for all users to be logged off of both servers involved in a migration. True or False?

17. A trial migration is important because _____.

18. If a Windows NT server is running FPNW, what must the NetWare client computer run to permit access to Windows NT resources?

    a. Microsoft client software such as Client Services for NetWare

    b. Novell client software such as Client32 or VLM

    c. nothing; FPNW makes the Windows NT server look like a NetWare server to NetWare clients

    d. none of the above; NetWare clients cannot access this server

19. Directory Services Manager for NetWare allows synchronization of user and group accounts between Windows NT and NetWare servers. What other features does DSMN provide?

  a. single user logon and password access

  b. resource sharing

  c. access to Windows NT directories from NetWare clients

  d. access to NetWare directories from Windows NT clients

20. Using FPNW, the Windows NT server:

  a. manages directory information and accounts and synchronizes them between Windows NT and NetWare

  b. acts as a gateway for access to NetWare resources

  c. looks like a NetWare server to the NetWare client

  d. is the protocol used to transfer information during a NetWare-to-Windows NT migration.

21. Which of the following NetWare rights have a Windows NT equivalent? (Choose all that apply.)

  a. Supervisor

  b. Modify

  c. Create

  d. File Scan

  e. Access Control

22. During a NetWare to Windows NT migration, the mapping file:

  a. provides information on where files should be mapped

  b. provides information on where volumes should be stored

  c. provides information on how user and group names should be translated

  d. all of the above

  e. none of the above

23. To edit the mapping file, you use:

  a. a text editor

  b. NWCONF.EXE

  c. User Manager for Domains

  d. none of the above; the mapping file is generated automatically and cannot be edited

10

HANDS-ON PROJECTS

For some or all of these projects you will need a functioning Windows NT Server on a network that includes one or more NetWare servers. You will also need the supervisor password for the NetWare Server. The NetWare server must be version 3.x or version 4.x in Bindery Emulation mode. You will also need the Services for NetWare CD (available from Microsoft for a nominal charge).

PROJECT 10-1

In this project you will install File and Print Services for NetWare (FPNW).

1. Click **Start**, point to **Settings**, click **Control Panel**, double-click the **Network icon**, click the **Services tab in the Network dialog box**, then click **Add**. The Select Network Service dialog box opens.

2. In the Network Service list, click **<Have Disk>**, then click the **Continue button**. The Insert Disk dialog box opens.

3. Insert the Services for NetWare CD-ROM into your CD-ROM drive.

4. Type the path **X:\FPNW\NT40***processortype*, where *X*: represent your CD-ROM drive and *processortype* is your hardware platform (i386, mips, alpha or ppc), then click **OK**. The Select OEM Option dialog box opens.

5. In the list box, select **File and Print Services for NetWare**, then click **OK**. The Install File and Print Services for NetWare dialog box opens.

6. In the Directory For SYS Volume text box, type the location for the SYSVOL directory that will be the NetWare SYS: volume. The default location is C:\SYSVOL, but you should choose a location that is on an NTFS partition.

7. In the Supervisor Account group text box, type a password for the Supervisor's account, then press **Enter**. The Password dialog box opens.

8. In the Password text box, type the password again to confirm it.

9. Click **OK** to complete the installation. You will see dialog boxes indicating that your bindings are being rebuilt and then reviewed. When prompted, click **Yes** to restart your server.

PROJECT 10-2

In this project you will install Directory Services Manager for NetWare (DSMN). To complete this project, you need both a Windows NT server and a NetWare server (version 3.x or 4.x operating in bindery emulation mode).

1. Click **Start**, point to **Settings**, click **Control Panel**, double-click the **Network** icon, click the **Services tab in the Network dialog box**, then click **Add**. The Select Network Service dialog box opens.

2. Click **Have Disk**.

3. Insert the Services for NetWare CD-ROM in the CD-ROM drive.

4. Type the path **X:\DSMN\NT40*processortype***, where *X:* represents your CD-ROM drive and *processortype* is your hardware platform (i386, mips, alpha, or ppc), then click **OK**. The Select OEM Option dialog box opens.

5. In the Select OEM Option list box, select **Directory Services Manager for NetWare**, then click **OK**. The Install Directory Service for NetWare dialog box opens.

6. In the password and confirm password text boxes, type a password for the DSMN user account, then click **OK**. (Make sure to type the same password in both boxes.) The Network Properties dialog box opens.

7. Click **Close** to close the Network Properties dialog box, and when prompted, click the button to restart your server.

10

PROJECT 10-3

In this project you will use the Migration Tool for NetWare in trial mode. To complete this project, you need both a Windows NT server and a NetWare Server (version 3.x or 4.x operating in bindery emulation mode).

1. From the Start menu, click **Run**.

2. In the Command Line box, type **NWCONV.EXE.**, then click **OK**.

3. Select the NetWare server(s) you want to migrate from and the computer(s) running Windows NT Server to which you want to migrate.

4. Click **User Options** to specify how users and groups will be transferred from the NetWare server to the Windows NT server.

5. Click **File Options** to specify which volumes (if any) on the NetWare server from which to transfer files and folders. For each volume you migrate, you can select which folders and files to actually transfer to the Windows NT server.

6. Click **Trial Migration**.

7. Click **Start Migration** to perform the migration. After the migration, the Migration Tool displays the log files for your review.

CASE PROJECTS

1. The Eden Restaurants network has a mixture of Novell NetWare servers and Windows NT servers. In the past, Windows NT users have not needed to access NetWare resources. Because of an upcoming project, however, several Windows NT users will require access to files on two of the NetWare servers. Write a brief report (two to three paragraphs) explaining how you will enable the Windows NT users to access the NetWare resources.

2. The Atwater Group wants to eliminate its NetWare servers and switch to Windows NT servers to allow single user logon and password access to server resources. In the future, only Windows NT clients will be added to the network. Write a brief report (three to five paragraphs) explaining how you will help the Atwater Group achieve its goal.

3. Your company, Sterling Enterprises, has recently merged with Platinum Productions. Sterling's network uses Windows NT, while the Platinum's network runs NetWare. You have been charged with the task of allowing some of the NetWare users to access resources on the Windows NT network. Write a brief report (two to three paragraphs) explaining how you will accomplish this task.

INSTALLING AND CONFIGURING MULTI-PROTOCOL ROUTING

Multi-protocol routing (MPR) is a Windows NT Server 4.0 feature that allows you to combine disparate LANs without a dedicated hardware-based router. A **router** is a piece of hardware or software that uses a data packet's header information to move that packet closer to its destination without passing it to a network to which it is not addressed. MPR can transmit network traffic between different network segments (both TCP/IP and IPX/SPX) and, depending on your environment, can also function as a **BOOTP/DHCP Relay Agent**. This type of routing is especially useful in networks that have relied on a NetWare server in the past to provide routing functionality. In this chapter you will learn the basics of how MPR operates in several environments (IP, IPX and AppleTalk).

AFTER READING THIS CHAPTER AND COMPLETING THE EXERCISES YOU WILL BE ABLE TO:

- Discuss multi-protocol routing on Windows NT
- Install the BOOT/DHCP Relay Agent
- Discuss IP routing
- Add static routes
- Install RIP for Internet Protocol
- Install RIP for NWLink IPX/SPX-compatible transport
- Configure routing for AppleTalk networks

MULTI-PROTOCOL ROUTING ON WINDOWS NT

Before you can understand how MPR works on a Windows NT network, you must be familiar with routing in general. Many networks are divided into segments (based on physical location) or logical groupings (based on, for example, department or functional responsibility). Routers allow information (in the form of packets) to travel between these network segments. They route packets from their source to their destination via the shortest path available; at the same time, they shield the packets from segments to which they are not addressed. The use of routers and segmentation can reduce traffic on the network, thereby producing a higher performance level for the same number of computers. In particular, routers can reduce bandwidth consumption (by limiting traffic to only the relevant traffic for that segment) and, in some cases, increase security (through the use of filters, compression, and/or encryption). They make it possible to share resources between different networks (or segments on the same network), and prevent the network manager from having to continually replicate data between unattached networks.

To understand the benefits of routing, imagine a company with three departments: Art, Marketing, and Finance. To minimize network traffic and maximize network performance, each of these departments has its own network. The existence of a network router, however, enables the Marketing department to access the Art department's color printer, thereby avoiding the need for the Marketing department to buy its own color printer.

With Windows NT Server's version of MPR, you can add routing functionality at the server level without the purchase of a hardware-based router. Further savings can be realized by selecting from a wide variety of local and wide area network cards supported by Windows NT Server. Thus you can select the solution that is most appropriate in your environment based on functionality, cost, or vendor.

MPR consists of three components: **Routing Information Protocol (RIP)** for Internet Protocol, RIP for NWLink IPX/SPX-compatible transport, and **BOOTP Relay Agent** for DHCP. RIP (for either Internet Protocol or IPX), allows a Windows NT server to function as a router and exchange routing information with other RIP-enabled routers. (You'll learn more about RIP later in this chapter.) As explained in the next section, BOOTP Relay Agent for DHCP allows a server to forward DHCP requests to other segments of the network.

BOOTP/DHCP RELAY AGENT

The BOOTP/DHCP Relay Agent is the simplest of the three MPR services. Because it allows a Windows NT server to relay DHCP messages, this service is useful in situations involving two LANs, only one of which has a DHCP server. The **BOOTP Relay Agent** for DHCP allows you to take advantage of DHCP without being forced to install a DHCP server on every network. It is fully compliant with RFC 1542, the standards document associated with BOOTP forwarding. The complete RFC (Request for Comments) can be found at *http://www.ietf.org*.

To install the BOOTP/DHCP Relay Agent, you use the Services tab of the Network applet. During the installation process, you will specify the address of the DHCP server on your network via the IP Address tab of the Microsoft TCP/IP Properties dialog box. (An illustration of this dialog box is provided in the Hands-On Projects at the end of this chapter.)

You can change the default values for the DHCP Relay Agent via the DHCP Relay tab in the Microsoft TCP/IP Properties dialog box, shown in Figure 11-1. The following values may be modified: seconds threshold, maximum hops, and the address of your DHCP servers. The seconds threshold mandates the number of seconds that must pass before the broadcast is issued from the local subnet. The maximum number of **hops** refers to the maximum number of times the packet can cross a router before reaching its host. (The packet will "time out" and be discarded if this number is exceeded.) You should accept the default values unless you are trying to accomplish a specific goal that requires a change. The address of the DHCP server, which is specific to your network, identifies a server running the DHCP Server service.

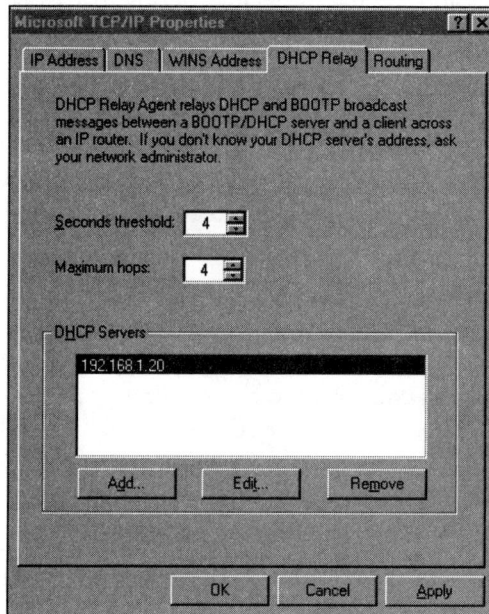

Figure 11-1   DHCP Relay tab of the Microsoft TCP/IP Properties dialog box

FUNDAMENTALS OF IP ROUTING

To understand RIP on Windows NT Server, you need to understand some common terminology. A **static route** is one that the systems administrator manually adds to the router's routing table (whether the router is hardware- or software-based). The **routing table** is a database that maintains paths (or routes) to other networks so the router will know where to send outbound data packets. With static routing, it does not matter whether a path is available; the route remains in the routing table in any event. The routing table stores routes to other **autonomous systems**, such as other corporate offices or different floors within a building, or to an ISP for connection to the Internet.

A **default route** is a path of last resort—the destination to which a packet will be sent if the routing table does not include a defined route. Default routing is the easiest way to implement routing if you have a single point of connection between two networks.

A **dynamic route** is one that is "learned" from internal or external routing protocols, such as RIP or OSPF. (**OSPF**—"Open Shortest Path First"—is a routing protocol for wide area networks.) Upon startup, these protocols send out a request for routes to other systems. Routers on other autonomous systems respond by providing information on the routes that they know, including the number of hops required for each route. The router compiles this information into a list of the shortest paths to a given network. As other routers come online or become unavailable, these routes are updated to reflect the new topology. If a route is unavailable, for example, it is removed from the routing table. Dynamic routing is more flexible and requires less maintenance than static routing or default routing (particularly in large networks), but it is also more prone to error.

RIP is a **distance vector routing protocol**, or a protocol that uses an algorithm to determine the least-cost path to a given destination. When using protocols other than RIP, the cost is based on the type or speed of the connection, or some mathematical function based on a combination of these elements. However, when using RIP, the cost is based on the number of hops. RIP computes the least-cost path to a destination by choosing the route with the smallest total hops required for a packet to reach that destination.

The router builds the routing table by making discovery requests beginning at the closest autonomous system and then extending a number of hops from 0 hops to infinity. Note that routing typically defines "infinity" as a number far smaller than the "infinity" found in mathematics—often as 16, which is the functional equivalent to being infinitely distant. If a router had an infinity value that matched the mathematical infinity, the routing table would become so large as to make the router unusable. The value of 16 is typically accepted as being distant enough to give excellent functionality but not overwhelming the routing table with data.

To build a routing table, RIP sends a message to neighboring routers that says all routes have a cost of infinity. The neighboring routers send back routing information showing that this assumption is not true. RIP then compiles this information into a routing table that extends to the infinity value.

Routing functions are not limited to routers. All hosts running TCP/IP make routing decisions even if they are **single-homed** (that is, contain one network interface). These decisions are dictated by the contents of the routing table. A Windows NT computer running TCP/IP builds a routing table automatically based on the host's IP configuration in much the same way as a dedicated router would.

To view the routing table on a Windows NT computer running TCP/IP, type "route print" in the Command Prompt window. Figure 11-2 shows the routing table for a single-homed host at 192.168.2.25. This routing table in Figure 11-2 includes five columns: Network Address, Netmask, Gateway Address, Interface, and Metric.

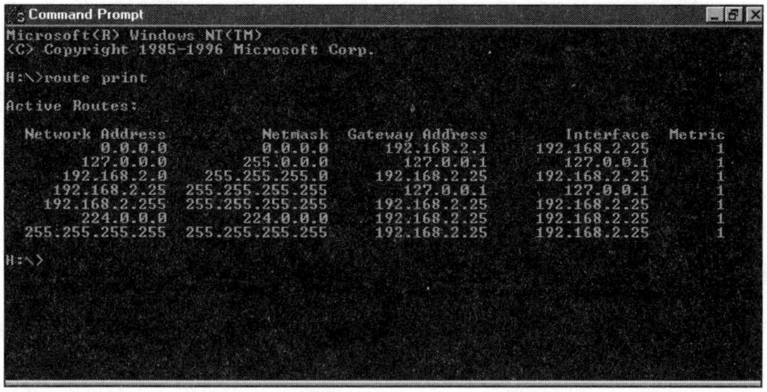

Figure 11-2   Routing table displayed in the Command Prompt window

The Network Address column lists the destination address to which a packet may be routed. The entries in this column go from the most unique (local address) to the most generic (default gateway). In Figure 11-2, the first entry in the Network Address column, 0.0.0.0, is the default route. The next entry, 127.0.0.0, is the loopback address. A **loopback address** is a special address that directs traffic back to the local machine. The remaining entries in the Network Address column are defined as follows: 192.168.2.0 is the local subnet address; 192.168.2.25 is the address of the network card in the local machine; 192.168.2.255 is the **broadcast address**, which will send data to all hosts on the local subnet; 224.0.0.0 is the **multicast address**, which will send data to all hosts registered to receive multicast packets; and 255.255.255.255 is the limited broadcast address, which says that the destination address must match exactly (as described below). (In binary form, 255.255.255.255 consists of all 1's.)

Each entry in the **Netmask** column defines the portion of the network address that must match for the route to be used. To understand the numbers in the Netmask column, you need to translate them to binary form (as explained in Chapter 3). In a binary netmask number, a 1 symbolizes "must match," while a 0 (zero) symbolizes "doesn't have to match." The number 255.255.255.0 would be written in binary as 11111111.11111111.11111111.00000000; thus the destination address of that packet must match exactly in the first three octets for the route to be used. The netmask 255.255.255.0 is the **subnet mask** for the network 192.168.2.0. The first three octets must match if traffic is to be routed to that subnet.

The **Gateway Address** column defines the IP address of a router that can locate that particular network—either the local network card or a gateway or router on the local subnet.

The Interface column defines the network card in the local host through which the packet should pass. The address 127.0.0.1 is the software loopback address and tells software (such as the PING utility) to send the request to itself.

The **Metric** column, which defines the number of hops to the destination address, helps determine the shortest route to a destination. In Figure 11-2, the metric is 1, indicating that the machine is single-homed and is therefore aware of only one network.

11

ADDING STATIC ROUTES

In some cases (for example, if you need to force packets to take a specific path to a specific destination or if a link in the chain between the source and destination is not visible), you may need to add a static route to the routing table. A static route will ensure that traffic flows in the required manner. You can add such a route by using the ROUTE ADD command in the Command Prompt window.

To add static route via the Command Prompt window:

1. Click the **Start button**, point to **Programs**, then click **MS-DOS Prompt**. The Command Prompt window opens.

2. At the command prompt, type **route add 192.168.2.0 mask 255.255.255.0 192.168.1.1 metric 2**.

The preceding steps create a static route in the routing table that specifies the following path: To get to the 192.168.2.0 network, which has a mask of 255.255.255.0, use the gateway at 192.168.1.1, which is two hops away. You now need to add a static route on the next router telling it how to find subnets reachable by the first router. Given the need to perform all of this manual configuration, static routing with more than a few routers can quickly become very complicated.

RIP FOR INTERNET PROTOCOL

In all but the simplest routing situations, you should use RIP (either RIP for IP or RIP for IPX/SPX-compatible protocol) instead of manual configuration. Both versions of RIP provide dynamic routing, which means that they query neighboring routers to find the fastest routes to a given network at any particular time and then add these routes to the routing table. RIP removes routes from the routing table when it receives information indicating that they are no longer available.

A Windows NT server running RIP can be referred to as a RIP router. A RIP router broadcasts its routing table every 30 seconds by default. In addition, it listens for broadcasts from other RIP routers, and updates its routing table from the information contained in those broadcasts. A RIP router cannot broadcast across a modem or an ISDN adapter; it will broadcast only across a LAN interface, such as a network adapter or T1 interface card. To install RIP for IP, you use the Services tab of the Network applet.

As soon as RIP for IP is installed, IP routing is enabled. To use static routing later, you must then turn off IP routing. To re-enable RIP for IP, you must reinstall it.

RIP FOR NWLINK IPX/SPX-COMPATIBLE TRANSPORT

The installation process for RIP for IPX is similar to that for RIP for IP. When installing RIP for IPX, Windows NT will also install NWLink Protocol, NWLink NetBIOS, and the SAP Agent service (if they are not already installed). SAP Agent allows Windows NT Server to propagate SAP Broadcasts. **SAP (Service Advertising Protocol)** is used by servers to advertise their services and addresses on a network.

The process of changing the RIP for NWLink configuration is similar to changing the configuration of RIP for IP. You will do both later in this chapter.

When you install RIP for NWLink, Enable RIP Routing is automatically activated. To disable it, deselect the Enable RIP Routing check box in the Properties page of the RIP for NWLink IPX/SPX-compatible service. Likewise, SAP Agent is automatically installed and initiated during the RIP for NWLink installation process. You can disable this service via the Services applet in the Control Panel.

Immediately after installing RIP for NWLink, you should assign an internal network number in the Protocol Properties dialog box. If you do not assign this number, a random number will be used.

> To minimize problems with IPX, manually select a frame type instead of using the auto detect feature.

11

Finally, keep in mind that you can use IPXROUTE.EXE to get information on RIP, SAP, routing, and statistics.

APPLETALK ROUTER

Windows NT Server also includes routing functionality for AppleTalk networks. AppleTalk routing is not handled by MPR, but rather by Services for Macintosh. Services for Macintosh allows the Windows NT server to function as either a seed router or a non-seed router.

AppleTalk networks differ significantly from PC networks. Most are actually multiple smaller networks connected together to form an **internetwork**. Because one core function of routers is the maintenance of a map of the physical network, this concatenation of smaller networks complicates the router's job. AppleTalk networks are further complicated by the need for **seed routers**, which initialize and broadcast routing information about one or more physical networks to the other routers on the network. (Not all routers are seed routers.) Non-seed routers use data received from seed routers to maintain a map of the physical network. Because the router then uses this to forward information to the correct physical network, it is important that the routing table be accurate.

To make it more fault-resilient, the network may include multiple seed routers. If multiple seed routers are present, all of them must transmit (seed) the same information for that network.

The order in which servers start is important on an AppleTalk network. The first seed router that starts will serve as the seed router for the entire network. Hence servers configured as seed routers must start first, so that other routers can contact it during their initialization process. A non-seed router cannot be activated until a seed router becomes available.

In AppleTalk networks, a zone is the equivalent of a Windows NT domain. A **zone** is a logical grouping of servers and resources that facilitates browsing the network for server and printer resources. LocalTalk networks can access only one zone at any given time; in contrast, EtherTalk, TokenTalk and FDDI networks can access multiple zones. This variation allows you to use creative zone designs. For example, you could group all of your EtherTalk printers into a single zone to make it easier for EtherTalk clients to find and access printers or to simplify administration.

To configure AppleTalk routing on a Windows NT server running Services for Macintosh:

1. Click the **Start button**, point to **Settings**, click **Control Panel**, double-click the **Network icon**, then click the **Services tab**.

2. In the Network Services list, click **Services for Macintosh**, then click **Properties**. The Microsoft AppleTalk Protocol Properties dialog box opens.

3. Click the **Routing tab**.

4. Select the **Enable Routing check box**, then select additional options (as explained below).

Figure 11-3 shows the Microsoft AppleTalk Protocol Properties dialog box with various options selected.

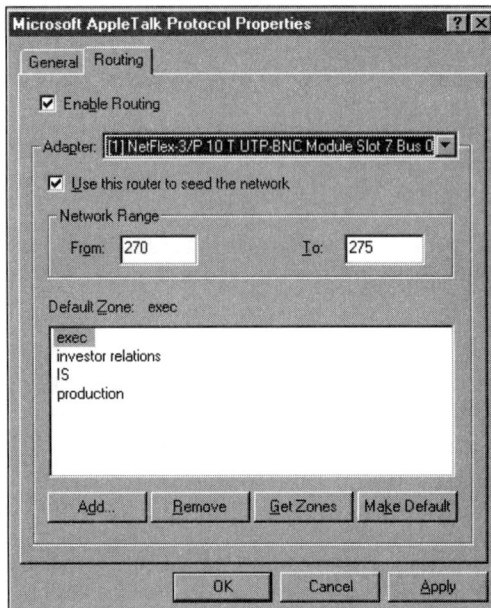

Figure 11-3 Microsoft AppleTalk Protocol Properties dialog box

When setting the options in the Microsoft AppleTalk Protocol Properties dialog box, you will need a good understanding of your network's layout. The Adapter list box contains a list of the network adapters found in your Windows NT server; knowing which adapter is connected to which network is crucial for proper routing configuration. You can enable seeding on any (or all) of the network adapters. You set options for each adapter individually by selecting the appropriate adapter from the drop-down list. To activate seeding for a specific adapter, choose that adapter from the list and then check the "Use this router to seed the network" check box.

To seed the network, you will use the Network Range. Each AppleTalk zone in a network is assigned a range of numbers, and each node in that zone is assigned a number within that range by which it can be addressed. The value you specify for the network must fall into the range 1 through 65,279. Make sure that your networks do not have overlapping ranges. If you choose an overlapping range, you will receive a warning.

> When setting ranges, allow adequate room for growth—that is, include enough numbers that will not be used today but may be needed in the future.

In the Default Zone section of the Routing tab, you can add, edit, and remove zones. You can also set the default zone, which will appear to any client that has not specified a particular zone.

For more information on Services for Macintosh, refer to Chapter 7.

11

Chapter Summary

- Multi-protocol routing (MPR) provides a low-cost routing solution. It allows a Windows NT server to route traffic between network segments. Routing enables resources on different networks to be shared while reducing the required bandwidth. MPR consists of three components: RIP for IP, RIP for IPX, and the BOOTP/DHCP Relay Agent.

- The BOOTP/DHCP Relay Agent is the simplest of the three MPR services. It allows a Windows NT server to relay DHCP messages, and thus it is useful in situations involving two LANs, only one of which includes a DHCP server. The BOOTP Relay Agent for DHCP allows you to take advantage of DHCP without being forced to install a DHCP server on every network.

- A static route is one that is manually added to the router's routing table by the systems administrator. The routing table is a database that maintains paths (or routes) to other networks so the router will know where to send outbound data packets. With static routing, it does not matter whether a path is available; the route remains in the routing table in any event. A default route is a path of last resort—the destination to which a packet will be sent if the routing table does not provide a defined route.

- RIP on Windows NT server uses dynamic routing, which is more flexible than static routing. The routing information is stored in routing tables, where it is updated every 30 seconds. RIP is a distance vector routing protocol that uses a least-cost path routing schema. Cost is calculated by number of hops or other predefined characteristics. Values for the hops range from 0 to infinity: Infinity is a set value—usually 16—that represents a point far enough away to be considered infinity without hurting performance.

- All hosts running TCP/IP make routing decisions based on the data found in routing tables. These tables can be displayed using the ROUTE PRINT command. IPX routing information and statistics can be viewed using a similar utility—IPXROUTE.

- In some cases you may need to add a static route to your routing tables. Such a route will ensure that traffic flows in the required manner. To add a static route to the routing table, you use the ROUTE ADD command in the Command Prompt window.

- AppleTalk routing is also possible on Windows NT using Services for Macintosh. Using this service, a Windows NT server can act as either a seed router or a non-seed router on a Macintosh network. While having multiple seed routers makes a network more resilient, only one seed router will be active at any given time. You can set routing options—including network addresses and AppleTalk zones—independently for each network adapter. AppleTalk zones fulfill the same function on Macintosh networks as domains on a Windows NT network.

KEY TERMS

- **autonomous systems** — A collection of hosts under control of a single entity.

- **BOOTP/DHCP Relay Agent** — The component of multi-protocol routing that relays DHCP and BOOTP broadcast messages between a BOOTP/DHCP server and a client across an IP router.

- **broadcast address** — An IP address used to send data packets to all hosts on the local network.

- **default route** — A path of last resort; the destination to which a packet will be sent if the routing table does not include a defined route.

- **distance vector routing protocol** — A protocol that uses an algorithm to determine the least-cost path to a given destination. The cost is generally an arbitrary number based on specific defined parameters, such as the number of hops.

- **dynamic route** — A route that is learned from neighboring routers through normal interactions and placed in the routing table.

- **gateway address** — Address that defines where the packet should be sent, either the local network card or to a gateway or router on the local subnet.

- **hops** — In routing, the transfer of a packet from one router to the next. Hops are used to calculate the least-cost path.

- **internetwork** — A group of connected networks.

- **loopback address** — The address 127.0.0.1, which tells a utility (for example, PING) to send a request to itself. The loopback address is most useful for troubleshooting.

- **metric** — The number of hops to the destination address, used to determine the shortest route to a destination.

- **multicast address** — The address 224.0.0.0, which is a reserved address in the TCP/IP standard. Multicasting allows multiple hosts to listen to a single stream of packets, a useful function in minimizing bandwidth when sending the same data to a group of hosts at the same time.

- **multi-protocol routing (MPR)** — A Windows NT feature that allows Windows NT to act as a router. MPR consists of three components: Routing Information Protocol (RIP) for Internet Protocol, RIP for IPX, and BOOTP/DHCP Relay Agent.

- **netmask** — The part of the routing table that defines which portion of the network address must match for that route to be used using a binary translation of the IP address.

- **OSPF** — "Open Shortest Path First," a routing protocol for wide area networks.

- **router** — A piece of hardware or software that uses a data packet's header information to move that packet closer to its destination without passing it to a network to which it is not addressed.

- **Routing Information Protocol (RIP)** — A protocol that enables a router to exchange routing information with another router. IPX or IP are the protocols used for the information exchange.

- **routing table** — A database that stores routes to other autonomous systems.

- **seed router** — A router that initializes and broadcasts routing information about one or more physical networks to other routers on the network.

- **Service Advertising Protocol (SAP)** — A protocol used by servers to advertise their services and addresses on a network.

- **single-homed** — A computer that has only one network adapter.

- **static route** — A route to a destination that is manually entered into the router. With static routing, it does not matter if a link is up or down; the route remains in the routing table in any event.

- **subnet mask** — When translated into binary, a number that is used to determine whether data can be sent to a particular network address.

- **zones** — In AppleTalk, the equivalent of domains for Windows NT networks. A zone allows the logical grouping of devices to reduce traffic and simplify browsing for network resources.

REVIEW QUESTIONS

1. Routers optimize network performance by routing packets from their source to their destination by the _____.

11

2. Multi-protocol routing consists of _____ components.

   a. 1

   b. 2

   c. 3

   d. 4

3. The DHCP Relay Agent allows a Windows NT server to:

   a. transfer datagrams between IPX networks

   b. pass DHCP messages between network segments

   c. broadcast type 20 packets between routers

   d. all of the above

   e. none of the above

4. The DHCP Relay Agent is compliant with _____.

5. Values for DHCP Relay Agents are configured:

   a. on the DHCP Relay tab of the DHCP Properties page

   b. in the DHCP Relay applet in Control Panel

   c. on the DHCP Relay tab in the Microsoft TCP/IP Properties dialog box

   d. The DHCP Relay Agent cannot be configured.

6. Static routing refers to routes that:

   a. are entered manually in the routing table

   b. are added to the routing table by routers on your own network

   c. are added to the routing table by routers more than one hop away

   d. can be used only when RIP for Internet Protocol is enabled

7. With a static route, the destination must always be available for the route to be retained. True or False?

8. A default route is the:

   a. destination to which a packet will be sent if the routing table does not include a defined route

   b. easiest way to implement routing between two networks where only a single point of contact exists

   c. both (a) and (b)

   d. neither (a) nor (b)

9. A dynamic route:

   a. is entered manually in the routing table

   b. is added to the routing table by hosts on your own network

   c. is added to the routing table by routers one or more hops away

   d. can be used only when RIP for Internet Protocol is enabled

10. Routing Information Protocol is a ——————— ——————— protocol.

11. RIP uses the ——————— ——————— ——————— to a given destination.

12. The number of hops can range from one to ———————.

13. The netmask defines:

   a. an IP octet that is all 1's

   b. where the packet needs to be sent—either to the local network card or to a gateway or router on the local subnet

   c. which portion of a network address must not match for the route to be used

   d. which portion of a network address must match for the route to be used

14. The metric: (Choose all that apply.)

   a. is the number of hops to the destination address

   b. is another term for subnet mask

   c. is used to determine the shortest route to a destination

   d. defines which network interface a packet should use

15. RIP routers broadcast their routing tables:

   a. every time they are requested

   b. only when a router requests them

   c. every minute

   d. every 30 seconds

16. When RIP for NWLink is installed, the following components are also installed if they are not already present: (Choose all that apply.)

   a. SAP Agent

   b. NWLink Protocol

   c. NWLink NetBIOS

   d. NWLink NetBEUI

17. To minimize the potential for problems using RIP for NWLink, you should:

   a. disable static routes

   b. manually select a frame type

   c. set IPX for auto detect

   d. all of the above

   e. none of the above

18. In a distance vector routing protocol, the least-cost path is determined by ———————.

11

19. Routing information can be obtained by:

   a. IPXROUTE.EXE

   b. ROUTE.EXE

   c. TCP/IP Properties page

   d. all of the above

   e. none of the above

20. A seed router:

   a. initializes and broadcasts routing information

   b. maintains only the addresses of the hosts on its network

   c. maps the physical network using type 20 packets

   d. uses static routes to set destination addresses

21. There can be _____ seed routers on a network.

22. AppleTalk routing is accomplished through the use of multi-protocol routing. True or False?

23. For an AppleTalk network, the range of network can be:

   a. from 1 to 65,536

   b. from 1 to 255

   c. from 1 to 65,279

   d. any number as long as no ranges overlap

HANDS-ON PROJECTS

For Projects 11-1 and 11-2 you will need a multihomed Windows NT server running TCP/IP, with static IP addresses on all adapters. For Project 11-3, you will need a multihomed Windows NT server running IPX. You might want to use the same server but reconfigure it for Project 11-3.

PROJECT 11-1

In this project you will install the BOOTP/DHCP Relay Agent. To do so, you will need a functioning Windows NT server running TCP/IP with static IP addresses on all adapters.

   1. Click the **Start button**, point to **Settings**, click **Control Panel**, double-click the **Network icon**, click the **Services tab**, then click **Add**. The Select Network Services dialog box opens.

   2. In the Network Service list box, click **DHCP Relay Agent**, then click **OK**. The Windows NT Setup dialog box opens.

3. In the Windows NT Setup text box, type the correct path for the Windows NT installation files. (These files are usually located on the I386 directory on the installation CD-ROM.) Click **OK**. The necessary files are copied, and you will return to the Network dialog box.

4. Click the **Protocol tab**, select **TCP/IP** in the Protocols list, then click **Properties**. The Microsoft TCP/IP Properties dialog box opens.

5. Click the **DHCP Relay** tab then click the **Add button**. In the DHCP Relay Agent Dialog Box, enter the IP Address of your DHCP Server and click **OK**. Your dialog box should resemble the one shown in Figure 11-4 (although your server's IP address will probably be different).

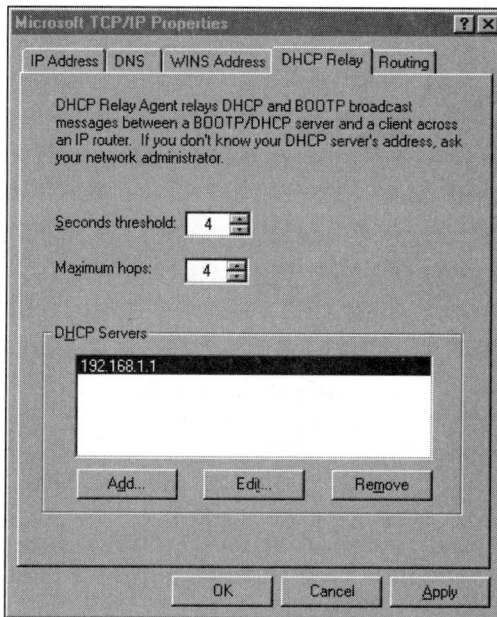

Figure 11-4   Setting the address of the DHCP server

6. Click **Apply**, click **OK** to close the Microsoft TCP/IP Properties dialog box, then click **OK** to close the Network Window.

7. Restart your computer when you are prompted to do so. The DHCP Relay Service is automatically enabled after you restart the computer.

PROJECT 11-2

In this project you will install RIP for Internet Protocol. Before beginning this exercise, you will need TCP/IP installed on your Windows NT server.

1. Click the **Start button**, point to **Settings**, click **Control Panel**, double-click the **Network icon**, click the **Services tab**, then click **Add**. The Select Network Service dialog box opens.

2. In the Network Service list box, click **RIP for Internet Protocol**, then click **OK**. The Windows NT Setup dialog box opens.

3. In the Windows NT Setup text box, type the correct path for the Windows NT installation files. (These files are usually located on the I386 directory on the installation CD-ROM.) Click **OK**.

4. Click **OK** to close the Network dialog box. A warning dialog appears stating that RIP Routing requires static IP addresses on all adapters. Click **OK**.

5. Restart your computer when prompted to do so.

PROJECT 11-3

In this project you will install RIP for NWLink.

1. Click the **Start button**, point to **Settings**, click **Control Panel**, double-click the **Network icon**, click the **Services tab**, then click **Add**. The Select Network Service dialog box opens.

2. In the Network Service list, click **RIP for NWLink** IPX/SPX compatible transport.

3. In the Windows NT Setup text box, type the correct path for the Windows NT installation files. (These files are usually located on the I386 directory on the installation CD-ROM.)

4. Click **Continue**.

5. The RIP for NW Link IPX Configuration dialog box appears (shown in Figure 11-5), indicating that NetBIOS Propagation is turned off and asking if you would like to turn it on. If you are using NetBIOS over IPX or are uncertain, click **Yes**. Broadcasting type 20 packets will have a significant impact on the bandwidth required and will propagate only a total of eight hops.

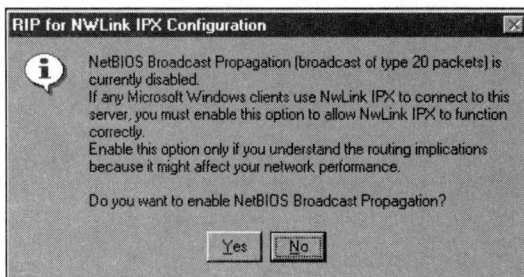

Figure 11-5 RIP for NWLink IPX Configuration dialog box

6. Click **OK** to close the Network dialog box. Then restart your computer when prompted to do so.

PROJECT 11-4

In this project you will remove RIP for Internet Protocol and enable static routing.

1. Click the **Start button**, point to **Settings**, click **Control Panel**, then double-click the **Network icon**.
2. Click the **Services tab,** then highlight **RIP for Internet Protocol**.
3. Click **Remove**. A warning message appears, asking if you wish to continue.
4. Click **Yes**.
5. Close the Network dialog box by clicking **OK**. Restart the computer when you are prompted to do so. When the computer has finished rebooting, log in. Reopen the Network properties as described in Step 1.
6. On the Protocols tab, highlight **TCP/IP Protocol**, then click **Properties**.
7. On the Routing tab, verify that the **Enable IP Forwarding check box** is checked, and then click **OK**.
8. Click **Start**, click **Run**, type **CMD** in the Open text box, then click **OK**.
9. At the command prompt, type **route print**.
10. Note the results on a piece of paper.
11. Type **route add 192.168.2.0 mask 255.255.255.0 192.168.1.1 metric 2**.
12. Type **route print** to display the routing table.
13. Compare the results of Step 10 to the results of Step 8. What changed?

11

To re-enable RIP for IP, you will have to re-install it following the steps in Project 11-2.

CASE PROJECTS

1. Thalia Graphics, Inc., has three departments: Art, Marketing, and Finance. Each department has its own separate network and servers. The Marketing department would like to access the Art department's color printer so that it will not have to buy its own color printer. You are fairly sure that, as soon as you set up this option, the Finance department will also want access to the color printer. Write a brief report (two to three paragraphs) explaining how you would provide access to the printer.

2. Embossed Design needs to connect its Los Angeles and Pasadena offices. The Los Angeles office is a mix of Macintosh and Windows clients connecting to a Windows NT server, while the Pasadena office is all Macintosh computers. Write a brief report (two to three paragraphs) explaining how you would connect the two offices.

3. Embossed Design loved your solution to their problem of connecting their two southern California offices and has invited you back to solve their latest dilemma. The company has decided to upgrade all of its Macintosh computers to PCs, but does not have the funds available to purchase a server for the Pasadena office. Also, the firm has no IS staff in Pasadena, so it does not want to use static IP addresses. Write a brief report (two to three paragraphs) explaining how you would achieve the company's goals.

4. Executive Management Services has hired you to coordinate a reworking of its network. Currently, the company has five networks distributed across the four floors of one building. On the third floor is the Art department, which uses only Macintoshes that are connected via EtherTalk over 10 Base T in a workgroup setting. On the fourth floor is the Legal department, which uses a mixture of Macintoshes and PCs. These Macintoshes are using TokenTalk, and the PCs are connected using Token Ring to a single Windows NT server 4.0 using TCP/IP. The clients on this floor use DHCP. On the seventh floor are the Production, Marketing, Sales, and Accounting departments. These departments use a combination of switched 10 Base T for their clients and switched 100 Base T for their servers. They also have four Novell servers and three Windows NT servers. The Novell servers run NetWare 3.12, with IPX as the protocol. The Windows NT servers run TCP/IP. Although your predecessor implemented switching to accommodate the latency introduced by running the multiple protocols to every client on this floor, performance is reported as only "adequate." The executives on the fourteenth floor use whatever they want and have a mix of multiple models of Macintosh and PC computers. Because of the variety of computers, your predecessor never set up the executives on a network. As a part of this project, they expect to gain access to all network resources, but the executives do not want to pay for a server on their floor.

Additionally, for security reasons (and perhaps a lack of understanding of networking) they insist that they be on a different subnet than anyone else and that their IP addresses be assigned dynamically.

What is your plan? Draw up a diagram of the finished network and describe completely all routing choices.

BASICS OF SERVER ANALYSIS AND OPTIMIZATION

Performance monitoring is the art and science of comparing the ongoing activity of a computer system with known operational parameters to gauge how well or how poorly the system is maintaining peak activity levels. As you will learn in this chapter, Windows NT includes several performance tuning, monitoring, and optimization features. You will begin by learning how to establish the known operational parameters, which take the form of a baseline.

AFTER READING THIS CHAPTER AND COMPLETING THE EXERCISES YOU WILL BE ABLE TO:

- Implement a performance baseline
- Locate bottlenecks
- Use all four views of Performance Monitor
- Use Network Monitor to capture packets
- Use filters to reduce the number of packets captured and displayed in Network Monitor
- Use other Windows NT tools to improve performance

IMPLEMENTING A MEASUREMENT BASELINE

The first step in performance monitoring is to assess a set of performance **metrics** or **counters** over an extended period of time to determine the normal operational parameters. For example, to measure the performance of a storage disk, you might monitor two counters for its Physical Disk object: % Disk Time and Avg. Disk Bytes/Transfer. This set of normal parameters is known as the **baseline**, or normal operation level.

Once a baseline is established, you can use it to measure your system's performance in the future. Deviations from the baseline may indicate problems with communication, misconfigurations, too much traffic, or failed components. The process of establishing a baseline, known as **baselining**, can help you identify and forecast network and computer problems before they result in downtime or data loss.

Establishing a baseline involves considerable work. Determining what is "normal" on a computer system can prove just as difficult as locating a transitive or non-repeating failure. A baseline should provide information on an entire computer system, from the smallest operational component to the network as a whole. Thus you must monitor performance on every computer individually, then in operational groups, and finally as a single network entity.

Most commonly a baseline is obtained by recording the performance activity of an object, computer, or network over a interval of at least 24 hours. (An object is any component, whether software or hardware, within a computer or a network.) By recording activity for 24 continuous hours, you can ensure that all levels of system activity encountered in a standard day of operation will be recorded. In some cases, when 24 hours is not sufficient time, then it may be necessary to expand the recording period to 48 hours or even 7 days.

When recording data for a baseline, keep in mind that the very act of measuring can skew your results, a phenomenon known as *measurement degradation*. In some situations, measurement degradation occurs because the act of measuring an object's performance increases its workload. The increased workload can degrade the object's performance, which in turn affects the measurement. For example, a storage disk's performance decreases when you attempt to measure it because the act of measuring the operation of a storage device causes that component to perform extra work.

Measuring a metric over a too-short interval can cause measurement degradation as well. To determine the ideal interval for a particular object, you should test and compare the results of intervals lasting 1, 2, 5, 10, 15, and 30 seconds, or even 1, 5, 10, 15, and 30 minutes. You may determine that longer intervals can provide you with sufficient information without creating an undue load or stress on the object being measured.

Measurement degradation may also result from measuring multiple objects on a single computer or network system, because the act of measuring increases workload and traffic, which may falsify the measurements. To avoid these problems, you must think intelligently about how, what, and when to measure. Divide your baseline measurements into sections whose components create the least degradation when measured together. After recording data for one section, continue to the next section. Of course, breaking measurements into such sections will greatly increase the time required to complete a full set of measurements.

Creating a performance baseline for most client computers is not as important as it is for network application and file servers. Your time as a network administrator may be spent more wisely in training your users to monitor their own clients independently and report suspect activity to you. This strategy will enable you to focus your efforts on the keystones of the network—the servers.

The older the baseline, the less likely that it reflects normal operation for your system. It is good practice to repeat the baseline process every month, or at least once every quarter. An updated baseline ensures that you have accurate information about the activity of your network. In addition, updating a baseline regularly gives you an ongoing perspective on the growth and development of your network. You can use this information to troubleshoot network problems and to improve your organization's computer systems.

BOTTLENECKS

The ultimate goal of baselining is to locate, isolate, and remove bottlenecks. A **bottleneck** occurs when a component of a computer system operates in such a way as to limit or restrict the optimum performance of other components; the constraints ultimately prevent the system as a whole from operating at its peak. Typically a bottleneck is related to the component with the least maximum throughput. Eliminating or improving the slowest component will not eliminate bottlenecks, however. Rather, it simply moves the bottleneck to the next slowest component.

Because computers comprise multiple components, each with a different operating capacity, every computer system has a bottleneck. The ultimate goal in the pursuit and elimination of bottlenecks is to improve the performance of a system to the point where its operator (the human user) is the limiting factor or bottleneck. Once the user represents the slowest component of the system, the computer can be said to be operating at peak performance, without limiting bottlenecks.

A bottleneck is not a directly measurable condition—that is, no alerts or alarms exist for bottlenecks, nor can they be measured directly. Instead, you must compare performance data to a baseline and, from that comparison, extrapolate the existence of a bottleneck. One good indicator of a bottleneck is a component that consistently operates near its maximum capacity, while several other components operate at extremely low utilization levels. Note, however, that this notion is just a rule of thumb. Components operating at low utilization levels may also be bottlenecks. Likewise, a component operating at 100% utilization may very well *not* be a bottleneck. The key to defining or locating a bottleneck is determining whether one component prevents another component from operating at its peak level. Bottlenecks can also be identified by the growth of task queues, the pattern or frequency of resource requests, and the time required for completion of each task.

12

OBJECT MONITORING

Windows NT is not strictly object-oriented, but it uses objects to represent operating system resources. Consequently, everything within the Windows NT environment is an **object**. As you will learn in the next section, Performance Monitor (the primary tool for monitoring system performance in Windows NT) measures, monitors, and tracks individual objects to determine how their operation affects the computing system as a whole.

Examples of Windows NT objects include the following:

- Devices (printers, CD-ROM drives, scanners, tape drives, storage devices, keyboards, and so on)
- Processes and threads
- Shared memory segments
- Access rights, permissions, and system policies
- User accounts, user groups, and user rights
- Files, directories, and volumes on storage devices
- Symbolic links, redirectors, and shares
- Messages, events, alerts, and alarms
- Ports, interfaces, communication links, and network links

A Windows NT object is composed of the following elements:

- Attributes—These program variables define the state of the object.
- Behavior—These methods, services, or code modules are used to modify attributes.
- Identity—A security ID, and often a NetBIOS name, may be employed to distinguish one object from another.

Each object includes multiple performance hooks. A **hook** (also called a metric or a counter) is an attribute or behavior that can be measured. Performance Monitor reads counters to glean specific details about the activity levels of an object, its attributes, and its resources. Four types of counters exist:

- Instantaneous—These counters obtain point measurements of activity.
- Averaging—These counters obtain the averaged value of two sequenced measurements. These values are displayed only after the second measurement has been taken.
- Difference—These counters obtain the difference between two sequenced measurements, by subtracting the earlier measurement from the later instance. A negative result is displayed as zero. Performance Monitor's basic or default set does not includes any difference counters.

- Extensible—These customized or application/device-specific counters are installed or added on to Performance Monitor to expand its range of functionality. Some third-party software products will automatically install extensible counters; others require manual installation. The Windows NT 4.0 Resource Kit includes some specialized extensible counters. You can create your own customized counters by using information included in the Win32 Software Development Kit.

USING PERFORMANCE MONITOR

Performance Monitor is the primary tool used to monitor system performance on Windows NT Server and Windows NT Workstation computers. An administrative tool, Performance Monitor is installed as a default component. This versatile utility reads the counters of Windows NT objects. The measurements from an object's counter can be used in real-time charting, logging, report generation, or issuing alerts. With a little practice, you can use Performance Monitor to analyze network operations, identify trends and bottlenecks, determine system capacity, notify administrators when thresholds are exceeded, track the performance of individual system devices, and monitor both local and remote computers. To start Performance Monitor, click the Start button, point to Programs, point to Administrative Tools (Common), then click Performance Monitor.

Performance Monitor offers features and functions that are often found only in high-end enterprise monitoring tools. Among other things, it can perform the following tasks:

- Monitor metrics from multiple computers simultaneously
- Watch in real time how modifications to a system affect performance
- Export recorded data for use in spreadsheets or database programs
- Launch batch files, initiate programs, or send alerts when a threshold is surpassed
- Record a log file of objects from multiple computers over long periods of time
- Save views and counter/object selections for use in later sessions

Performance Monitor has four views: chart, alert, log, and report. These views are explained in the following sections.

CHART VIEW

Chart view is used to display counter data in real time, as a graph or histogram. It is displayed by default when you first start Performance Monitor. To switch to chart view from another view, you can either select Chart on the View menu or click the chart button on the toolbar. Figure 12-1 shows Performance Monitor in chart view.

12

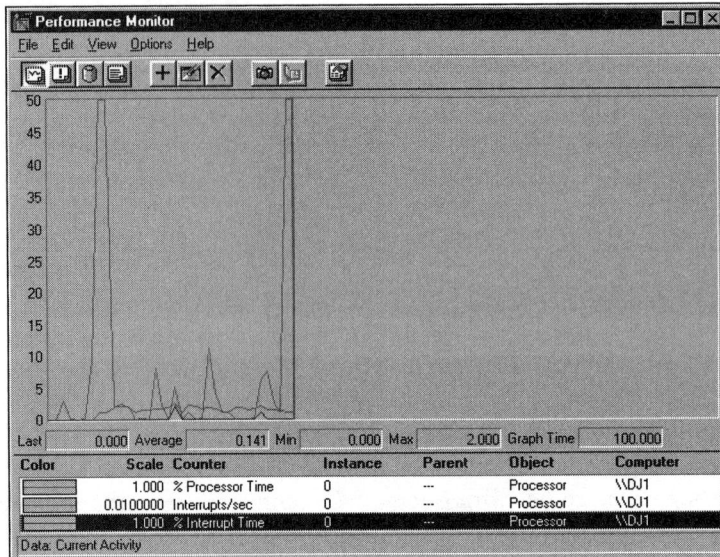

Figure 12-1   Performance Monitor in chart view

In Figure 12-1, counter data are displayed as a line graph, with each counter appearing as a separate colored line. You can add additional counters, so that multiple counters appear in the same chart. Because the display of so much data in a single chart can prove disorienting, you may want to adjust the color, width, and style for each counter on the chart. You can also adjust the scale, which determines the multiplier (0.0000001 to 100,000) applied to the counter data before those data appear on the chart. For example, Figure 12-1 shows three counters on one chart; the display properties for each counter have been adjusted to help you distinguish between the various counters.

You can also display data as a histogram, which shows the current and highest measurement achieved by each counter. (This display is similar to that found on many LCD audio/stereo equalizer panels.)

To add data from an additional counter to the graph:

1. Make sure Performance Monitor is open, in chart view.

2. Click **Edit** on the menu bar, then click **Add to Chart**. The Add to Chart dialog box opens. Figure 12-2 shows the Add to Chart dialog box with settings already specified. In the following steps, you will choose your own settings.

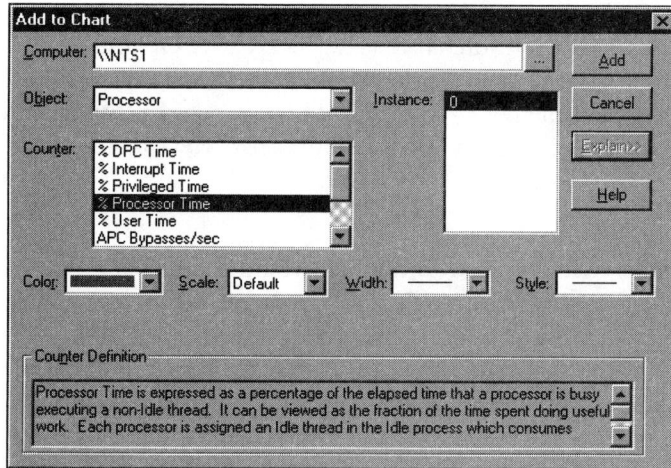

Figure 12-2 Add to Chart dialog box

> Figure 12-2 shows a brief description of the selected counter in the Counter
> Definition box. If this box is hidden, clicking Explain will display it.

3. First you need to select the computer (local or remote) whose data you want to add to the chart. To select a computer, click the **ellipsis button** beside the Computer text box, then use the dialog box to select a computer.

4. Next, you need to select the environment, resource, or service object whose data you want to chart. In the Object drop-down list box, select an object.

5. Now you need to select the specific counter to add to the chart. In the counter list box, select a counter.

6. Next, you need to designate the particular instance of the selected object. An **instance** is the identifier for a specific object when multiple versions of that object exist within the system. For example, if two hard drives are installed in the computer, then the Physical Disk object has two instances. In the Instance box, select either a single instance or a "total" instance to read the same counter for all objects of this type simultaneously.

7. You can now specify how the line for the new counter data should be displayed in the chart. Use the Color, Width, and Style list boxes to customize the line.

8. Use the Scale list box to specify a number (from 0.0000001 to 100,000) by which to multiply the counter data, to ensure that the counter's data fit on the chart.

9. Click **Add** to add this counter and its settings to the chart.

10. Repeat Steps 3–9 for any other counters you wish to add to the chart.

11. Click **Done** to exit the Add to Chart dialog box.

In addition to adding and adjusting the display for individual counters, you can modify the chart view as a whole. To modify the entire chart view, click Chart Options on the menu bar, then click Chart to open the Chart Options dialog box. Within this dialog box, you can choose from numerous options, such as whether to display grid lines or a legend, whether data should be displayed in a graph or a histogram, and how often the chart view should be updated.

ALERT VIEW

Performance Monitor's alert view is used to define threshold limits and issue alerts (such as messages or launches of programs or batch files). A **threshold** is a predefined level of activity for a particular counter. You can use alert view to specify what action should occur when a counter reaches its threshold. To switch to alert view, click View on the menu bar, then click Alert; alternatively, you can click the alert button on the toolbar. Figure 12-3 illustrates alert view.

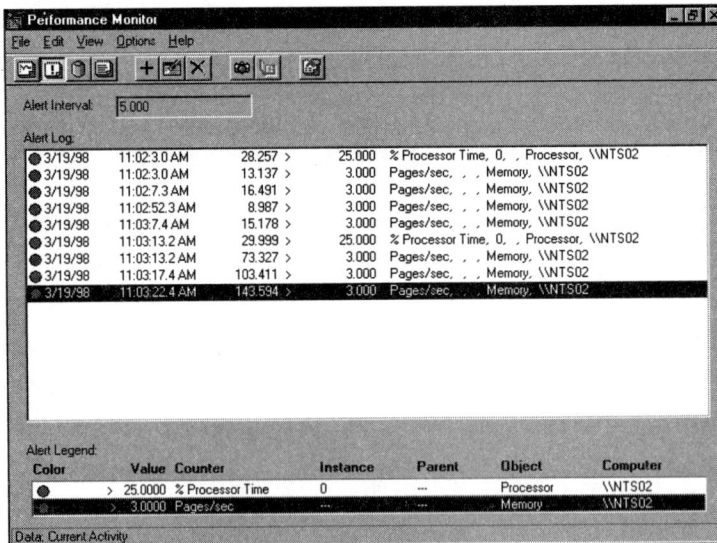

Figure 12-3   Performance Monitor in alert view

Alert view displays only those counters set with alarms, their threshold values, and any alerts. To add a counter to alert view, click Edit on the menu bar, then click Add to Alert; alternatively, you can click the Add counter button on the toolbar. The Add to Alert dialog box, shown in Figure 12-4, will open.

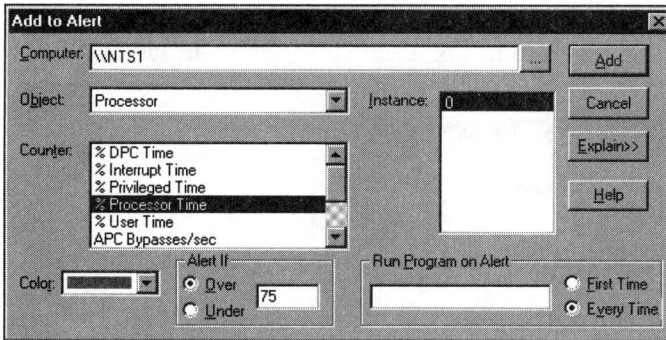

Figure 12-4   Add to Alert dialog box

You add a counter to alert view in the same way that you add a counter to chart view—that is, by specifying a computer, object, counter, and instance. In addition, in the Alert If section, you must define the counter's threshold. Finally, in the Run Program on Alert section, you can specify which program or batch file (if any) should run when the counter reaches its threshold.

To specify general alert activities (such as recording the alert in the Application log of the Event Viewer, sending a network alert message to a single user, and polling the counters for their current activity levels), you click the Alert command on the Options menu.

LOG VIEW

The log view of Performance Monitor is used to record all of the counters from one or more objects. You can then analyze the data from these counters in any of the other three views. To switch to log view, click the Log button in the toolbar. Figure 12-5 illustrates log view.

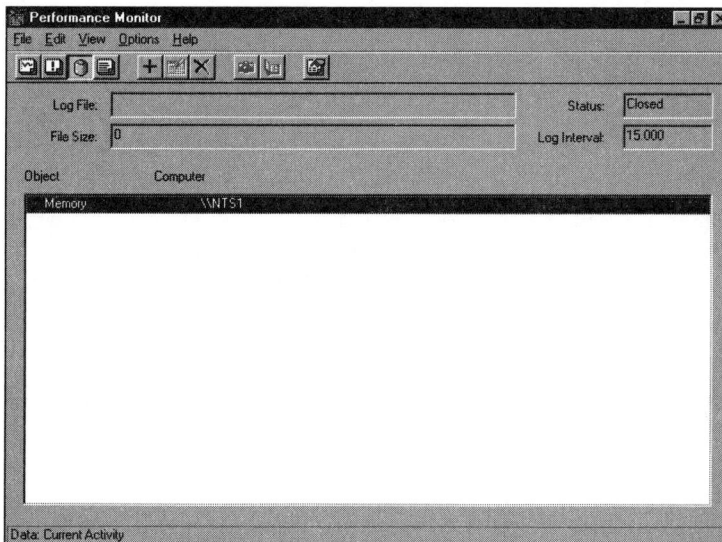

Figure 12-5   Performance Monitor in log view

To add a counter to log view, click the Add to Log command on the Edit menu, or click the Add button on the toolbar. The Add to Log dialog box, shown in Figure 12-6, will open.

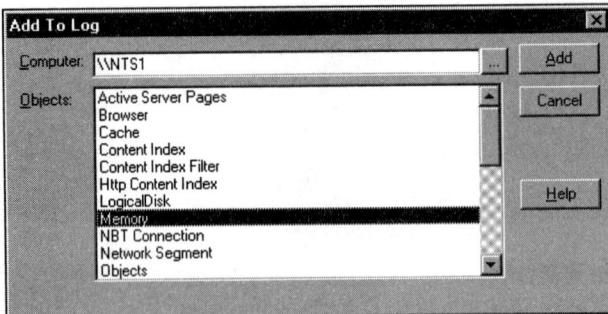

Figure 12-6   Add to Log dialog box

Adding a counter to log view is similar to adding a counter to the other views, except that you add an entire object instead of individual counters.

To perform other log view activities (such as starting or stopping logging, defining a log file, or setting the measurement interval) click Options on the menu bar, then click Log to open the Log Options dialog box.

REPORT VIEW

Report view, shown in Figure 12-7, is used to display a snapshot record of one or more counters. Adding a counter to a report is similar to adding a counter to chart view. In the report, all added counters are displayed in groups according to computer, object, counter, and instance.

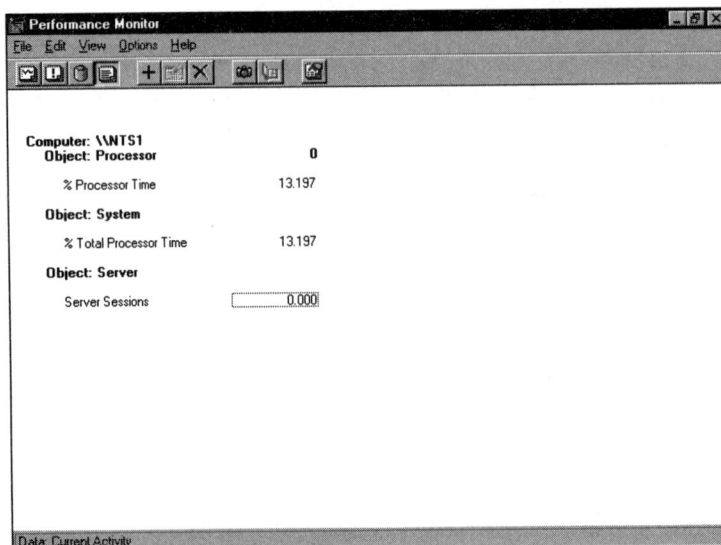

Figure 12-7   Performance Monitor in report view

Report view includes only one option: changing the update interval. To change the update interval, click the options button, type in a new interval, then click OK to return to the report view.

USING PERFORMANCE MONITOR IN THE REAL WORLD

To help you gain even more insight from Performance Monitor, here are some additional important tips and features to consider:

- Unlike most other objects, the Physical Disk and Logical Disk objects are not enabled by default, because their measurement degrades the performance of storage devices. To enable these objects, use the Run command on the Start menu to execute DISKPERF -Y, then reboot. Once these disk-related objects have been measured, turn off the counters with the "diskperf -n" command.

- To measure network activity, you must install Network Monitor Agent via the Network applet's Service tab. This installation will enable the Network Segment object.

- Multiple instances of Performance Monitor can operate simultaneously.

- Performance Monitor must be running to record real-time data, monitor for alerts, record a log file, or to create reports.

- The view and counter setups for each view can be saved separately or together for use in other Performance Monitor sessions on the computer where Performance Monitor is active or on other computers.

12

USING PERFORMANCE MONITOR TO IDENTIFY BOTTLENECKS

Performance Monitor is typically used to locate and identify bottlenecks. To use it effectively for this purpose, you need to have some perspective on the normal operation of your network—that is, you need a baseline. In addition, you need to know about some common bottlenecks. Tables 12-1, 12-2, and 12-3 identify the objects and counters associated with various types of bottlenecks.

Table 12-1   Memory-Related Bottleneck Identifiers

Object	Counter	Explanation
Memory	Available Bytes	When available memory falls below a threshold, Windows NT will take memory back from applications to maintain the required minimum.
Memory	Pages/sec	A reading higher than 5 may indicate that the system has too little physical RAM.
Memory	Page Faults/sec	A high reading indicates that a great deal of page swapping is occurring and that some pages are failing. In this situation, more physical RAM is needed.
Paging File	% Usage	If this value is near 100%, you need to increase the size of the paging file and possibly add more physical RAM.

Table 12-2   Processor-Related Bottleneck Identifiers

Object	Counter	Explanation
Processor	Interrupts/sec	If this number suddenly increases, check hardware settings and drivers.
Processor	% Processor Time	If this number is consistently above 80%, your CPU may be a bottleneck.
System	Processor Queue Length	If this number is greater than 2, the CPU is a bottleneck.

Table 12-3   Disk-Related Bottleneck Identifiers

Object	Counter	Explanation
Physical Disk	Avg. Disk sec/Transfer	A value that is consistently 3 or higher may indicate a slow controller or write failures on the drive.
Physical Disk	% Disk Time	A value higher than 85% may indicate a slow drive.

USING NETWORK MONITOR TO MONITOR NETWORK TRAFFIC

Windows NT Server 4.0 includes its own network analysis tool—Network Monitor. The version included with Windows NT Server 4.0 is a scaled-down version of the tool found in Microsoft Systems Management Server (SMS). Network Monitor can be used to capture and display protocol frames (or packets) to detect and troubleshoot problems on local area networks. Its only significant restriction is that it can monitor only traffic that is sent to or from its host computer. In contrast, the SMS version can monitor remote traffic. One benefit of Network Monitor's constraint is that the NIC on the host computer does not need to be set to promiscuous mode. Instead Network Monitor captures data using NDIS 4, resulting in a 30% performance improvement.

Network Monitor is installed through the Services tab of the Network applet, where it is listed as "Network Monitor Tools and Agent." If you select "Network Monitor Agent," you will not install the Network Monitor utility, but only the Performance Monitor hook for remote network segment monitoring. The Windows NT Server 4.0 Network Monitor window is shown in Figure 12-8.

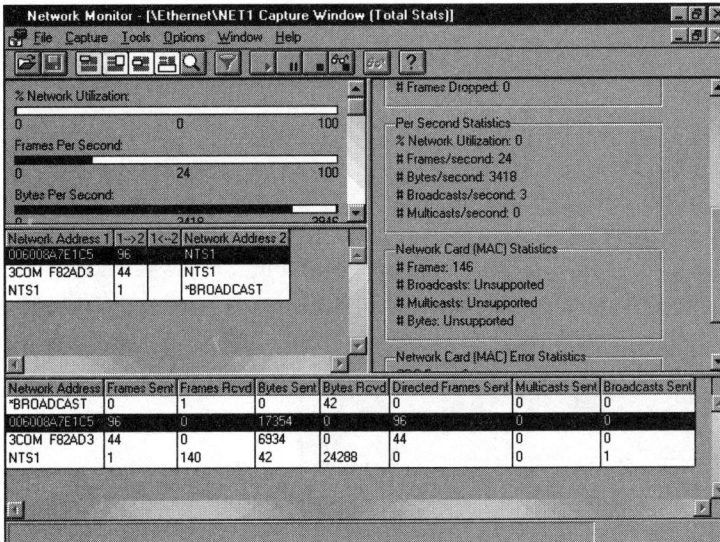

Figure 12-8   Windows NT Server 4.0 Network Monitor

Network Monitor works by capturing network packets or frames to a buffer. During the capture operation, you can obtain session, station, network, and total statistics. After capturing has ceased, you can inspect the captured data through filtering (explained later in this section) and by examining individual frames (also explained later in this section). To initiate the capture of data sent to or from the host server, click Capture on the menu bar, then click Start. To stop this process, click Capture on the menu bar, then click Stop.

Network Monitor stores all data in a memory buffer. When this buffer becomes full, the oldest pieces of data are deleted to make room for newly captured data items. To change the size of the buffer, click Capture on the menu bar, then click Buffer. The buffer size is 1 MB by default, but it can be increased to 8 MB less than the total physical RAM installed on the host server. Only after frame capture is completed can you save the captured data to disk. Thus you can capture only a small segment of time before the buffer begins to overwrite itself. By default, the .CAP capture files are stored in the WINNT\System32\Netmon\Capture directory.

During the capture operation, Network Monitor's statistics windows display real-time information about the captured data and the state of the network. The Graph pane displays percent network utilization and the number of frames, bytes, broadcasts, and multicasts per second in the form of thermometer bars. The Session Stats pane records the number of communications between the host server and other computers on the network. The Station Stats pane displays cumulative details on network conversations, including MAC addresses, frames, and bytes. The Total Stats pane displays a wide variety of metrics, including network, captured, per-second, network card (MAC), and network card error statistics.

CAPTURE FILTER

You can use **Capture Filter** to reduce the number of packets captured by Network Monitor. To begin using Capture Filter, click Capture on the menu bar, then click Filter.

By default, Network Monitor captures all packets sent to or from the host computer's network interface. You can reduce this number to only those packets that are likely to contain the elements or data you need. Using the Capture Filter, you can limit the packets captured by Network Monitor based on protocol (as shown in Figure 12-9), address (as shown in Figure 12-10), and data pattern (or content, as shown in Figure 12-11). You'll have a chance to use the Capture Filter in the Hands-on Projects at the end of this chapter.

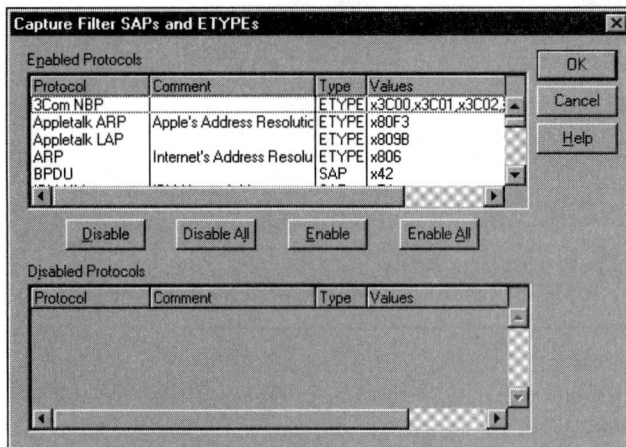

Figure 12-9 Network Monitor's Capture Filter Protocol dialog box

Capture Filter limits which packets are captured via simple include/exclude statements. By using the extensive list of packet components, you can pinpoint exactly which packets should be captured.

CAPTURE TRIGGERS

Capture triggers are similar to Performance Monitor's alert thresholds. A **capture trigger** specifies what action occurs when a defined set of conditions are met. To automatically trigger the capture of data, you can specify conditions involving pattern matching, buffer filling, or a combination of the two. When the conditions are met, the trigger action (such as stopping the data capture and launching a program or batch file) is initiated. Figure 12-12 shows the Capture Trigger dialog box.

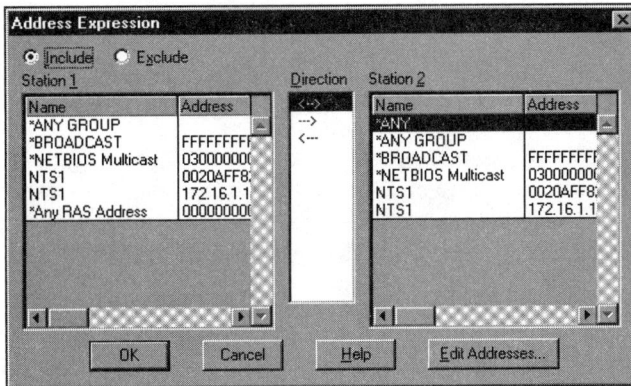

Figure 12-10   Network Monitor's Address Expression dialog box

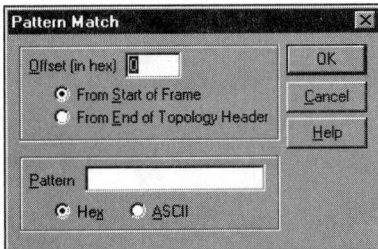

Figure 12-11   Network Monitor's Pattern Match dialog box

12

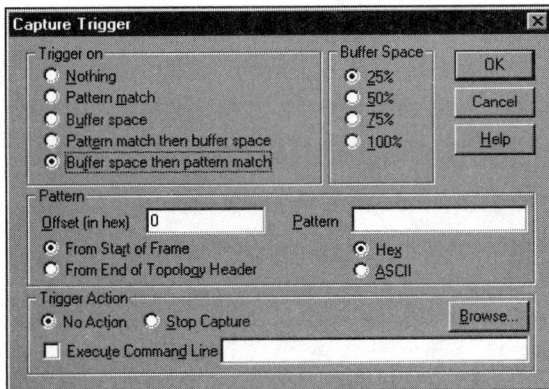

Figure 12-12   Network Monitor's Capture Trigger dialog box

ADDITIONAL CAPTURE ISSUES

Other items of which you should be aware so as to improve your use of Network Monitor include the following:

- Dedicated Capture Mode—Using the Dedicated command on the Capture menu, you can switch Network Monitor into a capture-only state in which the only statistic calculated and displayed is the number of packets captured. This restriction reduces CPU load and increases your ability to capture packets on a high-traffic network.

- Security—The Monitoring Agent applet in the Control Panel can be used to specify a display-and-capture password. A password can prevent unauthorized users from gathering or viewing packets. If you do not specify a password, any user with the SMS version of Network Monitor can capture any data packet to and from your server.

- Addresses—You can view a list of all of the MAC and NetBIOS names encountered during a Network Monitor session via the Addresses command on the Capture menu. In addition, the Find All Names command on this menu allows you to force Network Monitor to attempt to resolve all MAC addresses to NetBIOS names.

- Partial Packets—You can use the Buffer command on the Capture menu to instruct Network Monitor to capture only part of a packet. In this way you can restrict capture to between 64 and 65,472 bytes of a packet.

- Multi-homed—Multi-homed servers running Network Monitor can select which NICs to record and which to suspend. This option helps isolate communication inspection to a known segment or portion of a network.

- Limitations—The Windows NT Server 4.0 version of Network Monitor does not include the Find Routers or Resolve Addresses From Name commands on its Tools menu. These commands are available only in the SMS version.

DISPLAYING CAPTURED DATA

Once you have stopped Network Monitor from capturing data, you can view the packets stored in the buffer. To display a list of captured packets, click Capture, then click Display Captured Data. Double-click any packet in the list to divide the window into three panes, as shown in Figure 12-13. The top pane displays the list of captured frames, the middle frame gives the header and delivery details, and the bottom pane shows a hex/ASCII representation of content.

Even with the use of Capture Filter, the number of captured packets can still prove daunting. To resolve this problem, Network Monitor offers yet another tool, the **Display Filter**. It allows you to specify which packets to display and which to hide according to the protocol, address, and packet/protocol/service property. The hundreds of thousands of possible combinations from which you can choose ensure that you will be able to construct a display filter that will reduce your data to a manageable level.

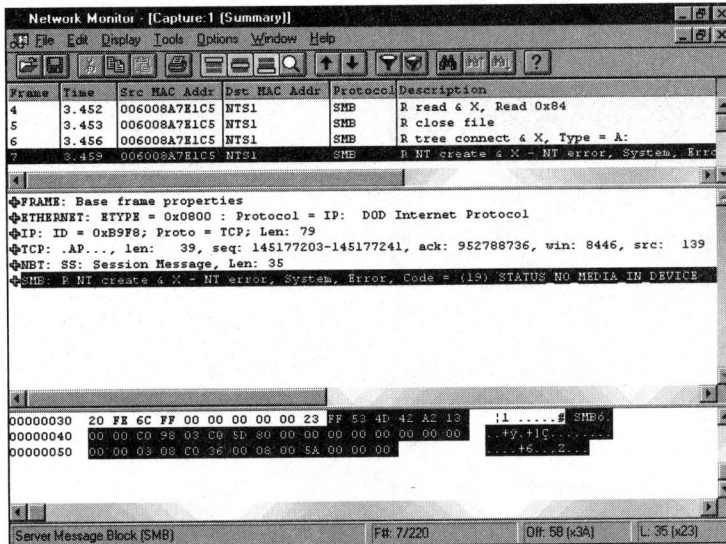

Figure 12-13   Captured data display

OTHER PERFORMANCE TOOLS

Performance Monitor and Network Monitor are not the only performance tools included with Windows NT Server 4.0. In the following sections, you will learn about other tools available to improve your system's performance.

TASK MANAGER

The Task Manager is used to gain a perspective on the active processes, applications, and performance of a system. It can help you terminate hung applications and processes and gain a quick view of the system's memory. The Task Manager can be accessed in two ways:

- Right-click over an empty area of the taskbar, then select Task Manager from the pop-up menu.

- Press CTRL-ALT-DEL to open the Win Logon dialog box, then click Task Manager.

Once opened, the Task Manager offers you useful information on three tabs. The first of these tabs, the Applications tab, is shown in Figure 12-14. It lists all currently active applications and displays their current status. If the application is hung, the status will be listed as "not responding." In the figure, all the applications are functioning, and so are listed as "running." To terminate an application, select it in the Task list, then click End Task. You can also launch new applications by clicking the New Task button (which acts much like the Run command on the Start menu).

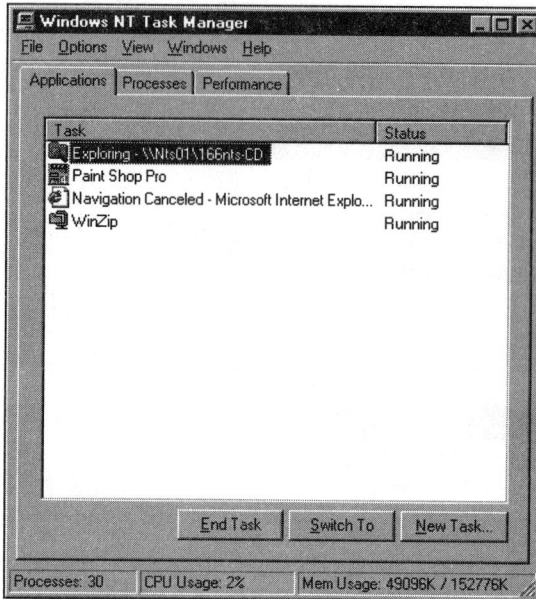

Figure 12-14   Applications tab of the Windows NT Task Manager

The second tab in the Task Manager, the Processes tab, is shown in Figure 12-15. It lists all currently active processes, with metrics for each process. For example, in Figure 12-15, you can see metrics such as PID (which indicates Process ID number), CPU (which indicates the percentage of CPU time used by the process), and Mem Usage (which indicates memory usage). You can modify the metrics displayed via the Columns command on the View menu. To re-sort the display by a particular column, double-click that column. To terminate a process, select it in the list, then click the End Process button. To change a process' operating priority, right-click the process, then click Set Priority in the shortcut menu.

The third tab in the Task Manager, the Performance tab, is shown in Figure 12-16. It displays graphical and numerical information about the current and historical usage of the CPU and memory. To display the amount of kernel CPU usage in red, click the Show Kernel Times command on the View menu.

Windows NT Task Manager

File Options View Help

Applications | Processes | Performance

Image Name	PID	CPU	CPU Time	Mem Usage
System Idle Process	0	91	268:26:02	16 K
System	2	00	0:01:37	120 K
smss.exe	21	00	0:00:01	120 K
csrss.exe	30	00	0:00:02	388 K
WINLOGON.EXE	35	00	0:00:01	40 K
SERVICES.EXE	41	00	0:00:31	2572 K
LSASS.EXE	44	00	0:00:19	2328 K
MSPADMIN.EXE	61	00	0:00:00	36 K
TASKMGR.EXE	63	04	0:00:01	1308 K
WSPSRV.EXE	65	00	0:00:00	128 K
llssrv.exe	66	00	0:00:07	1020 K
SPOOLSS.EXE	72	00	0:00:06	792 K
PSTORES.EXE	75	00	0:00:00	32 K
RPCSS.EXE	87	00	0:00:09	824 K
NTVDM.EXE	90	00	0:00:15	236 K
wowexec.exe		00	0:00:00	
mdm.exe	91	00	0:00:00	1716 K
msdtc.exe	101	00	0:00:04	536 K
NDDEAGNT.EXE	103	00	0:00:00	84 K

End Process

Processes: 30   CPU Usage: 9%   Mem Usage: 49280K / 152776K

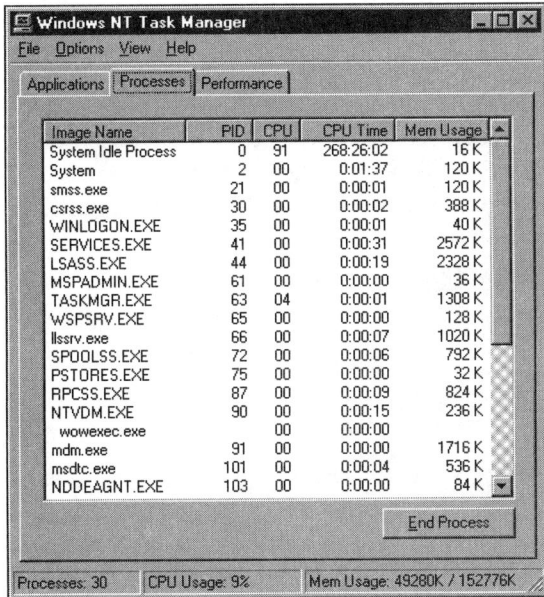

Figure 12-15   Processes tab of the Windows NT Task Manager

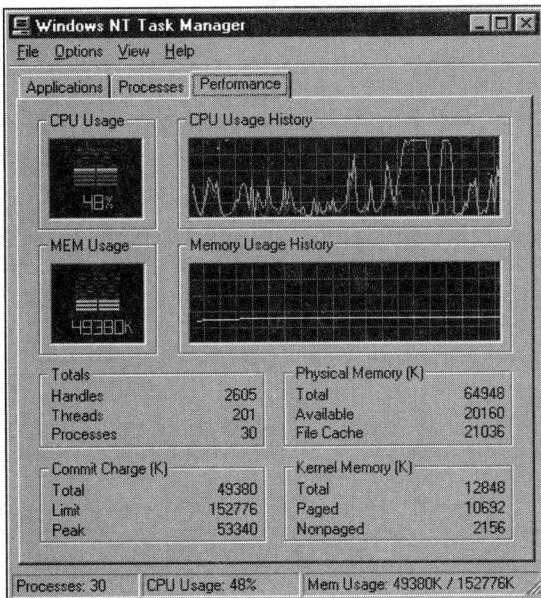

Windows NT Task Manager

File Options View Help

Applications | Processes | Performance

CPU Usage
48%

CPU Usage History

MEM Usage
49380K

Memory Usage History

Totals		Physical Memory (K)	
Handles	2605	Total	64948
Threads	201	Available	20160
Processes	30	File Cache	21036

Commit Charge (K)		Kernel Memory (K)	
Total	49380	Total	12848
Limit	152776	Paged	10692
Peak	53340	Nonpaged	2156

Processes: 30   CPU Usage: 48%   Mem Usage: 49380K / 152776K

Figure 12-16   Performance tab of the Windows NT Task Manager

12

Virtual Memory and Paging

Many performance issues are related to memory. When the addition of physical RAM is impossible or when a temporary solution is needed to circumvent a memory shortage, you can try manipulating the virtual memory settings. To access the virtual memory settings, double-click the System icon in the Control Panel, click the Performance tab, then click Change. The Virtual Memory dialog box, shown in Figure 12-17, will open.

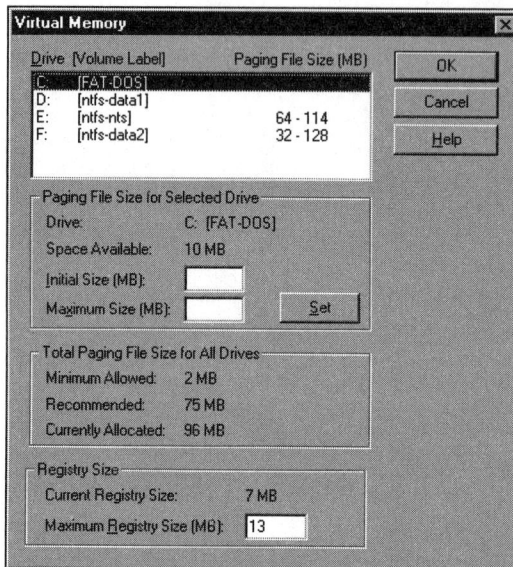

Figure 12-17   Virtual Memory dialog box

In the Virtual Memory dialog box, you can define one or more locations for Windows NT to store memory page files. Microsoft recommends defining page files to be 12 MB larger than the physical RAM installed on your computer. In practice, however, a page file that is twice the size of installed physical RAM is preferred. Remember: if you place a paging file on a slow, older, or full storage device, performance will degrade even further.

Chapter Summary

- Performance monitoring is the art and science of comparing the ongoing activity of a computer system with known operational parameters to gauge how well or how poorly the system is maintaining peak activity levels.

- Establishing a baseline is the act of monitoring a set of performance metrics over an extended period of time to determine the normal operational parameters. Once established, a baseline can be used to measure the performance of a system at a later time. Deviations from the baseline may indicate problems with communication, misconfigurations, too much traffic, or failed components.

- The ultimate goal of baselining is to locate, isolate, and remove bottlenecks. A bottleneck occurs when a component of a computer system operates so as to limit or restrict the optimum performance of other components, ultimately preventing the system as a whole from operating at its peak level. Typically a bottleneck is related to the component with the least maximum throughput. Eliminating or improving the slowest component does not remove bottlenecks entirely, but rather shifts the bottleneck to the next slowest component.

- Although Windows NT is not strictly object-oriented, it uses objects to represent operating system resources. Thus everything within the Windows NT environment is an object. Consequently, every object can be measured, monitored, and tracked to determine how its operation affects the computing system as a whole.

- Performance Monitor is the primary tool used to monitor system performance on Windows NT Server and Windows NT Workstation computers. This administrative utility is installed as a default component. A versatile tool, it reads the counters (or metrics) of any Windows NT object for use in real-time charting, logging, report generation, or issuing alerts. With a little practice, you can use Performance Monitor to analyze network operations, identify trends and bottlenecks, determine system capacity, notify administrators when thresholds are exceeded, track the performance of individual system devices, and monitor both local and remote computers.

- Windows NT Server 4.0 includes its own network analysis tool—Network Monitor. The version included with Windows NT Server 4.0 is a scaled-down version of the tool found in Microsoft Systems Management Server. It can be used to capture and display protocol frames and packets to detect and troubleshoot problems on local area networks. Its main restriction is that it can monitor only traffic that is sent to or from its host computer. One benefit of this constraint is that the NIC on the host computer does not need to be set to promiscuous mode. Instead it captures data using NDIS 4, resulting in a 30% performance improvement.

- The Capture Filter is a tool that pares down the number of packets captured by Network Monitor. By default, all packets sent to or from the host computer's network interface are captured; using Capture Filter, you can reduce this number considerably, to only those packets that are likely to contain the needed elements or data. Using the Capture Filter, you can limit the packets captured by Network Monitor based on protocol, address, or data pattern (content).

- Capture triggers are similar to Performance Monitor's alert thresholds. A capture trigger is an action that must take place when a defined set of conditions are met. It is used to automate the process of capturing network data and monitoring network communications. A capture filter can be specified based on pattern matching, buffer filling, or a combination of the two. When the conditions are met, the trigger action is initiated. For example, the computer might stop data capture and execute a command (perhaps launching a program or batch file).

- Once you have stopped Network Monitor from capturing data, you can view the packets stored in the buffer. The Capture|Display Captured Data command will bring up the list of captured packets. Double-clicking on any listed packet splits the display into three panes: a list of captured frames, header/delivery details, and hex/ASCII representation of content.

- Even with a capture filter, the number of packets to review can still prove daunting. To overcome this problem, Network Monitor offers yet another tool—the Display Filter. As with the capture trigger, you can define which packets to display and which to hide according to their protocol, address, and packet/protocol/service property. Hundreds of thousands of possible combinations of the offered selections exist, ensuring that you will be able to construct a display filter that will reduce your data to a manageable level.

- Performance Monitor and Network Monitor are not the only performance tools included with Windows NT Server 4.0. Other tools available to improve the performance of your system include the Task Manager, which is used to gain a perspective on the active processes, applications, and performance of a system.

- Many performance issues are related to memory. When the addition of physical RAM is impossible or a temporary fix is needed, you can attempt a solution by manipulating the virtual memory settings. The Virtual Memory dialog box is accessed through the Change button on the Performance tab of the System applet from the Control Panel. Here you can define one or more locations for Windows NT to store memory page files. Microsoft recommends defining page files that are 12 MB larger than the physical RAM installed on your computer, although a page file that is twice the size of installed physical RAM is preferred in practice. Placing a paging file on a slow, older, or full storage device will, however, degrade performance even further.

KEY TERMS

- **averaging counter** — A counter used to obtain the averaged value of two sequenced measurements. The value of an averaging counter is displayed only after the second measurement has been taken.

- **baseline** — A set of normal operational parameters.

- **baselining** — The process of monitoring a set of performance metrics over an extended period of time to determine the normal operational parameters.

- **bottleneck** — The condition where a component of a computer system operates so as to limit or restrict the optimum performance of other components, ultimately preventing the system as a whole from operating at its peak level.

- **Capture Filter** — A Network Monitor tool that limits or restricts the amount of data captured by storing only those packets that meet a specified criteria.

- **capture trigger** — A feature of Network Monitor that, when its criteria are met, can stop the capture of data and launch programs or batch files.

- **counter** — A facet, feature, function, service, or resource to be measured on an object.

- **difference counter** — A counter that obtains the difference between two sequenced measurements by subtracting the earlier measurement from the later instance. A negative result is displayed as zero.

- **Display Filter** — A Network Monitor tool that hides all packets that do not meet a specified criteria to simplify the packet-by-packet inspection process.

- **extensible counter** — An application/device-specific counter added to Performance Monitor to expand its range of functionality. Some products will automatically install extensible counters; others require manual installation.

- **hook** — An attribute that can be measured. Also called a metric or a counter.

- **instance** — A designation used to distinguish between multiple objects of the same type.

- **instantaneous counter** — A counter used to obtain point measurements of activity.

- **metric** — A facet, feature, function, service, or resource to be measured on an object.

- **object** — In performance monitoring, any component, whether software or hardware, within a computer.

- **threshold** — A predefined activity level for a particular counter.

REVIEW QUESTIONS

1. The first step in performance monitoring is:
   a. looking for bottlenecks
   b. establishing a baseline
   c. changing server settings to optimize performance
   d. increasing the virtual memory paging file

2. Establishing a baseline is:
   a. the act of monitoring a set of performance metrics over an extended period of time to determine their normal operational parameters
   b. uninstalling all software to return a computer to its initial post-install state
   c. launching all applications simultaneously to determine the system's ability to support them
   d. restricting access to a client machine to administrators during nonwork hours

3. After a baseline is established, a computer's deviation from that baseline can indicate:
   a. communication problems
   b. misconfigurations
   c. too much network traffic
   d. failed components

12

4. A baseline is most effective when it is covers what period of time?

   a. 2 hours

   b. 8 hours

   c. 24 hours

   d. every other hour for 3 days

5. For which portions of a network should a baseline be established?

   a. each individual computer

   b. operational groups

   c. only application servers

   d. the entire network

6. The use of short measurement intervals (such as 1, 2, or 5 seconds) can cause the item measured to show a less-than-optimal value due to interference from the act of measuring. True or False?

7. Once a baseline is established, it can be used over and over again to compare and evaluate current activity without requiring the re-creation of a new baseline for as long as the network/server remains operational. True or False?

8. What is the ultimate goal of baselining?

   a. to provide competitive comparisons of network performance

   b. to familiarize administrators with the network

   c. to test the operational functioning of a network

   d. to locate, isolate, and remove bottlenecks

9. A bottleneck is a component of a computer system that operates so as to limit or restrict the optimum performance of other components, ultimately preventing the system as a whole from operating at its peak level. True or False?

10. Locating and removing a bottleneck causes what to happen?

   a. The performance of the computer degrades.

   b. The performance of a system approaches near-infinite speed.

   c. All bottlenecks are eliminated from the system.

   d. The bottleneck shifts to the next slowest component.

11. In a system that has been tuned to its maximum level of performance, which component is the bottleneck?

   a. CPU

   b. memory

   c. human user

   d. storage devices

12. Bottlenecks are always components that are operating at 100% utilization, because components operating at a lower level of utilization cannot be constraining other components from functioning at their full capacity. True or False?

13. What types of counters or metrics does Performance Monitor support?

    a. extensible

    b. averaging

    c. intransitive

    d. difference

14. Which view of Performance Monitor allows you to see the current and historical values of multiple counters in real time?

    a. chart

    b. alert

    c. log

    d. report

15. Which view of Performance Monitor allows you to set thresholds for counters and actions to take when these thresholds are exceeded?

    a. chart

    b. alert

    c. log

    d. report

16. While using Performance Monitor, you add two counters to the chart view. One counter's values are displayed clearly in the middle of the chart area. The other counter's values are so large that they run off the chart. What can you do?

    a. Change the scale of the second counter.

    b. Change the style of the second counter.

    c. Change the color of the first counter.

    d. Select a different counter that fits on the chart better.

17. Which Performance Monitor counters are not available by default?

    a. Logical Disk

    b. Session

    c. Network Segment

    d. Cache

18. Which of the following values for counters are indications of possible bottlenecks?

    a. Memory:Pages/sec—greater than 5

    b. Paging File: % Usage—less than 25%

    c. Processor: % Processor Time—less than 45%

    d. System:Processor Queue Length—greater than 3

12

19. The Network Monitor included with Windows NT Server 4.0 uses promiscuous mode to capture packets, so it provides a 30% performance improvement over the SMS version, which uses NDIS 4. True or False?

20. Network Monitor captures packets in a buffer. What is the maximum size of this buffer?

    a. 1 MB

    b. 8 MB less than the total physical RAM

    c. 8 MB less than the total virtual memory

    d. 8 MB less than the total free storage space

21. If your network hosts a lot of traffic, but you wish to view only data sent to your host from a specific machine, what can you do?

    a. Use Capture Filter.

    b. Use a capture trigger.

    c. Use Display Filter.

    d. Use an alert threshold.

22. On what basis can Capture Filter differentiate between packets?

    a. address

    b. MIME type

    c. protocol

    d. pattern matching

23. When a capture trigger's criteria are met, it can perform what actions?

    a. start a new capture session

    b. execute a command line

    c. stop a capture session

    d. issue an Event Viewer log message

24. To minimize the impact that Network Monitor has on your system when performing extended captured sessions, what feature can you use?

    a. dedicated capture mode

    b. capture trigger

    c. partial packet capture

    d. Capture | Find All Names

25. Which tool can be used to alter the priorities of active processes?

    a. Performance Monitor

    b. Task Manager

    c. Network Monitor

    d. Services applet

HANDS-ON PROJECTS

For some or all of these projects you will need one Windows NT server with Network Monitor installed.

PROJECT 12-1

In this project you will alter Performance Monitor scale values. To complete this project, you need to have Windows NT installed on your computer.

1. Click the **Start button**, point to **Programs**, point to **Administrative Tools (Common)**, then click **Performance Monitor**. The Performance Monitor window opens.

2. Click the **Add counter button** in the toolbar. The Add to Chart dialog box opens.

3. Because you want to view objects and counters from the computer where Performance Monitor is operating, do not change the Computer field.

4. The Processor object is already selected by default.

5. In the Counter list, locate and select the **% Processor Time counter**, then click **Add**.

6. Select and add both the **% User Time** and **% Privileged Time counters**.

7. Click **Done**. You will return to the chart view of Performance Monitor.

8. Click **Options** on the menu bar, then click **Chart**. The Chart Options dialog box opens.

9. Change the vertical maximum to **1000**, then click **OK**. You will return to Performance Monitor.

10. Double-click the **% Processor Time counter**. The Edit Chart Line dialog box opens.

11. Click the **Scale list arrow**, select **10.0**, then click **OK**. You will return to Performance Monitor.

12. Repeat Steps 10 and 11 for % User Time and % Privileged Time.

13. Exit Performance Monitor.

PROJECT 12-2

In this project, you will view disk metrics in Performance Monitor. To complete this project, you need to have Windows NT installed on your computer.

1. Click the **Start button**, point to **Programs**, point to **Administrative Tools (Common)**, then click **Performance Monitor**. The Performance Monitor window opens.

2. Click the **Add button** on the toolbar. The Add to Chart dialog box opens.

12

3. Select the **PhysicalDisk object** from the Object pull-down list.

4. Select **Avg. Disk sec/Transfer** in the Counters list, click **Add**, then click **Done**. You will return to Performance Monitor.

5. Notice that no readings are taking place.

6. Click the **Start button**, click **Run**, type **diskperf -y**, then click **OK**.

7. Reboot the computer.

8. Click the **Start button**, point to **Programs**, point to **Administrative Tools (Common)**, then click **Performance Monitor**. The Performance Monitor window opens.

9. Click the **Add counter button** on the toolbar. The Add to Chart dialog box opens.

10. Select the **Physical Disk object** from the Object pull-down list.

11. Select **Avg. Disk sec/Transfer** in the Counters list, click **Add**, then click **Done**. You will return to Performance Monitor.

12. Notice that readings are now taking place.

13. Click the **Start button**, click **Run**, type **diskperf-n**, then click **OK**.

14. Reboot the computer.

PROJECT 12-3

In this project, you will set a Performance Monitor alert. To complete this project, you need to have Windows NT installed on your computer.

1. Click the **Start button**, point to **Programs**, point to **Administrative Tools (Common)**, then click **Performance Monitor**. The Performance Monitor window opens.

2. Click the **Alert button** on the toolbar to change to the alert view.

3. Click the **Add button** on the toolbar. The Add to Alert dialog box opens.

4. Note that the Processor object is already selected in the Objects list by default.

5. Select **% Processor Time** in the Counters list.

6. Type **25** in the Alert if Over field, click **Add**, then click **Done**. You will return to Performance Monitor.

7. Click the **Options button** on the toolbar to open the Alert Options dialog box.

8. Select the **Send network message check box**.

9. Type your **user name**, then click **OK**. You will return to Performance Monitor.

10. Open and close any application to force the CPU above 25% usage. This action will cause the threshold to be met and, as a result, an alert message will appear.

11. Click **OK** on the alert message.

12. Exit Performance Monitor.

PROJECT 12-4

In this project, you will use a capture filter in Network Monitor. To complete this project, you must have Network Monitor already installed.

1. Click the **Start button**, point to **Programs**, point to **Administrative Tools (Common)**, then click **Network Monitor**. The Network Monitor window opens.

2. Click **Capture** on the menu bar, then click **Filter** to open the Capture Filter dialog box. Click **OK** on the pop-up message.

3. Select the **SAP/ETYPE line**, then click the **Line button** under the Edit heading. The Capture Filter SAPs and ETYPEs dialog box opens.

4. Click **Disable All**.

5. Using the scroll bar for the Disabled Protocols list, locate and select all instances of **IP** in the protocol list, then click **Enable**.

6. Click **OK** to close this dialog box and return to the Capture Filter dialog box. Click **OK** again to close the Capture Filter dialog box.

7. Click **Capture** on the menu bar, then click **Start** to initiate a capture.

8. Minimize Network Monitor by pressing the **minimize button** on the application's title bar.

9. Double-click on **Network Neighborhood** on your desktop to open it. Double-click on any computer names that appear in the Network Neighborhood dialog box. A dialog box opens, listing the shared resources for the selected computer.

10. Close the dialog box that appeared when you double-clicked a computer name, then close the Network Neighborhood dialog box.

11. Restore the Network Monitor by clicking its **icon** on the taskbar.

12. Click **Capture** on the menu bar, then click **Stop** to stop the capture.

13. Do not close Network Monitor. You will use this captured data in the next project.

PROJECT 12-5

In this project, you will use Display Filter with Network Monitor. To complete this project, you need to have Network Monitor already installed and to have completed Project 12-4.

1. Click **Capture** on the menu bar, then click **Display Captured Data** to switch Network Monitor into display mode.

2. Click **Display** on the menu bar, then click **Filter** to open the Display Filter dialog box.

3. Click the **Expression button**. The Expression dialog box opens.

4. Select the **Property tab**.

5. Use the scroll bar in the Protocol:Property window to locate **NBT** in the Protocol list, then double-click **NBT** to expand its contents. The properties for this protocol will appear in the same window.

6. Using the scroll bar, locate and select **SS**.

7. In the Relation list, select **exists**.

8. Click **OK** to close the Expression dialog box, then click **OK** again to close the Display Filter dialog box.

9. Notice that the long list of captured packets has been reduced to only those packets that match the criteria you specified.

10. Double-click on any packet to view its header and hex/ASCII contents.

11. Exit Network Monitor without saving the capture.

CASE PROJECTS

1. You've just installed a new storage device on your network's file server. You want to be warned when this new device reaches 75% capacity. Write a brief report explaining how you can achieve this goal.

2. Your computer issues a warning that you are running low on virtual memory. How can you set up Performance Monitor to track memory usage so you are more aware of memory usage on servers with which you do not regularly interact?

3. Using Performance Monitor, you read the following metrics:

   Memory:Pages/sec = 15

   Memory:Page Faults/sec = 8

   Physical Disk:% Disk Time = 80%

   Processor:% Processor Time = 15%

   What is the problem? How can you resolve it?

4. Your network is experiencing extremely slow communications. You suspect that a server is performing multiple broadcasts that are overloading the network. How can you determine which computer is flooding the network?

5. All network traffic directed toward the Internet passes over your multi-homed routing server. You suspect that a user is accessing data on a known illegal FTP site. If you know the IP address and domain name of the FTP server, how can you determine whether communication is occurring with that server and from which client computer it is originating?

PRINTING

On any network, printing is probably the most commonly shared and used resource. Windows NT Server 4.0 simplifies the printing process by providing a print system that can be used by nearly any network client, including those running Windows NT Workstation, Windows 95, Windows for Workgroups, DOS, Macintosh, UNIX, and other TCP/IP clients. In this chapter you will learn how the Windows NT printing system works, how to install printers, how to share printers with the network, how to configure and manage printers, and how to troubleshoot common printing problems.

AFTER READING THIS CHAPTER AND COMPLETING THE EXERCISES YOU WILL BE ABLE TO:

- Define the terms associated with the Windows NT printing system
- Explain and understand the Windows NT printing model
- Create, share, and connect to print devices
- Understand print management
- Configure a print device
- Fine-tune the printing process for various situations
- Connect to remote print providers
- Troubleshoot common printing problems

A Lexicon of Windows NT Printing

The printing environment of Windows NT is very easy to configure and use. Nevertheless, the terminology involved can prove somewhat confusing. Microsoft has slightly altered the meanings of some common printing terms and redirected others. To fully understand printing in Windows NT, you need to be familiar with the new nomenclature:

- **Client Application** A software program that initiates a print job. A client application can reside on a client/workstation computer, a server computer, or even the computer hosting the print server.

- **Connecting to a Printer** The act of creating a logical printer to be referenced and used by client applications to send print jobs. A logical printer can connect to a locally attached printer or to a network printer share. To connect to a printer, you use the Add Printer icon in the Printers folder. This folder is reached through the Start menu, My Computer, or the Control Panel.

- **Creating a Printer** The act of installing drivers for a print device on the machine locally hosting the physical device. Creating a printer also involves naming the printer, setting printer-specific configurations, and, optionally, sharing that printer with the rest of the network. To create a printer, you use the Add Printer icon in the Printers folder.

- **Logical Printer** The term used by Microsoft to refer to the software interface that defines, names, and points to a physical printer (whether local or remote). The software component that appears in the Printers folder, a logical printer, redirects print jobs to the appropriate print server for processing. Logical printers serve as the interface point at which user access and printer functions are managed.

- **Network-Attached Printer** A print device that is physically connected to the network, instead of being directly connected to a computer host. Such a device is equipped with a network interface card, such as the Hewlett-Packard JetDirect. Network-attached printers are accessed using the DLC protocol.

- **Print Client** A client computer on the network that submits print jobs from a client application to a print server.

- **Print Device** The physical electronic mechanism that, in non-Microsoft environments, is simply called a printer. It is also referred to as the physical printer.

- **Print Job** The electronic package that contains the document to be printed, as well as process and control data. The print job is initiated by a client application on a client computer, sent to a print server, and eventually dispatched to a physical printer.

- **Print Queue** The series of print jobs received by a print server that are waiting for access to the physical print device; sometimes referred to simply as the "queue." Print queues operate in a default "first in, first out" mode.

- **Print Resolution** A measurement of pixel density that relates to the sharpness and clarity of a printed image. Resolution is measured in dots per inch (DPI). Typically, greater DPI will produce a higher-quality printed output. Most modern printers (laser and ink-jet) print at more than 300 DPI.

- **Print Server** The computer that hosts the spool file for a physical printer; print jobs are temporarily stored and managed in this file. The print server controls the printer, manages the print queue, and maintains the link with the network to offer the printer share. Any Windows NT or Windows 95 computer with a local printer is considered a print server.

- **Print Server Services** Specialty Windows NT services that extend the capabilities of the standard print system. They include Services for Macintosh, File and Print Services for NetWare, and TCP/IP Print Services. Typically, print server services extend a print server's ability to accept print jobs from a wider variety of clients and protocols.

- **Print Spooler** A component of the print system that receives, processes, stores, and distributes print jobs. Print spooling is the process through which the print system writes a print job to disk into a "spool file," where print jobs await their turn in the print queue. Despooling occurs as the stored print jobs are retrieved, printed, and then removed from the spool.

- **Printer Driver** The device driver that enables the print server to communicate with the physical print device.

- **Rendering** The Windows NT print system's recreation of an image viewed on the computer screen in printer-specific language, enabling the image to be properly reproduced on the paper.

The Windows NT printing environment is not primarily concerned with the physical print devices, but rather with the logical printers used to link and redirect print-related traffic (such as print jobs, printer access, and printer management). This approach represents a change from other network operating systems' printing environments. Once a physical printer is attached to a computer (or the network) and the correct driver is installed, nearly everything else that occurs in relation to printing remains software-based. Thus, after the initial installation, the only time you'll ever deal or interact with the physical print device is to add paper and retrieve hard copies of documents.

13

THE PRINT MODEL OF WINDOWS NT

Windows NT Server and Windows NT Workstation 4.0 both take a modular approach to printing. Each module, or component, of the printing system focuses on a single task or job. The components of the print model are stacked logically, similar to the layers of the OSI model discussed in Chapter 4. In the following sections, you will learn about each component of the Windows NT printing system.

GRAPHICS DEVICE INTERFACE (GDI)

The **graphics device interface (GDI)** supplies client applications with a method for representing graphical information. The GDI is used not only by the print system, but also by the video system. In fact, the GDI makes Windows' WYSIWYG (What You See Is What You Get) interface possible. The GDI interprets and translates the graphical data seen by a user in a client application into the correct data type and form needed by the printer to reproduce or render the image correctly on paper.

PHYSICAL PRINT DEVICE

As explained earlier, the print device comprises the actual computer hardware that creates some output in response to the instructions defined by the print job. It usually takes the form of an ink-jet or laser printer that prints on paper. Nevertheless, the print device could also be a slide printer, a printer-plotter, a punch-card machine, a fax modem, or even a file. The type of device used as the physical printer does not affect the rest of the print model, as long as the correct device driver (explained in the next section) is installed.

PRINTER DRIVER

Without the correct printer driver, the print system and the physical printer (of whatever type) cannot communicate. If the driver is lacking, the print job will not be completed because the print server will be unable to send the print job to the device.

The **printer driver** (sometimes called the device driver) is the piece of software code that gives the print server the commands and language needed to communicate with the physical print device. It is usually written specifically for the particular model of printer and the particular operating system. As explained in the following sections, a printer driver typically includes individual drivers for graphics and interface, plus a characterization data file.

Printer Graphics Driver

The printer graphics driver is the component that transforms GDI information into printer-specific language. This language is a collection of Device Driver Interface (DDI) commands that represent the correct syntax and command options for the specific printer. Each printer may accommodate multiple graphics drivers, each designed to handle a specific type of print request. For example, the graphics driver PSCRIPT.DLL handles all PostScript printing requests, PLOTTER.DLL handles all HPGL/2 plotter language requests, and RASDD.DLL handles requests involving raster or bitmapped images.

Printer Interface Driver

The printer interface driver has a simple task: it connects the user portion of the print system (such as the Printers folder) with the printer itself and retrieves information from the characterization data file.

Characterization Data File

The **characterization data file** includes printer-specific information that is stored in the printer's memory. This data file informs the print system of the device's make and model, print functions, available resolutions, available paper trays, method of paper selection, and more.

PRINT SPOOLER

The print spooler comprises the print router, local print provider, print processor, and the print monitor. The spooler itself (SPOOLSS.EXE) and a large collection of Dynamic Link Libraries (DLLs) manage the processing and distribution of print jobs.

The Windows NT spooler service receives print jobs from the client application after they are interpreted by the GDI. By default, these files are saved to a storage device, in a process called spooling. The data stored in a spool file may be one of several data types:

- **EMF (Enhanced Metafiles)**—The native print and rendering data type of Windows, which is generated by the GDI. EMF files are portable (that is, they can be sent to any print device) and more compact than the RAW data type (explained below). After creating an EMF version of a print job, the application returns to user control.

- **RAW**—A data type generated by the printer driver, rather than the GDI. Using the RAW data type requires the client application to remain in communication with the print system until the print job has been completely sent to the print device.

- **RAW (FF Appended)**—A variation of RAW that instructs the print server to add a form-feed character to the end of the print job, ensuring that the last page of the job will be printed.

- **RAW (FF Auto)**—Another variation of RAW, in which the print server inspects the print job to determine whether a form-feed character is needed.

- **TEXT**—A data type consisting of ANSI characters only.

- **PSCRIPT1**—A data type used for PostScript code, typically generated by a Macintosh or specialized graphical application when the targeted print device is a non-PostScript device. This data type instructs the print server to create a bitmap-equivalent rendering of the print job to send to the device.

13

Print Router

A print router is the component of the Windows NT print system that communicates a print job from a print client to the print server. The print router is simply a collection of Remote Procedure Calls (RPCs) that perform the redirection or communication of the print job from the client to the server. The RPCs pass between the client's print router (WINSPOOL.DRV) and the print server's print router (SPOOLSS.DLL). Once received by the print server's router, the print job is directed to the appropriate print provider—either the local print provider, for local jobs, or another networked print provider, for remote jobs.

Print Provider

Print providers poll the available print processors to determine which one recognizes the print job's data type and destination printer name. Once recognized, the print job is transmitted to that print processor. Two of the more commonly used print providers of Windows NT are as follows:

- Windows NT print provider (WIN32SPL.DLL)—Transfers print jobs to Windows network print servers.

- NetWare print provider (NWPROVAU.DLL)—Transfers print jobs to NetWare print servers.

Once the print processor receives the print job, the job is spooled to disk. By default, each print job is stored in its own spool file (with an .SPL extension) in the WINNT\System32\Printers\Spool directory. Spool files provide fault tolerance for printing. If the power fails or communication with the printer becomes disrupted, the spooled print job can be restarted or sent to another printer. Once a print job has successfully been sent to the print device, it is deleted from the Spool directory. It is possible, however, to configure the print server so that spool files are always retained.

A NetWare print provider will handle the task of sending the print job to a NetWare print server. To send print jobs from a Windows NT client to a NetWare-hosted printer, File and Print Services for NetWare must be installed on the client. To route print jobs from a Windows NT server to a NetWare print server, the Windows NT server must have Gateway Services for NetWare installed.

Print Processor

The **print processor** makes any final modifications to a print job after it is read from the spool file but before it is sent to the print monitor. Windows NT uses two types of print processors: one for Windows clients and another for Macintosh clients. The Windows print processor uses the EMF option, all three RAW data types, and TEXT data types. The Macintosh print processor uses only PSCRIPT1 and is present only if Services for Macintosh is installed.

Print Monitor

The final component in the chain, the print monitor passes a print job on to the physical print device. The print monitor, however, is more than just a hand-off mechanism; it can also communicate with the printer in bidirectional mode to maintain information about print status and errors. In addition, it manages the flow of data over the port (or other communication pathway) to the print device. The monitor must maintain orderly control of multiple print jobs, and feed data to the printer only as fast as the imaging device can process the job.

The Windows NT print system can manage the printer queue for Windows NT clients even when the physical printer is attached to a different network or operating system. For example, such clients can use NetWare or UNIX printers. A print server manages the print jobs on the Windows NT side, but the jobs are sent to the print server on the other network or another operating system type for final processing. Thus a second print server may be involved in the print process.

THE PRINTERS FOLDER

The Printers folder is the centralized control area for all events associated with printing in the Windows NT environment. To open the Printers folder, you can do one of the following:

- Click the Start button, point to Settings, and then click Printers.
- Double-click the My Computer icon on the desktop, then double-click the Printers folder icon.
- Open Windows NT Explorer, then scroll down to display the Printers folder in the left pane.

After the installation of Windows NT, the Printers folder initially contains only one item—the Add Printer applet (sometimes referred to as the Add Printer wizard; see Figure 13-1). This applet is used to add new local printers or to connect to existing network printer shares. Once a local printer is created, it can be shared and managed.

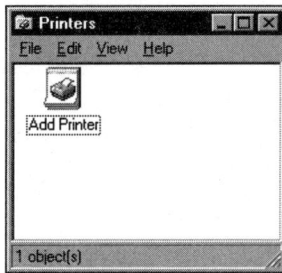

Figure 13-1   Printers folder

13

INSTALLING LOCAL PRINTERS

When you install a local printer via the Add Printer wizard, you create a logical printer (in the Printers folder) that connects to a physical print device. (You will learn how to install a network printer via the Network print share selection later in this chapter.) To begin installing a local printer, double-click the Add Printer icon in the Printers folder, then click My Computer. You will be prompted for information about the printer, such as the following:

- The port to which the physical device is attached
- The make and model of the print device
- A name for the logical printer
- Whether the printer should be shared
- If you are sharing the printer, a share name
- If you are sharing the printer, other operating system print drivers to install on the print server
- Whether a test page should be printed to verify the installation of the new printer

Once this process is complete, an icon for the new logical printer will appear in the Printers folder. For example, Figure 13-2 shows a Hewlett-Packard LaserJet added to the Printers folder. (You may need to refresh the view in the Printers Folder to see this icon—press the F5 key or click View on the menu bar, then click Refresh.)

Figure 13-2   Printers folder with new printer added

Typically, this configuration is enough to enable client applications to use the new printer. If further configuration is required, you can modify any of the settings originally defined with the Add Printer wizard. Details about altering the configuration of a logical printer are discussed later in this chapter.

PRINT JOB MANAGEMENT

All printer management begins with the Printers folder. To manage print jobs, double-click the icon for the printer in question. This action opens a print queue window similar to the one shown in Figure 13-3.

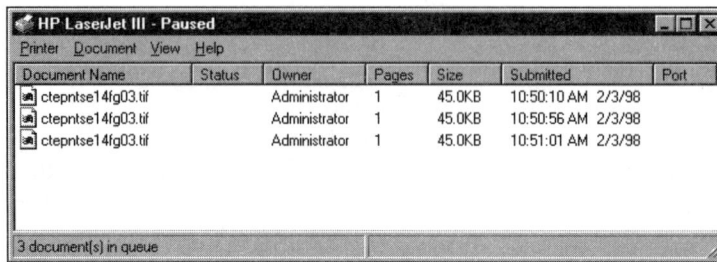

Figure 13-3   Print queue window

To manage print jobs, you simply select one or more print jobs listed in the queue and then choose one of four commands from the Document menu:

- Pause—Prevents a print job from printing or halts the printing of an in-process print job. If the print job is not already occupying the print device, other non-paused print jobs behind the paused job will then be sent to the printer.

Pausing a print job or the entire print queue will not immediately stop the printer from printing. The printer will continue to print as long as data are stored in its memory and buffers. Pausing printing simply prevents the print server from sending more data to the print device. Only after the print device has cleared its memory and buffer will it stop printing.

- Resume—Continues a previously paused print job.

- Restart—Starts a print job from its beginning. This command is used to reprint documents that failed to print properly on the physical device.

- Cancel—Deletes a print job from the print queue. Any portion of the print job already sent to the physical printer will continue printing from the device's buffer.

You can also perform management actions on the entire print queue at one time. The relevant commands are found in the Printer menu:

- Pause Printing—Stops the printing of the entire print queue, including print jobs currently being transmitted to the printer. All print jobs sent to the printer will be added to the end of the queue, where they will wait for the printer to resume printing. Instead of using a separate Resume Printing command, you turn off Pause Printing by reselecting this command. When this option is in use, a check mark appears beside the command in the menu; when it is not in use, no check mark is visible.

- Set as Default Printer—The operating system designates a default printer to which print jobs will be sent when an alternative or specific printer is not defined. When a printer serves as the default printer, a check mark is present beside the Set as Default Printer command in the Printer menu. To change the default printer, you must define another device as the default printer. Most client applications include two ways of sending a document to be printed. First, you can use the print icon in the application's toolbar; this option sends the print job to the default printer using current printing default settings. Second, you can use the Print command (usually found in the application's File menu); this option opens the Print dialog window, where you can select alternative printers and designate other print settings.

- Document Defaults—This command opens the Default Document Properties dialog box (shown in Figure 13-4), where you can set the default parameters for this printer regarding how documents are printed. These parameters include paper size, paper source, number of copies, and print orientation. You may also have access to advanced printer-specific features if the print device supports bidirectional communication.

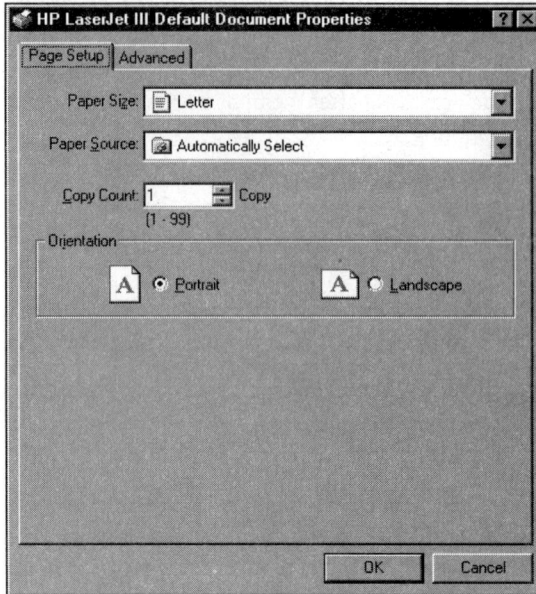

Figure 13-4 Default Document Properties dialog box

- Sharing—This command opens the Sharing tab of the Printer Properties dialog box. This tab allows you to enable or disable sharing, define the share name, and indicate what other operating system driver types to host on the printer server.

- Purge Print Documents—This command deletes all jobs currently in the print queue.

Your ability to manage a printer and print jobs is determined by the permission level assigned to your user account for that specific printer. If this level is set at No Access, you cannot perform any management activities or even send a print job to that printer. If it is designated as Print access, you can send and manage your own computer's print jobs in the queue. Manage Documents access enables you to pause, resume, restart, and cancel any print job in the queue. If you have Full Control, you can perform any print management activity. (Setting user permission levels will be discussed later in this chapter.)

ATTACHING TO A NETWORK PRINTER

Connecting to a network printer is similar to creating a local printer; you begin by double-clicking the Add Printers icon in the Printers folder. To connect to an existing network printer share, select Network printer server in the first Add Printer wizard dialog box. The Connect to Printer dialog box (shown in Figure 13-5) will then display all of the printer shares currently available on the network. Select the appropriate share in the Shared Printers list box, verify that the UNC for the selected share appears in the Printer text box at the top of the dialog box, then click OK. If the printer server has stored printer drivers for your local operating system, then setting up the logical printer is complete. If you need drivers locally, you will be prompted for them.

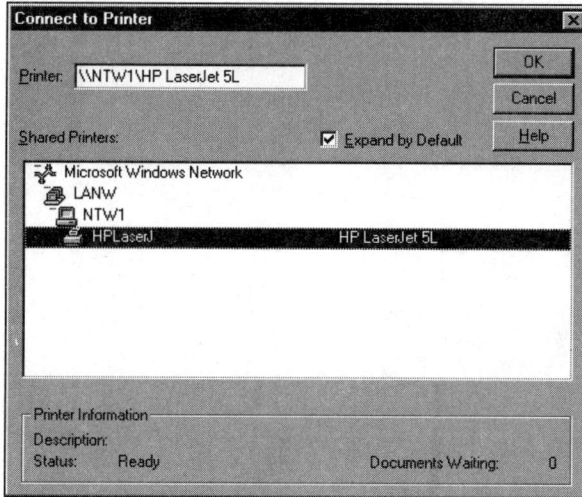

Figure 13-5   Connect to Printer dialog box

PRINTER CONFIGURATION

After you have installed or defined a logical printer pointing to a local printer or attached to a network printer, further configuration of that printer is handled through the printer's Properties dialog box. You can open this dialog box in several ways:

- In the Printers folder, right-click the icon for the specific printer, then click Properties in the shortcut pop-up menu.

- In the Printers folder, select the icon for the printer you want to configure, click File on the menu bar, then click Properties.

- In the Printers folder, double-click the icon for the specific printer to open the queue window. Click Printer on the menu bar, then click Properties.

The following sections explain the six tabs found in a printer's Properties dialog box.

GENERAL TAB

The General tab is shown in Figure 13-6. On this tab, you can:

- Define a comment for the printer.

- Describe the location of the printer.

- Select installed drivers or add new drivers.

- Specify a separator page (explained below).

- Set the print processor and data type.

- Print a test page.

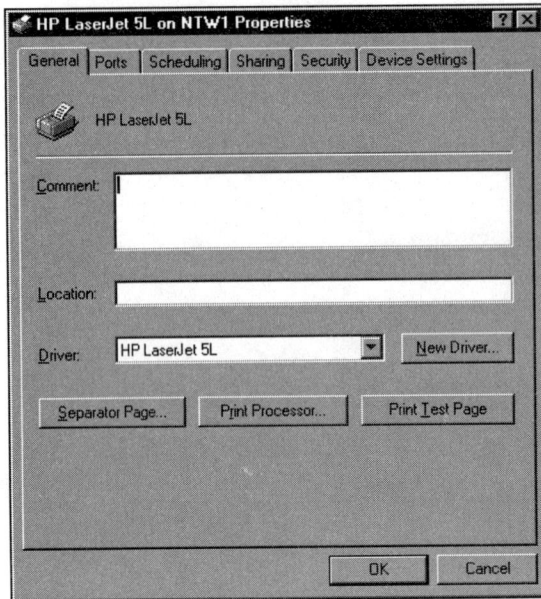

Figure 13-6   General tab of the Properties dialog box

A **separator page** is a short document that is printed automatically between each print job; it identifies the sender (and other details) and thereby helps the user find his or her documents on the office printer. You can create your own separator pages or use one of the three pages provided with Windows NT—PCL.SEP, PSCRIPT.SEP, and SYSPRINT.SEP. These premade pages are located in the WINNT\System32 directory. PCL.SEP is compatible with PCL printers— it switches the printer into PCL printing mode and prints a page before each document. Both PSCRIPT.SEP and SYSPRINT.SEP are compatible with PostScript printers; the former does not print a page before each document, while the latter does.

To create your own separator pages, you need to use a text editor, such as Notepad. You can start from scratch, but it easiest to copy one of the existing SEP files and edit it. For details on creating a SEP file, please consult Windows NT online Help or the Resource Kit.

PORTS TAB

The Ports tab of the Properties dialog box is shown in Figure 13-7. On this tab, you can:

- Set the ports to which the logical printer should send print jobs.

- Enable bidirectional communication.

- Enable printer pooling (discussed later in this chapter).

- Add, delete, or configure ports (local printers only).

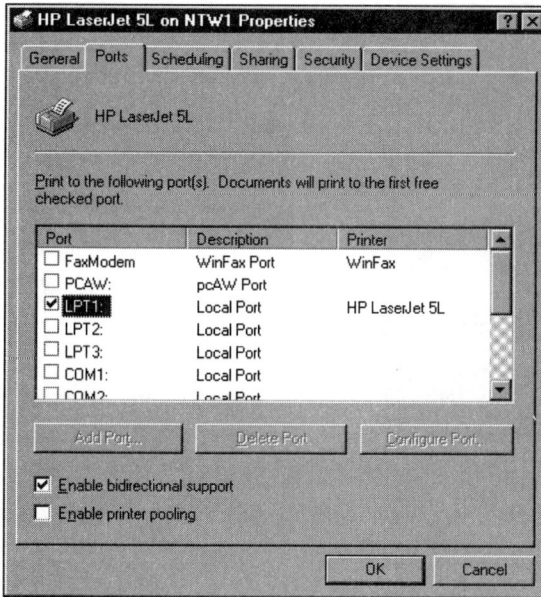

Figure 13-7 Ports tab of the Properties dialog box

SCHEDULING TAB

The Scheduling tab of the Properties dialog box is shown in Figure 13-8. On this tab, you can:

- Define the printer as being always available or as being available only within a specific time range. Any print jobs sent when the printer is unavailable will be stored until the printer becomes available.

- Set the print priority of the printer. If multiple logical printers are defined for the same physical printer, the logical printer with the highest priority will send its print jobs to the physical printer first. On the Scheduling tab, 1 is the lowest and default priority, while 99 is the highest priority.

- Order the printer to spool documents or to print directly to the print device. If spooling is enabled, the print job is stored to disk quickly and control of the client application returns to the user. If print jobs are sent directly to the printer, the client application will remain tied up until the entire print job has been sent to the print device; only then will control of the client application return to the user.

- If spooling is enabled, set the print processor to print the job after the completion of spooling or as soon as possible.

- Set the print processor to examine the print job's intended destination before attempting to complete it. If its destination, data type, or processor type do not match those of the print device, printing will not begin. If a mismatched document is sent to a printer, the printer may fail or other documents may not print.

13

- Print spooled documents first. If this option is selected, all spooled print jobs will be printed before any direct-to-printer jobs begin. This setup can produce extremely long delays before a client application returns control to the user.

- Keep the spooled files after the print job finishes. By default, all spool files are deleted once the print job is successfully sent to the print device.

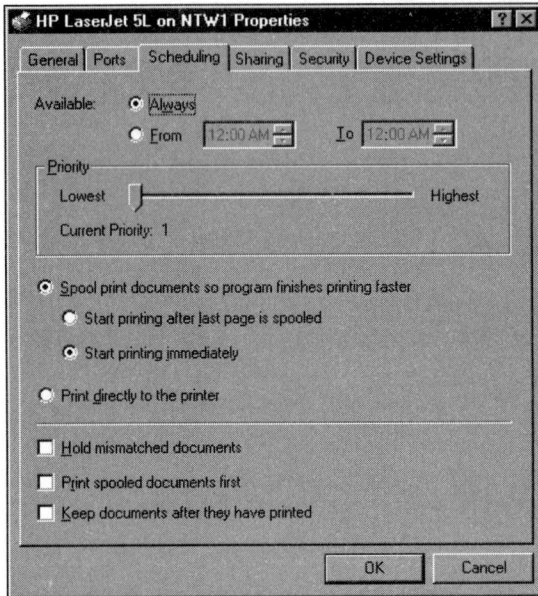

Figure 13-8   Scheduling tab of the Properties dialog box

SHARING TAB

The Sharing tab of the Properties dialog box is shown in Figure 13-9. On this tab, you can:

- Share the printer with the rest of the network.

- Define the printer's share name.

- Set alternative drivers to be stored on the print server based on operating system. If a client computer uses the same operating system as one of the print driver types stored on the print server, a local driver is not required. The print system will transfer the print driver to the client computer each time printing begins, which simplifies driver management by centralizing the location of the drivers. Currently, only Windows 95 and Windows NT 3.5 or later drivers can be stored on the print server; all other operating system types require the installation of a local printer driver to access a network printer share.

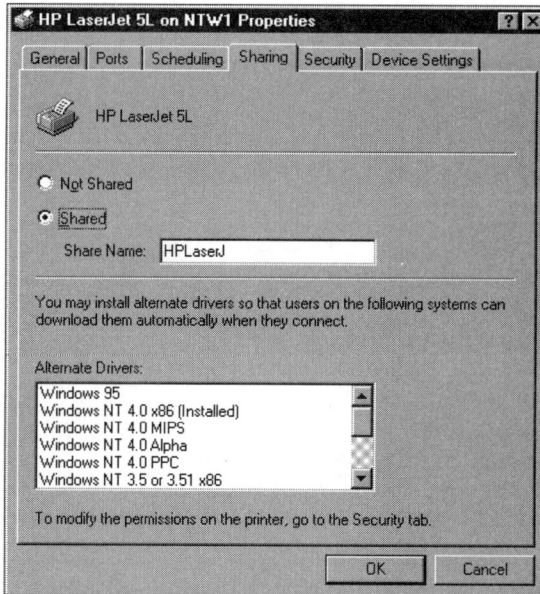

Figure 13-9   Sharing tab of the Properties dialog box

SECURITY TAB

The Security tab of the Properties dialog box is shown in Figure 13-10. As explained in the following sections, this tab gives you access to the Permissions, Auditing, and Ownership dialog boxes for the logical printer.

Permissions

The Permissions button on the Security tab opens the Printer Permissions dialog box, which is shown in Figure 13-11. In this dialog box, you can specify which users and groups can access the printer and what level of access those users enjoy. The same settings and permission types are used for both local printers and network shares. The available options for printer access are as follows:

- No Access—Users have no access to the printer.

- Print—Users can print and manage their own documents.

- Manage Documents—Users can print and manage any document in the print queue.

- Full Control—Users have full control over the logical printer itself and can manage all documents in the print queue.

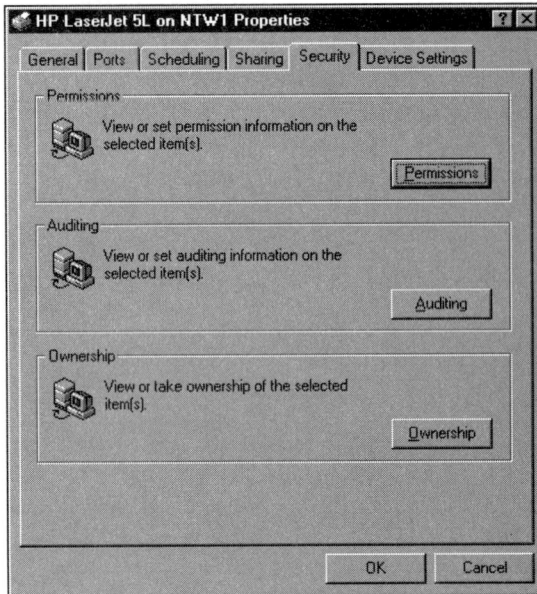

Figure 13-10   Security tab of the Properties dialog box

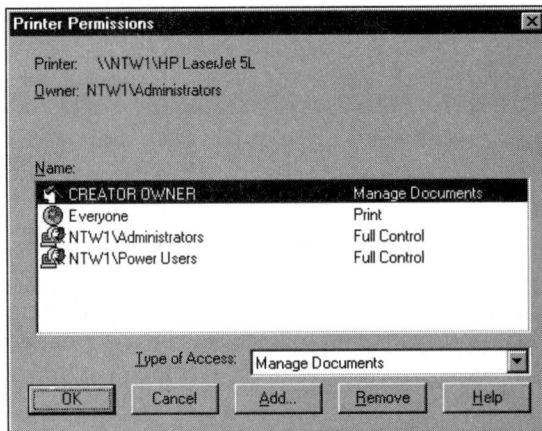

Figure 13-11   Printer Permissions dialog box

The default permissions settings for a new printer are explained in Table 13-1.

Table 13-1   Default Permissions Settings for a New Printer

Permission	Assigned to
Print	Everyone group
Manage Documents	Creator/Owner
Full Control	Administrators, Server Operators, Print Operators

Auditing

The Auditing button on the Security tab opens the Printer Auditing dialog box, which is shown in Figure 13-12. In this dialog box, you can specify which print events to audit and for which users and groups. The available print events to audit are the success or failure of printing, using Full Control permissions, deleting print jobs, changing permissions, and taking ownership.

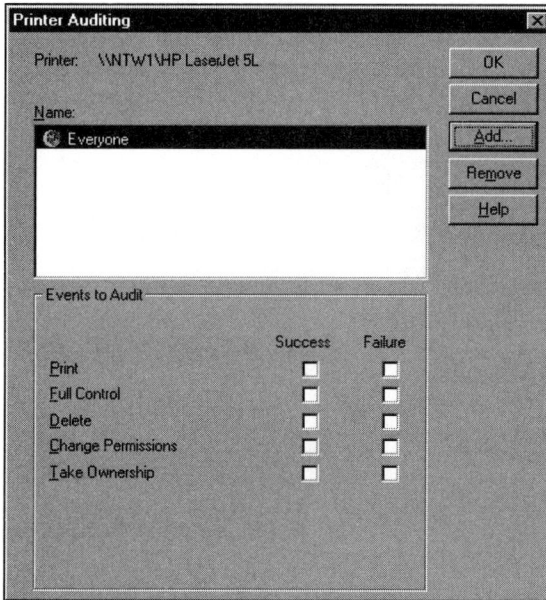

Figure 13-12   Printer Auditing dialog box

Ownership

The Ownership button on the Security tab opens the Owner dialog box, which indicates who currently owns the printer. By clicking the Take Ownership button in the Ownership dialog box, you can take ownership of this printer. Remember, however, that you must have Full Control permissions or be a member of the Administrators group to use this feature.

DEVICE SETTINGS

The final tab in the Properties dialog box is the Device Settings tab, which is shown in Figure 13-13. In this tab, you can configure specific settings for the print device. Using an easy-to-use GUI interface, this dialog box displays the complicated feature selections often set on the print device via a multibutton LED display. Features that commonly appear on this tab include memory, paper trays, accessories, fonts, halftone/graphics, and page protection.

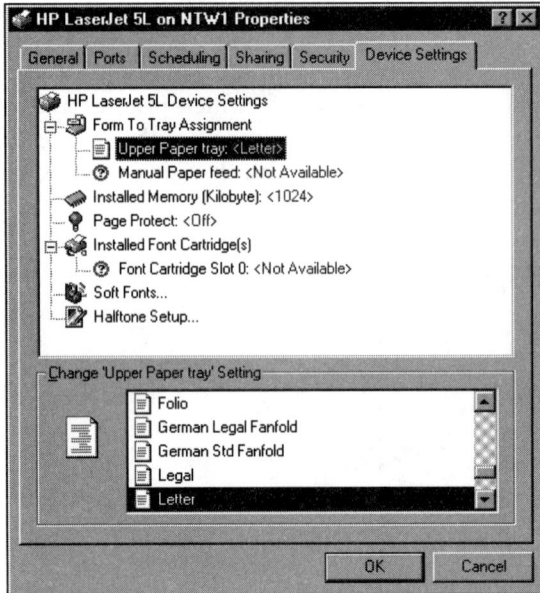

Figure 13-13   Device Settings tab of the Properties dialog box

PRINTER POOLING

Printer pooling, illustrated in Figure 13-14, is a feature of the Windows NT print system that enables a single logical printer to send print jobs to multiple printers. All of the printers managed in such a print pool must be identical models and configurations. When one printer in a print pool is busy with a print job, the logical printer directs the next print job to the next available printer in the pool.

Print job   Logical printer   Printer device / Printer device

Figure 13-14   Printer pooling

Windows NT also allows the opposite of print pooling, in which multiple logical printers target a single print device (see Figure 13-15). In this type of setup, you can alter the settings of one logical printer without changing the normal operation of the other logical printer, even though both send print jobs to the same print device. For example, you might define a high-priority printer for management, a printer to use letterhead paper in a secondary paper tray, or even a printer to cache all nonessential documents to print overnight.

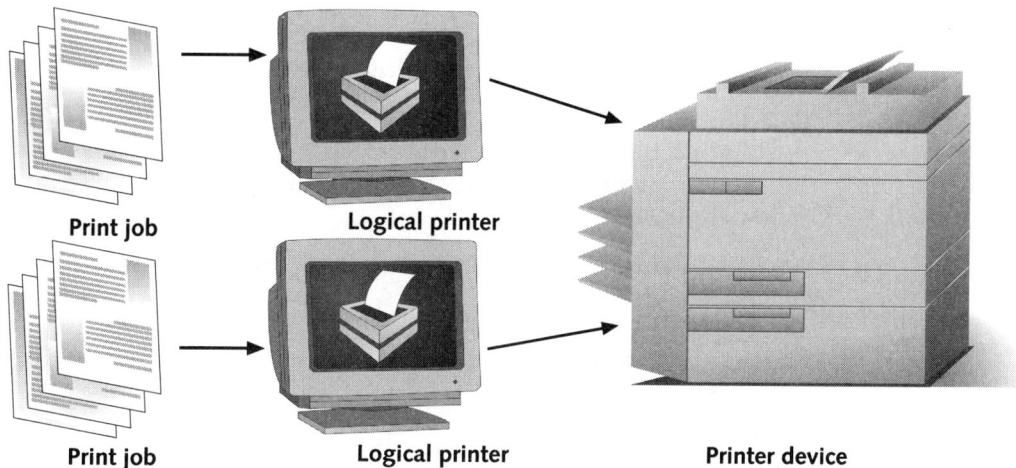

Figure 13-15   Multiple logical printers defined for a single print device

As illustrated in Figure 13-16, by combining the features of multiple logical printers and printer pooling, you can create complex printing scenarios to meet the unique needs of your office.

13

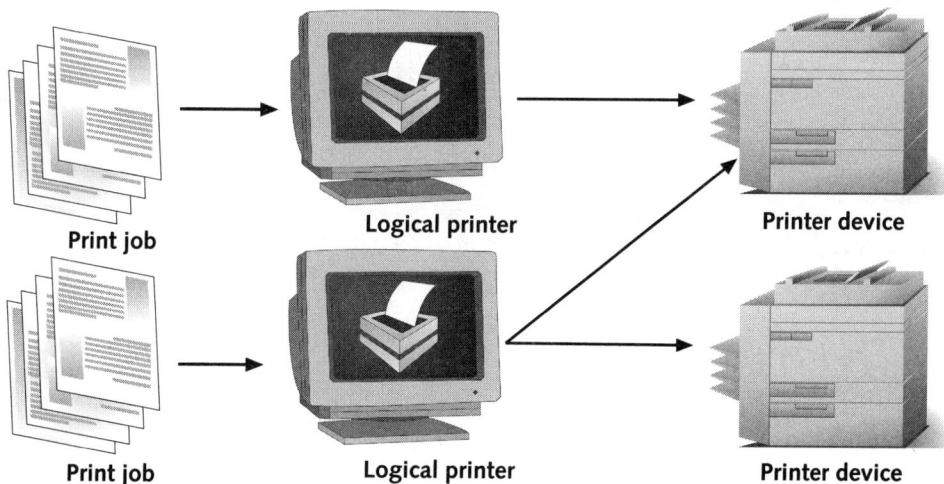

Figure 13-16   A possible printing setup

PRINT SERVER MANAGEMENT

In addition to managing the individual printers, the print server itself can be configured. To manage the Print Server, open the Printers folder, click File on the menu bar, then click Server Properties. The Print Server Properties dialog box will open. The three tabs of this dialog box are explained in the following sections.

FORMS TAB

The Forms tab of the Print Server Properties dialog box is shown in Figure 13-17. On this tab, you can:

- Delete any available form from the print server. A form is a defined paper type. Windows NT uses forms instead of the tray designations employed by most non-Windows operating systems.

- Create new forms, including naming the form, defining the paper size, and designating margin areas.

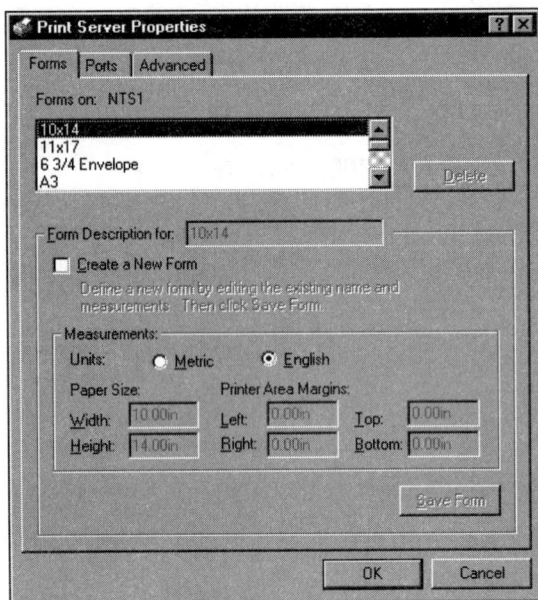

Figure 13-17   Forms tab of the Print Server Properties dialog box

PORTS TAB

The Ports tab of the Print Server Properties dialog box is shown in Figure 13-18. On this tab, you can:

- Review the defined ports and the print devices attached to them.

- Add, delete, or configure ports.

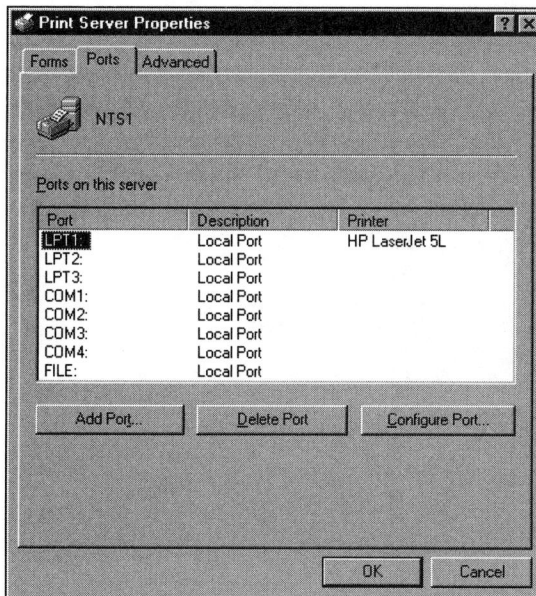

Figure 13-18   Ports tab of the Print Server Properties dialog box

ADVANCED TAB

The Advanced tab of the Print Server Properties dialog box is shown in Figure 13-19. On this tab, you can:

- Specify the folder location for the spool files (the default is WINNT\System32\spool\PRINTERS).

- Enable logging of spool errors.

- Enable warning and informational spool events (such as pop-up messages).

- Enable audio signals for remote document errors.

- Enable local notification when documents have completed printing on remote printers.

13

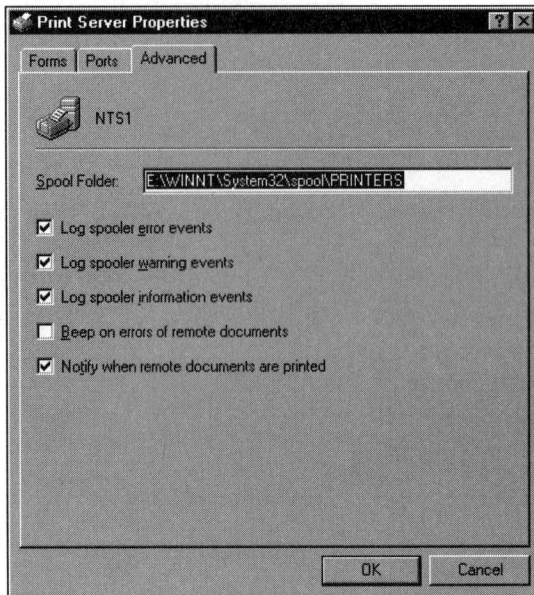

Figure 13-19   Advanced tab of the Print Server Properties dialog box

DLC PRINTERS

The **DLC** protocol was originally created to allow servers to interoperate with IBM mainframes, but it can also be used to connect to Hewlett-Packard network-attached printers. Like other LAN protocols, it is installed through the Protocol tab of the Network applet. (You'll need to know the 12-byte network adapter card's physical MAC address, which generally appears in the printer or network adapter user manuals.) Once DLC is installed, you can use the Add Printer wizard to install the logical printer for the network-attached printer. The computer where you install this logical printer will become that printer's print server—as a result, the spool file will be stored on it locally. When prompted to select a port, click the Add Port button, then select the Hewlett-Packard Network Port. You must then define a printer name and provide the card address. The resulting logical printer for the network attached printer can be configured, managed, and shared just like any other printer.

TCP/IP AND UNIX PRINTERS

The Windows NT TCP/IP Print Services enables UNIX and other TCP/IP clients to print to Windows NT-hosted printers and allows Windows NT clients to print to UNIX print queues. This service adds the Line Printer Daemon (LPD) and Line Printer Remote (LPR) UNIX utilities to Windows NT. TCP/IP Print Services is installed through the Services tab of the Network applet and requires the TCP/IP protocol to be present on the print server. Once this service is in place, you can use the Add Printer wizard in the Printers folder to create a new logical printer. Be sure to select the LPR port, directing this port to either the Windows NT print share or a UNIX print queue.

TROUBLESHOOTING

When troubleshooting printing and printer problems, check the simple and obvious places first, and then move on to more complex and subtle possibilities. Thus, you should initially check the physical aspects of the print device—cable, connectors, power, paper, toner, jams, and so on. Next, attempt to print to the same logical printer with another client application, another computer, and other user accounts (including an administrator). Then, check the permissions and configuration settings on the logical printer and the printer share. Finally, reinstall the print driver, create a new logical printer, or move the printer to a different computer.

Some print problems are associated with the print spooler itself. If you have determined that the spooler is (or could be) the culprit, several options exist for eliminating the problem.

First, stop and restart the spooler. Using the Services applet, locate and select "Spooler," click Stop, then click Start. If a hung spooler created the problem, this action should restore the print server to operation.

Second, verify that the spooler has enough storage space to perform the required operations. In general, 50 to 100 MB of free space (or more) are needed to handle spool files. If the driver hosting the spool folder is full, remove files or change the spool folder's location.

CHAPTER SUMMARY

13

- The print system for Windows NT Server 4.0 can be used by nearly any network client, including those running Windows NT Workstation, Windows 95, Windows for Workgroups, DOS, Macintosh, UNIX, and other TCP/IP clients. Some of the terminology used by Microsoft to describe the printing environment varies from industry standards. To fully understand printing in Windows NT, you'll need to be aware of the new nomenclature.

- The Windows NT printing environment is not primarily concerned with the physical print devices, but rather with the logical printers used to link and redirect print-related traffic (such as print jobs, printer access, and printer management). This setup differs from other network operating system printing environments. Once a physical printer is attached to a computer or to the network and the correct driver is installed, nearly everything else that occurs in relation to printing is software-based. Thus, after the initial installation, you'll only interact with the physical print device so as to add paper and retrieve hard copies of documents.

- The Printers folder is the centralized control area for all events associated with printing in the Windows NT environment. After the installation of Windows NT, it contains only a single applet icon. This Add Printer applet or wizard is used to add new local printers or to connect to existing network printer shares. A local printer can then be shared and managed.

- Installing a local printer is a simple process—you just create a logical printer in the Printers folder that connects to a physical print device. To initially install printer drivers and create the logical printer, you use the Add Printer wizard in the Printers folder.

- All printer management is performed through the Printers folder (or at least starts there). To manage print jobs, double-click the icon for the targeted logical printer.

- Connecting to a network printer is just as easy as creating a local printer. Once again, logical printer setup is performed using the Add Printer wizard in the Printers folder. After you have installed or defined a logical printer, further configuration of that printer is handled through its Properties dialog box.

- Printer pooling is a feature of the Windows NT print system that allows a single logical printer to send print jobs to multiple devices. All of the printers within a print pool must be identical models and configurations. When one printer in a print pool is busy, the logical printer directs the next print job to the next available printer in the pool.

- In addition to managing the individual printers, the print server itself can be configured. Print server management is performed via the Print Server Properties dialog box.

KEY TERMS

- **characterization data file** — A collection of printer-specific information that is stored in the printer's memory.

- **client application** — A software program that initiates a print job. A client application can reside on a client/workstation computer, a server computer, or even the computer hosting the print server.

- **connecting to a printer** — The act of creating a logical printer to be referenced and used by client applications to send print jobs. A logical printer can connect to a locally attached printer or to a network printer share. Connecting to a printer is carried out via the Add Printer wizard found in the Printers folder.

- **creating a printer** — The installation of drivers for a print device on the machine locally hosting the physical device. Creating a printer also involves naming the printer, setting printer-specific configurations, and, optionally, sharing that printer with the rest of the network.

- **DLC** — A protocol that was originally created to allow servers to interoperate with IBM mainframes; it can also be used to connect to Hewlett-Packard network-attached printers.

- **EMF (Enhanced Metafiles)** — The native print and rendering data type of Windows that is generated by the GDI. EMF files are portable (that is, they can be sent to any print device) and more compact than the RAW data type.

- **graphics device interface (GDI)** — The print architecture component that enables client applications to represent graphical information.

- **logical printer** — The term used by Microsoft to refer to the software interface that defines, names, and points to a physical printer (either local or remote). This component, which appears in the Printers folder, redirects print jobs to the appropriate print server for processing. User access and printer functions are managed at this interface point.

- **network-attached printer** — A print device that is physically connected to the network, rather than being directly connected to a computer host. It is equipped with a network interface card, such as the Hewlett-Packard JetDirect, and accessed using the DLC protocol.

- **print client** — A client computer on the network that submits print jobs from a client application to a print server.

- **print device** — The physical electronic mechanism that is more commonly called a printer (outside the world of Microsoft). This hardware component, which produces the printed document, is also called the physical printer.

- **print job** — The electronic package that contains the document to be printed as well as process and control data. It is initiated by a client application on a client computer, sent to a print server, and eventually dispatched to a physical printer.

- **print processor** — The portion of the Windows NT printing model that makes modifications to a print job after it is read from the spool file but before it is sent to the print monitor.

- **print queue** — The series of print jobs received by a print server waiting for access to the physical print device. A print queue operates in a default "first in, first out" mode. Sometimes referred to simply as the "queue."

- **print resolution** — A measurement of pixel density that relates to the sharpness and clarity of a printed image. Resolution is measured in dots per inch (DPI). Typically, greater DPI yields a higher-quality printed output. Most modern printers (laser and ink-jet) print at more than 300 DPI.

- **print server** — The computer that hosts the spool file for a physical printer where print jobs are temporarily stored and managed. It controls the printer, manages the print queue, and maintains the link with the network to offer the printer share. Any Windows NT or Windows 95 computer that has a local printer is considered a print server.

- **Print Server Services** — Windows NT services that extend the capabilities of the standard print system. They include Services for Macintosh, File and Print Services for NetWare, and TCP/IP Print Services. Typically, these services extend the print server's ability to accept print jobs from a wider variety of clients and protocols.

- **print spooler** — A component of the print system that receives, processes, stores, and distributes print jobs. Print spooling is the process in which the print system writes a print job to disk into a "spool file," where it awaits its turn in the print queue. Despooling occurs as the stored print jobs are retrieved, printed, and removed from the spool.

13

- **printer driver** — The device driver that enables the print server to communicate with the physical print device.

- **printer pooling** — A feature of the Windows NT print system that enables a single logical printer to send print jobs to multiple printers.

- **PSCRIPT1** — A data type used for PostScript code, typically generated by a Macintosh or specialized graphical application, when the targeted print device is a non-PostScript device. It instructs the print server to create a bitmap-equivalent rendering of the print job.

- **RAW** — A data type generated by the printer driver rather than the GDI. Using RAW requires the client application to remain in communication with the print system until all of the print job has been sent to the print device.

- **RAW (FF Appended)** — A variation of RAW that instructs the print server to add a form-feed character to the end of the print job, ensuring that the last page of the job will be printed.

- **RAW (FF Auto)** — A variation of RAW in which the print server inspects the print job to determine if a form-feed character is needed.

- **rendering** — The Windows NT print system's process of recreating an image on the computer screen in printer-specific language so that the image can be properly reproduced on paper.

- **separator page** — A short document that is printed automatically between each print job; it identifies the sender (and other details) to aid in locating your documents on the office printer.

- **TEXT** — A data type consisting of ANSI characters only.

REVIEW QUESTIONS

1. Which component of the Windows NT print system is responsible for representing graphical information?

   a. print router

   b. graphics device interface (GDI)

   c. print processor

   d. print spooler

2. Which devices can be used as the print devices with the Windows NT printing system?

   a. plain-paper printers

   b. fax modems

   c. color-slide printers

   d. files on storage devices

3. Print drivers are make/model/manufacturer-specific as well as operating-system-specific. True or False?

4. Which printer graphics driver file handles requests based around raster or bitmapped images?

   a. PSCRIPT.DLL

   b. PLOTTER.DLL

   c. RASDD.DLL

5. Which native or default print job data type does Windows NT use?

   a. RAW

   b. PostScript

   c. EMF

   d. TEXT

6. Where are the spool files stored by default?

   a. in Printers\Temp on the client computer

   b. in WINNT\System32\Printers\Spool on the print server

   c. in WINNT\System32\Printers\Spool on the client computer

   d. in Program Files\Spooler on the print server

7. Which print job data types does the Windows normal or default print processor handle?

   a. EMF

   b. RAW

   c. TEXT

   d. PostScript

8. While using the Add Printer wizard, you can define a share name, alternate operating system drivers, and group permission levels. True or False?

9. Issuing the Pause Printing command will:

   a. stop the print device immediately

   b. allow the print device to complete the entire print job

   c. stop the print monitor from sending data to the print device

   d. prevent new print jobs from joining the queue

10. If a piece of paper jams in the print device while printing the third page of a long document, which command should you use after removing the paper jam?

   a. Restart

   b. Resume

   c. Cancel

   d. Purge Print Documents

13

11. You have two logical printers defined on your workstation. One points to a locally attached printer; the other points to a shared network printer. The management and configuration dialog boxes accessible through the logical printers will differ significantly. True or False?

12. On which tab of the Printer Properties dialog box are new drivers installed?

   a. General

   b. Schedule

   c. Ports

   d. Security

13. On which printer Properties dialog box tab is printer auditing configured?

   a. General

   b. Schedule

   c. Share

   d. Security

14. On which printer Properties dialog box tab are print-device-specific settings such as memory, paper trays, accessories, fonts, halftone/graphics, and page protection configured?

   a. General

   b. Security

   c. Ports

   d. Device Settings

15. Printer pooling is:

   a. defining multiple logical printers to send print jobs to a single print device

   b. defining a single print device to send print jobs to multiple, identical print devices

   c. defining multiple logical printers each with a different priority level

   d. defining multiple user groups and assigning each a different printer access level

16. It is not possible to define multiple logical printers that point to the same print device. True or False?

17. Where is the destination folder for spool files defined?

   a. in each Printer Properties dialog box on the Ports tab

   b. on the Advanced tab of the Server Properties dialog box

   c. through the Network applet

   d. via the Server Manager utility

18. The DLC protocol can be used to:

    a. distribute e-mail

    b. interoperate with IBM mainframes

    c. communicate with network-attached printers

    d. remotely monitor a Windows NT server's performance

19. UNIX client are able to print to Windows NT-hosted printers if what service is installed?

    a. UNIX Services

    b. File and Print Services for UNIX

    c. TCP/IP Print Services

    d. Macintosh Services

20. The spooler service can be stopped and restarted through which utility?

    a. Services applet

    b. Server Manager

    c. Printers folder

    d. System applet

21. The collection of processing and control data, plus a document of some sort, within the print system is commonly known as a:

    a. print queue

    b. print job

    c. print processor

    d. print monitor

22. What characteristic of a printed image is measured in DPI?

    a. size

    b. available time

    c. print priority

    d. resolution

23. Any Windows 95 or Windows NT computer with an attached printer is known as a print server. True or False?

13

24. When you pause an individual print job, what happens to other print jobs currently in the queue or being added to the queue?

    a. They wait for the paused print job to be deleted or to complete printing.

    b. All print jobs from the same logical printer are paused, but jobs from other logical printers can still print.

    c. Nonpaused print jobs are sent to the printer normally, and only the paused job is held back.

    d. It is not possible to pause individual print jobs.

25. Which components of the Windows NT print system make up the spooler?

    a. print router

    b. print monitor

    c. print processor

    d. print provider

HANDS-ON PROJECTS

For some or all of these projects you will need one Windows NT server and one Windows NT workstation. A printer is optional, but not necessary.

PROJECT 13-1

In this project, you will install a locally attached printer. To complete this project, you need to have Windows NT installed. A physical printer is not required, unless you want to print a test document.

    1. Open the **Printers folder** as described in the chapter, then double-click the **Add Printer icon**. The Add Printer wizard dialog box opens.

    2. On the first page of this dialog box, click **My Computer**, then click **Next**. The Port Selection dialog box opens.

    3. Select **LPT1** as the port, then click **Next**. The Manufacture and Print Model Selection dialog box opens.

    4. Select **HP** in the Manufacturers list and **HP LaserJet 5L** in the Printers list, then click **Next**. The Define Printer Name dialog box opens.

    5. Define a printer name, select this printer as the default by clicking **Yes**, then click **Next**. The Sharing dialog box opens.

    6. Click the **Not shared option button**, then click **Next**. The Print Test Page dialog box opens.

7. Click the **No option button** to indicate that you do not want to print a test page, then click **Finish**. You will return to the Printers folder.

8. You will be prompted for the location of the Windows NT setup files. Enter the information and click **OK**.

PROJECT 13-2

In this project, you will share the local printer you installed in Project 13-1. To complete this project, you need to have Windows NT installed. A physical printer is not required.

1. Open the **Printers folder**.
2. Right-click the **icon for the printer** you installed in Project 13-1, then click **Sharing** in the shortcut menu. The Sharing tab of the printer's Properties dialog box opens.
3. Select the **Shared option button**, define a share name in the Share Name text field, then click **OK**. You will return to the Printers folder.
4. Close the Printers folder.

PROJECT 13-3

In this project, you will connect to a network printer share. To complete this project, you need to have Windows NT installed. A physical printer is not required. A network-shared printer is required. You cannot perform this project by attempting to connect to the printer shared from the same computer.

1. Open the **Printers folder**, then double-click the **Add Printer icon**. The Add Printer wizard dialog box opens.
2. Click the **Network printer server option**, then click **Next**. The Connect to Printer dialog box opens.
3. Use the browser list to locate and select a printer share, then click **Next**. The Default Printer dialog box opens.
4. Verify that this printer is *not* the default, then click **Next**. The final Add Printer wizard dialog box opens.
5. Click **Finish**. You will return to the Printers folder.
6. Close the Printers folder.

13

PROJECT 13-4

In this project, you will set permissions on a logical printer shared with the network. To complete this project, you need to have Windows NT installed. A physical printer is not required.

1. Open the **Printers folder**.

2. Right-click the **icon for the printer** you shared in Project 13-3, then click **Properties** in the shortcut menu. The Properties dialog box for that printer opens.

3. Click the **Security tab**, then click the **Permissions button**. The Printer Permissions dialog box opens.

4. Click **Add**. The Add Users and Groups dialog box opens.

5. Locate and select the **Domain Admins group**, then click **Add**. The Domain Admins group appears in the Add Names field.

6. Click the **Type of Access list arrow**, select **Manage Documents**, then click **OK**. You will return to the Printer Permissions dialog box.

7. Click **OK** to close the Printer Permissions dialog box, then click **OK** again to close the Properties dialog box. You will return to the Printers folder.

8. Close the Printers folder.

PROJECT 13-5

In this project, you will manage a printer queue. You will begin by pausing the printer you created in Project 13-1. You can then create print jobs for that printer, without dealing with the process of sending print jobs to a physical printer. To complete this project, you need to have Windows NT installed. A physical printer is not required.

1. Open the **Printers folder**, then double-click the **icon for the printer** you created in Project 13-1. The printer's queue window opens.

2. Click **Printer** on the menu bar, then click **Pause Printing**. Now that you have paused the printer, you can create print jobs for it without those print jobs being sent to a real printer. Pausing the printer simply prevents the spooler from processing the print queue and sending print jobs to the printer. You can still perform all of the print-job-specific management activities just as if the printer was not paused.

3. Click **Start**, point to **Programs**, point to **Accessories**, then click **Notepad**. The Notepad window opens.

4. Type your name once.

5. Click **File** on the menu bar, then click **Print**.

6. Repeat Step 5 four times.

7. Exit Notepad. You will return to the printer's queue window, where you can manage the print jobs you just created.

8. Select **one of the print jobs**, click **Document** on the menu bar, then click **Cancel**. This print job is deleted from the queue.

9. Select another **print job**, click **Document** on the menu bar, then click **Pause**. If the printer were not already paused, this action would pause the individual print job.

10. Select another **print job**, click **Document** on the menu bar, then click **Restart**. If the document were actually being transmitted to a real printer, it would stop going to the printer and start over from the beginning.

11. Select the **paused print job**, click **Document** on the menu bar, then click **Resume**. If the printer were not paused, this action would allow the individual print job to continue printing from the point at which it was paused.

12. Click **Printer** on the menu bar, then click **Purge Print Documents**. This action removes all print jobs from the queue.

13. Click **Printer** on the menu bar, then click **Pause Printing**. This action returns the printer to normal operation.

14. Close the printer queue window. You will return to the Printers folder.

15. Close the Printers folder.

13

CASE PROJECTS

1. You have a single printer on your network. Your manager has been complaining that it takes too long for his print jobs to reach this printer. How can you give him priority access?

2. Users at your company complain that the print device is not printing their print jobs. They have restarted the print device, but it still will not work. You check the printer's queue and see that all of the print jobs sent for the last few hours remain in the queue. What actions can you take to attempt to get the print system operating again?

3. The accounting department prints large documents, often 50 pages or more, that are given to an intern to file on a weekly basis. The marketing department prints single-page press releases, which are needed for immediate faxing. How can you configure the single office printer to maximize this situation?

4. You have recently connected the central office's LAN to another remote network using a leased WAN link. Both networks use TCP/IP. While the central office LAN mostly relies on Windows NT, however, the remote network uses all UNIX computers. How can you enable clients from either network to print to either network's printers?

5. You have purchased a high-speed, color laser printer for the office network. After the printer was installed, many users printed nonproductive materials on it—each costing more than $1 per page in terms of paper and toner consumption. You need to restrict color printing to those individuals responsible for printed presentations, while still allowing other users to print standard black-and-white documents on normal paper. How can you accomplish this goal?

CHAPTER FOURTEEN

CHOOSING AN APPROPRIATE RESPONSE FOR PROBLEMS

In this chapter, you will learn about common troubleshooting issues. First, you will examine problems involving installation and booting. You will see how to address problems with printers and printing. You will look at connectivity issues, involving both dial-up and LAN connections, and see how best to proceed with the resolution of these problems. You will also consider the all-too-common problem of resource access rights and security, and see how you can use the Event Viewer to redress their associated problems. Finally, you will learn how to restore your system if your fault-tolerant systems fail.

AFTER READING THIS CHAPTER AND COMPLETING THE EXERCISES YOU WILL BE ABLE TO:

- Troubleshoot installation failures
- Troubleshoot boot failures
- Troubleshoot printer problems
- Troubleshoot RAS connectivity problems
- Troubleshoot other connectivity problems
- Troubleshoot resource access problems
- Troubleshoot fault-tolerance failures

INSTALLATION FAILURES

When troubleshooting installation problems, you should start by considering several important issues, many of which are explained in Table 14-1.

Table 14-1   Common Causes of Installation Problems

Problem	Explanation
Incorrect information provided during the text-based portion of the installation	During this stage of the setup, Windows NT checks for basic configuration information regarding drivers, the CPU, the motherboard, hard-drive controllers, file systems, free space on hard drives, and memory. Windows NT Setup uses this information to construct a miniature version of Windows NT that will be used for the rest of the setup. For setup to run properly, you must provide accurate and complete information.
Hardware not included on Microsoft's **Hardware Compatibility List (HCL)**	If your hardware is not on the HCL, either you will not be able to install Windows NT or you will experience unexpected results. In addition, you will not be able to obtain technical support from Microsoft. Verify that all your hardware components are on the HCL before proceeding with your troubleshooting. Search for the latest HCL at *http://www.microsoft.com/hwtest*.
System does not meet the minimum requirements	In Windows NT, hardware drivers are written to and polled heavily for input/output (I/O) instructions. Thus hardware problems that have gone unnoticed or seemed to be minor under other operating systems may be amplified in Windows NT. To avoid such problems, make certain that your system meets at least the minimum requirements, which can be found at *http://www.microsoft.com/ntserver*.
Incorrect detection of controllers and settings	Windows NT may incorrectly detect controllers and settings if the system is using nonstandard or proprietary bus components or enhancements that do not follow industry standards (such as SMP 1.1, PCI 2.1, special bus drivers, or caching chips for burst-mode transfer). If Setup detects these items incorrectly, it will most likely fail at a later stage.
Old drivers	Some drivers that were available in Windows NT 3.51 were not updated either by the hardware manufacturer or by Microsoft. Check both the README.DOC and SETUP.TXT files on the installation CD-ROM to see whether the driver has been moved to the "retired drivers" directory. If it was, you will find complete installation instructions there. You can also contact the hardware manufacturer for an up-to-date driver.

Table 14-1   Common Causes of Installation Problems (continued)

Problem	Explanation
Booting from the CD-ROM drive fails after the installation	To boot directly from the Windows NT 4.0 compact disc, your computer's BIOS must support the El Torito Bootable CD-ROM format natively. Check with your computer manufacturer if you are unsure whether your BIOS has this feature.
Incorrect drivers loaded	Choosing the wrong driver during the setup process will create serious problems, often preventing the setup from moving into the graphical portion of the installation, as evidenced by a blue-screen Stop error or as an unreadable screen. For more on blue-screen Stop errors, see Chapter 15.
Use of an evaluation copy of Windows NT	Evaluation versions of Windows NT are **time-bombed**, meaning they become inoperable after a specified period of time (often 120 days). Check your installation media carefully before installing to make sure yours is *not* an evaluation copy. If you do accidentally install the evaluation version, you will have to reinstall your server to correct the problem.
Use of the wrong installation procedure for your processor type	The installation procedure differs for different processor types (such as Intel, RISC, and Power PC); using the wrong procedure could cause your installation to fail.

After you have ruled out the problems described in Table 14-1, you should consider the issues described in the following section.

DOCUMENT YOUR SETTINGS

To make it easier to restore your system in the event of an installation failure, you should document all configurations, including the IRQ and memory address, any extended settings, and hardware information for every adapter in your system. There are two reasons for taking this step. First, Windows NT sometimes has difficulty detecting correct memory addresses and IRQ settings. Without these data, you will not have a proper installation or installation will fail in the middle of the setup process. Windows NT does not handle installation properly if it cannot access one or more devices. Second, and probably more important, in the case of a catastrophic failure, you may need to return the system to a known good state before attempting to continue. Make sure you have the documentation described in Table 14-2.

14

Table 14-2   Required Documentation by Adapter Type

Adapter Type	Necessary Information
Video	Adapter or chipset type
Network	IRQ, I/O address, DMA (if used), connector type (BNC, twisted-pair, and so on)
SCSI controller	Adapter model or chipset, IRQ, bus type
Mouse	Mouse type, port (COM1, COM2, bus, or PS/2)
I/O port	IRQ, I/O address, DMA (if used) for each I/O port
Sound card	IRQ, I/O address, DMA
External modem	Port connections (COM1, COM2, and so on)
Internal modem	Port connections or IRQ and I/O address (for nonstandard configurations)

Windows NT does not support a number of nonstandard controller and Basic Input/Output System (BIOS) enhancements, including 32-bit BIOS switch, enhanced drive access, multiple-block addressing or rapid integrated device electronics (IDE), write-back cache on disk controllers, and power management features. If you are using any of these features, you should disable them prior to installation or replace the device with one found on the HCL.

HARD DRIVE PROBLEMS

If you encounter an error during setup that you suspect is related to the hard drive or controller, you should immediately power down, then check all cables to ensure that the device is connected properly. After confirming the physical aspects of the devices, check for other potential problems, as explained in Table 14-3.

> **Note**
> If you are running Setup on a system with a SCSI device that is not supported by one of the supplied drivers, you should copy the proper Windows NT device driver onto the boot floppy disk before beginning the Setup process. Be sure to check the HCL for notes regarding SCSI adapters and any limitations associated with specific adapters.

If you are installing Windows NT on a mirrored partition, you must disable mirroring before running Setup and then reestablish mirroring after the installation is complete. If these steps do not resolve the problem, consult with your hardware manufacturer.

Table 14-3   Troubleshooting Drive Issues

Type of Drive	Troubleshooting Issues
SCSI	■ Is there a valid boot sector on the drive? ■ Are all SCSI devices properly terminated? ■ If you are using a passive terminator, upgrade to an active terminator. ■ Is BIOS enabled on the boot (initiating) SCSI adapter? ■ Is BIOS disabled on all non-initiating SCSI adapters? When BIOS is enabled on a non-initiating SCSI adapter, it can fail at startup and/or interfere with hardware interrupt 13 calls to the initiating hard-drive controller, preventing your computer from starting and creating random hangs during installation. ■ Is the SCSI ID for your boot drive set at zero? ■ Have you checked your cables for problems? ■ Does your SCSI configuration comply with the appropriate standards?
EIDE	■ Verify that the system drive is the first drive on the first IDE controller on the motherboard. ■ In the system BIOS, verify that file I/O and disk access are set to standard. Most computers ship with access set to either 32-bit or enhanced access.
IDE	■ Verify that the controller is functional in a different computer, if possible. ■ If the drive is larger than 1024 cylinders, make certain you are using a supported disk configuration utility. ■ Verify that the drive jumpers are set correctly for a master, slave, or single drive.

INSTALLING A SECOND INSTANCE OF WINDOWS NT FOR TROUBLESHOOTING

14

During the setup process, you may see error messages that state that necessary files are missing or corrupt or you may have problems with drivers that prevent you from reaching the graphical portion of the installation process. You can place a second basic installation of Windows NT on your system to assist you in recovery should your primary installation become unstable. If you take this route, you can edit the BOOT.INI file to remove reference to the second installation from the startup list, thereby protecting it from changes. In an emergency, you can then restore the entry to direct the OS loader to the location of the protected version.

If you are installing to a drive other than C: and the primary drive is FAT, edit your BOOT.INI file and change the partition information by taking the following steps:

1. At the command prompt, type **ATTRIB –S –R C:\BOOT.INI**. This command removes the Read Only and System File attributes from the BOOT.INI file.

2. Open Notepad or another text editor.

3. Change the Windows NT line in BOOT.INI as follows: **multi(0)disk(x) rdisk(0)partition(y)\winnt="Windows NT on z:"** where x is the drive number, y is the partition number, and z is the drive where Windows NT resides. This command will change the location BOOT.INI looks for Windows NT.

4. At the command prompt, type **ATTRIB +S +R C:\BOOT.INI**. This command restores the proper attributes to the file.

INCORRECT HAL

You should also ensure that the correct hardware abstraction layer (HAL) is installed, especially when dealing with multiprocessor systems. Table 14-4 describes several problems involving an incorrect HAL.

Table 14-4   Problems Resulting from Installing the Wrong HAL

Problem	Result
Attempt to install a multiprocessor HAL on a single-processor machine	Installation fails.
Attempt to install a single-processor HAL on a multiprocessor machine	Installation succeeds but only one CPU can be used until the HAL is updated to the proper level.
Attempt to install an incorrect multiprocessor HAL on a multiprocessor machine	During restart from the character-based mode within the Setup wizard, an error message appeared, stating that HAL.DLL is missing or corrupt. Alternatively, you receive a message that states: "HAL: Bad APIC version. HAL: This HAL.DLL requires an MPS version 1.1 system. Replace HAL.DLL with the correct HAL for this system. The system is halting."

To solve a problem relating to an incorrect HAL:

1. Restart Setup.

2. As soon as the message "Windows NT is examining your hardware configuration" appears, press **F5**. A list of various computer types appears.

3. Select your computer type in the list. For example, if you are using an Intel Pentium-based computer with a single processor, choose "Standard PC." If your computer type does not appear on the list, select "Other" and then insert the disk containing the HAL supplied by your computer manufacturer.

4. Press **Enter** to continue with Setup.

BOOT FAILURES

Failures can also occur while the Window NT server is booting. An error at this stage can be difficult to diagnose, as not enough of the system is operational to take advantage of any utilities that could provide additional information. This situation is further complicated by the lack of displayed information. In such a case, you must rely on your knowledge of the behind-the-scenes action to identify and resolve the dilemma.

UNDERSTANDING THE BOOT PROCESS

To determine the cause of a boot process error, you need to understand the various stages of the boot process. The first part of the boot process, the preload sequence, goes as follows:

1. NTLDR (NT Loader) reads BOOT.INI and displays its contents for selection.

2. OS selection occurs or a timeout selects the default selection.

3. If Windows NT is the selected operating system, OS Loader invokes NTLDR.

4. NT Loader runs NT DETECT and builds a hardware list that includes all settings, such as IRQ, port address, DMA, and so on.

5. NT Loader loads the kernel.

6. NT Loader loads the HAL.

7. HKEY_LOCAL_MACHINE\System is loaded.

8. Drivers with a start value of zero (such as SCSI and network) are loaded.

9. The kernel (NTOSKRNL.EXE) takes over. Windows NT is loaded. The CurrentControlSet is copied to the Clone Set and creates the Hardware hive from the data gathered by NT DETECT.

Any error that occurs during the preload sequence is at a very low level and probably relates to a driver or other system file that has been deleted or corrupted. To resolve such an error, you will almost certainly need to use an emergency repair disk or reinstall Windows NT.

After the preload sequence, the kernel initialization phase occurs. During this phase, the drivers (such as the keyboard, mouse, and video drivers) that are set for "START=1" load.

14

After the kernel initializes, the services load. During this phase, drivers with "START=2" are loaded, as are the session manager (SMSS.EXE) and the Win 32 Subsystem. SMSS.EXE checks each partition by using AUTOCHK.EXE to set up pagefiles as defined in HKEY_LOCAL_MACHINE\SYSTEM\CurrentControlSet\Control\Session Manager\Memory Management. After all drives are checked and memory management is resident, the Software hive is loaded along with required subsystems (by default, only the Win 32 Subsystem is required).

Next, the Windows Subsystem starts loading WINLOGON.EXE, LSASS.EXE, and SCREG.EXE. LSASS.EXE, the local security authority, is responsible for displaying the Welcome logon box. SCREG.EXE, the Service controller, is responsible for loading services in the order determined by their dependencies.

When a user logs on, the CLONE control set is set to replace the LastKnownGood setup. Once CLONE is copied, the system considers the boot to be successful.

It is a good idea to wait a few moments before logging in (particularly after making changes). This delay allows the system to discover faulty device drivers and report a problem while you still have the potential to restart with the LastKnownGood settings.

If a Windows NT Server computer does not initialize all services successfully, you can still verify that the files required for each service have been successfully loaded. Drivers are loaded in many phases of the Windows NT system initialization.

NTLDR attempts to load all drivers with a START value of 0 during the boot sequence. During the load sequence, the kernel attempts to initialize those drivers loaded by NTLDR; it then loads all drivers with a START value of 1. The Session Manager loads all drivers with a START value of 2 during its processing. Device drivers with a START value of 3 are loaded as required by the initializing services.

The DRIVERS.EXE utility, which is included in the Windows NT Resource Kit, verifies that each driver was successfully loaded. To determine if drivers are missing from the list that DRIVERS.EXE generates, run DRIVERS.EXE on a similar computer and compare the results.

You can repair or replace a corrupted file in several ways. EXPAND.EXE, when run with an −R switch, will install a new version of the missing or corrupt file. The emergency repair process (discussed in the next section) will produce the same results. It can also identify which files are corrupt or missing in some cases. The emergency repair disk is a particularly good way to restore a missing or corrupt registry hive file.

> When a service is behaving improperly, you can often stop and restart the service to either correct the behavior or produce an error message that provides more information about the problem.

EMERGENCY REPAIR PROCESS

In the event of a system failure, the emergency repair process is one of the most important tools available to you.

To begin the emergency repair process:

1. Insert the **Windows NT Setup Disk 1** in drive A, then start the computer.

2. Insert **Disk 2** when prompted.

3. When the Windows NT Setup Welcome window opens, type **R**.

4. Select the desired repair options, as described in Table 14-5, and follow the prompts.

Table 14-5   Repair Options

Repair Option	Explanation
Inspect registry files	This option prompts for the replacement of each registry file on the system. Any changes to the registry hives SECURITY and SAM will be lost, and these files will be restored as they were upon system installation. Changes to SOFTWARE and SYSTEM are restored as of the last update to the emergency repair information.
Inspect startup environment	This option verifies that Windows NT is a choice in the Operating System Select menu. If this selection is not listed in the BOOT.INI file, the option adds a Windows NT choice for the next boot attempt.
Verify Windows NT system files	This option identifies and offers to replace files that have been altered from their original state on the Windows NT CD-ROM. It also verifies that boot files, such as NTLDR and NTOSKRNL.EXE, are present and valid. To discover whether one or more service packs need to be reinstalled, check FILES.LST for each service pack.
Inspect boot sector	This option verifies that the primary boot sector still references NTLDR, and updates the boot sector if it does not. This feature is useful if someone uses the MS-DOS SYS.COM utility on the hard disk, wiping out the Windows NT boot sector and replacing it with MS-DOS. It can also be helpful when certain viruses infect the master boot record. Inspecting and repairing the boot sector will restore it to Windows NT, and preserve the ability to dual-boot to MS-DOS.

If you know the name of the missing or damaged file, you can use EXPAND -R to retrieve the file from the Windows NT CD-ROM, uncompress it, and store it in the proper directory. If Windows NT is not functioning, using EXPAND –R is more difficult, because EXPAND is a Windows NT command. Try using EXPAND from another Windows NT machine to restore the file if it has connectivity to the targeted drive. You can also uncompress the file and copy it to a bootable floppy disk, then transport the floppy to the computer that needs it. If you cannot access the machine (perhaps because it has an NTFS partition), you can install another copy of Windows NT in a different directory (or use a copy that you preinstalled for this purpose); you can expand the necessary file into the appropriate location via the second installation.

Windows NT creates a REPAIR directory under %SystemRoot% in which it stores the emergency repair disk files. You can use the RIDISK.EXE utility to update the SOFTWARE and SYSTEM hives in the REPAIR folder and create an emergency repair disk.

To update all of the emergency repair disk files, you can click the Start button, click Run, then type "rdisk /s" in the Open text box. Using the "/s" switch forces the Repair Disk program to update the registry keys in the %SystemRoot%\Repair folder. You can use either the diskette or the REPAIR directory to make any needed repairs.

CORRUPTION OF THE BOOT SECTOR BY MBR VIRUSES

A corrupt boot sector can prevent access to BOOT.INI, making it difficult to load the operating system. The most common cause of a corrupt boot sector is a master boot sector virus. Even if the drive is formatted as an NT File System (NTFS), the master boot record (MBR) can become infected. In such a case, Windows NT may not see the hard drive properly. If you are concerned about the presence of a virus, scan each drive for viruses.

PRINTER PROBLEMS

Printing problems on Windows NT can be hard to solve because of the many variables and the wide variety of print devices and clients supported by this operating system. To troubleshoot printing problems, you must determine the point in the printing process at which the failure occurred or, at the very least, stages in the process that took place without error.

Each troubleshooting step should be aimed at eliminating one stage of the printing process until you have honed in on the actual problem. If necessary, review the explanation of the printing process in Chapter 13. You should also search for documented solutions to similar problems in the product documentation, online help material, and the Microsoft Knowledge Base.

By default, Windows NT stores a number of the modules needed for printing in \%systemroot%\SYSTEM32\SPOOL. Table 14-6 describes these files in more detail.

Table 14-6   File Locations for Printing Files

Subdirectory	Contents
\DRIVERS	All locally used print drivers are stored here. Subdirectories of this directory separate the drivers by platform (for example, Intel, MIPS, and Alpha).
\PRINTERS	Spool files are stored in this directory while a print job is spooling.
\PRTPROCS	This directory for the print processor includes subdirectories for each platform, similar to \DRIVERS. These subdirectories will themselves have subdirectories for each print provider. For example, for Intel-based machines, the default print processor, WINPRINT.DLL, is stored in \PRTPROCS\W32X86\WINPRINT\.
\%SystemRoot%\SYSTEM32\	All other components are stored in this directory, with each component being listed under HKEY_LOCAL_MACHINE\ SYSTEM\CurrentConrolSet\Control\Print.

RAS CONNECTIVITY PROBLEMS

Because of the large number of subsystems involved in the Remote Access Service (RAS), a methodical approach to troubleshooting RAS problems is absolutely essential. In addition, you need to understand how the connection sequence works to help identify where a problem may be occurring. This process is covered in depth in Chapter 5.

The following sections describe some of the most common RAS troubleshooting issues.

RAS-SPECIFIC LOGS

You can use the PPP log, Device log, and auditing when troubleshooting RAS. To enable these features, you must modify the registry. If you are using the **Routing and Remote Access Service (RRAS)** update, the PPP log and Device log do not apply. Instead, refer to the RRAS logging section for information on enabling connection trace information. The PPP and Device logs are text only and cannot be viewed in Event Viewer.

PPP Log

The PPP log records all **Point-to-Point Protocol (PPP)** events to the file %systemroot%\ SYSTEM32\RAS\PPP.LOG. You can use this file to help determine the stage of the connection at which a failure is occurring. PPP logging is most helpful if you have a good understanding of the PPP protocol (described in RFC 1332, 1334, 1549, 1552, and 1661). Even without this knowledge, however, you can use this log to search for valuable clues to the PPP connection process.

To enable the PPP log, go to the following key and change the Logging value to 1:

HKEY_LOCAL_MACHINE\SYSTEM\CurrentControlSet\Services\RasMan\PPP

Device Log

The Device log records communication between the serial port and the RAS device (modem or otherwise). Logging stops after a successful connection is established. This process can help to determine whether your problem is related to communication between the port and the device attached. The Device log, found at %systemroot%\SYSTEM32\RAS\DEVICE.LOG, is enabled by setting the following registry key to a value of 1:

HKEY_LOCAL_MACHINE\SYSTEM\CurrentControlSet\Services\RasMan\Parameters

Auditing

It is also possible to audit RAS, thereby recording successes and failures in Windows NT's event log. To enable auditing, set the following registry subkey to 1:

HKEY_LOCAL_MACHINE\SYSTEM\CurrentControlSet\Services\ RemoteAccess\Parameters

14

As described in Table 14-7, you can choose to audit several different kinds of events.

Table 14-7   Event Types

Event Type	Description
Audit—Success	Normal behavior that includes most information about client connections
Audit—Failure	Normal behavior that indicates a session has been inactive too long or that a user tried to log on with invalid credentials
Warning	Any irregular event that does not have an impact on system functionality
Error	A major event or failure that has an impact on functionality

RRAS Trace Information

If you are using RRAS Update, the audit events described in Table 14-7 are not applicable. Instead, you can take advantage of as many as 27 different types of logging or "tracing" that can be enabled through the registry and output to a file or to the console. These log files are located in the %SystemRoot%\Tracing directory.

To enable tracing:

1. Click **Start**, click **Run**, then type **Regedt32.exe** in the Open text box.

2. Go to the following key in the registry:
   HKEY_LOCAL_MACHINE\SYSYTEM\CurrentControlSet\Services\Tracing

The value of EnableConsoleTracing determines whether console tracing will be permitted or denied for all subkeys; 0 is "off" and 1 is "on." Once console or file tracing is enabled, tracing is turned on or off individually for each of the subkeys.

You can trace the following subkeys: IPRIP2, IPRouterManager, MIB-II Subagent, MIB-II Utility, OSPF, OSPFMIB, PPP, RASADHLP, RASAPI32, RASCHAP, RASCPL, RASDLG, RASIPCP, RASIPHLP, RASMAN, RASMON, RASSCRIPT, Router, IPBOOTP, IPX Traffic Filter Logging, IPXCP, IPXRIP, IPXRouterManager, IPXSAP, IPXWAN, RASAUTO, and RASNBFCP.

Which subkeys are traced depends on which protocols and services are installed on the computer.

TROUBLESHOOTING PROTOCOL PROBLEMS WITH RAS

After eliminating connection issues as the potential source of your system's problems, you should start your troubleshooting from the RAS service itself. To simplify matters, begin with the core service. The first step is to ensure that the same protocol is running on both ends of the connection. Once you have determined that both ends of the connection are speaking the same language, you should consider the issues explained in the following sections. Although the following discussion centers on troubleshooting TCP/IP RAS connections, the same principles can be applied to other protocols as well.

As you learned in Chapter 3, the TCP/IP suite provides several utilities to assist you in gaining low-level information about a given connection. This section assumes that you have reviewed the "Troubleshooting TCP/IP" section in Chapter 3.

The first TCP/IP utility, PING, can be used to test whether traffic from your station can reach a host on a TCP/IP network. Table 14-8 explains how to gain troubleshooting information using the PING utility.

Table 14-8   Using PING to Troubleshoot RAS Connections

Command	Response	Meaning
ping *IP address*	Reply from IP address	Host is reachable. You are connected properly.
ping *IP address*	Request timed out	Host is not reachable. There is a connectivity problem of some kind.
ping *IP address*	Destination net unreachable	A routing issue exists. The RAS server cannot communicate with that IP address.
ping *host name*	Bad IP address	Problem with the name server (either WINS or DNS).

> **Note**
> If you are using **Point-to-Point Tunneling Protocol (PPTP)**, PING may not work for troubleshooting. If the administrator has set up PPTP filtering, the server will accept only PPTP packets. In this case, the server will not accept PING requests.

As explained in Table 14-9, you can use Net View to help determine if hosts on your TCP/IP network are reachable by name via WINS.

Table 14-9   Using Net View for RAS Troubleshooting

Command	Response	Meaning
net view *server name*	Returns information about the server	Server can be reached via WINS
net view *server name*	No information returned	Either a problem with WINS exists or the specified server is not available

WNTIPCFG is a graphical tool that gives you information about your current IP configuration. This tool can be found in the Windows NT Server 4.0 Resource Kit (Supplement 2). The DOS-based IPCONFIG provides much of the same information.

To use WNTIPCFG:

1. Click **Start**, click **Run**, and then type **wntipcfg**. The WNTIPCFG utility opens. Here you can see your IP address and the IP address of your default gateway.

2. Click **More info**.

3. The IP Configuration dialog box opens (as shown in Figure 14-1), giving your IP address, the subnet mask, and the default gateway for each of your network interfaces, including the interface for your network adapter, your dial-up networking (DUN) interface, and your PPTP interface.

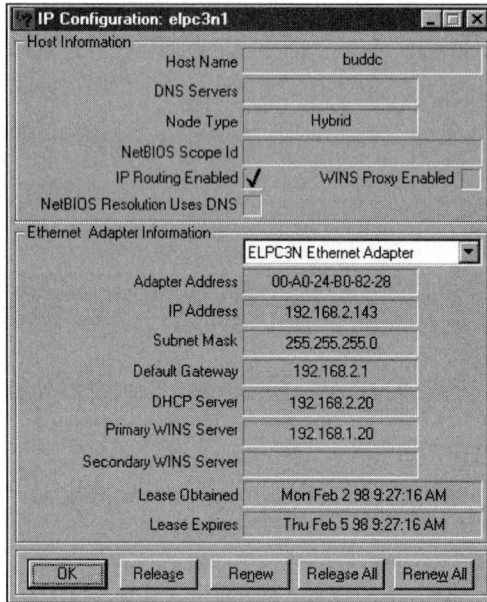

Figure 14-1   IP Configuration dialog box

You can use the DUN Monitor (accessed via the Control Panel) to monitor elements of a call. As Figure 14-2 shows, the Status tab of the DUN Monitor dialog box allows you to review the speed at which you connected, the duration of the connection, the names of users connected to a RAS server, protocols used during the connection, and the devices that are part of a connection.

RASADMIN, the RAS Administrator utility, provides real-time information about users, ports, modems, and data transmissions. To use it, you must log on as an Administrator. To access this utility on a computer running RAS, look in the Administrative Tools (Common) group on the Programs menu.

MULTIPLE VERSIONS OF RAS

When troubleshooting RAS problems, remember that several different versions of the RAS client have been released to accompany the various versions of Microsoft's operating systems. The versions included in the following list should be interoperable, but they may behave differently depending on your environment. Newer RAS features, such as the Multilink protocol, are available only in Windows NT 4.0 and later versions.

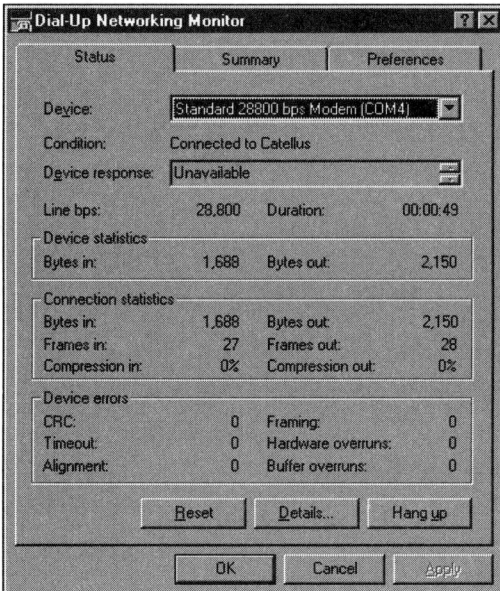

Figure 14-2   Status tab of the DUN Monitor dialog box

The list of RAS versions includes the following:

- Microsoft Remote Access for MS-DOS, versions 1.0, 1.1, and 1.1a
- Microsoft Remote Access for OS/2 (version 1.3), versions 1.0 and 1.1
- Microsoft Windows for Workgroups, version 3.11
- Microsoft Windows 95
- Microsoft Windows NT operating system, version 3.1
- Microsoft Windows NT Advanced Server, version 3.1
- Microsoft Windows NT Workstation, versions 3.5, 3.51, and 4.0
- Microsoft Windows NT Server, versions 3.5, 3.51, and 4.0

RAS HARDWARE ISSUES

If you suspect hardware-based RAS problems, you should first verify that the selected hardware is on the HCL. Next, consider the issues explained in the following sections.

Testing Modems Using HyperTerminal

You can use HyperTerminal to make sure a modem is functioning properly. To test a modem with HyperTerminal:

1. Click **Start**, point to **Programs**, point to **Accessories**, then click **HyperTerminal**. When the Hyperterminal folder opens, double-click **HYPERTRM.EXE**. The Connection Description dialog box opens.

2. In the Name text box, type the name you wish to assign to this connection, then click **OK**. The Connect To dialog box opens. HyperTerminal will test the first modem listed in the Connect using list box.

3. Click **Cancel** to accept the default setting. The HyperTerminal window opens.

4. In the HyperTerminal window, type **AT**.

5. Your modem should return the text "OK" if it is functioning properly. Some modems return 0, depending on their settings. If HyperTerminal returns the appropriate value, you have ruled out that modem as a potential cause of the problem.

Connection Problems with Supported Modems

A modem can be on the HCL and still be the source of a RAS connectivity problem. For example, your modem might not work at the speeds supported by other modems. To avoid a conflict between modems, you should use the same model of modem with the same firmware on each end of the connection.

If you are using supported modems and have a connectivity problem:

1. Make sure your cabling is correct and that all connections are secure.

2. Check the modem's documentation to verify that the modem has been correctly installed.

3. Using a terminal emulator program (such as Windows NT HyperTerminal), try to issue commands to the modem.

4. Turn on device logging in the registry, as described earlier.

Connection Problems with Unsupported Modems

It is possible that a modem not listed on the HCL will work with RAS. If you must use such a modem, make sure that it supports one or more standards described in Table 14-10. Except where mentioned, the information in this table comes from the ITU-T (formerly CCITT) standard. ITU is an international organization that focuses on telecommunications.

Table 14-10 Supported Modem Standards

Standard	Speed
V.22	1200 bps
V.22 *bis*	2400 bps
V.32	4800–9600 bps
V.32 *bis*	4800–14,400 bps
V.fc and V.fast (proprietary modulation schemes)	2400–28,800 bps
V.34	2400–33,600 bps
V.90	2400–57,600 bps

When configuring an unsupported modem for RAS, you should select a device from the list of supported modems that matches your modem's capabilities as closely as possible. If you are unsure of which modem matches best, compare entries in the MODEM.INF file with commands for your modem as listed in the modem's documentation.

If you have trouble establishing a connection with an unsupported modem, test the modem's compatibility as follows:

1. Check the modem's documentation to make sure it is installed and configured correctly.

2. Make sure your modem is powered up and connected to a serial port on your computer; in addition, verify that your software is set for the same port.

3. Check to see whether the modem works properly with HyperTerminal. If this test works, you can rule out the possibility that the modem is malfunctioning.

4. If the modem doesn't work after Step 3, contact the manufacturer and request a modem command file compatible with the RAS Modem.inf file.

SECURITY

When troubleshooting RAS problems, you need to ensure that the party dialing in has sufficient rights on the server. Permission to dial in can be set in the Remote Access Administrator or in User Manager. Failure to give such permission prevents authentication at the server. You also need to consider the hours during which a user may dial in. If the server's clock shows the time to be outside of the permitted hours, the connection will fail. If the user is already logged on at a point where permission then becomes invalid, the user's session will terminate.

BAD PHONE LINE

Another common problem in maintaining a connection is the quality of the phone line. A phone line with a great deal of static or intermittent signal drop can have an adverse effect on your RAS session. If, after troubleshooting, you suspect this situation to be the case, you should contact your local exchange carrier for line repair.

14

POINT-TO-POINT TUNNELING PROTOCOL (PPTP)

A RAS server is usually connected to a telephone network, whether it is analog (**PSTN**), digital (**ISDN**), or **X.25**, allowing remote users to access a server through these networks. With Windows NT Server 4.0, RAS allows remote users to gain access through the Internet via the new PPTP.

PPTP supports multi-protocol **virtual private networks (VPNs)**, enabling users to establish secure access to corporate resources over an untrusted network, such as the Internet. Given the additional level of complication that protocols such as PPTP add, you will want to remove it from the troubleshooting process as early as possible. If you have exhausted other possibilities, and the problem seems to arise from PPTP, you need to consider the following issues.

Verifying Your PPTP Configuration

A PPTP connectivity problem could lie with either the server or the client. Ruling out the client as a possibility is fairly easy if other users can connect successfully. Otherwise, you should verify the following:

1. Make sure that your workstation and its applications support the protocols native to the target network (the network to which you will be tunneling).

2. If you are tunneling through the Internet, make sure your Internet connection is working properly.

3. Using the Network applet, make sure that you have added the PPTP protocol.

4. Using the Network applet, make sure that you have configured at least one VPN port.

5. Check the phonebook entry for the PPTP server to make sure it applies to a VPN device, not a modem.

6. Make sure you have a valid account on the PPTP server.

7. Check the phonebook entry for the PPTP server to ensure that it includes the IP address or host name of the PPTP server.

8. Check the phonebook entry for the PPTP server to ensure that it includes all of the protocols used on the target network.

9. If the target network uses TCP/IP, check the phonebook entry for the PPTP server to verify that the TCP/IP settings are correctly configured for the target network.

> **Note** When you make a PPTP connection, dial-up networking changes your default gateway to be the IP address of the PPTP server.

10. If you are making two connections, make sure that the second connection is a VPN connection.

Troubleshooting Your PPTP Connection

If you cannot connect to a PPTP server, try the following steps:

1. Ping a known good host, such as *www.microsoft.com*.

2. If the PING text does not reach *www.microsoft.com*, ping a known good host by its IP address. For *www.microsoft.com,* this address would be ping 207.68.156.16.

3. If the PING test succeeds, you are properly connected to the Internet, but not properly configured for your DNS server.

4. If the PING test fails, you might not be connected to the Internet. Ask your ISP to confirm that you are set up properly.

5. After you have confirmed your settings with your ISP, ping the IP address of the PPTP server.

6. If you receive a response, you are properly connected to the PPTP server. Verify that you did not originally enter an incorrect user name or password.

7. If you do not receive a response, the administrator of the PPTP server might have turned on PPTP filtering, which prevents you from pinging this server. Contact the administrator of the PPTP server.

8. Check for a firewall. **Firewalls**, or systems that protect a network from the Internet, are often configured with security settings that filter out PPTP packets. If you believe that this situation may apply in your case, contact your administrator and the ISP and ask if a firewall exists. If it does, ask them to pass TCP port 1723 and IP protocol 47 (GRE, Generic Routing Protocol).

9. Check for a proxy server. At the time of this writing, you cannot create a PPTP tunnel that passes through a proxy server. Therefore, if your internal network uses a proxy server to handle all Internet traffic, you will not be able to create a tunnel so as to access resources on the corporate network. An exception occurs if you configure the proxy server to act as a PPTP server as well. This setup will allow you to securely access resources on the proxy server and, in so doing, access corporate resources. The PPTP process will answer all PPTP requests, and the proxy server will answer all other requests.

10. Increase the number of retransmissions. If your server does not respond, you can increase the number of attempts that PPTP makes to transmit data. Edit the PPTPTcpMaxDataRetransmissions registry entry, in the following registry path:

    HKEY_LOCAL_MACHINE\System\CurrentControlSet\Services\ Tcpip\Parameters

14

> The default value of this parameter is 9h. You should not increase the value to exceed 25h.

11. Determine whether you have high latency in your PPTP connection. If your PPTP connection is slow, check to see if you have latency to other sites on the Internet by using PING. If your PING test to Internet sites such as *www.microsoft.com* and *www.compaq.com* shows a response time of more than five seconds, you have a slow Internet connection. In this case, you should contact your ISP.

12. Check the load on your PPTP server. If you do not experience problems with other sites on the Internet, but have latency issues with your PPTP server, the PPTP server may be overloaded. Contact the administrator of the PPTP server or use Perfmon on that server.

Partial Connectivity via PPTP

If you can connect via PPTP, but cannot access all of the servers that you should be able to reach, it may indicate the presence of a segmentation issue or a problem with the default gateway. Keep in mind that PPTP uses the PPTP connection as the default gateway. This change to the gateway may introduce network routing problems on networks that possess more than one segment, because more than one default gateway cannot exist at any one time. Figure 14-3 shows a configuration with a default gateway defined. In contrast, Figure 14-4 shows the same network once a PPTP connection is established.

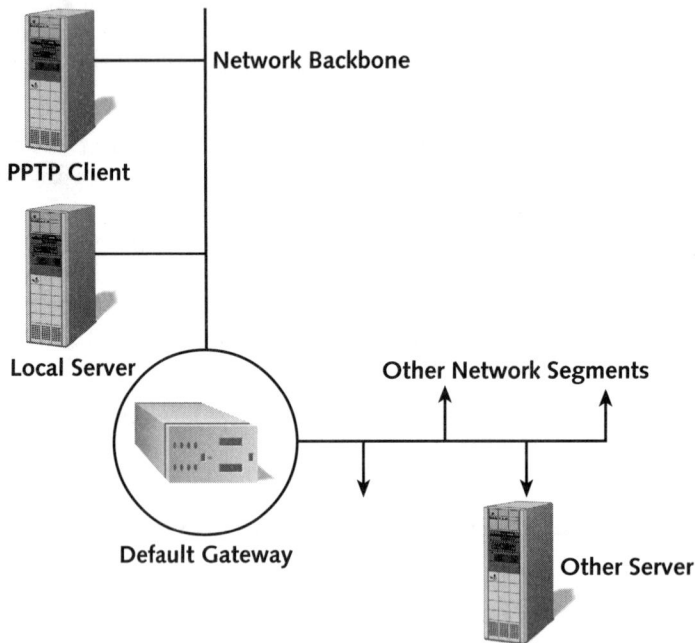

Figure 14-3   Default gateway

> You can circumvent the problem arising from a change to the default gateway by using the ROUTE command to manually add routes to servers you wish to access.

Removing PPTP

If the presence of PPTP makes troubleshooting too difficult, you may wish to remove it. The process for removing PPTP is as follows:

1. In the Control Panel, click **Add/Remove Programs**.
2. Remove all dial-up networking components.
3. Restart your computer.
4. Reinstall dial-up networking without the PPTP component.

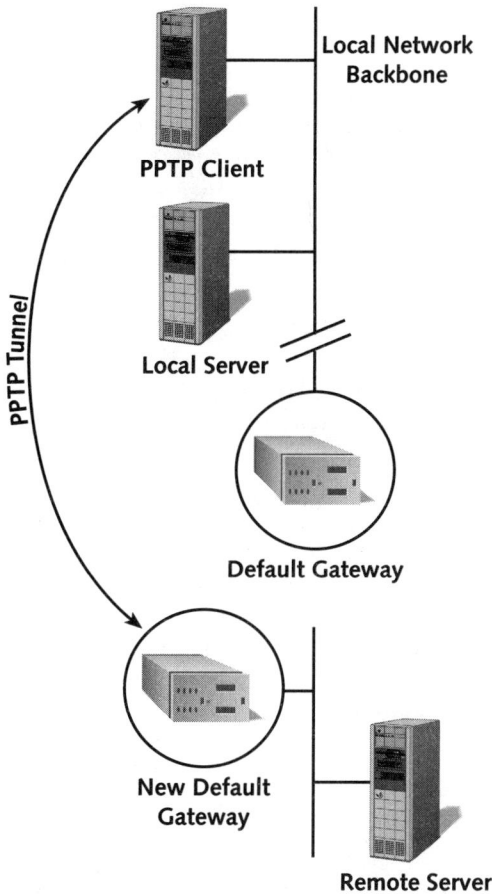

Figure 14-4   Same network as in Figure 14-3 after tunneling to a different server

14

MULTILINK CONNECTIONS

Multilink connections take multiple phone lines and concatenate them into a single connection. From a troubleshooting perspective, any of these lines could create problems, as could the Multilink service itself. Multilink will work only if multiple WAN adapters (ISDN, modem, or X.25) are available on the computer. Both the client and the server must have Multilink available to successfully use this service.

Configuring RAS for dial-back service can also cause problems with Multilink. If RAS is configured for dial-back, only one device will be called, as only one phonebook entry exists for each user. In this situation, one multilinked device will connect and the rest will fail, thus causing a loss of Multilink functionality (and bringing a corresponding reduction in connection speed). An exception to this situation occurs when an ISDN adapter is configured for two channels that have the same phone number.

CONNECTIVITY PROBLEMS

Most connectivity problems involve a Windows NT server and a client running Windows 3.x, Windows 95, or Windows NT Workstation. When faced with connectivity problems, you must first determine whether the trouble relates to the workstation or in the server. Think of connectivity troubleshooting in terms of the **Open Systems Interconnect (OSI)** model—that concept that will force you to work in a systematic manner. When troubleshooting a workstation or server, therefore, you should first verify connectivity at Level 1 of the OSI model by ensuring that everything is plugged in and properly connected. When checking the connection, also check that the appropriate OK lights on the networking hardware are working (for example, green lights on the NIC and hub). Often, these lights will help you verify Level 2 connectivity, or at least tell you whether these components are indicating a problem. Once you have verified Level 1 and Level 2 connectivity, then you are ready to move up the OSI model and consider Level 3, the Networking level.

NETWORK CONNECTIVITY

To verify Level 3 connectivity, check whether the NIC can send its frames onto the network via Level 3 protocols such as IP and IPX. You can verify this fact by using utilities such as PING and TRACERT, which can determine whether two machines on a network are able to successfully deliver packets between them, identify missing or unreachable hosts on the network, and point to misconfigured local TCP/IP settings.

If tools such as PING reveal problems with the workstation's ability to exchange packets with other hosts on the network, you can use tools like those described below to further isolate the problem. You can use PING not only to identify basic connectivity problems, also use it to point out host name and NetBIOS name resolution problems on a TCP/IP network. If you can PING by direct IP address but not by name, then you have identified a problem with either DNS or WINS. You should then check your DNS and WINS settings for that workstation.

> Depending on the troubleshooting utility you are using (such as Net View or PING), you will be working with either NetBIOS names or host names. While they are often considered identical, slight but important differences separate the two. True TCP/IP-based utilities and applications (such as PING and DNS) rely on host names. Windows NT networking services, such as WINS and its related commands (such as the Net View command), rely on NetBIOS names. Because host names and NetBIOS names; are separate entities, it is possible for there to be differences between NetBIOS and host names; these differences can create difficulties in troubleshooting IP-based networks.

If your problem relates to the resolution of a NetBIOS name to an IP address, then the problem is ultimately an LMHOSTS or WINS issue. In this case, try using the NBTSTAT utility (accessed via the Run dialog box) to check the states of all current **NetBIOS over TCP**

(NBT) connections. It allows you to view and update the LMHOSTS cache of NetBIOS names, and determine the registered name and scope ID. Table 14-11 explains the various NBTSTAT commands.

Table 14-11   NBTSTAT Commands

Command	Description
NBTSTAT –c	Checks the local copy of the NetBIOS name cache
NBTSTAT –R	Purges and reloads the NetBIOS name cache
NBTSTAT –r	Lists the NetBIOS names that have been resolved

The NSLOOKUP utility helps isolate and troubleshoot DNS problems by allowing you to send directed name lookup queries to DNS servers; you can then review the information returned on DNS resolved requests. At the command prompt, type NSLOOKUP, the host name you are seeking, and the name server that should perform the lookup. The DNS server you specified will return the information on the host you specified. Remember, however, that NSLOOKUP is a host name utility. If you have not implemented DNS–WINS integration, this tool will tell you only what is provided for host name resolution, not NetBIOS name resolution. You must use NBTSTAT or some other NetBIOS-based utility to handle NetBIOS name resolution issues.

> HOSTS and LMHOSTS files are primarily supported for backward-compatibility reasons. The HOSTS file does play a role in host name resolution, and the LMHOSTS file does play a role in NetBIOS name resolution. Check these files early in the troubleshooting process if you experience resolution problems.

If you are able to verify network connectivity via PING, then you can safely rule out problems in the first three OSI layers. You should then turn your attention to the higher application layers of the OSI model, as explained in the next section.

14

NETWORKING SERVICES PROBLEMS

In troubleshooting the networking services, which lie in the Application layer of the OSI model, remember that NetBIOS forms the heart of Windows NT networking. Even if you are running IPX or IP without NetBEUI on your network, Windows NT will rely on NetBIOS to provide most of its Transport-level networking (Layer 6 in the OSI model).

If you are running a routed IP network, be sure to enable the NetBIOS ports (TCP and UDP Ports 137–139) on your router. If your routers block these ports, your Windows NT servers and Windows-based client workstations will be unable to access one another across the router. Windows NT servers will not be able to exchange directory information, making it impossible for backup domain controllers to synchronize their actions with primary domain controllers.

You have several tools at your disposal in troubleshooting workstation connectivity issues. The Application and System event logs in Event Viewer may illuminate obvious problems within the operating system, such as networking drivers that fail to load, duplicate NetBIOS names on the network, or networking services that fail to start. If Event Viewer does not reveal any obvious operating system problems, then you need to gather more information by testing the system.

A very useful tool at this stage is the Net View command (accessible via the command line). To test for NetBIOS-level connectivity between machines, type *net view \\ NetBIOS name*. If your command is successfully executed, it will return a list of shared resources, similar to the one shown in Figure 14-5.

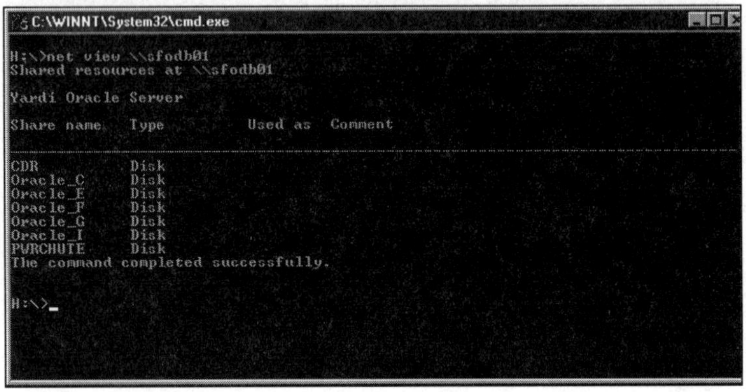

Figure 14-5   Result of Net View command

Using Net View helps identify problems by letting you use the same NetBIOS-based commands that Windows NT uses for basic network connectivity. Not all of Windows NT-based networking is NetBIOS-based, however. Many of the newer Windows NT networking features employ Remote Procedure Call (RPC). If you suspect RPC problems, try using the RPCPING utility (included in the BackOffice Resource Kit for testing Microsoft Exchange Servers), which executes on both the server and the workstation. RPCPING mimics the functionality of the PING utility by sending test data back and forth between the specified workstation and server; it can, therefore, help verify whether all of the core Windows NT components have full connectivity to one another.

RESOURCE ACCESS AND PERMISSION PROBLEMS

When considering resource and access problems, you are generally asking the question, "Which part of Windows NT is denying access, and why?" To answer that question, start by looking at the Windows NT Security log, which you can access by opening Event Viewer and selecting the Security command on the Log menu. Figure 14-6 shows a sample Security log.

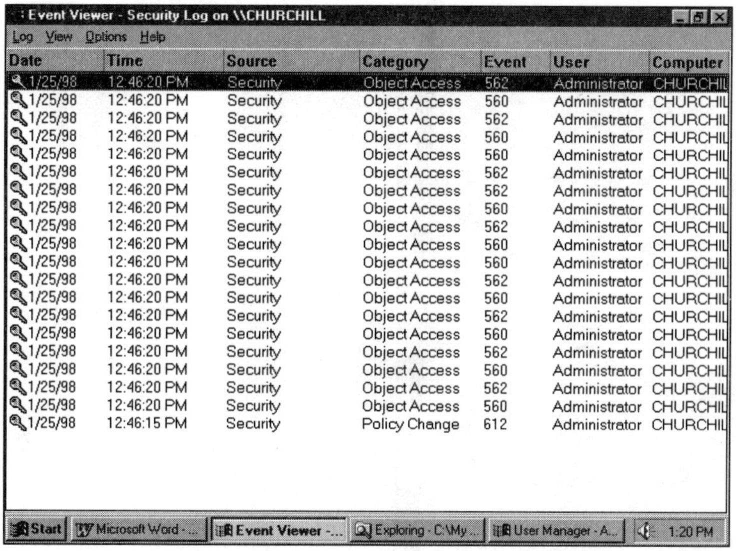

Figure 14-6 Windows NT Security log displayed in Event Viewer

When you audit in Windows NT, you target object access, such as file and directory access. All audited events are placed in the Security log. A gold key indicates a successful event; a gray lock indicates an unsuccessful event. Each entry includes time, category, and user information. Remember that all events happening under Windows NT occur within some account security context. When SYSTEM is shown as the user, for example, it indicates that the Windows NT system account actually performed the actions in question.

To see details on any item, double-click the item. Figure 14-7 shows the details for one such event.

To enable event or file auditing in Windows NT, you must first enable event auditing through the User Manager. To configure event or file auditing, you need to understand the differences between these types of audits. Each tracks slightly different information, and each is configured as a separate feature.

14

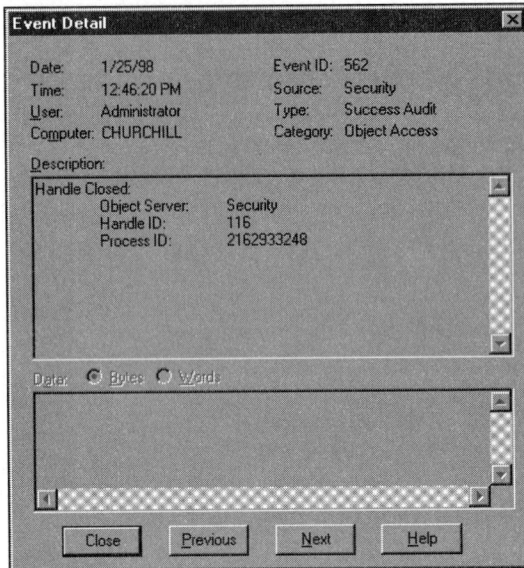

Figure 14-7   Event Detail dialog box

EVENT AUDITING

As explained in Chapter 8, you can configure your system to audit events by clicking Policies on the menu bar, then clicking Auditing. The Audit Policy dialog box will open, allowing you to choose audit events such as users logging on and logging off, the use of user rights, and restart or shut down of the system. You can also choose to audit the access of files or objects. When Windows NT audits file access, it also audits directory access.

FILE AUDITING

To enable file auditing, you must first enable event auditing for file and object access. File (and directory) auditing allows you to monitor failed attempts to access information, identify the accounts in use, and determine the source of the denial. To enable auditing for a file or directory, open Windows NT Explorer, right-click the directory or file you wish to audit, click Properties, click the Security tab, then click Auditing. The Directory Auditing dialog box, shown in Figure 14-8, will open.

Notice in the dialog box that you can configure the system to track access for Local Groups, Global Groups, Special Built-in Groups, and individual users.

> **Note**
> Before you make any changes to the registry, no matter how small, you should make a backup of the entire registry, in case you need to revert to the old configuration. While most backup software programs, including Windows NT Backup, include the ability to backup and restore the registry, this can also be done through the Registry Editor. For example, use the Export Registry file or Import Registry file commands in REGEDIT to perform these tasks.

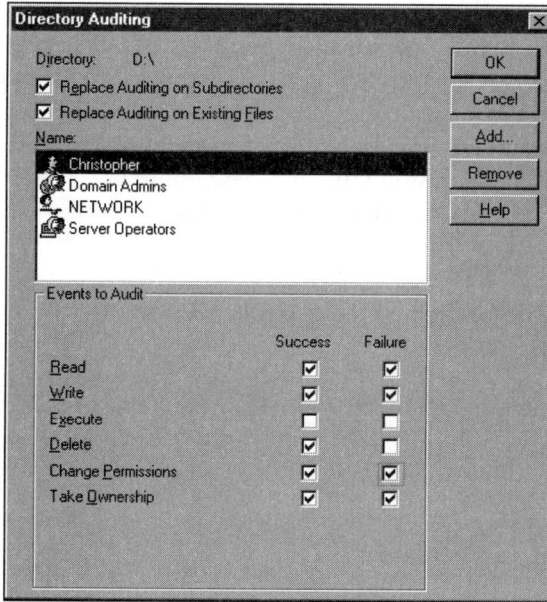

Figure 14-8   Directory Auditing dialog box

FAULT-TOLERANCE FAILURES

This section covers problems involving Windows NT software-based fault tolerance. Because your backup strategy should figure prominently in any fault-tolerance strategy, it will also cover troubleshooting steps for Windows NT-based backup.

CREATING A MIRROR SET BOOT FLOPPY DISK

To use your Windows NT mirrored or duplexed drive for recovery during a failure, you must create a Windows NT bootable floppy disk that will allow your system to access and run the operating system contained on that drive. This floppy disk is necessary because of the very structure of Windows NT. Remember that both the BOOT.INI file (on Intel) and the firmware profile (on RISC) tell OS Loader where the Windows NT system partition is located and how it should be loaded. The syntax of BOOT.INI specifies the location of the system partition not by traditional drive letter names, but through a convention called **Advanced RISC Computing (ARC)**. (This setup applies even for Intel-based CISC systems.) ARC conventions specify the system partition based on the disk's controller number, the disk's own number on that controller, the SCSI ID of the disk (in some instances), and the partition number on which the system partition resides.

On RISC machines, the firmware in the system performs this function. To boot off of a mirrored copy of Windows NT, a **firmware profile** (much like the profile of BOOT.INI) must be created, with each profile pointing to a loadable system partition.

The BOOT.INI and firmware profile from your original installation of Windows NT maintain a pointer to the partition into which you installed Windows NT. When you create a mirrored system partition, however, it will be located in a different physical location than the original installation. (For mirroring, your mirrored copy will occupy a different partition number. For duplexing, the mirrored copy will be on a different controller number.) Thus, to access and use your mirrored copy of Windows NT, you must use a BOOT.INI or firmware profile that specifies the physical location of the mirrored partition—not the live partition.

PREPARING AN INTEL SYSTEM FOR MIRRORED RECOVERY

To prepare your Intel system for mirrored recovery, you will create a bootable Windows NT floppy disk and modify a copy of BOOT.INI. You accomplish this goal by creating a Windows NT boot floppy disk with a modified BOOT.INI that points to your mirrored installation.

To create the boot floppy for Intel mirror recovery:

1. Open **Windows NT Explorer**, click **View** on the menu bar, click **Options**, click the **View tab**, then click **Show all files**.

2. Insert a floppy disk into the disk drive, right-click the **disk drive** in the left pane, then click **Format** in the pop-up menu.

3. For each file you copy, in Windows NT Explorer, click **File** on the menu bar, click **Properties**, click the **General tab**, then deselect the **Read Only**, **System**, and **Hidden check boxes**.

4. Find the following files in the root of your system partition and copy them to the floppy: **NTLDR**, **BOOT.INI**, and **NTDETECT.COM**.

5. In the left pane, right-click **BOOT.INI** on the floppy disk, then click **Open** in the pop-up menu.

> **Note**
> If your BOOT.INI uses SCSI rather than MULTI syntax, copy the file NTBOOTDD.SYS as well. NTBOOTDD.SYS is a renamed copy of the SCSI driver that your system needs to see the controller card.

This process creates the bootable Windows NT floppy disk. Now you need to change the BOOT.INI file you copied from your live Windows NT system so that it points to your mirrored system partition.

BOOT.INI contains two entries for Windows NT. Figure 14-9 shows an example of a typical BOOT.INI.

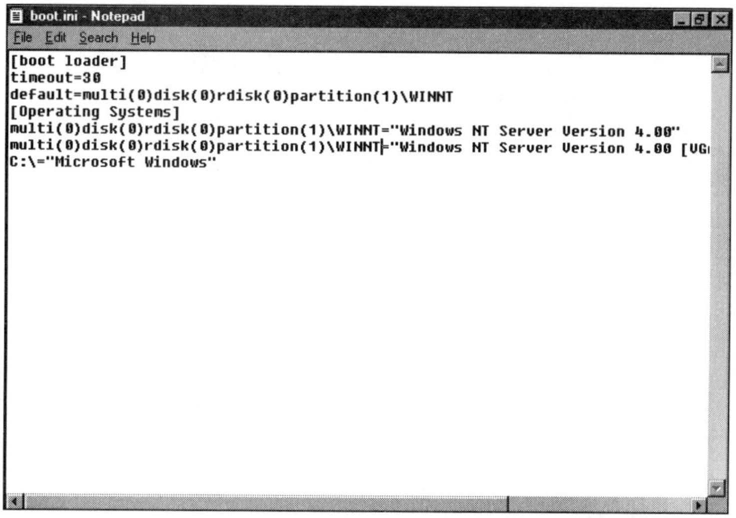

```
boot.ini - Notepad                                           _ 6 X
File  Edit  Search  Help
[boot loader]
timeout=30
default=multi(0)disk(0)rdisk(0)partition(1)\WINNT
[Operating Systems]
multi(0)disk(0)rdisk(0)partition(1)\WINNT="Windows NT Server Version 4.00"
multi(0)disk(0)rdisk(0)partition(1)\WINNT="Windows NT Server Version 4.00 [VG
C:\="Microsoft Windows"
```

Figure 14-9   BOOT.INI file

The syntax is broken into four parts, with each part providing information on the physical location of the system partition.

- Multi() or SCSI(): This section tells the system the type and number of the controller that holds the Windows NT system partition. Use Multi if the system BIOS is used for system files. If a SCSI BIOS controller is used, choose SCSI(X) where X represents the ordinal number of the disk controller as identified by its driver.

- DISK(): For Multi() entries, this entry is always 0. For SCSI entries, it is the SCSI ID of the disk.

- RDISK(): For Multi() entries, this part is the ordinal number of the disk on the controller. For SCSI() entries, it is the SCSI logical unit number of the disk, and will often be 0.

- Partition(): For both Multi() and SCSI() entries, this part will be the number of the partition on which the system resides. For this entry, note that counting begins at 1, rather than 0 like the other entries.

With this syntax in mind, you can now alter your BOOT.INI file to point to your mirrored Windows NT system partition. Figure 14-10 shows you the same BOOT.INI file modified to point to a mirrored copy of Windows NT.

14

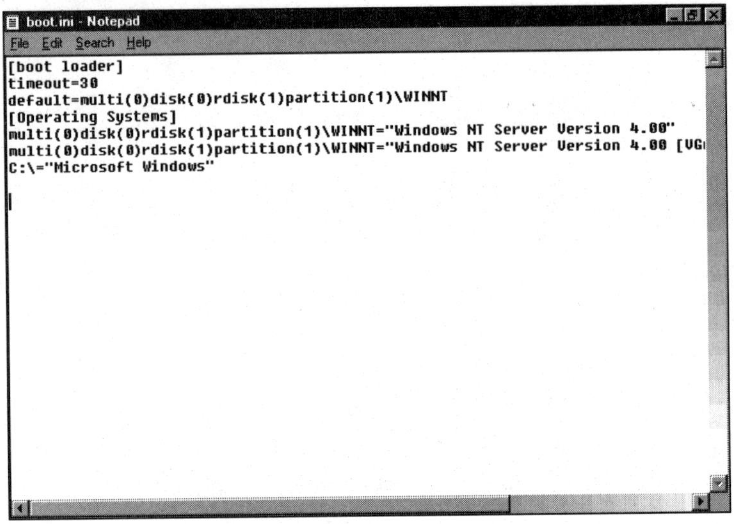

Figure 14-10   Modified BOOT.INI file

Preparing a RISC System for Mirrored Recovery

To prepare a RISC system for mirrored recovery, you will need to create a bootable Windows NT floppy disk and a new firmware profile.

1. Open **Windows NT Explorer**, click **View** on the menu bar, click **Options**, click the **View tab**, then click **Show all files**.

2. Insert a floppy disk into the disk drive, right-click the **disk drive** in the left pane, then click **Format** in the pop-up menu.

3. Create a directory called **Os\Winnt40** on the floppy disk.

4. For each file you copy, in Windows NT Explorer, click **File** on the menu bar, click **Properties**, click the **General tab**, then deselect the **Read Only**, **System**, and **Hidden check boxes**.

5. Find the following files on the root of your system partition and copy them to the floppy disk: **Osloader.exe** and **HAL.DLL**. For AXP-based computers, also copy ***.pal**.

This process creates the bootable floppy disk. Next, you need to create a firmware profile that points to the mirror. Each hardware platform differs in this respect, and you will have to check your manufacturer's documentation for more details.

To reboot a machine to the mirrored copy of the operating system, simply insert the bootable floppy disks that you created and select the appropriate firmware profile for RISC machines. If properly configured, your system should boot seamlessly from the mirrored partition. At this point, you can treat the recovery of your system partition like any other partition recovery in a mirrored set.

RECOVERING FROM A FAILURE

General mirror recovery under Windows NT is actually a fairly simple process. For partitions other than the boot partition, the fail-over should be invisible at the operating system level as Windows NT begins to use the mirror copy rather than the original. Member disk failures will generate Windows NT error messages. Thus, although such a failure may be invisible to the users, the network administrator will be aware of the problem.

When you receive notification of a failed member of a mirror set, you should immediately perform a full backup of the system. Until the fault-tolerant volume is replaced, your system remains vulnerable to data loss from a second failure. If both disks of a mirror set fail, all you have left is the backup.

Once you have completed a full backup, you need to take the system down to replace the failed member. If your system has other unallocated drives installed or includes hot-pluggable drives, you will not need to restart the system to perform this operation. Otherwise, you should schedule a shutdown as soon as possible and replace the failed member of the set.

Once you make a new mirror set, Windows NT copies the data from the current hard drive to the new mirror.

> **Caution**
> Make sure your BOOT.INI or firmware profiles are still accurate. If you booted off of a copy of the system partition, and the replacement drive does not have identical ARC characteristics, your system may not restart without the boot floppy disk.

STRIPE SET WITH PARITY

Because RAID 5 cannot be used to protect a system partition, there are no extra steps to take to recover a system partition under this setup. Recovery simply cannot be done at the Windows NT level. Hardware-based RAID 5 is an option, however, and Windows NT system partitions can reside on hardware-based RAID 5.

When you experience a RAID 5 failure under Windows NT, your first action should be to perform a full backup of the system. As with RAID 1, your system remains vulnerable to total data loss from a second failure after the initial fault-tolerant failure. While RAID 5 spreads data across more disks than RAID 1, it does not provide any extra protection from a second failure.

Once you have completed a backup of the system, you must replace the failed member as soon as possible. This procedure requires a restart of the system to install the replacement unit, unless you have unallocated drives already in the system or your hardware supports hot-pluggable drives.

14

Once a replacement drive is available for RAID, Windows NT can regenerate the data on the lost member. To accomplish this task, open Disk Administrator, select the array with the failed member, select the unpartitioned space in the drive you have made available, click Fault Tolerance on the menu bar, then click Regenerate. Data will be regenerated on the new member from the parity stripe on the remaining members of the original array. Once regeneration is complete, the array is fully functional and your data are protected again.

TAPE BACKUP

If you are faced with a situation where you must rely on your tape backup to recover your system when dealing with fault-tolerance issues, you are most likely addressing a complete loss of the system. In this case, backup is more complicated than just simply restoring a few files. You must rebuild your entire Windows NT system—a process involving several steps.

The first step is to repair any failures that led to the loss of your system. If you experienced two failed drives on a RAID 5 array, replace both of them. Once your system is bootable off of the Windows NT setup disks, you are ready for the next step.

When using the Backup utility that ships with Windows NT (and most third-party backup applications), a working copy of Windows NT must be present on the machine to permit the restore operation. Thus you need to perform a fresh installation of Windows NT into a different destination directory. (You will delete this copy of Windows NT when you are finished.) The version you install must be the same base version as the version you are trying to restore. You should also load the service packs present on the dead system to bring it into parity (SP1, SP3, and so on).

After you finish installing Windows NT, you should be able to log on to the system once again. At this point, the crucial issue is that you gain access to the drives on the system from within Windows NT. Once you reach Windows NT, open Disk Administrator and recreate your Windows NT drive configuration. If you have a copy of your old configuration on disk, load it by using your Disk Configuration floppy disk. If you do not have this configuration, you must reconstruct it manually from memory or documentation. You should recreate your partition information, drive letter assignments, and any fault tolerance, such as RAID 5.

Once your new disk configuration has become identical to that on your old system, you are ready to restore the system using the Windows NT backup program or a third-party application. If you are using a third-party application, you must load that application first. When your backup application is ready, you can then load your tapes from your last complete, good backup.

> **Tip**
> When restoring a server that is a primary domain controller, you may want to consider promoting one of your backup domain controllers to primary status. This approach will allow you to continue adding accounts to the domain and will minimize complications caused by a missing PDC. If you take this route, be sure to forcibly demote the old PDC to backup status to synchronize it with the current PDC. Otherwise, your old PDC may overwrite the current directory with its older, out-of-date copy.

You will probably want to perform a full restore of all files on your old system, including the operating system. If your backup spans several tapes, you will probably need to perform a cataloging operation before you begin the restore steps.

> You will probably have to edit BOOT.INI to point to the restored installation of Windows NT in addition to your temporary copy.

Once the restore operation is complete and BOOT.INI has been changed, if necessary, restart the system. During the boot sequence, choose the restored copy of Windows NT. Allow the system to finish starting and check the event log for any error messages. Check Windows NT Explorer to ensure that all of the files you restored are in their proper locations, with the correct permissions. Once you have verified that the restoration was successful and that no errors occurred, your system should be fully operational.

CHAPTER SUMMARY

- Installation problems can be caused by several things, including incorrect information provided during the text-based portion of installation, hardware not included on Microsoft's Hardware Compatibility List (HCL), a system that does not meet minimum requirements, incorrect detection of controllers and settings, and old drivers.

- To make it easier to restore your system in the event of an installation failure, you should document all configurations, including the IRQ and memory addresses, any extended settings, and hardware information for every adapter in your system. If you encounter an error during setup that you suspect is related to the hard drive or controller, you should first verify all connections and then check for other issues related to your particular type of drive. You can install a second basic installation of Windows NT on your system to assist you in recovery should your primary installation become unstable. In that case, you can edit the BOOT.INI file to remove it from the startup list to protect it from changes; in an emergency, you can then restore the entry to point the OS loader to the location of that version. You should also make sure that the correct hardware abstraction layer (HAL) is installed, especially when dealing with multiprocessor systems.

- To determine the cause of a boot process error, you need to understand the various stages of this process. You may then be prepared to use the emergency repair process to resolve the problem. A corrupt boot sector can prevent access to BOOT.INI, making it difficult to load the operating system. If you are concerned about a virus, scan each drive for viruses.

- Printing problems on Windows NT can be difficult to solve because of the many variables and wide variety of print devices and clients supported by Windows NT. To troubleshoot printing problems, you must determine the point in the printing process at which the failure occurred or, at the very least, stages where failure did not occur.

14

- Because of the great number of subsystems involved in Remote Access Service (RAS), a methodical approach to troubleshooting RAS problems is absolutely essential. You can use the PPP log, Device log, and auditing when troubleshooting RAS. After eliminating connection problems as a potential source of trouble, you should start your troubleshooting from the RAS service itself. To simplify matters, begin with the core service. First, ensure that the same protocol is running on both ends of the connection. Next, consider issues such as incompatible versions of RAS, a malfunctioning modem, the rights of the party dialing in relative to the server, and the quality of the phone line. If you are using the Point-to-Point Tunneling Protocol (PPTP) or Multilink, you should also consider issues specifically related to those features. When you encounter connectivity problems, you should structure your troubleshooting around the Open Systems Interconnect (OSI) model, beginning with verifying connectivity at Levels 1 and 2, and then moving up to Level 3, the Networking level.

- When assessing resource and access problems, you are generally asking the question, "Which part of Windows NT is denying me access, and why?" To answer that question, look first at the Windows NT Security log, which should provide information on event and file auditing.

- For problems involving Windows NT software-based fault tolerance, you need to consider several issues. To use your Windows NT mirrored or duplexed drive for recovery during a failure, you must create a Windows NT bootable floppy disk that will allow your system to access and run the operating system contained on that drive. To prepare your Intel system for mirrored recovery, you will need to create a bootable Windows NT floppy disk and modify a copy of BOOT.INI. To prepare a RISC system for mirrored recovery, you must create a bootable Windows NT floppy disk and a new firmware profile.

- When you receive notification of a failed member of a mirror set, you should immediately perform a full backup of the system. You will then need to take the system down to replace the failed member. Once you have made a new mirror set, Windows NT copies the data from the current hard drive to the new mirror. Note that you cannot recover a system partition at the Windows NT level under RAID 5. If you face a situation in which you must rely on your tape backup to recover your system, you must rebuild your entire Windows NT system—a process involving several steps.

KEY TERMS

- **Advanced RISC Computing (ARC)** — A set of naming conventions developed for RISC-based systems that have been adopted for Windows NT under all architectures. ARC names locate system partitions by pointing to the actual physical controller, drive, and partition for the system partition.

- **firewall** — Hardware exposed on the Internet whose purpose is to secure a connection to the Internet.

- **firmware profile** — The functional equivalent of the BOOT.INI file under Intel-based architecture. It contains configuration information for the loading of system partitions and operating systems.

- **graphical device interface (GDI)** — The graphics engine in Windows NT. It provides a standard set of functions that mediate between applications and graphics devices.

- **Hardware Compatibility List (HCL)** — A list maintained by Microsoft of all computer equipment that has been tested for and is known to work properly with Windows NT.

- **Integrated Service Digital Network (ISDN)** — A digital telephone service that allows for transmission rates of up to 128 Kbps over existing copper telephone wires.

- **Multilink** — A technology that allows concatenation of multiple physical dial-up connections into a single logical dial-up connection. Requires multiple WAN adapters to function.

- **NetBIOS over TCP (NBT)** — An extension of TCP/IP that allows NetBIOS to run on top of TCP/IP. Described in RFCs 1001 and 1002.

- **Open Systems Interconnect (OSI)** — A seven-layer networking model put together by the International Standards Organization (ISO). Used as a common point of reference when comparing implementation of protocols.

- **Point-to-Point Protocol (PPP)** — A standard protocol for connecting systems over dial-up connections. PPP is used in Windows NT as the basis for dial-up networking.

- **Point-to-Point Tunneling Protocol (PPTP)** — An extension of PPP that adds encryption to allow for secured communication between hosts across wide area networks. Usually implemented across the Internet to provide a private secure channel.

- **Public Switched Telephone Network (PSTN)** — A term for the collected matrix of the analog phone lines. Sometimes called Plain Old Telephone Service (POTS).

- **Routing and Remote Access Service (RRAS)** — An update to Windows NT 4.0 that adds routing functionality and allows Windows NT to function as a low-end router over dial-up connections or local LAN connections.

- **time-bomb** — A modification to commercially released software that makes the software inoperable after a defined period of time has elapsed, such as 120 days. Usually installed in evaluation copies of software to ensure licensing compliance.

- **virtual private network (VPN)** — A secure communications channel over the Internet between hosts established through the use of shared encryption. Allows for the transport of sensitive information across unsecure networks.

- **X.25** — A communication standard set by the ITU that breaks up packets for transmission across different physical paths for reassembly at the destination. Best known as the precursor frame relay.

14

REVIEW QUESTIONS

1. The Hardware Comparability List (HCL):

   a. is generated when you install Windows NT Server and lists which components (if any) are compatible with the optional components you have selected

   b. lists hardware that has been tested by Microsoft and is known to be compatible with the operating system

   c. is a graphical utility that helps you to design a Windows NT server

   d. all of the above

   e. none of the above

2. If your hardware is not listed on the HCL (check all that apply):

   a. Windows NT will not install

   b. Windows NT will sometimes install but may have problems

   c. it will not be supported by Microsoft

   d. it could lead to corruption of data

3. Windows NT supports the following (check all that apply):

   a. enhanced drive access

   b. symmetric multitasking

   c. power management

   d. 32-bit BIOS

4. You must _____ mirroring before installing Windows NT.

5. If you attempt to install an incorrect HAL on your computer:

   a. installation will fail

   b. installation will succeed but leave you with only partial capability until you apply the correct HAL

   c. you will receive an error message and the system will halt

   d. any of the above

   e. none of the above

6. When you log on to Windows NT Server, the clone set becomes the
   _____.

7. If a driver is found to be missing or corrupt, you can replace the driver by:

   a. installing the operating system into a new directory

   b. the Emergency repair disk

   c. EXPAND.EXE

   d. all of the above

   e. none of the above

8. The data used to create the emergency repair disk by default is located at _____.

9. The Windows NT printing architecture is _____ to allow great flexibility.

10. The Device log records communication between the _____ and the _____.

11. Auditing on RAS is viewed in:

    a. the Event Log

    b. the registry

    c. AUDIT.LOG

    d. RASADMIN.EXE

12. You enable the Device log and the PPP log in _____.

13. When auditing RAS events, you may see _____ events (check all that apply).

    a. device

    b. warning

    c. alert

    d. all of the above

    e. none of the above

14. A RAS audit failure will occur when:

    a. a session has been inactive too long

    b. a modem does not answer

    c. any irregular event that does not have an impact on system functionality occurs

    d. all of the above

    e. none of the above

15. Routing and Remote Access Service can output its data to (check all that apply):

    a. a file

    b. the Event Log

    c. the console

    d. the Device log

    e. the PPP log

16. When using PING with an IP address, if you receive a "Request Timed Out" it indicates that:

    a. there is a routing problem

    b. the host is not reachable due to a connectivity problem

    c. the host is reachable but you do not have permission

    d. there is a problem with the name server

14

17. DUN monitor can be used to gather information about the following (check all that apply):

    a. connection speed

    b. protocols used in the connection

    c. how long the connection has been in effect

    d. which devices are part of a connection

    e. which users are logged in

18. In a PPTP connection, if you cannot reach the PPTP server:

    a. your Internet configuration is misconfigured

    b. there may be a firewall between you and the server

    c. you may not have permission to access the server

    d. all of the above

    e. none of the above

19. The protocol most important to Windows NT is:

    a. NetBIOS

    b. TCP/IP

    c. NetBEUI

    d. OSI

20. The Security log contains information about (check all that apply):

    a. system shutdown

    b. failures in accessing a file

    c. logons

    d. changes in policy

21. Windows NT has software support for the following RAID levels (check all that apply):

    a. 0

    b. 1

    c. 2

    d. 3

    e. 4

    f. 5

22. The firmware profile is the RISC equivalent to the _____ on the Intel platform.

23. The Windows NT Server software support for RAID 5 can be used to protect any volume. True or False?

24. Using Windows NT software support for RAID 5, if you lose a single drive (check all that apply):

   a. the server will continue operating with no effects being apparent to the user

   b. the failed drive can be swapped with a fresh drive while the system is running and will regenerate itself

   c. you will lose data

   d. after replacing the failed drive, you will need to run the emergency repair disk

25. For the Windows NT Backup applet to operate, your operating system must
   _____.

HANDS-ON PROJECTS

For some or all of these projects you will need a working NT Server running TCP/IP that has two drives configured for mirroring.

PROJECT 14-1

In this project you will use the Disk Administrator to break a mirror set. This strategy is useful if you must remove a failed member.

1. Click the **Start button**, point to **Programs**, point to **Administrative Tools (Common)**, then click **Disk Administrator**. The Disk Administrator window opens.

2. Highlight a mirrored volume.

3. Click **Fault Tolerance** on the menu bar, then click **Break Mirror**.

4. Exit Disk Administrator.

14

PROJECT 14-2

In this project you will use IP utilities to learn about your network. As you proceed through the steps, consider how the information you find could be used when troubleshooting a network problem.

1. From the Start menu, select **Run**.

2. In the Open box, type **CMD**, then press **Enter**.

3. At the DOS prompt, type **ping 127.0.0.1**.

4. Note the information that is returned about your machine.

5. At the DOS prompt, type **ping** *server name*. (Replace *server name* with the name of a server on your network.)

6. Note the information that is returned about your server.

7. At the DOS prompt, type **arp −g**.

8. Note the information that is returned. What does this information tell you? How can it be used when you are troubleshooting a network problem? Write a brief answer (three to four paragraphs).

PROJECT 14-3

In this project you will enable auditing on the %SystemRoot% folder. To complete this project, your %SystemRoot% directory must be on an NTFS partition.

1. Open **Windows NT Explorer**, then select the **WINNT directory**.

2. Click **File** on the menu bar, click **Properties**, then click the **Security tab**.

3. Click **Auditing**. The Directory Auditing dialog box opens.

4. Click **Add**.

5. Click **Show Users**, then, in the Names list box, select the account under which you have been authenticated.

6. Click **OK**. You will return to the Directory Auditing dialog box.

7. Verify that all of the check boxes in the Events to Audit section are selected. Click **OK**.

8. Copy a file from the WINNT directory to your desktop.

9. Close any open dialog boxes. Click **Start**, point to **Programs**, point to **Administrative Tools** (**Common**), and then click **Event Viewer**.

10. Click **Log** on the menu bar, then click **Security**.

11. Note the log entries related to copying the file.

PROJECT 14-4

After completing the steps in Project 14-3, you may want to disable auditing. To disable auding, use the following steps.

1. Open **Windows NT Explorer**, then select the **WINNT directory**.

2. Click **File** on the menu bar, click **Properties**, then click the **Security tab**.

3. Click **Auditing**. The Directory Auditing dialog box opens.

4. Uncheck all boxes, then close the Directory Auditing window.

5. Exit Windows NT Explorer.

CASE PROJECTS

1. You are the network manager for Amalgamated Biotech. You have recently implemented Remote Access Service (RAS) on a pair of Windows NT Server 4.0 servers to connect your Chicago branch office to your corporate headquarters in San Francisco. As several users will be sharing this connection, you are using Point-to-Point Multilink Protocol (PPMP) to concatenate four 33.6K modems into a single connection. Because of the confidential nature of the data being transferred, members of senior management are concerned about security setup. You are using Point-to-Point Tunneling Protocol (PPTP) to address this concern. You had a short timeframe and small budget to put this system together and so were forced to pull various modems from other uses on a temporary basis. As a result, the modems are not exactly identical (although the speeds correlate exactly). Users in the remote office report that they cannot connect to the PPTP server at headquarters. Describe in detail the procedure you would use to isolate the cause of the problem.

2. You have just been hired by Dan Caroll International, an award-winning advertising agency that has experienced huge growth over the past several months. On your first day (a Friday), you were told that you must set up the Des Moines, Iowa, office by the end of the weekend. You arrive in Des Moines to find that hardware and software have already been delivered. The server is a new eight-processor machine but the version of Windows NT is the standard version that could be purchased at any software store. Given that it is a weekend, you cannot reach the server vendor. Describe your plan of action.

3. Your company, Darrian Productions, is a comic book publisher headquartered in Los Angeles. The firm is preparing to file with the SEC a motion to purchase a controlling interest in your rival, New York-based Curium Press, in a cooperative takeover bid. As a part of the due-diligence process, your legal and finance staffs will need 24-hour access to Curium's e-mail and all files that reside on the company's network. After investigation, you determine that your first choice of a frame relay connection will take 45 business days to implement—far too long to be acceptable to senior management. How can you connect your network to the Curium Press network both soon enough and with sufficient bandwidth to maintain a high level of productivity? Cost is not an issue because of the huge amount of money that Darrian Productions will make from the takeover.

4. You work for the law firm of Harmuth, Gerhard, Kemper and Sacks. You have added RAS and PPTP with the goal of improving the productivity of the legal clerical staff. Because downtime is unacceptable in your organization, you installed these new services at one time, without restarting the server. The company works two shifts—one from 8 A.M. to 5 P.M. and another from 5 P.M. to 2 A.M. Because you are on the first shift, you plan to come in early the next day to perform the restart at 6 A.M. You

14

come in and restart the server as planned. After the restart, however, you receive a message you have not seen before—that one or more services failed to start. You manage to get the server up and running to cover normal business but the three new services are not yet operational. Management expects that the services will be operational on Monday. Over the weekend, you will have time to troubleshoot. Describe the process you will take to identify and resolve the cause of the problem.

5. You have successfully completed the RAS setup for the law firm Harmuth, Gerhard, Kemper and Sacks. The RAS connectivity will be used to connect your firm to the accounting firm of Canalita, Chinn, and Vold, with which you are working on a major case. Because the relationship between the two firms is not entirely cordial, what steps should you take to make certain no improper file accesses occur? Write a brief report explaining how you would accomplish this goal.

PERFORMING ADVANCED PROBLEM RESOLUTION

When errors occur within the kernel, they will often take the entire operating system down, because the error affects the core of the operating system, rather than remaining localized within an environment subsystem, such as the Win 32 subsystem. When a critical error occurs at the kernel level, Windows NT will provide as much information as possible to help isolate the problem. Unfortunately, because this error affects the core of the operating system, Windows NT cannot trap it and let you work within the operating system to resolve it. Instead, Windows NT will provide all the information it can about the error and its operating environment in the form of a blue-screen Stop error.

In this chapter you will learn how to prepare your system to log critical errors in the Event Viewer. You will also learn to interpret blue-screen errors. Finally, you will learn about some tools for troubleshooting kernel errors.

AFTER READING THIS CHAPTER AND COMPLETING THE EXERCISES YOU WILL BE ABLE TO:

- Configure your Windows NT server to create a dump file and to use other recovery tools
- Configure your Windows NT server to send alert messages
- Configure your Windows NT server to log kernel-level error messages to the Event Log
- Diagnose and interpret kernel-level errors
- Analyze the dump file

THE DUMP FILE AND OTHER RECOVERY TOOLS

Severe errors that cause Windows NT Server to reboot (sometimes known as a kernel error, or a **Stop error**) can prove very difficult to resolve, because the act of rebooting may remove the problem's symptoms. In the event of a Stop error (or blue screen error), however, you do have several useful tools available via the Startup/Shutdown tab of the System Properties dialog box, shown in Figure 15-1.

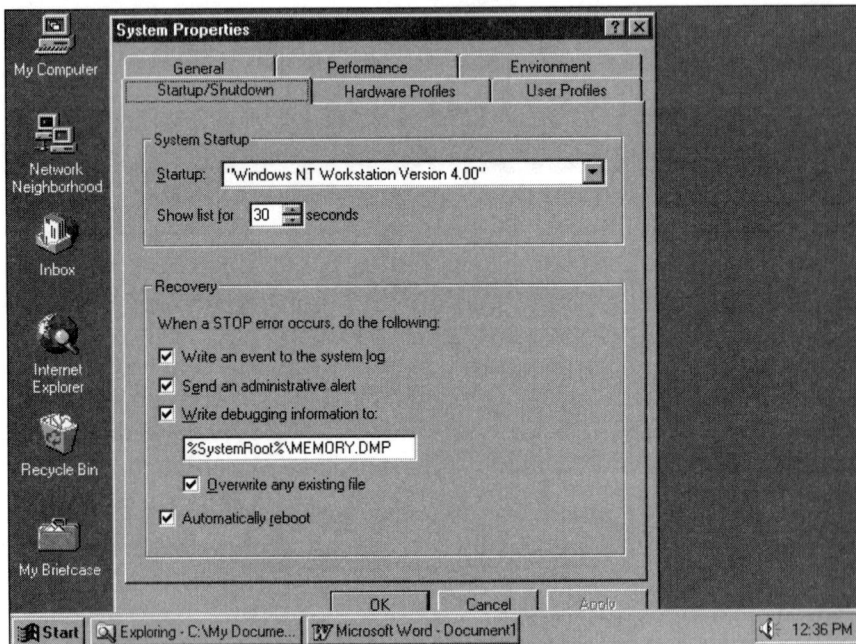

Figure 15-1   Startup/Shutdown tab of the System Properties dialog box

The Recovery section of the Startup/Shutdown tab contains settings related to Stop errors. Among the most important Recovery tools is the ability to write debugging information to a **dump file**. This information includes data on the state of the server from the time that a problem first manifests itself. To configure your server to write to a dump file, select the "Write debugging information to" check box. This and other options are explained in the following list.

- **Write an event to the system log**. This option will add information in the system log prior to a restart regarding the cause of a problem.

- **Send an administrative alert**. In the event of a Stop error, this option will send a popup message to a predetermined workstation (or workstations) via the Windows Messaging service.

- **Write debugging information to**. In the event of a Stop error, this option will capture the contents of memory and write it to a dump file (a process sometimes referred to as a **memory dump**). You can accept the default location for the dump file or type a new location. Once the dump file is created, you can analyze it using tools described later in this chapter. The dump file, which is usually called MEMORY.DMP, takes up the same amount of space in megabytes as the total RAM plus 1 MB. Thus, if you have 128 MB of RAM on your server, you will need 129 MB of available drive space at the specified location to write this file. In addition, you must have a pagefile on your %SystemRoot% drive that at least equals the size of your RAM.

- **Overwrite any existing file**. If you select this option, Windows NT will write over the existing dump file every time a crash occurs. If you choose to overwrite the existing file, you should rename the MEMORY.DMP file after a crash to save its data for analysis at a later time. If you do not choose the overwrite option, and a crash occurs, Windows NT will check to see if a MEMORY.DMP already exists at the specified location; if such a file is present, Windows NT will *not* write a new dump file.

- **Automatically reboot**. This option tells Windows NT to automatically reboot after a Stop error. In most cases, this option is very desirable because it reduces the amount of time during which the server is unavailable. In some cases, however, it can put the server into a loop of crash, reboot, crash, reboot, and so on. If you do enable the Automatically restart option, you will certainly want to select the "Write an event to the system log" check box, and probably the "Send an administrative alert" check box as well.

> The crash recovery settings are stored in the registry under the key HKEY_LOCAL_MACHINE\SYSTEM\CurrentControlSet\Control\CrashControl. This key contains entries that correspond to every setting in the Control Panel System applet. While you should make your changes via the Control Panel System applet whenever possible, knowing the location of the registry keys can prove helpful when you are administering a number of servers over a wide area.

15

CONFIGURING ALERTS

You can configure your server to send administrative alerts (about problems with user sessions, security access, printing, server shutdown, and so on) to a predefined list of users and computers. If you specify a computer, the alert will go to that machine regardless of the user logged on. This option is particularly useful for an administrative workstation that is shared by more than one technician. If you specify a user name, and the user is logged on at more than one location, the alert will go to only one machine. In this case, the user may not see the alert.

For alerts to be sent, both the "Alerter" and "Messenger" services must be running on the computer sending the alert. To receive an alert, the Messenger service must be running on the receiving machine. After you have determined where alerts should be sent, you must restart the Alerter and Server services to implement the changes.

If you stop the Server service on a remote computer using Server Manager, you will not be able to restart that service, because Server Manager needs this service to accomplish that task.

THE EVENT LOG

An event in Windows NT is either an occurrence that is significant to the system or a notification from an application of some predetermined behavior. The Event Log service starts automatically at startup. Services and applications generate events both during startup and throughout the course of normal operations, recording this information to the event log.

There are three types of event logs—the System log, Application log, and Security log. Each is responsible for recording a different type of event. When an event is written to one of these logs, it will contain the following information:

- Date of the event

- Time of the event

- Source of the event (the creator of the event, such as Microsoft Exchange or SNMP)

- Category (additional information on the source that is used when multiple event types exist for a single source; for example, if Microsoft Exchange is the source, the category could be replication)

- Event ID number (an identification number used for looking up additional information)

- User (the user or service account that triggered the event)

- Computer name (the computer on which the event occurred)

Double-clicking on an event in the Event Viewer will often display additional details. For some events, the event log may list additional details, such as text descriptions or binary data. Descriptions of the various event numbers are available in the Windows NT and Back Office Resource kits and supplements.

The System log contains errors, warnings, or information generated by components of the operating system itself, such as the Server and Net Logon services. The selection of events to be recorded is determined by the operating system. Examples of system events include a service failing to start at boot time or a print job completing successfully.

The Application log contains errors, warnings, or information generated by installed applications and services. The application's developer will determine which behavior should generate an event in this event log. Examples of applications that write to the Application log include the various products in Microsoft Back Office (Exchange Server, SMS, SNA Server, SQL Server, and so on) as well as optional services such as Directory Replication.

The Security log shows events generated by the security subsystem. It can contain information on valid and invalid logon attempts and events related to resource use, such as creating, opening, or deleting files or other objects. The determination of which events appear in the Security log depends on the auditing policies you have set for your computer. You specify which events will appear in this event log by making selections in the Auditing Policy dialog box. To view the Security log, you must be logged in with administrative rights.

VIEWING EVENT LOGS

To view an event log, click Start, click Programs, select Administrative Tools (Common), then click Event Viewer. The Event Viewer window, shown in Figure 15-2, will open.

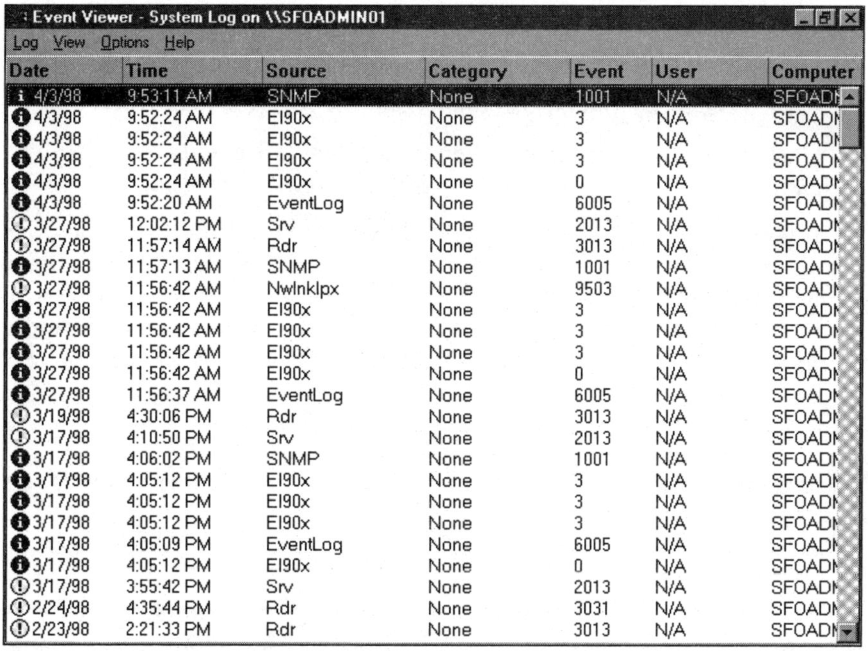
Event Viewer - System Log on \\SFOADMIN01
Log View Options Help

Date	Time	Source	Category	Event	User	Computer
4/3/98	9:53:11 AM	SNMP	None	1001	N/A	SFOADI
4/3/98	9:52:24 AM	El90x	None	3	N/A	SFOADI
4/3/98	9:52:24 AM	El90x	None	3	N/A	SFOADI
4/3/98	9:52:24 AM	El90x	None	3	N/A	SFOADI
4/3/98	9:52:24 AM	El90x	None	0	N/A	SFOADI
4/3/98	9:52:20 AM	EventLog	None	6005	N/A	SFOADI
3/27/98	12:02:12 PM	Srv	None	2013	N/A	SFOADI
3/27/98	11:57:14 AM	Rdr	None	3013	N/A	SFOADI
3/27/98	11:57:13 AM	SNMP	None	1001	N/A	SFOADI
3/27/98	11:56:42 AM	Nwlnklpx	None	9503	N/A	SFOADI
3/27/98	11:56:42 AM	El90x	None	3	N/A	SFOADI
3/27/98	11:56:42 AM	El90x	None	3	N/A	SFOADI
3/27/98	11:56:42 AM	El90x	None	3	N/A	SFOADI
3/27/98	11:56:42 AM	El90x	None	0	N/A	SFOADI
3/27/98	11:56:37 AM	EventLog	None	6005	N/A	SFOADI
3/19/98	4:30:06 PM	Rdr	None	3013	N/A	SFOADI
3/17/98	4:10:50 PM	Srv	None	2013	N/A	SFOADI
3/17/98	4:06:02 PM	SNMP	None	1001	N/A	SFOADI
3/17/98	4:05:12 PM	El90x	None	3	N/A	SFOADI
3/17/98	4:05:12 PM	El90x	None	3	N/A	SFOADI
3/17/98	4:05:12 PM	El90x	None	3	N/A	SFOADI
3/17/98	4:05:09 PM	EventLog	None	6005	N/A	SFOADI
3/17/98	4:05:12 PM	El90x	None	0	N/A	SFOADI
3/17/98	3:55:42 PM	Srv	None	2013	N/A	SFOADI
2/24/98	4:35:44 PM	Rdr	None	3031	N/A	SFOADI
2/23/98	2:21:33 PM	Rdr	None	3013	N/A	SFOADI

Figure 15-2 The Event Viewer window

You can view the three log types on your server or on other Windows NT machines on your network. To select the specific log type or computer, use the File menu. The title bar will reflect the computer and the log being viewed.

The event type is indicated by the icon at the left. A stop sign indicates an error, a yellow exclamation point indicates a warning, a blue "i" indicates information, a yellow key indicates a successful audited event, and a gray key indicates a failed audited event. You can also sort and filter events based on specific characteristics, such as the event ID, date range, or event source.

Managing Event Logs

To set parameters for each event log, you can use the Log Settings command in Event Viewer's Log menu. Among other things, you can specify a maximum size for each log. You can also specify whether the log file overwrites events as needed, overwrites events after a specified number of days, or never overwrites events. The last option requires the administrator to clear the log manually.

> ⚠ **Caution**
> When making your selection, keep in mind that your server will fail if the Event Log service cannot record an event due to a lack of space.

To manually clear a log file:

1. Open **Event Viewer**.

2. Click **Log** on the menu bar, then select the log you want to clear.

3. Click **Log** on the menu bar, then click **Clear all events**. A dialog box appears, asking if you want to save the events before clearing the log.

4. If you want to save the log data, click **Yes**, enter a name for the log file, then select the file type you wish to use. (You can choose from among log file format, text only, and comma delimited for the file type. If you save in any format other than log file format, then you will lose any extended information and will be unable to view the archived log with Event Viewer.) If you do not want to save the log data, click **No**. In this case, your events will be unretrievable.

> 📝 **Note**
> You can also save your log data (without clearing the log) by using the Save As command on the File menu.

Diagnosing and Interpreting Kernel-Level Errors

Once you have taken the preliminary steps to enable Event Viewer logging and memory dumps, your system is ready for you to begin troubleshooting, should a kernel-level error occur.

When a kernel-level error occurs, you will see either a blue-screen Stop error message or a character-based Windows NT error message that identifies hardware failures in your system, such as memory errors or CPU failures. These hardware-based error messages are easier to interpret than Stop error messages are, but they are not necessarily less important than Stop error messages. Both hardware- and Stop-related error messages emanate from the Windows NT Executive, and are sometimes referred to as **Executive error messages**.

BLUE-SCREEN STOP ERROR MESSAGES

A blue-screen Stop error message is a serious matter—so serious that it is sometimes referred to as the "blue screen of death." Unlike other types of errors, blue-screen errors often require the assistance of Microsoft Tech Support. Nevertheless, you can gather information from Stop errors that point you in the right direction, making it possible to resolve some blue-screen Stop errors on your own.

When troubleshooting Stop errors, you should first establish when the error occurred. One category of Stop errors occurs only during the initialization of the kernel. As you probably know, kernel initialization is one of the last phases of this sequence. Thus, if your machine generates a Stop error during this sequence, then the problem very likely relates to initialization.

> To determine the time of the Stop error, you can check Event Viewer for the Stop error's entry. In addition, you can use Event Viewer to get a feel for the current activity at the time of the Stop error, which may in turn point you toward the cause of the error.

Keep in mind that a Stop error message is generated at the same time that the system creates the dump file. Thus, if you choose not to configure your system to create a dump file, you lessen your chances of actually viewing the blue-screen Stop error message. What's more, if you choose not to configure your system for event logging, you may miss a Stop error entirely. For this reason, it is crucial that you configure some form of logging. Note, however, that these recovery options pertain to Stop errors, not hardware errors. Hardware errors will stop the system until you perform a cold reboot (usually by cycling power on the system).

Another type of Stop error, a **software-trap error**, occurs when the CPU detects a problem in the executing instruction, which is located within the kernel part of the executive services. Software-trap Stop messages can result from divide by zero errors or invalid memory address allocation or access attempts. If your Stop error is neither a software trap nor a kernel initialization failure, you will have to consult the actual Stop message and interpret the information it provides to gain insight into what happened when the Stop was raised. You will learn how to interpret a Stop error message later in this chapter.

15

HARDWARE ERROR MESSAGES

Hardware failures that affect the Executive directly (for example, uncorrected memory parity errors) generate hardware error messages. These messages are similar to blue-screen Stop errors insofar as they are character-based and displayed on a blue screen. By convention, however, they are not referred to as "blue screen" or "blue screen of death" errors. Like blue-screen Stop Errors, these Executive-level errors will bring your system down immediately.

Hardware messages differ depending on the hardware component that caused the error and the manufacturer of that component. The appropriate response to a hardware error will also vary accordingly. Whatever form it takes, the error will provide information specific to the operating environment, helping to identify the cause of the hardware failure. For example, errors regarding EISA devices will sometimes include EISA slot number information.

As with all error messages, when a hardware error occurs, you should write down the exact text of the resulting message. Next, you should consult with the component's manufacturer to determine the appropriate response. Usually, some form of hardware diagnostics is in order to test the accuracy of the Windows NT error and to identify the true cause of the error. Sometimes Windows NT is aware of only one part of what is actually a sequence of failures. Thus the hardware error message may point not to the actual cause of the initial failure, but rather to one of the initial results of that failure.

INTERPRETING THE BLUE-SCREEN STOP ERROR MESSAGE

As mentioned earlier, you can identify kernel-initialization Stop errors based on the time of their occurrence. For all other Stop errors, the exact type will not be immediately obvious. Instead, you will need to interpret the jumble of blue and white on the screen by dividing it into meaningful parts. A sample blue-screen Stop error message is shown in Figure 15-3.

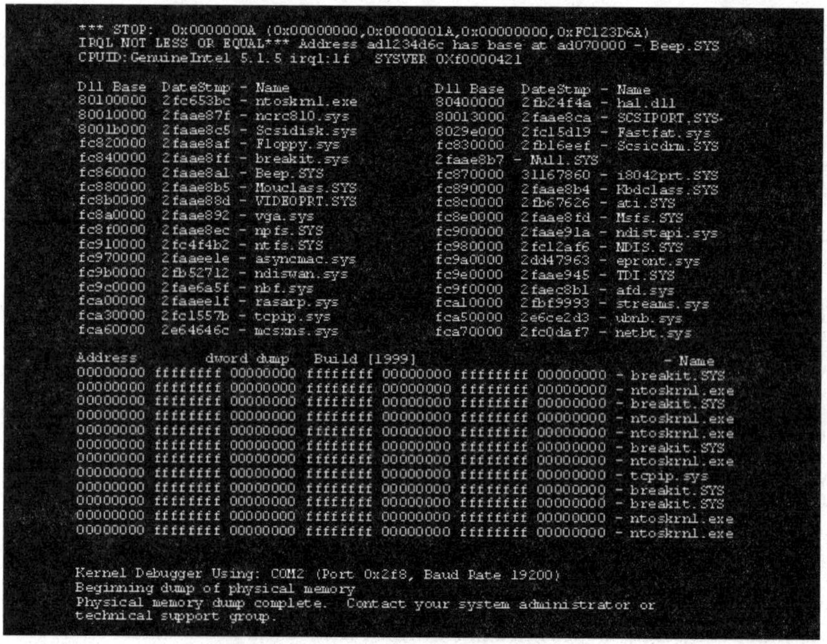

```
*** STOP:  0x0000000A (0x00000000,0x0000001A,0x00000000,0xFC123D6A)
IRQL NOT LESS OR EQUAL*** Address ad1234d6c has base at ad070000 - Beep.SYS
CPUID:GenuineIntel 5.1.5 irql:1f    SYSVER 0Xf0000421

Dll Base   DateStmp - Name                 Dll Base   DateStmp - Name
80100000   2fc653bc - ntoskrnl.exe         80400000   2fb24f4a - hal.dll
80010000   2faae87f - ncrc810.sys          80013000   2faae8ca - SCSIPORT.SYS
8001b000   2faae8c5 - Scsidisk.sys         8029e000   2fc15d19 - Fastfat.sys
fc820000   2faae8af - Floppy.sys           fc830000   2fb16eef - Scsicdrm.SYS
fc840000   2faae8ff - breakit.sys                     2faae8b7 - Null.SYS
fc860000   2faae8al - Beep.SYS             fc870000   31167860 - i8042prt.SYS
fc880000   2faae8b5 - Mouclass.SYS         fc890000   2faae8b4 - Kbdclass.SYS
fc8b0000   2faae88d - VIDEOPRT.SYS         fc8c0000   2fb67626 - ati.SYS
fc8a0000   2faae892 - vga.sys              fc8e0000   2faae8fd - Msfs.SYS
fc8f0000   2faae8ec - npfs.SYS             fc900000   2faae91a - ndistapi.sys
fc910000   2fc4f4b2 - ntfs.SYS             fc980000   2fc12af6 - NDIS.SYS
fc970000   2faaeele - asyncmac.sys         fc9a0000   2dd47963 - epront.sys
fc9b0000   2fb52712 - ndiswan.sys          fc9e0000   2faae945 - TDI.SYS
fc9c0000   2fae6a5f - nbf.sys              fc9f0000   2faec8bl - afd.sys
fca00000   2faaeelf - rasarp.sys           fcal0000   2fbf9993 - streams.sys
fca30000   2fc1557b - tcpip.sys            fca50000   2e6ce2d3 - ubnb.sys
fca60000   2e64646c - mcsxns.sys           fca70000   2fc0daf7 - netbt.sys

Address       dword dump  Build [1999]                     - Name
00000000 ffffffff 00000000 ffffffff 00000000 ffffffff 00000000 - breakit.SYS
00000000 ffffffff 00000000 ffffffff 00000000 ffffffff 00000000 - ntoskrnl.exe
00000000 ffffffff 00000000 ffffffff 00000000 ffffffff 00000000 - breakit.SYS
00000000 ffffffff 00000000 ffffffff 00000000 ffffffff 00000000 - ntoskrnl.exe
00000000 ffffffff 00000000 ffffffff 00000000 ffffffff 00000000 - ntoskrnl.exe
00000000 ffffffff 00000000 ffffffff 00000000 ffffffff 00000000 - breakit.SYS
00000000 ffffffff 00000000 ffffffff 00000000 ffffffff 00000000 - ntoskrnl.exe
00000000 ffffffff 00000000 ffffffff 00000000 ffffffff 00000000 - tcpip.sys
00000000 ffffffff 00000000 ffffffff 00000000 ffffffff 00000000 - breakit.SYS
00000000 ffffffff 00000000 ffffffff 00000000 ffffffff 00000000 - breakit.SYS
00000000 ffffffff 00000000 ffffffff 00000000 ffffffff 00000000 - ntoskrnl.exe
00000000 ffffffff 00000000 ffffffff 00000000 ffffffff 00000000 - ntoskrnl.exe

Kernel Debugger Using: COM2 (Port 0x2f8, Baud Rate 19200)
Beginning dump of physical memory
Physical memory dump complete.  Contact your system administrator or
technical support group.
```

Figure 15-3   Blue-screen Stop Error Message

As you can see in Figure 15-3, the Stop screen is divided into five distinct sections, each of which contains specific information to help you troubleshoot the cause of the Stop error and possibly isolate its cause. These sections are described below.

- **Debug Port Status Indicators**. Located in the upper right-hand corner of the screen, this flashing text (which is not visible in Figure 15-3) provides information on the debug port status. The debug port is the serial port used for communication. You will learn how to configure debugging later in this chapter. For now, remember that if you use kernel debugging, you will need the information contained in this section. It provides serial communication information, much like the lights on a modem. The flashing letters *SND* indicate that the kernel information is being sent through the serial port listed in the Debug Port Information section (explained later in this list).

- **Bug Check Information.** This section, which is often mistaken for the Debug Port Status Indicators section, contains the error code (or bug check code). The error code is the hexadecimal number to the immediate right of the word "STOP", followed by four parameters in parentheses. Immediately below the word "Stop" is a rather cryptic-looking string called the **symbolic string.** The error code and symbolic string are explained in more detail later in this section.

- **Driver Information**. This section provides a three-column list of all drivers that were loaded and present in the system when the Stop error occurred. The first column, which lists the preferred base address in physical RAM, depicts the physical RAM of your system at the time of your system crash. The second column provides the time–date stamp for the creation of the driver, calculated in seconds since 1970. (You can use CVTIME.EXE to convert the listed file-date stamp into the standard date/time format.) The final column provides the driver's filename. In Figure 15-3, the first driver listed is NTOSKRNL.EXE. The filename information can be very useful, because a number of Stop errors contain the address of the driver or program that generated the error in the list of four parameters following the bug check code. When using the driver information in conjunction with the Stop message to identify the offending driver, remember that memory addresses are reckoned in hexadecimal format.

- **Kernel Build and Stack Dump.** This section provides a snapshot of the system at the time of the failure. It includes the build number, which tells you the build of the operating system (without third-party device drivers or service packs) and indicates the original version of Windows NT installed on your system. These data give you definitive information on the operating system code base. This section also includes a stack dump, which displays a portion of the contents of the system's RAM. The information displayed includes the name of the drivers in RAM that are associated with the failed module. In some cases, you might find addresses referenced in the symbolic string at the top of the error. They can help you to confirm the source of the error referenced in the Bug Check Information and Driver Information sections.

- **Debug Port Information.** When you are engaged in kernel debugging (as explained later in this chapter), you can consult this section for information about the debug configuration under which you are currently operating. This information, combined with the information at the top of the blue screen, helps you determine your debug configuration and its current status.

To interpret blue-screen Stop error messages, you need to access Microsoft's complete database of Windows NT messages. This information is available via TechNet and Microsoft's

Web site (among other ways). In general, you will find that most blue-screen troubleshooting involves checking TechNet or the Microsoft Web site for information on the error code or symbolic string, and then checking some or all of the four parameters of the error code. With that information, you can then cross-reference information in the drivers portion of the blue screen and possibly isolate the problem.

INTERPRETING ERROR CODES

This section provides more detailed information on the bug check information discussed in the previous section.

Two types of kernel level initialization errors exist: phase 0 errors and phase 1 errors. Both of these phases occur during the startup sequence, when the kernel is loaded. During phase 0, hardware interrupts are disabled and only a few Executive components, such as the HAL, are actually active. If you receive a phase 0 Stop message, you should run diagnostics on your hardware. If the diagnostics do not identify any errors, Microsoft recommends reinstalling Windows NT. If you get the same Stop message after the reinstallation process, you probably need the assistance of a hardware technician to isolate the problem. Table 15-1 lists bug check codes and symbolic strings for phase 0 Stop errors:

Table 15-1   Bug Check Codes and Symbolic Strings for Phase 0 Stop Errors

Symbolic Strings	Bug Check Code
0x0031	PHASE0_INITIALIZATION_FAILED
0x005C	HAL_INITIALIZATION_FAILED
0x005D	HEAP_INITIALIZATION_FAILED
0x005E	OBJECT_INITIALIZATION_FAILED
0x005F	SECURITY_INITIALIZATION_FAILED
0x0060	PROCESS_INITIALIZATION_FAILED

Once phase 0 has completed, phase 1 initialization begins. It marks the broader initialization of the kernel and enables the hardware interrupts and the remaining components of the Executive. If you experience a phase 1 Stop error, try reinstalling Windows NT. If the error occurs again after the reinstallation, you should contact Microsoft to obtain technical support. Table 15-2 lists phase 1 initialization errors.

Table 15-2   Bug Check Codes and Symbolic Strings for Phase 1 Initialization Errors

Symbolic Strings	Bug Check Code
0x0032	PHASE1_INITIALIZATION_FAILED
0x0061	HAL1_INITIALIZATION_FAILED
0x0062	OBJECT1_INITIALIZATION_FAILED
0x0063	SECURITY1_INITIALIZATION_FAILED
0x0064	SYMBOLIC_INITIALIZATION_FAILED
0x0065	MEMORY1_INITIALIZATION_FAILED
0x0066	CACHE_INITIALIZATION_FAILED
0x0067	CONFIG_INITIALIZATION_FAILED
0x0068	FILE_INITIALIZATION_FAILED
0x0069	IO1_INITIALIZATION_FAILED
0x006A	LPC_INITIALIZATION_FAILED
0x006B	PROCESS1_INITIALIZATION_FAILED
0x006C	REFMON_INITIALIZATION_FAILED
0x006D	SESSION1_INITIALIZATION_FAILED
0x006E	SESSION2_INITIALIZATION_FAILED
0x006F	SESSION3_INITIALIZATION_FAILED
0x0070	SESSION4_INITIALIZATION_FAILED
0x0071	SESSION5_INITIALIZATION_FAILED

Unlike kernel initialization errors, all software trap errors use the same bug check number and symbolic string, as follows:

> Stop: 0x0000007F (0x0000000N, 00000000, 00000000, 00000000)
> UNEXPECTED_KERNEL_MODE_TRAP

The first entry in the parentheses provides the specific details for software trap errors. Table 15-3 lists possible values for the first parameters and their meanings.

This information will help you to determine what sort of software error is being trapped by the operating system. Unfortunately, it does not immediately indicate which software component is involved. You can, however, gather more information from other parts of the Stop screen to further troubleshoot the problem.

If you do not recognize your Stop error as a kernel-initialization or software-trap error, then it is one of the many other Stop errors defined within Windows NT. You will need to gather more information from the rest of the Stop screen to resolve the problem.

15

Table 15-3 Explanations of First Parameters

First Parameter	Meaning
0x00000000	An attempt to divide by zero
0x00000001	A system-debugger call
0x00000003	A debugger breakpoint
0x00000004	An arithmetic operation overflow
0x00000005	An array index that exceeds the array bounds
0x00000006	Invalid operands in an instruction or an attempt to execute a protected-mode instruction while running in real mode
0x00000007	A hardware coprocessor instruction, with no coprocessor present
0x00000008	An error while processing an error (also known as a "double fault")
0x0000000A	A corrupted task state segment
0x0000000B	An access to a memory segment that was not present
0x0000000C	An access to memory beyond the limits of a stack
0x0000000D	An exception not covered by some other exception—a protection fault that pertains to access violations for applications

ANALYZING THE DUMP FILE

Once a Stop error occurs, you need to analyze the dump file. This section introduces the tools you can use to analyze the dump file and shows how to implement and configure these tools.

> As with other advanced tools, the best means of learning how to analyze the dump file is through practice. While you do not want to crash a production server to play with blue screens, you should take the time to configure your systems to log Stop errors and prepare them for kernel debugging and dump analysis.

UNDERSTANDING DUMP ANALYSIS

Before you can successfully analyze a dump file (a process known as **dump analysis**), you need to know something about the process of commercial software development. Most software comes in two versions: a checked build (also known as a debug version) and an unchecked build (also known as a free version). You may see checked versions of software available on the Microsoft Developer's Network (MSDN) subscription CD-ROMs and from other sources. Checked builds are not readily available for commercial use. Instead, they are primarily intended for use by software developers. The most important difference between checked and unchecked builds is that **checked builds** contain code that facilitates debugging. While useful, this extra code introduces a performance penalty, which is why it is not made commercially available. It also explains why most beta software performs more slowly than its final-release counterpart: the beta code usually consists of a checked build. Unchecked builds run faster, because they lack the extra debugging code.

All of the compiled executable and system files in Windows NT's commercial releases (as opposed to beta versions or explicit checked builds) are unchecked build files. For each of these files, Microsoft offers a checked-build counterpart file that contains the extra debugging code. This debug code is not used during regular execution, but is available for debugging purposes. Thus you get the best of both worlds: fast performance and in-depth debugging information.

The checked debug files are usually found on the Windows NT CD-ROM under Support\Debug*architecture*\symbols. For example, you would look at the support\debug\ i386\symbols directory to find Intel-based systems. Within the symbols directory, you will see a directory for each type of file available, forming what is called a symbol tree. The standard directories that make up the Windows NT symbol tree are as follows:

- ACM: Microsoft Audio Compression Manager files
- COM: Executable files (.com)
- CPL: Control Panel programs
- DLL: Dynamic-link library files (.dll)
- DRV: Driver files (.drv)
- EXE: Executable files (.exe)
- SCR: Screen-saver files
- SYS: Driver files (.sys)

> **Note** When using the symbol files for Windows NT, it is imperative that you use the same version of symbols as the operating system. In addition, you should place your symbol tree under the symbols directory under the %SystemRoot% directory—for example, C:\WINNT\SYSTEM32\SYMBOLS. Some utilities allow you to place the symbol tree in a different location and then specify that location by using switches at the command line. As a general rule, however, the symbols directory under the SystemRoot is the standard location for the symbol tree. It is a good idea to stick with the standard, unless a compelling reason exists to do otherwise.

15

Once you have loaded the debugging symbols (or are running a checked build), your system stands ready to perform debugging. Before you can analyze the dump file, you need to know the location of the dump file on your system and have access to it. If you cannot perform dump analysis on the failed computer, you need to move the file to another machine and analyze it there.

Three dump analysis tools are at your disposal. These tools can be found in the support\debug*architecture* directory on the Windows NT CD-ROM. (For Intel-based systems, for example, you would look under support\debug\i386.) These tools are as follows:

- **DUMPFLOP.EXE**. This utility is used to copy your dump file to a floppy disk. Because it contains the entire contents of RAM at the time of the failure, the dump file can be quite large, especially on production servers. If you need to send the contents of this file to support personnel for outside analysis, you are faced with a tricky question: How do you break up a file that may be 256 MB in size? DUMPFLOP.EXE addresses this need. It will perform its own compression to minimize the number of floppy disks required. Although FTP is a better option for transferring such large files, if you need to move the Dump file onto a floppy disk, then DUMPFLOP.EXE is the best choice. You will rarely need to use this tool, but it is nevertheless important to be aware of its existence. The syntax for DUMPFLOP is DUMPFLOP *DUMPFILE*. If your dump file is in the default location, for example, you would use DUMPFLOP C:\WINNT\SYSTEM32\MEMORY.DMP.

- **DUMPCHK.EXE**. This utility verifies the integrity of the dump file. If you plan to analyze your dump file, you should first run this utility to verify that the file was successfully created without any errors. DUMPCHK will report back any errors it finds in your dump file. If your dump file is corrupt or was not completely generated, you will need to generate a new one. The syntax for DUMPCHK is DUMPCHK *DUMPFILE*. Using our previous example, the syntax would be DUMPCHK C:\WINNT\SYSTEM32\MEMORY.DMP.

- **DUMPEXAM.EXE**. This utility actually analyzes the content of your dump file and writes its analysis to a straight-text file that, by default, is located in the same directory as the dump file. The syntax for DUMPEXAM is DUMPEXAM −y *symbols path* −f *output file DUMPFILE*. Using our previous example, the DUMPEXAM for a Windows NT system that has no service packs applied and that takes the default path for the output file would simply be DUMPEXAM C:\WINNT\SYSTEM32\MEMORY.DMP. If you wanted to redirect the output file, you could use DUMPEXAM −f d:\logs\DEBUG.TXT C:\WINNT\SYSTEM32\MEMORY.DMP. If you have loaded the symbol tree into a different location, you would use DUMPEXAM −y d:\symbols C:\WINNT\SYSTEM32\MEMORY.DMP.

When dealing with systems that have applied service packs, you must point DUMPEXAM to the symbol tree for both the operating system and the service pack. This step is crucial, because service packs update files on the system; failing to direct to the service pack symbols will create a mismatch between the unchecked file and its checked symbol file. Multiple symbol trees are specified by separating the references with semicolons (";"). The following example points explicitly to the symbols for Windows NT 4.0 and Service Pack 3: DUMPEXAM −y d:\symbols\winnt; d:\symbols\sp3 d:\C:\WINNT\SYSTEM32\MEMORY.DMP.

After you run DUMPEXAM, you need to interpret its output. This output contains much of the information included in the blue-screen Stop message, along with a great deal of assembly-level information on the state of the operating system. The DUMPEXAM output (sometimes referred to as the **dump log**) does not include the equivalent of the first and fifth sections of the Stop screen. Because these sections are relevant to the live debugging session, they are not included in the dump file.

The error code is located at the top of the dump log. To find the symbolic string (which is not included), you can cross-reference the bug check error code in any Microsoft documentation. Following the bug check error code, you will see the four bug check parameters. For software-trap errors, you will find the specific failure parameter here. As with the parameters on the Stop screen, you can sometimes find the base address of a driver that is creating the problem. You can then take this parameter and search for more details.

The equivalent of the third section of the Stop screen, which contains the driver information, can be found in the !drivers portion of the output file. In this area, you will find the name of a driver whose base address you have obtained from the bug check parameters.

The build number, seen at the top of the dump log, is listed as the MinorVersion. Stack information, which corresponds to the rest of the fourth section of the Stop screen, mainly appears under the !process section. As with the stack information on the Stop screen, you will use this section infrequently.

CONFIGURING DEBUGGING

As helpful as dump analysis tools are, they are only as good as the dump file available for them. In some rare and very frustrating circumstances, even these tools cannot isolate the cause of your Stop. In these extreme cases, support personnel will ask you to configure kernel debugging.

Kernel debugging provides support personnel with information on the failed system as it is happening, through serial connections with the failed system. Because you will undertake kernel debugging only in conjunction with trained support personnel, this section covers merely the basics of kernel debugging.

Kernel debugging requires two computers: a host computer and a target computer. The target computer is the Windows NT server that has experienced the Stop error. The host computer is the computer you will use in the actual debugging process.

When configuring host and target computers, you have two options:

- **Remote Debug Session.** This session takes place between your failed target computer and an off-site host computer (such as one at Microsoft's technical support department). It is carried out as the error occurs. The remote host computer connects to your target computer through a modem connection and performs kernel debugging over the modem connection.

- **Local Debug Session.** This session occurs between your failed target and local host. A null modem cable is used to connect your target and host computer to one another. You can then use your host computer as a gateway and connect to a remote host via RAS or another asynchronous connection. In this scenario, your local target will act as a gateway between your failed host and the remote target computer. You can also analyze debugging information at the local target computer.

As these options indicate, the first step in configuring for debugging is to set up an external modem or null-modem cable on the failed target machine. You will find information on the specific steps for configuring a modem on your target system in the Windows NT Workstation Resource Kit. If you are connecting a host machine at your site to your target system, then you must configure the dial-up session between your host computer and the technical support's dial-up server. Your support technician will provide details on this portion of the setup.

15

For your failed target system to work with debugging, it must boot up using special parameters in the BOOT.INI for Intel-based machines or in the firmware menu for RISC-based machines. These changes to your system's boot sequence are also available, in the Windows NT Workstation Resource Kit or from your support technician.

If you are using the local debug session, then the host system will have to be configured with the symbol tree for debugging. The symbol tree must match the retail build version and service pack of the target system, just as the DUMPEXAM utility needs the proper symbols. Unlike with DUMPEXAM, however, your use of a remote system means that you must manually install the appropriate HAL symbols on the host system. Finally, the debugger and its support files must be installed on the host system. Details on the specific files and where they must be loaded are available in the Resource Kit or from your support technician. After you load all files, you can load the debugger itself on the local host system. Your support technician will provide details on how to accomplish this goal.

CHAPTER SUMMARY

- When errors occur within the kernel, Windows NT will provide all the information it can about the error and its operating environment in the form of a blue-screen Stop error.

- To resolve a Stop error, you can take advantage of several useful tools available via the Startup/Shutdown tab of the System Properties dialog box. Keep in mind, however, that to use these tools you must configure your system before a Stop error actually occurs. Among the most important recovery tools is the ability to write information on the state of the server from the time a problem first manifests itself to a dump file. In addition, you can choose to send an administrative alert in the event of a Stop error and automatically reboot after a Stop error occurs.

- You can configure your server to send administrative alerts about problems other than Stop errors (such as problems with user sessions, security access, or printing). In addition, you can choose to send alerts to a predefined list of users and computers. To send alerts, both the Alerter and Messenger services must be running on the computer transmitting the alert. To receive an alert, the Messenger service must be running on the receiving machine. After you have determined where alerts should be sent, you must restart the Alerter and Server services to implement these changes.

- An event in Windows NT is either an occurrence that has significance for the system or a notification from an application of some predetermined behavior. Services and applications generate events both during startup and throughout the course of normal operations, recording this information to the event logs. Three types of event logs exist—the System log, Application log, and Security log. The System log contains errors, warnings, or information generated by components of the operating system itself, such as the Server and Net Logon services. The Application log contains errors, warnings, or information generated by installed applications and services. The Security log shows events generated by security subsystems. It can contain information on valid and invalid logon attempts and events related to resource use, such as creating, opening, or deleting files or other objects. The type of events that appear in the Security log depends on the

Auditing policies set for your computer. To view an event log, click Start, click Programs, select Administrative Tools (Common), then click Event Viewer. Use the Log Settings command in Event Viewer's Log menu to set the parameters for each event log.

- Once you have taken the preliminary steps to enable Event Viewer logging and memory dumps, your system is ready to begin troubleshooting should a kernel-level error occur. When such an error occurs, you will see either a blue-screen Stop error message (sometimes referred to as the "blue screen of death") or a character-based Windows NT error message that identifies hardware failures in your system, such as memory errors and CPU failures. One category of Stop errors occurs only during the initialization of the kernel, which is one of the last phases of the boot and startup sequence. Another type of Stop error—the software trap—occurs when the CPU detects a problem in the executing instruction, which is located within the kernel part of the Executive services.

- Hardware failures that affect the Executive directly (for example, uncorrected memory parity errors) generate hardware error messages. These messages differ depending on the hardware component that causes the error and the manufacturer of that component. The appropriate response to a hardware error will vary accordingly.

- A blue-screen Stop error is divided into five distinct sections, each of which contains specific information that will help you troubleshoot and possibly isolate the cause of the error. The most important section is the bug check information, which includes the error code (or bug check code). This code identifies the actual error. To interpret the error codes, you need to access Microsoft's complete database of Windows NT messages, which is available via TechNet and Microsoft's Web site. You should also familiarize yourself with the most common error codes.

- Once a Stop error occurs, you must analyze the dump file to find the source of the error. Before you can take this step, you need to know the location of the dump file on your system and have access to it. (If you cannot perform dump analysis on the failed computer, you need to move the file to another machine and analyze it there.)

- Several tools are available for analyzing the dump file. For each of the compiled executable and system files in Windows NT's commercial releases, Microsoft offers a checked-build counterpart file that contains extra debugging code. These checked debug files are usually found on the Windows NT CD-ROM under Support\Debug*architecture*\symbols (where architecture stands for the hardware platform on which you are running Windows NT, such as i386). In addition to the checked debug files, you can use the following debugging utilities: DUMPFLOP.EXE, which copies your dump file to floppy disk; DUMPCHK.EXE, which verifies the integrity of the dump file; and DUMPEXAM.EXE, which analyzes the contents of your dump file and writes its analysis to a straight-text file After you run DUMPEXAM, you must interpret its output, which contains much of the information included in the blue-screen Stop message, plus assembly-level information on the state of the operating system.

- In some rare circumstances, even dump analysis tools cannot isolate the cause of your Stop error. In these extreme cases, support personnel will ask you to configure kernel debugging. Kernel debugging provides support personnel with information on the failed system as the error is happening, through serial connections with the failed

15

system. In general, you will undertake kernel debugging only in conjunction with trained support personnel. This process requires two computers: a host computer and a target computer. The target computer is the Windows NT server that has experienced the Stop error. The host computer is the computer you will use in the actual debugging process.

KEY TERMS

- **Blue screen error** — *See* STOP error.
- **Checked build** — Software that includes code designed to facilitate debugging.
- **Dump analysis** — The process of analyzing a dump file.
- **dump file** — A binary file that contains a complete copy ("dump") of the contents of physical RAM.
- **Executive error messages** — A hardware or STOP-related error message emanating from the Windows NT Executive.
- **Kernel debugging** — The process of resolving a STOP error via a serial connection between support personnel and the failed system.
- **software-trap error** — A kernel-level software error. The Windows NT Executive catches ("traps") these errors and stops processing. Examples include division by zero errors and memory address errors.
- **Stop error** — An Executive-level error in Windows NT characterized by a blue screen that contains current environment information.
- **symbolic string** — A string error message that is associated with a numeric error code. Symbolic strings are provided to make it easier to identify and remember error messages.

REVIEW QUESTIONS

1. A binary file that contains the contents of physical RAM is called a
   _____ .
2. When configuring recovery options, to which directory and filename does Windows NT default for its dump file?
3. How much free disk space do you need to hold a dump file for a system with 256 MB of RAM?
4. Your server is configured to log Stop events. Where can you get information when a Stop error occurs?
   a. Application log
   b. System log
   c. Security log
   d. %SYSTEMROOT%\DEBUG.LOG

5. If you want to be notified the moment that a server goes down due to a Stop error, which parameter should you configure?

6. Stop errors are raised by which portion of the Windows NT architecture?

7. Your junior network engineer was working on a production server when a Stop error was raised. He admits he was running Pinball on the server when it went down, and is afraid he caused the Stop error. Is he correct? Why or why not?

8. Stop errors are the only type of messages reported from the kernel. True or False?

9. You are examining a Stop error on your production machine. Where can you find the bug check information?

10. To correctly perform dump analysis, you must copy the entire contents of the Windows NT Server CD-ROM under %SYSTEMROOT%\DEBUG. True or False?

11. You have a dump file you need to send on floppy disk to tech support for analysis. Which utility do you use to copy the file to the floppy disk?

12. DUMPEXAM is a graphical utility that examines dump files and reports the likely cause of errors. True or False?

13. To configure kernel debugging, you need to load Visual Studio on your Windows NT Server. True or False?

14. How many phases does kernel initialization have?

    a. 8

    b. 5

    c. 2

    d. 1

15. When installing service packs in Windows NT, you must overwrite the installed debug symbols with the newer versions in the service packs. True or False?

16. When setting up for debugging, you mainly need a parallel cable to connect a printer so you can print the blue screen. True or False?

17. A _____ _____ of software contains additional code for debugging.

18. WINDGB replaces DUMPEXAM starting with Windows NT 3.51. True or False?

19. The bug check error is displayed in _____ notation.

    a. binary

    b. decimal

    c. hexadecimal

    d. octal

20. Executive-level hardware errors will report information specific for the type of component that has failed. True or False?

21. When Windows NT raises a software-trap error, it writes a copy of the code that caused the error into a file called ERROR.WRI. True or False?

15

22. When performing debugging, you should refer to the failed computer as the
    _____ computer.

23. For remote debugging, you must connect to an ISP or have an Internet connection.
    True or False?

24. Which symbols must be loaded on the local host machine during remote debugging?

    a. symbols from the same retail version as the failed target

    b. symbols from the same or a later retail version as the failed target

    c. symbols from the last service pack applied to the failed target

    d. symbols from the same retail version and last service pack applied to the failed target

25. You should try reinstalling Windows NT when phase 1 kernel initialization errors
    arise. True or False?

HANDS-ON PROJECTS

For some or all of these projects you will need a functioning Windows NT server with free
disk space in excess of the amount of the server's RAM. More free space would be even better.

PROJECT 15-1

In this project, you will add alerting capabilities to a machine. As a part of this process, you
will need to stop and restart the Alerter and Server services.

1. Click **Start**, point to **Programs**, point to **Administrative Tools (Common)**, then
   click **Server Manager**. The Server Manager window opens.

2. Select the appropriate computer from the list of computers by highlighting it.

3. From the Computer menu, choose **Properties**, then click the **Alerts button**.

4. Add the names of users and computers to which you want alerts sent. Click **OK** to
   close the dialog box. Exit Server Manager using the Exit entry of the Computer menu.

5. Click **Start**, click **Settings**, then choose **Control Panel**. The Control Panel opens.

6. Double-click the **Services icon**. The Services window opens.

7. In the list, highlight the **Alerter service**, then press the **Stop button**. This action
   will stop the Alerter service. You will receive a message box that asks if you are sure
   you want to stop the Alerter service. Click **Yes**.

8. From the list of services, highlight the **Server service**, then press the **Stop button**.
   A dialog box will appear, listing any dependent services, such as Net Logon,
   Computer Browser, and perhaps others, depending on your configuration. Make a
   note of these services, as you will need to restart them all. After you have copied the
   services down, click **OK** to stop the services.

9. Restart each of the services in your list and the Alerter service by highlighting the relevant service name in the list of services and pressing the Start button. When you have restarted all of the services, close the Services applet.

PROJECT 15-2

In this project, you will enable your server to provide an alert in the event of a Windows NT Stop error.

1. Right-click **My Computer**, then right-click **Properties**. The System Properties dialog box opens.
2. Click the **Startup/Shutdown tab**.
3. If it is not already selected, select the **Send Administrative Alert** check box.
4. Click **OK**.

PROJECT 15-3

In this project, you will configure Windows NT to automatically reboot during Stop errors.

1. Right-click **My Computer**, then right-click **Properties**. The System Properties dialog box opens.
2. Click the **Startup/Shutdown tab**.
3. If it is not already selected, select the **Automatically Reboot** check box.
4. Click **OK**.

PROJECT 15-4

In this project, you will configure Windows NT to create a dump file.

1. Right-click **My Computer**, then right-click **Properties**. The System Properties dialog box opens.
2. Select the **General tab**.
3. Locate the amount of RAM installed in the system under Computer. You will need this information to ensure that you are making your dump file large enough.
4. Click the **Startup/Shutdown tab**.
5. Click **Start**, point to **Programs**, then click **Windows NT Explorer**. The Windows NT Explorer window opens.
6. Highlight the system partition.

15

7. Compare the available free space on the system partition with the amount of RAM installed (see Step 3). If the free space on the system partition is less than the amount of RAM installed, check other drives on the server for enough free space.

8. Close Windows NT Explorer.

9. If it is not already selected, select the **Write Debugging Information to:** check box.

10. If there is enough space on your system partition, accept the default location for the dump file. Otherwise, locate the file on a partition with enough space.

11. Click **OK**.

CASE PROJECTS

1. Noveck Pharmaceutical Company has an office in Fairbanks, Alaska, with no technical staff and a Windows NT server. As the IS manager, you are worried about Stop errors, because no one in the office is qualified to restart the server or to note the details on a blue-screen Stop error message. How can you address this concern? How can you guarantee that you receive a notification on your Windows NT workstation when this server goes down?

2. You are working on your main Windows NT server at Amalgamated Biotech Company when it suddenly restarts itself unexpectedly. You think this restart might be a Stop error, but you are confused because you didn't see a blue-screen Stop error message. How might you check to see whether dump files are being created? To which location will the dump file default? What are some things that might prevent your dump file from being created once you have configured the system to create dump files?

3. Your Windows NT server at your publishing subsidiary in Bonn, Germany, has crashed with a blue-screen Stop error message. The junior technician on-site in Bonn has sent you the dump file from the server. How do you verify its integrity and begin to examine this file? Is it possible to obtain the bug check error code raised during the Stop error? Suppose you find that a software trap caused the error. How can you identify the specific type of software-trap error?

4. Despite your best efforts at troubleshooting, you cannot identify the cause of a blue screen, which is raised after your server has been running for 10 days. Because of the pattern of the occurrences, do you think it would be worthwhile to contact Microsoft for more assistance? What steps, if any, can the company's technical support take to resolve the problem that you cannot? Suppose the support technician requires local debugging to isolate this problem. What configuration steps might this debugging require and what equipment will you need?

5. You are working on your Windows NT server in Chicago when a blue-screen Stop error message suddenly appears. What information should you write down immediately? From reading the screen, you believe that a bad device driver is the cause. Can you identify the driver from this screen? If so, where can you find out which driver caused this Stop error?

GLOSSARY

A

account policies A set of rules that govern user account settings, such as password length.

acknowledgment (ACK) messages Message sent by the receiver to acknowledge the receipt of a data packet.

Adapter Card Drivers layer One of the five layers of the Microsoft Networking model. Roughly equivalent to the Physical layer of the OSI model. Handles formatting of data for physical access to the network adapter card and the network wire.

Address Resolution Protocol (ARP) A protocol in the TCP/IP suite that obtains the MAC (physical) address of a host, matches it to an IP (logical) address, and stores this information in the ARP cache.

Advanced RISC Computing (ARC) Set of naming conventions developed for RISC-based systems that have been adopted for Windows NT under all architectures. ARC names locate system partitions by pointing to the actual physical controller, drive, and partition for the system partition.

AppleTalk A protocol used to connect Apple computers to a Windows NT network.

Application layer One of the four layers of the TCP/IP model, or stack. Roughly equivalent to the Application and Presentation layers of the OSI model. Allows applications access to the network.

Application/File System Drivers layer One of the five layers of the Microsoft Networking model. Roughly equivalent to the Application and Presentation layers of the OSI model. Holds the two application programming interfaces.

Application Programming Interface (API) A set of programmed routines that operates at the Application layer of the OSI model.

approachable Term used to describe the ease of using a new network operating system for the first time.

archive bit A file attribute used to determine which files will be backed up and which ones will not be backed up. When a file is modified, the archive attribute is turned on, indicating that the file has changed since the last backup.

ARP A command prompt utility used to display the current ARP cache entries.

ARPAnet A network of U.S. Department of Defense and university computers that preceded the Internet. It allowed for only 256 computers on the network at one time.

ARP cache A database that maintains a list of IP address that have recently been matched (or resolved) to MAC addresses.

Asynchronous NetBEUI (Microsoft RAS Protocol) A protocol that enables clients that do not support PPP to establish communications with Windows NT.

AutoDial A feature of RAS that enables the system to automatically reconnect to remote systems to retrieve previously accessed resources.

autonomous systems A collection of hosts under control of a single entity.

averaging counter A counter used to obtain the averaged value of two sequenced measurements. The value of an averaging counter is displayed only after the second measurement has been taken.

B

backup browser A computer that receives a copy of the browse list from the master browser and distributes it to the browser clients upon request.

base code operating systems Multiple operating systems that utilize the same basic code to form their structure. Windows NT Server and Windows NT Workstation fall into this category.

baseline A set of normal operational parameters.

baselining The process of monitoring a set of performance metrics over an extended period of time to determine the normal operational parameters.

bind Configure protocols to function on a network computer.

bindery NetWare's equivalent to the SAM (Security Accounts Manager) database; it keeps track of NetWare users and privileges. The Migration Tool for NetWare converts bindery information to SAM information.

BOOTP/DHCP Relay Agent The component of multi-protocol routing that relays DHCP and BOOTP broadcast messages between a BOOTP/DHCP server and a client across an IP router.

bottleneck The condition where a component of a computer system operates so as to limit or restrict the optimum performance of other components, ultimately preventing the system as a whole from operating at its peak level.

broadcast address An IP address used to send data packets to all hosts on the local network.

brownouts Power fluctuations associated with lights dimming for extended periods of time. Brownouts can occur when an electrical device nearby drains the common current to low levels, or the needs of a geographic area cannot be met.

browse list The list of available resources distributed to specially assigned computers known as browser computers.

built-in accounts User and group accounts that are automatically created upon installation of Windows NT.

business/mission-critical Term used to describe a network in which business stops if the network goes down. Monetary losses can be measured during downtime.

C

Callback A feature of RAS in which the server disconnects clients and then calls them back to establish a communications link.

Capture Filter A Network Monitor tool that limits or restricts the amount of data captured by storing only those packets that meet a specified criteria.

capture trigger A feature of Network Monitor that, when its criteria are met, can stop the capture of data and launch programs or batch files.

Certificate Server An optional Windows NT service that enables an organization to manage the issuance, renewal, and termination of Secure Socket Layer (SSL) certificates without using the services of a third-party certificate issuer.

characterization data file A collection of printer-specific information that is stored in the printer's memory.

checksum A method used to determine whether data have been transmitted correctly.

client A stand-alone computer that has been integrated into a network so that it may access information from a server.

client application A software program that initiates a print job. A client application can reside on a client/workstation computer, a server computer, or even the computer hosting the print server.

client-based network administration tools Utilities that can be executed on a workstation and are used to administer one or more servers.

client rollout The process of loading and configuring software on multiple computers simultaneously.

client/server application An application with components that execute both locally and at the server.

client/server revolution The transition from dumb terminal/mainframe environments to desktop PCs and servers.

client Services for Netware (CSNW) A service provided with Windows NT Workstation that allows it to connect seamlessly to NetWare volumes and access information, provided that a valid user account has been created on the NetWare server.

Commerce Server An optional Windows NT service (formerly known as Merchant Server) that allows users to create secure, shopping-cart applications for the Internet, develop sales promotions based on real-time information, and process orders online.

complete trust model A network structure in which every domain has a two-way trust relationship with every other domain.

Computer Browser Service A core Windows NT service that creates a centralized list of available network resources.

computer policy A collection of Registry settings that specifically define the operating environment for a specific workstation.

connecting to a printer The act of creating a logical printer to be referenced and used by client applications to send print jobs. A logical printer can connect to a locally attached printer or to a network printer share. Connecting to a printer is carried out via the Add Printer wizard found in the Printers folder.

connectionless Term used to describe a protocol that does not guarantee delivery of data packets in the proper sequence.

connection-oriented Term used to describe a protocol that guarantees delivery of data packets in the proper sequence.

core service A service that is shipped with Windows NT and installed in the typical Windows NT environment. These services include Computer Browser Service, Dynamic Host Configuration Protocol Server (DHCP), Windows Internet Naming Service (WINS), Domain Naming Service (DNS) Server, and directory replication.

counter A facet, feature, function, service, or resource to be measured on an object.

creating a printer The installation of drivers for a print device on the machine locally hosting the physical device. Creating a printer also involves naming the printer, setting printer-specific configurations, and, optionally, sharing that printer with the rest of the network.

D

data-critical Term used to describe a network in which servers store highly important information that absolutely cannot be lost.

Data Link Control (DLC) A protocol used to connect to IBM SNA devices and Hewlett-Packard Jet network printers.

default route A path of last resort; the destination to which a packet will be sent if the routing table does not include a defined route.

Dial-Up Networking (DUN) The outbound call initiation interface of RAS.

difference counter A counter that obtains the difference between two sequenced measurements by subtracting the earlier measurement from the later instance. A negative result is displayed as zero.

directory replication A core Windows NT service that maintains identical copies of specified files and directories on different computers. Changes made to files on one computer are automatically replicated to other computers configured to receive the changes.

Directory Services The Windows NT features used to manage domains.

Directory Services for Netware The Windows NT service that copies user and group account information from a Novell network to a Windows NT server.

Directory Services Manager for NetWare (DSMN) A Windows NT service that enables the management of NetWare users and groups from the Windows NT server.

Disk Administrator A Windows NT utility used to create, format, and delete partitions, volume sets, stripe sets, mirror sets, and stripe sets with parity.

disk duplexing The process in which a separate disk controller exists for each disk in a mirrored set.

Display Filter A Network Monitor tool that hides all packets that do not meet a specified criteria to simplify the packet-by-packet inspection process.

distance vector routing protocol A protocol that uses an algorithm to determine the least-cost path to a given destination. The cost is generally an arbitrary number based on specific defined parameters, such as the number of hops.

DLC A protocol that was originally created to allow servers to interoperate with IBM mainframes; it can also be used to connect to Hewlett-Packard network-attached printers.

domain An administrative group of servers and resources. In a Windows NT network environment, a collection of users and network resources in which security is managed by a primary domain controller.

domain administrators Personnel responsible for managing the master domain.

domain model A description of the way domains are associated in a network.

Domain Naming Service (DNS) The database used by computers on the Internet to look up one another's addresses. Installed as a core Windows NT service.

DOS (Disk Operating System) An operating system widely used on early PCs that requires the user to type lines of commands. DOS is available through emulation in Windows NT.

dotted decimal notation The method of presenting IP addresses in four 8-bit fields.

dumb terminal A screen and keyboard that connect, via standard asynchronous or telephone line, to a mainframe computer.

dump file A binary file that contains a complete copy ("dump") of the contents of physical RAM.

Dynamic Host Configuration Protocol (DHCP) A network protocol that enables a DHCP server to automatically assign an IP address to an individual computer's TCP/IP stack.

dynamic route A route that is learned from neighboring routers through normal interactions and placed in the routing table.

E

election The process that ensures that only one master browser exists in each domain or workgroup. An election is triggered when a network client cannot locate a master browser, a backup browser attempts to update its browse list but cannot locate a master browser, or a second computer configured as a preferred master browser is turned on.

EMF (Enhanced Metafiles) The native print and rendering data type of Windows that is generated by the GDI. EMF files are portable (that is, they can be sent to any print device) and more compact than the RAW data type.

enterprise network A network that encompasses at least two domains.

Event Viewer A utility used to provide a record during server or workstation startup and operation.

extensible counter An application/device-specific counter added to Performance Monitor to expand its range of functionality. Some products will automatically install extensible counters; others require manual installation.

F

fault tolerance The ability of a system to respond to hardware failures without losing or corrupting data.

fiber channel A data transfer method that uses fiber-optic cables instead of copper to increase the speed and distance over which data can be transferred.

File and Print Services for NetWare (FPNW) A Windows NT service that allows NetWare clients to access resources on a Windows NT server without installing any additional client software.

firewall A device used to isolate a network and prevent external intrusion..

firmware profile The functional equivalent of the BOOT.INI file under Intel-based architecture. It contains configuration information for the loading of system partitions and operating systems.

G

gateway A software component that facilitates the translation of different protocols and allows computers running different protocols to communicate with one another.

gateway address Address that defines where the packet should be sent, either the local network card or to a gateway or router on the local subnet.

Gateway Services for NetWare (GSNW) A Windows NT service that enables a Windows NT server to access NetWare file and print resources directly and acts as a gateway for other Microsoft clients, allowing them to access the NetWare resources without requiring additional software on the clients.

global group A group of users that is granted access to a domain.

graphical device interface (GDI) The graphics engine in Windows NT. It provides a standard set of functions that mediate between applications and graphics devices.

group account A logical collection of users that are assigned access rights and permissions. Each user in the group receives the same access rights and permissions as the rest of the group.

group policy A collection of Registry settings that define the operating environment for a specific group of users.

GUI Graphical user interface. A screen display that allows the user to use a mouse to point at and click on pictures (graphics) rather than typing lines of commands.

GUI revolution The transition from text-based interfaces, such as DOS, to graphics-oriented interfaces, such as Windows.

H

HAL Hardware abstraction layer. A layer of the Windows NT operating system that hides many differences in hardware platforms from the operating system.

Hardware Compatibility List (HCL) A list maintained by Microsoft of all computer equipment that has been tested for and is known to work properly with Windows NT.

high-availability Term used to describe a network that places the strongest focus on server uptime and performance.

home directory A location on a server or local hard drive used to store user data.

hook An attribute that can be measured. Also called a metric or a counter.

hop A point during data transmission in which the data packet passes through a router.

host A host computer is a central computer resource on which data and applications are stored for access by clients.

host bus adapter (HBA) A device that controls the flow of data to each device on the bus, and acts as the interface between the SCSI bus and the rest of the computer.

hotspot Long-lasting voltage surge. Hotspots are rare and are usually caused by utility company failures.

I

Index Server A search engine integrated into Internet Information Server that provides users with access to documents on the Web site.

installation disk set A set of disks that contains all software, files, and settings needed to access a Windows NT server.

instance A designation used to distinguish between multiple objects of the same type.

instantaneous counter A counter used to obtain point measurements of activity.

Integrated Service Digital Network (ISDN) A digital telephone service that allows for transmission rates of up to 128 Kbps over existing copper telephone wires.

internal logic board A device on a SCSI disk that keeps track of cylinders, heads, and sectors, so that the bus controller does not have to.

Internet Control Message Protocol (ICMP) A protocol in the TCP/IP suite that notifies the sender if something goes wrong during data transmission and packets remain unsent.

Internet Information Server An optional Windows NT file service that enables a Windows NT 4.0 server to become a robust and secure vehicle for publishing information.

Internet layer One of the four layers of the TCP/IP model, or stack. Roughly equivalent to the Network layer of the OSI model. Holds protocols concerned with routing messages and host address resolution.

Internet Protocol (IP) An unreliable, connectionless protocol in the TCP/IP suite that does not guarantee delivery of data. Provides the unique addresses that make the TCP/IP suite so useful.

internetwork A group of connected networks.

Internetwork Packet Exchange/Sequenced Packet Exchange (IPX/SPX) Novell's proprietary network protocol.

InterNIC The Internet authority that controls the distribution of IP addresses.

interoperable Term used to describe an operating system that can communicate, share information, and cooperate with other network servers and devices.

IP address A unique number assigned to a computer in the TCP/IP addressing scheme. Takes the form of a 32-bit number broken up into four 8-bit fields separated by periods, with each field numbered from 0 to 255. An example might be 131.127.3.22.

IPCONFIG A command-prompt utility used to show TCP/IP configuration details for a host.

IPDatagram A broadcast messaging process used by Internet Control Message Protocol (ICMP) to address packets. Does not allow for acknowledgment of receipt.

IP header The means by which the Internet Protocol (IP) provides information about how and where data should be delivered. A maximum of 20 octets long, the IP header contains a number of fields, such as packet destination address and Time to Live.

ISDN adapter card (ISDN modem) A communication device used to connect a computer to an ISDN line. Similar to but not the same as a modem.

J

JBOD (Just a Bunch of Disks) A slang acronym used to refer to a volume configuration in which each hard disk is its own volume and receives its own drive letter.

L

local group A set of related users that are granted access to resources on a particular computer.

local user profile A profile that controls the settings for a user on a specific computer.

log file A file generated by a software program that tracks processes performed by the software.

logical printer The term used by Microsoft to refer to the software interface that defines, names, and points to a physical printer (either local or remote). This component, which appears in the Printers folder, redirects print jobs to the appropriate print server for processing. User access and printer functions are managed at this interface point.

logon script A list of commands that execute when the user logs on to the network.

loopback address The address 127.0.0.1, which tells a utility (for example, PING) to send a request to itself. The loopback address is most useful for troubleshooting.

M

mainframe An environment in which one or more primary servers (usually called mainframe computers) effectively centralize all processing and data gathering. Users communicate with the mainframe computer via dumb terminals.

mandatory profile A roaming profile that cannot be modified by the user.

map To assign a local designator to a remote resource. For example, you could map a storage resource to a drive letter.

mapping file A file that shows how NetWare users and groups are to be migrated to Windows NT servers; it is primarily used to preserve NetWare passwords.

master browser The computer that maintains a database (or browse list) of available resources on the domain or workgroup; it distributes this list to the backup browsers.

master domain In a network with more than one domain, the domain that acts as a central administrative unit for user and group accounts in other domains.

mean time between failures The predicted average time between installation and failure of hardware.

media access control (MAC) address Physical address of a network interface card that is hard-coded to the device by the manufacturer.

member server A server that is part of a domain but does not participate in the domain controller process.

metric A facet, feature, function, service, or resource to be measured on an object. In RIP, the metric is the number of hops to the destination address, used to determine the shortest route to a destination.

Migration Tool for NetWare A Windows NT utility that allows users and groups, along with their associated rights and permissions, to be recreated on (or migrated to) Windows NT servers.

mirroring The process by which data on one disk are duplicated onto an identical drive, providing a complete "live" backup of all data. If one disk fails, the other disk continues to work, and no interruption in service occurs.

modem (modulator/demodulator) A communications device that translates digital computer signals into analog signals for transmission over standard telephone lines.

multicasting The process by which data packets are directed to more than one host simultaneously.

multicast address The address 224.0.0.0, which is a reserved address in the TCP/IP standard.

Multicasting allows multiple hosts to listen to a single stream of packets, a useful function in minimizing bandwidth when sending the same data to a group of hosts at the same time.

multi-homed router A Windows NT computer with two or more network adapter cards, enabling the computer to act as a node on two or more networks.

Multilink A technology that combines multiple physical dial-up connections into a single logical dial-up connection. Requires multiple WAN adapters to function.

multiple master domain model A network structure that divides resources into resource domains, and uses two or more master domains.

multiple protocol binding The Windows NT Server feature that allows you to use one or all available protocols on a single adapter card.

multi-protocol routing (MPR) A Windows NT feature that allows Windows NT to act as a router. MPR consists of three components: Routing Information Protocol (RIP) for Internet Protocol, RIP for IPX, and BOOTP/DHCP Relay Agent.

N

NBTSTAT A Command Prompt utility used to display the current TCP/IP connections using NetBIOS over TCP/IP. May help resolve name resolution problems.

NetBEUI (NetBios Enhanced User Interface) Simple, nonroutable protocol used for traffic over small LANs of up to 200 clients with Microsoft operating systems.

NetBIOS Gateway A RAS service that provides access to resources for NetBIOS clients even though NetBIOS is not routable.

NetBIOS over TCP (NBT) An extension of TCP/IP that allows NetBIOS to run on top of TCP/IP. Promulgated in RFCs 1001 and 1002.

Net Logon Service The Windows service that is used to authenticate user accounts and provide pass-through authentication.

netmask The part of the routing table that defines which portion of the network address must match for that route to be used using a binary translation of the IP address.

NETSTAT A command-prompt utility that displays TCP/IP statistics as well as the state of the current TCP/IP connections.

network-attached printer A print device that is physically connected to the network, rather than being directly connected to a computer host. It is equipped with a network interface card, such as the Hewlett-Packard JetDirect, and accessed using the DLC protocol.

Network Control Protocol (NCP) A predecessor of TCP/IP, developed by the U.S. Department of Defense.

network driver Software that facilitates communication between the operating system and the network card.

Network Driver Interface Specification (NDIS) Boundary layer One of the five layers of the Microsoft Networking model. Roughly equivalent to the Data Link layer of the OSI model. Provides interfaces between the protocols and the Adapter Card Drivers layer.

network interface card (NIC) The card that connects the server or client to the network cabling. Also called a network adapter.

Network Interface layer One of the four layers of the TCP/IP model, or stack. Roughly equivalent to the Data Link and Physical layers of the OSI model. Handles the formatting of data and transmission to the network wire.

network protocols The language or rules used by computers to communicate on a network to ensure that data is transmitted whole, in sequence, and without error.

nonbrowser A computer (typically a client computer) that does not maintain a network resource list.

nonpaged pool memory RAM that is reserved and cannot be paged out to the hard disk to free up space for other data.

Novell NetWare A DOS-based network operating system.

NS Lookup A TCP/IP utility that queries the DNS system to determine the status of a name server, its IP address, and hostname.

NTCONFIG.POL file The system policy file that contains settings for users, groups, and Windows NT computers; it is placed on a network-shared folder so that system policies can be uniformly or selectively enforced across the domain.

NT Diagnostics A utility that displays environment information about a remote or local host, general information about network settings and transports, and statistics about network connections.

NTUSER.DAT file The user profile file that contains the settings that maintain network connections, Control Panel configurations that are unique to the user (such as the desktop color and mouse), and specific application settings.

NWLink Microsoft's implementation of the IPX/SPX protocol. Required for communication with NetWare clients and servers.

O

object In performance monitoring, any component, whether software or hardware, within a computer.

octet One of the four 8-bit fields in an IP address.

one-way trust relationship The simplest form of trust relationship, in which one domain (the trusting domain) grants users in another domain (the trusted domain) access to its resources.

open database connectivity (ODBC) A protocol used for providing access to multiple data sources using a common language.

Open Systems Interconnect (OSI) A seven-layer networking model put together by the International Standards Organization (ISO). Used as a common point of reference when comparing implementation of protocols.

operating system Software that allows a computer to run programs, store data, and communicate with networks.

optional service A service that is included in the Windows NT BackOffice suite. The list of BackOffice products includes Microsoft SQL Server, Exchange Server, SNA Server, System Management Server, Transaction Server, Proxy Server, Site Server, and Commercial Internet Systems. In addition, a number of products, while not part of the BackOffice family, are considered optional services.

OSPF "Open Shortest Path First," a routing protocol for wide area networks.

outsourcing The act of hiring an outside firm to conduct some element of your business. Generally outsourcing is done to alleviate manpower shortages.

overhead Resource utilization on a network.

P

Packet Internet Groper (PING) A command-prompt utility used to check for correct TCP/IP configuration and to verify network connection.

parity Term used to describe an algorithm that is used to regenerate lost stripes of data in the event of a disk failure.

pass-through authentication The process by which a request for user account authentication is passed to the domain controller on which the user account was created.

performance monitor A utility used to identify any server or workstation performance issues.

phonebook entry A collection of settings that define the parameters for establishing a RAS connection with a specific server or system.

ping The process of sending out a test signal using the PING utility.

Point-to-Point Protocol (PPP) A standard protocol for connecting systems over dial-up connections. PPP is used in Windows NT as the basis for dial-up networking.

portable Term used to describe an operating system that adapts itself to many different processor revisions and hardware platforms.

potential browser A computer that can maintain a network resource list, but will not take this step unless specifically instructed to do so by a master browser.

PPP Multilink protocol A version of PPP that enables multiple physical connections to be aggregated into a single, larger communication pipeline.

preferred master browser A NT Windows server or workstation that designates itself as the master browser if no other master browser exists on the network. If another computer already serves as the master browser, the preferred master browser sends a broadcast message that forces an election.

print client A client computer on the network that submits print jobs from a client application to a print server.

print device The physical electronic mechanism that is more commonly called a printer (outside the world of Microsoft). This hardware component, which produces the printed document, is also called the physical printer.

printer driver The device driver that enables the print server to communicate with the physical print device.

printer pooling A feature of the Windows NT print system that enables a single logical printer to send print jobs to multiple printers.

print job The electronic package that contains the document to be printed as well as process and control data. It is initiated by a client application on a client computer, sent to a print server, and eventually dispatched to a physical printer.

print processor The portion of the Windows NT printing model that makes modifications to a print job after it is read from the spool file but before it is sent to the print monitor.

print queue The series of print jobs received by a print server waiting for access to the physical print device. A print queue operates in a default "first in, first out" mode. Sometimes referred to simply as the "queue."

print resolution A measurement of pixel density that relates to the sharpness and clarity of a printed image. Resolution is measured in dots per inch (DPI). Typically, greater DPI yields a higher-quality printed output. Most modern printers (laser and ink-jet) print at more than 300 DPI.

print server The computer that hosts the spool file for a physical printer where print jobs are temporarily stored and managed. It controls the printer, manages the print queue, and maintains the link with the network to offer the printer share. Any Windows NT or Windows 95 computer that has a local printer is considered a print server.

Print Server Services Windows NT services that extend the capabilities of the standard print system. They include Services for Macintosh, File and Print Services for NetWare, and TCP/IP Print Services. Typically, these services extend the print server's ability to accept print jobs from a wider variety of clients and protocols.

print spooler A component of the print system that receives, processes, stores, and distributes print jobs. Print spooling is the process in which the print system writes a print job to disk into a "spool file," where it awaits its turn in the print queue. Despooling occurs as the stored print jobs are retrieved, printed, and removed from the spool.

protocol A prearranged method of communication between computers.

protocol binding The connections between network interfaces, protocols, and services installed on a Windows NT computer.

protocols See *Network protocols.*

protocols layer One of the five layers of Microsoft's Networking model. Roughly equivalent to the Transport and Network layers of the OSI model.

Contains protocols responsible for translating data so that other operating systems can understand them.

Proxy Server An optional Windows NT service that allows a company to access the Internet, while providing security for the internal network, and does not require TCP/IP to be running on the client computer.

PSCRIPT1 A data type used for PostScript code, typically generated by a Macintosh or specialized graphical application, when the targeted print device is a non-PostScript device. It instructs the print server to create a bitmap-equivalent rendering of the print job.

PSTN (Public Switch Telephone Networks) Standard telephone lines, sometimes called POTS (Plain Old Telephone Service).

Public Switched Telephone Network (PSTN) A term for the collected matrix of the analog phone lines. Sometimes called Plain Old Telephone Service (POTS).

R

RAW A data type generated by the printer driver rather than the GDI. Using RAW requires the client application to remain in communication with the print system until all of the print job has been sent to the print device.

RAW (FF Appended) A variation of RAW that instructs the print server to add a form-feed character to the end of the print job, ensuring that the last page of the job will be printed.

RAW (FF Auto) A variation of RAW in which the print server inspects the print job to determine if a form-feed character is needed.

redirector Software that intercepts software requests for data from network drives, converts them into network I/O requests, and passes the I/O requests to the network driver to be packaged.

redundancy A state in which a second device is available to take over the duties of the primary device in case of failure.

Redundant Array of Independent Disks (RAID) Techniques used to group sets of drives so that they can perform a single task as a team. RAID techniques provide redundancy and, in some cases, performance advantages. Several levels of RAID exist, each of which is designed to satisfy a different need.

Remote Access Admin (RAA) The administration utility used to manage and observe the activity of RAS.

Remote Access Service (RAS) The service that adds remote network communication functionality to Windows NT.

Remoteboot A Windows NT Server feature that starts MS-DOS and Microsoft Windows computers over the network.

rendering The Windows NT print system's process of recreating an image on the computer screen in printer-specific language so that the image can be properly reproduced on paper.

resource domain A domain containing resources that users in other domains need to access.

resource domain administrators Personnel responsible for relatively simple, GUI-based tasks, such as creating shares and computer accounts.

roaming profile A user profile stored on a network-shared directory that can be accessed from any networked computer.

routable The characteristic that allows protocols to be recognized and passed on by a router.

ROUTE A command-prompt utility that, among other things, displays the current routing table showing the routes and number of hops that a packet takes to reach a specific destination.

router A device that connects more than one network segment and intelligently transfers data between segments.

routing The process of forwarding data packets from a source computer on one network segment to a destination computer on another network segment.

Routing and Remote Access Service (RRAS) An update to Windows NT that combines routing and RAS into a single service, thus providing improved performance, security, and features.

Routing Information Protocol (RIP) A protocol that enables a router to exchange routing information with another router. IPX or IP are the protocols used for the information exchange.

routing table A table that provides information to a router about which paths to take when transferring data.

S

scalable Term used to describe an operating system that takes full advantage of multiple processors by balancing the processing load and ensuring optimal performance. A scalable operating system can accommodate both large and small networks.

scope The range of numbers assigned to a network that DHCP uses when assigning IP addresses to an individual computer within that network.

Security Accounts Manager (SAM) database The security account database located on a domain's primary domain controller, containing user and resource security data including all user settings.

security authentication The process by which users log onto the network.

Security Identifier (SID) A unique number assigned to a user, group, or computer account in the SAM database.

seed In the AppleTalk protocol, a router that functions much like a Windows NT RIP-enabled router.

seed router A router that initializes and broadcasts routing information about one or more physical networks to other routers on the network.

separator page A short document that is printed automatically between each print job; it identifies the sender (and other details) to aid in locating your documents on the office printer.

Serial Line Internet Protocol (SLIP) An early protocol developed to establish communications over telephone lines; it has since been superceded by PPP.

server In early networks, a PC that acted as the central repository of documents and applications. In modern networks, a computer that provides services by responding to client requests.

Server Services for NetWare A service that allows a NetWare client to log on to a Windows NT Server as if it were a NetWare Server.

Service Advertising Protocol (SAP) A protocol used by servers to advertise their services and addresses on a network.

share A local designator for a remote resource.

single domain model A network structure in which the entire network is one domain, with a single primary domain controller for the entire network.

single-homed A computer that has only one network adapter.

single master domain model A network structure in which the master domain acts as a central administrative unit for user and group accounts and controls access in other domains (resource domains).

Small Computer System Interface (SCSI) A standard developed so that hard disks would have a uniform presentation across the computer industry. This standard has gone through several revisions.

software-trap error A kernel-level software error. The Windows NT Executive catches ("traps") these errors and stops processing. Examples include division by zero errors and memory address errors.

source quench messages Messages sent by the Internet Control Message Protocol (ICMP) telling senders to suspend sending packets for a period of time.

spikes Sudden changes in voltage that can instantly destroy a server. Also called *surges*.

stand-alone server Similar to a member server, a stand-alone server is not part of a domain, but provides server functions in a workgroup network.

static route A route to a destination that is manually entered into the router. With static routing, it does not matter if a link is up or down; the route remains in the routing table in any event.

Stop error An Executive-level error in Windows NT characterized by a blue screen that contains current environment information.

stripe set A data volume that spans multiple physical disks, writing data in blocks or stripes to each physical disk. Also called RAID-0, stripe sets write to more than one physical disk simultaneously and can improve data retrieval times by a significant margin.

subnet A section of a larger network, as logically defined through TCP/IP configurations.

subnet mask When translated into binary, a number that is used to determine whether data can be sent to a particular network address.

Subprotocols *See TCP/IP core protocols.*

symbolic string A string error message that is associated with a numeric error code. Symbolic strings are provided to make it easier to identify and remember error messages.

symmetric multiprocessing (SMP) An operating system process that takes full advantage of multiple processors in the same machine by balancing the operating load across all of them.

synchronization The process of maintaining an identical database, such as the user and groups database, on one or more servers.

system group A special group of users that is populated automatically by the server.

system policy A collection of Registry settings that defines the domain resources that are available to a group of users or an individual user.

System Policy Editor A utility that allows the administrator to manage the user desktop by changing the Default User settings and to manage the logon and network settings by changing the Default Computer settings.

T

TCP/IP core protocols Protocols in the TCP/IP suite concerned with providing communications between hosts on a network.

TCP/IP suite A widely used suite of protocols that connect large networks over a large area.

Telephony application programming interface (TAPI) A standard interface between software, hardware, and communication media.

Text A data type consisting of ANCII characters only.

threshold A predefined activity level for a particular counter.

time-bomb A modification to commercially released software that makes the software inoperable after a defined period of time has elapsed, such as 120 days. Usually installed in evaluation copies of software to ensure licensing compliance.

Time To Live (TTL) The time allotted for the delivery of a data packet. The default TTL on the Internet is 32 seconds.

TRACERT A command-prompt utility used to display the route that TCP/IP packets take through a network.

Transmission Control Protocol (TCP) A connection-oriented protocol that guarantees delivery of data packets in the proper sequence. It is the most widely used protocol.

Transport Driver Interface (TDI) Boundary layer One of the five layers of Microsoft's Networking model. Roughly equivalent to the Session layer of the OSI model. Handles requests to and from the lower protocol layer and provides session services.

Transport layer One of the four layers of the TCP/IP model, or stack. Roughly equivalent to the Session and Transport layers of the OSI model.

transport protocols Networking protocols that operate at the Transport layer of the OSI model. Transport Protocols include NWLink, NetBEUI, DLC, AppleTalk, and TCP/IP.

trusted domain In a trust relationship, the domain containing users who need access to resources in the trusting domain.

trusting domain In a trust relationship, the domain containing resources that can be accessed by the trusted domain.

trust relationship A relationship between two or more domains, in which one domain (the trusting domain) allows users in another domain (the trusted domain) to access its resources.

two-way trust relationship Two one-way trust relationships, in which both domains act as both trusted and trusting domains.

U

uninterruptible power supply (UPS) A device that maintains full power when AC power fails, monitors external power for fluctuations, absorbs spikes, and reconditions power to an acceptable steadiness through the use of batteries or AC/DC-DC/AC converters.

User Datagram Protocol (UDP) A connectionless-oriented protocol in the TCP/IP suite that offers unreliable delivery of data packets with low overhead.

user domain A domain devoted to managing user accounts.

user policy A collection of Registry settings that define the operating environment for a user logged on to the domain.

user profile A collection of files that define the Windows NT configuration for a specific user, including the user's environment and preference settings.

user rights Permissions assigned to a group of users to allow them to perform specific functions on the server, such as backing up files and directories.

V

virtual private network (VPN) A secure communications channel over the Internet between hosts established through the use of shared encryption. Allows for the transport of sensitive information across unsecure networks.

volume One or more partitions on one or more hard disks that are spanned together as a single formatted entity and can be assigned a single drive letter.

volume/set Any group of hard drives configured to act as a single volume. A volume set with a single drive letter can span multiple disks, making use of irregularly sized chunks of free space.

W

Windows Internet Naming Service (WINS) A Windows NT feature that enables client computers to resolve NetBIOS computer names of other network computers to their IP addresses by providing a dynamic database that automatically keeps track of IP addresses. WINS has 2 parts: **WINS server**, a server component which maintains the database, and **WINS client**, which seeks this information from the server component.

workgroup A network of computers that act as both clients and servers.

workgroup A collection of computers that work together, each acting as both a client and a server to the other group members.

workstation A computer within a workgroup.

X

X.25 A communication standard set by the ITU that breaks up packets for transmission across different physical paths for reassembly at the destination. Best known as the precursor frame relay.

Z

zones In AppleTalk, the equivalent of domains for Windows NT networks. A zone allows the logical grouping of devices to reduce traffic and simplify browsing for network resources.

INDEX

N